Digital Convergence – Libraries of the Future

Rae Earnshaw and John Vince (Eds)

Digital Convergence – Libraries of the Future

 Springer

Rae Earnshaw, PhD, FBCS, FRSA, CEng, CITP
Pro Vice-Chancellor (Strategic Systems Development)
University of Bradford, UK

John Vince, MTech, PhD, DSc
Emeritus Professor in Digital Media
Bournemouth University, UK

Festschrift in honour of Dr Reg Carr

British Library Cataloguing in Publication Data
A catalogue record for this book is available from the British Library

ISBN-13: 978-1-84996-672-6   e-ISBN-13: 978-1-84628-903-3

Printed on acid-free paper

9 8 7 6 5 4 3 2 1

Springer Science+Business Media
springer.com

Contents

Foreword ix

List of Contributors xi

Introduction xxiii

Part 1
The Organization and Delivery of Digital Information

1   **From "Boutique" to Mass Digitization: the Google Library
    Project at Oxford** 3
    Ronald Milne

2   **Digital Services in Academic Libraries: the Internet is Setting
    Benchmarks** 11
    Norbert Lossau

3   **The Early Years of the United Kingdom Joint Academic
    Network (JANET)** 31
    Mike Wells

Part 2
**The World Library – Collaboration and Sharing of
Information**

4   **World-Class Universities Need World-Class Libraries and
    Information Resources: But How Can they be Provided?** . . . 55
    Sir Brian K. Follett

5   The International Dimensions of Digital Science and
    Scholarship: Aspirations of the British Library in Serving the
    International Scientific and Scholarly Communities 65
    Lynne Brindley

6   CURL – Research Libraries in the British Isles 75
    Peter Fox

Part 3

Cultural and Strategic Implications of Digital Convergence for Libraries

7   For Better or Worse: Change and Development in Academic
    Libraries, 1970–2006 85
    Bill Simpson

8   Combining the Best of Both Worlds: the Hybrid Library 95
    David Baker

9   Beyond the Hybrid Library: Libraries in a Web 2.0 World . . . 107
    Derek Law

10 Libraries and Open Access: the Implications of Open-Access
    Publishing and Dissemination for Libraries in Higher
    Education Institutions 119
    Stephen Pinfield

Part 4

Shaking the Foundations – Librarianship in Transition

11 Scholarship and Libraries: Collectors and Collections 137
    Fred Ratcliffe

12 When is a Librarian not a Librarian? 155
    Frederick Friend

Part 5

New Dimensions of Information Provision: Restructuring, Innovation, and Integration

13 From Integration to Web Archiving 163
    John Tuck

14 Not Just a Box of Books: From Repository to Service
    Innovator 173
    Sarah E. Thomas and Carl A. Kroch

15 Learning Enhancement through Strategic Project
    Partnership 181
    Mary Heaney

16 Libraries for the 21st Century 191
    Les Watson

Part 6
Preserving the Content – The Physical and the Digital

17 Tomorrow, and Tomorrow, and Tomorrow: Poor Players on the
    Digital Curation Stage 207
    Chris Rusbridge

18 Some Key Issues in Digital Preservation 219
    Marilyn Deegan and Simon Tanner

Part 7
From Information to Knowledge – the Human–Computer Interface

19 From the Information Age to the Intelligence Age: Exploiting
    IT and Convergence 241
    Rae Earnshaw and John Vince

20 Cognitive Implications of Information Spaces: Human Issues
    in the Design and Use of Electronic Library Interfaces 253
    *Sherry Chen, Jane Coughlan, Steve Love, Robert D. Macredie
    and Frankie Wilson*

21 Mobile Media – From Content to User 273
    Antonietta Iacono and Gareth Frith

Part 8
Historic Collections and Case Studies

22 Special Collections Librarianship 295
    Richard Ovenden

23 **Defending Research and Scholarship – United Kingdom Libraries and the Terrorism Bill 2005** 303
    Clive D. Field

24 **Politics, Profits and Idealism: John Norton, the Stationers' Company and Sir Thomas Bodley** 327
    John Barnard

25 **William Drummond of Hawthornden: Book Collector and Benefactor of Edinburgh University Library** 345
    John Hall

26 **de Gaulle and the British** 359
    David Dilks

Part 9
High Level Applications of Content and its Governance

27 **Great Libraries in the Service of Science** 381
    Alan Eyre

28 **Governance at Harvard University Library** 401
    Dudley Fishburn

29 **Higher Education Libraries and the Quality Agenda** 407
    John Horton

Author Index 415

Foreword

Sir Colin Lucas

I first met Reg Carr when I was a young Lecturer at Manchester University and he was a young Assistant Librarian there. I came across him again some 25 years later when he was appointed Bodley's Librarian and Director of the University Library Services at Oxford, shortly before I became Vice-Chancellor there. The new addition to that old title of "Bodley's Librarian" symbolized obliquely how much had changed in the challenges facing libraries between those two moments of encounter. Reg Carr had become in Leeds, and was to continue to be in Oxford, one of the principal influences in trying to think how to adapt to them.

I learned to do historical research at a time when major libraries were fine and private places. As one entered them, their characteristic and reassuring smell announced already the mysteries that awaited – card indexes, printed catalogues (or even ones with slips pasted in by hand) and bibliographies to be perused with imagination as much as method, references to be culled and followed, inspired guesses at the contents behind seemingly irrelevant titles, books patiently read in search of a single fact or an idea sparked by something apparently outside one's line of enquiry, the sense of treading where few others had been, and so on. The lone scholar can still have this sort of experience, although immeasurably enhanced and hastened by the appearance of electronic catalogues. However, it echoes a time when knowledge was closely held by the few, difficult to acquire in depth and to handle in breadth. That is decreasingly what libraries are centrally about now.

The purpose of libraries would have been limited indeed if they had served only to preserve the accumulation of human knowledge, belief and imagination by locking it away. Even so, the revolution that has been wrought in our world generally by IT, digitization and telecommunications has transformed libraries rapidly and profoundly (and continues to do so), not only in how they do their business but also in some senses in what they are.

To traditional and new library users the most immediate effect is on access. What is (perhaps glibly) referred to as the "Google generation" has quite different expectations about access to information and quite different assumptions about how research is to be done. Across the spectrum of research – whether academic, commercial, creative or personal – users expect speed and convenience in work, comprehensiveness combined with sensitivity in search engines, and the capacity to manipulate large data sets.

The digitization of holdings responds to this, most obviously to date in the initiatives launched by Google and Microsoft. Other forces push in the same direction. Digitization seems to offer one solution to the endless effort of preservation, though we are already learning that its own particular forms of obsolescence and decay are as daunting as the physical deterioration of objects. Further, the electronic revolution clearly reduces costs in processing and transmission and also by compressing storage requirements dramatically.

Beyond this, however, the function of libraries is changing into a future as yet unclear. Libraries are only part of a complex information system globally accessible and thereby seemingly ever more present, ephemeral and voluminous. At the most ordinary level, libraries face new problems on how to capture this information, especially when born digital, how to adapt their traditional function as preserver and authenticator of text in all its forms, and how to manage copyright issues in an electronic world. At a more innovative level, libraries have to confront the problem of the continuing evolution in how their users relate to them. How far will they eventually travel towards something more closely resembling a website and a virtual resource for readers endowed with unforeseen desktop power by successive Web types and the progeny of broadband? What kind of information hunger will be generated in what kind of public hitherto innocent of libraries and how to reach and satisfy it? And what should libraries do to engage more directly in a fecund way with the creative impact of ideas which will fuel our growing knowledge economies?

This collection of essays, written by those who best understand these themes, is a fitting tribute to Reg Carr. His career illustrates these issues. If I may express it in purely personal terms, in Manchester I remember him as someone who was extraordinarily helpful and imaginative in acquiring strange and neglected publications from the 1940s in France, Belgium and Switzerland, on which I wanted to work without having to travel from library to library looking through their collections. At the turn of the century in Oxford, he was undertaking the process of integrating a fragmented university library system into a single usable whole as well as developing the hybrid library with digitization and hyperlinks so that people like myself could begin to read widely and more subtly without having to travel from library to library. Certainly, in his leadership of national and international library organizations, Reg has been an intelligent observer and force for change – a change whose direction we understand but whose ultimate destination we probably do not yet know. The library world and the world of scholarship have benefited mightily from his devotion to them.

Sir Colin Lucas
Chair, British Library Board
Warden, Rhodes House, and Chief Executive, Rhodes Trust
Vice-Chancellor, University of Oxford, 1997–2004
April 2007

Contributors

Professor David Baker, Principal, College of St Mark and St John

David Baker was born in Bradford, West Yorkshire, in 1952. He gained an open organ scholarship to Sidney Sussex College, Cambridge, graduating with First Class Honours in Music in 1973. He subsequently undertook postgraduate studies in both music and librarianship. In 1985 he became Chief Librarian of the University of East Anglia, becoming Pro-Vice Chancellor there in 1997 and moving to his present post six years later. He has published widely in his field of professional interest, including 14 monographs and over 40 refereed articles. His hobbies include creative writing, history and archaeology and watching cricket.

Email: principal@marjon.ac.uk

Professor John Barnard

John Barnard was Professor of English Literature at the University of Leeds until his retirement in 2001. He has published extensively on seventeenth century literature and book history, and on Keats and the second generation Romantics.

Email: jon_barnard@hotmail.com

Dr Lynne Brindley, Chief Executive, British Library

Lynne Brindley has been the Chief Executive of the British Library since 2000. She is the first woman and the first Library/Information professional to hold the post. Since her appointment, Lynne has led a major strategic repositioning and modernization programme to ensure that the BL continues to provide relevant services to users in the 21st century, and that the library is recognized for its contribution to research, innovation and culture. Lynne came to the BL from the University of Leeds where she was Pro-Vice-Chancellor and University Librarian. She previously held positions as Librarian & Director of Information Services at the London School of Economics, Principal Consultant at KPMG, and Pro-Vice-Chancellor and Director of Information Services at Aston

University. She spent the early part of her career at the British Library. Lynne is also active in national and international bodies concerned with cultural, library and digital information strategy. She is a Visiting Professor at City and Leeds universities. Her research and professional interests are in knowledge management, digital library developments, strategy and leadership. She has received a number of honorary degrees, including from the universities of Oxford, Leeds, Sheffield and UCL. She enjoys music, buying modern art and hill-walking and has recently become the first woman on the Court of Goldsmiths' Company.

Email: Lynne.Brindley@bl.uk

Marilyn Deegan, Kings College, London

Marilyn Deegan has a PhD in medieval studies: her specialism is Anglo-Saxon medical texts and herbals and she has published and lectured widely in medieval studies, digital library research, and humanities computing. She is currently Director of Research Development in the Centre for Computing in the Humanities at King's College, London and was formerly Digital Resources Director of the Refugee Studies Centre at Oxford University. She has held a number of posts in digital library research and humanities computing over the past fifteen years. She is Editor-in-Chief of *Literary and Linguistic Computing*, the Journal of the Association for Literary and Linguistic Computing, and Director of Publications for the Office for Humanities Communication based at King's College London.

Marilyn Deegan and Simon Tanner are Series Editors of the Digital Futures series for Facet Publishing, and co-authors of *Digital Futures: Strategies for the Information Age* in that series.

Email: marilyn.deegan@kcl.ac.uk

Professor David Dilks FRHistS FRSL

Professor Dilks is a Professor of International Relations at Leeds University. He was born in Worcester in 1938 and attended The Royal Grammar School before winning a scholarship to Hertford College, Oxford to read History. He remained in Oxford to do research at St Antony's College before becoming research assistant to Anthony Eden and Harold MacMillan. He was the official biographer of the latter as well as producing a two-volume biography of Viscount Curzon of India and Neville Chamberlain. In 1977 he became a Visiting Fellow of All Souls College, Oxford. Professor Dilks became Vice Chancellor of the University of Hull in 1991, in which position he remained until 1999. He remains on many political and international committees including *The Guardian* politics advisory council, Politea and the International Committee for the History of the Second World War (of which he was president). He was also president of the Churchill Society and has recently written a book on Churchill's time in Canada.

Email: dndilks@tiscali.co.uk

Dr Alan Eyre, University of West Indies, Jamaica

Alan Eyre has been associated with the University of the West Indies for the past fifty years as student, senior lecturer, reader, and senior research fellow. During this time he spent six years as a research analyst at the Library of Congress, Washington DC (1966–72). This was not only crucial to his own scientific area as an earth and space scientist, but was spent when that greatest of all world libraries was undergoing tremendous expansion and fundamental change. He has also spent time at other institutions such as USGS Reston hunting data on comet impacts, USAA Oak Ridge, the Marciana Library in Venice, Staatsbibliotek Vienna, the Czartoryski Library in Krakow during martial law in Poland, the University Library of Cluj-Napoca, the National Library of South Africa, and the Royal Botanic Library at Kew. As academic dean of the International College of the Cayman Islands (1998–2001), he had ultimate responsibility for the Library, and personally strengthened its holdings in the sciences.

Email: lawrencealaneyre@cwjamaica.com

Dr Clive Field, FRHistS, formerly Director of Scholarship and Collections, British Library

Clive Field is an Oxford-educated historian who is currently Honorary Research Fellow in the Department of Modern History at the University of Birmingham, specializing in the social history of religion in modern Britain, on which he has written widely. His book on Church and Chapel in Early Victorian Shropshire was published in 2004. His career as a professional librarian spanned the years 1977–2006 during which he held posts at the Universities of Manchester and Birmingham and at the British Library (where he was the inaugural Director of Scholarship and Collections from 2001 to 2006). He was active on the national and international stages for library and information services, including nine years as a Director of the Consortium of Research Libraries in the British Isles. He also led the successful library campaigns to extend legal deposit in Britain, through the Legal Deposit Libraries Act 2003, and to amend what is now the Terrorism Act 2006, to protect the interests of libraries and their users. The latter campaign is the subject of his contribution to this volume.

Email: c.d.field@bham.ac.uk

Dudley Fishburn

Dudley Fishburn is a director of HSBC Bank plc. He served as a Harvard University Overseer for six years and then chaired Harvard library's Visiting Committee from 1996–2006. He has been Member of Parliament for Kensington and Executive Editor of *The Economist*. He chaired the Trustees of the Open University and is on the Council of Reading University.

Email: dudley@fishburns.co.uk

Professor Sir Brian Follett FRS, University of Oxford

Sir Brian Follett read Chemistry at the University of Bristol, followed by a PhD in Pharmacology. After a period at Washington State University, he held a number of academic posts at Leeds University and the University of Wales, Bangor. In 1978 he was appointed Professor of Zoology at the University of Bristol, where he also chaired the Department of Zoology until 1993. He was the Biological Secretary and Vice-President at the Royal Society from 1987 until 1993 and was Vice-Chancellor of the University of Warwick from 1993 until 2001. Since then he has chaired the Arts and Humanities Research Council (AHRC), and the Training and Development Agency for Schools (TDA) along with being a nonstipendiary Professor in the Department of Zoology at Oxford where he teaches. He chaired the committee that drew up the library report for HEFCE that was published in 1992, its implementation group and the second report that created RIN. He chairs the British Library Advisory Council. He was knighted in 1992 for services to science.

Email: bkfollett@btinternet.com

Peter Fox, Librarian, University of Cambridge

Peter Fox has been University Librarian at the University of Cambridge since 1994. This follows 10 years at Trinity College Dublin as Librarian and College Archivist (1984–1994). He has published many contributions to books and learned journals, and edited several books, including *Cambridge University Library: the great collections* (CUP 1998), *Treasures of the Library: Trinity College Dublin* (Royal Irish Academy 1986), and the commentary volume to *The Book of Kells, MS 58, Trinity College Library Dublin* (Faksimile Verlag Luzern 1998). He has chaired a number of national committees, including the Advisory Board for the CEDARS digital archiving project, the Wellcome Trust Library Advisory Committee, the Board of the National Preservation Office, and the Board of CURL (Consortium of University Research Libraries). He is currently a member of the Lord Chancellor's Advisory Council on National Records and Archives, the Legal Deposit Advisory Panel (reporting to the Department of Culture, Media and Sport) and General Secretary of LIBER (Ligue des Bibliothèques Européennes de Recherche).

Email: pkf20@cam.ac.uk

Frederick J. Friend, University College London

Fred Friend grew up by the sea in Dover, read most of the books in his local public library, and with the help of supportive parents went to study history at Kings College London. He had the good fortune to enter academic libraries at a time of growth. His first post was in Manchester University Library as a SCONUL Trainee and then as Assistant Librarian. Fred moved from university to university in the UK and obtained his first library director post at the University of Essex. This was followed by a move to University College London, where he was library director for 15 years before moving into a role as Honorary Director Scholarly Communication which enables him to explore new developments in information services. Fred is involved in many initiatives through work for organizations such as JISC in the UK and international organizations such as the Open Society Institute. He is one of the authors of the Budapest Open Access Initiative.

Email: ucylfjf@ucl.ac.uk

Gareth Frith, University of Leeds

Gareth Frith is Mobile Technologies Project Manager for the Assessment and Learning in Practice Settings (ALPS) Project funded by the Higher Education Funding Council for England. He is responsible for developing and coordinating the ALPS mobile technologies plan and will be working closely with the Partner Site Implementation Groups to help them develop and implement the infrastructure and mobile technologies needed.

Email: G.S.Frith@leeds.ac.uk

Dr John T. D. Hall, University Librarian, University of Durham

John Hall has been University Librarian of Durham University since 1989, with responsibilities for libraries, extensive heritage collections of archives, manuscripts and rare books and two museums. Before that he held appointments at the Universities of Manchester, Edinburgh and Cambridge. John is active professionally at a national level through CURL and SCONUL; he was active in establishing the Archives Hub as a national service and managed the introduction of SCONUL Research Extra, the national borrowing scheme for researchers. Regionally he works closely with MLA North East through the Collections Care Scheme for libraries, archives and museums and is currently a Board member.

Email: j.t.d.hall@durham.ac.uk

Mary Heaney, Director of Services, Manchester Metropolitan University

Mary Heaney's focus at Manchester Metropolitan University is to create effective learning, teaching and research environments appropriate for students and staff in a modern 21st-century university. More than half of her career has been with the BBC: she worked for the Policy and Planning Unit in London for a short period and spent 16 years with BBC Scotland, firstly as a film librarian then as manager of all library services before taking on the role of Deputy Head of Post-Production Facilities. Leaving the BBC for higher education, she was appointed Director of Administration at St Andrew's College of Education in Glasgow (now the Faculty of Education at Glasgow University), directing all support services and serving as Secretary to the College. She was Director of Learning Centres at Wolverhampton University and led the transformation of libraries into student-focused facilities offering open access IT, learning support, self-directed and peer-group learning environments and resources to support courses and modules.

Email: m.heaney@mmu.ac.uk

John J. Horton MA, MPhil, DipLib, ALA, University Librarian, University of Bradford

John Horton gained his first degree at Oxford University and qualified on the inaugural year of the Postgraduate School of Librarianship and Information Studies at the University of Sheffield. After early experience working for the late and much lamented West Riding County Library Service, he joined the University of Bradford, where he acquired his MPhil, and filled several positions in the University Library prior to being appointed in 2000 to his current role as University Librarian and Head of Academic Library Services. He has researched and published widely in the field of Icelandic and Yugoslav Studies and is a member of the Council of the Inter-University Centre for Postgraduate Studies in Dubrovnik, Croatia. He is also a member of the Council of the University of Bradford, and was until recently an institutional auditor for the QAA. Extramurally he is a trained theatre director, but his general disposition is entirely dependent upon the fortunes of Barnsley Football Club.

Email: J.J.Horton@bradford.ac.uk

Antonietta Iacono, University of Bradford

Antonietta graduated with a first-class BSc degree in Interactive Systems and Video Games Design from the Department of Electronic Imaging and Media Communications at the University of Bradford. Part-time lecturer specializing in multimedia development, user interface design and mobile content. Recent Projects include GRID – Growing Interest in the Development of Science Teaching – a two year EU Socrates-funded project, and ALPS – Assessment and Learning in Practice Settings, and Mobile Technologies Review.

Email: A.Iacono@bradford.ac.uk

Professor Derek Law, Head of the Information Resources Directorate, University of Strathclyde

Derek Law has been Head of the Information Resources Directorate and University Librarian since 1999. As such he is a member of the University's Senior Management Team. He was educated at Arbroath High School, George Watson's College and the Universities of Glasgow and Strathclyde. Before joining Strathclyde he held appointments at King's College London and at the universities of Edinburgh, St Andrews and Glasgow. He was awarded the Barnard Prize for contributions to Medical Informatics in 1993, Fellowship of King's College London in 1997, Fellowship of the Royal Society of Edinburgh in 1999, an honorary degree by the Sorbonne in 2000, the IFLA medal in 2003 and Honorary

Fellowship of CILIP in 2004. As head of the Information Resources Directorate he is responsible for IT Services, Learning Services and Library Services. He holds a chair in the Department of Computing and Information Science and is a member of the Centre for Digital Library Research. Professor Law has written extensively on the development of digital libraries, on the role of information in e-learning, on digital information systems and has a subsidiary interest in naval history.

Email: d.law@strath.ac.uk

Dr Norbert Lossau, University of Goettingen, Germany

Dr Norbert Lossau is the University Librarian at the University of Gottingen. He was previously Librarian at Bielefeld, Germany, where he moved in 2002 from his post as first Head of the Oxford Digital Library, University of Oxford, UK. Previous to Oxford, he was the Head and founding Director of the Digitization Centre at Göttingen State and University Library, Germany (1997–2001), one of two national supply centres funded by the Deutsche Forschungsgemeinschaft (DFG). Dr. Lossau has been the main organizer of the International Bielefeld Conference since 2004, having taken overall responsibility for this biannual strategic forum for academic librarians in Europe. He is co-author of a paper on the "Implementation of New Directions in German HE Information and Publishing Systems", the official Statement from the Library Working Group of the German State Ministries in response to the respective "Recommendations" of the German University Presidents and member of a new "eScience" group of experts at the German Federal Ministry of Education and Research. He represents Bielefeld University Library for the national "Distributed Document Server" project within the German Digital Library "Vascoda", and has initiated strategic partnerships and collaboration with international libraries and enterprises (such as Oxford University Library Services, UK; Sheridan Libraries at Johns Hopkins University, Baltimore, U.S. and FAST Search & Transfer ASA, Norway).

Email: Norbert.Lossau@sub.uni-goettingen.de

Professor Robert Macredie, Pro Vice-Chancellor, Brunel University

With over 15 years of research experience, Robert Macredie has worked with a range of organizations, ranging from large, blue-chip companies, through small businesses, to government agencies. Robert's key interest lies in the way in which people and organizations use technology, and his research aims to determine how work can be more effectively undertaken by improving the way that we understand how people and technology interact in organizational (and social) settings. He is Professor of Interactive Systems and Pro-Vice-Chancellor, Brunel University. He has undertaken work on a range of issues associated with people, technology and organizations and has over 180 published research contributions in these areas.

Email: Robert.Macredie@brunel.ac.uk

Ronald Milne, Acting Director of Oxford University Library Services, University of Oxford

Acting Director of Oxford University Library Services and Bodley's Librarian since August 2004, Ronald Milne has had a regular career in university libraries in the UK. He has worked at the University of London (on the staff of the Library Resources Co-ordinating Committee), Glasgow University, Trinity College Cambridge and King's College London. Prior to taking up the post of Deputy Director at Oxford, in November 2002, he was based at the University of Edinburgh, where he was Director of the Research Support Libraries Programme, a £30M initiative for UK university libraries funded by the Higher Education Funding Councils.

Email: ronald.milne@bl.uk

(From February 2007, Ronald Milne is Director of Scholarship and Collections, British Library)

Richard Ovenden, University of Oxford

Richard Ovenden is a librarian and scholar working in the fields of the history of the book and the history of photography. He is the author of *John Thomson (1837–1921): Photographer* (1997), *A Radical's Books* (1998) and a chapter in *The Cambridge History of Libraries*, volume one (2006). He was educated at Sir Roger Manwood's School, Kent, at St Chad's College, Durham University, and at University College London. He has worked at Durham University Library, the House of Lords Library, the National Library of Scotland and at the University of Edinburgh, where he was Director of Collections. Since 2003 he has been Keeper of Special Collections and Associate Director at the Bodleian Library, University of Oxford, and a Professorial Fellow at St Hugh's College. He is a member of the JISC's Collections Committee and Chair of the CILIP's Rare Books and Special Collections Group.

Email: richard.ovenden@ouls.ox.ac.uk

Stephen Pinfield, University of Nottingham

Stephen Pinfield is Deputy Chief Information Officer and Director of Research and Learning Resources at the University of Nottingham. He is also Director of SHERPA, a cluster of projects focusing on research and development activities for open-access institutional repositories. He has a particular interest in scholarly communication and digital library management, and publishes and speaks widely on these topics. He is currently the Chair of the Joint CURL-SCONUL Scholarly Communication Group which represents all UK higher education libraries in the area of scholarly communication and publishing. He is also a member of the JISC Scholarly Communication Group and a member of the Steering Group of the European DRIVER project, which is setting up a Europe-wide digital repository infrastructure. His previous professional experience has been at the London Business School, University of Leeds (under Reg Carr) and University of Birmingham.

Email: stephen.pinfield@nottingham.ac.uk

Dr Fred Ratcliffe, CBE JP, Emeritus University Librarian of Cambridge

Dr Ratcliffe held senior positions in the university libraries of Glasgow and Newcastle upon Tyne before returning to the University of Manchester as University Librarian in 1965. In 1972, he organized the merger of the John Rylands Library with that of the University and became the first University Librarian and Director of the John Rylands University Library of Manchester until 1980. He then became the first non-Oxbridge graduate to be invited to the University Librarianship of Cambridge, retiring from that post in 1994. In the same year he was appointed Parker Librarian of Corpus Christi College Cambridge, of which he is a Life Fellow, retiring again in 2000. He was a founder member of the CVCP Library Committee, serving for twenty seven years, the founder of CURL and its "Hon. President" until retiring from the University, founder chairman of the National Preservation Office, Trustee of St Deiniols Library for twenty three years, later Hon. Fellow, founder member of the Welcome Library Advisory Committee, and other bodies. He has published widely in English and German on university librarianship, conservation and various academic topics. He served as member of the Stockport and Cambridge Magistrates' Benches for twenty five years.

Email: frederick@ratcliffe7375.freeserve.co.uk

Chris Rusbridge, Director, Digital Curation Centre, University of Edinburgh

Chris Rusbridge is Director of the Digital Curation Centre, funded by JISC and the e-Science Core Programme to provide support services, development and research in digital curation and preservation. This follows five years as Director of Information Services at Glasgow University. There his responsibilities included the library and archives, together with IT, MIS, and A/V services. For the previous five years, he was Programme Director of the JISC Electronic Libraries Programme (eLib), a major digital library R&D Programme (where he worked closely with Reg Carr). During his tenure at JISC, one of his major interests was preservation of digital materials, the subject of a set of JISC-funded studies, two major international preservation workshops in 1995 and 1999, held at Warwick, and two preservation projects, CEDARS (involving both Leeds and Oxford) and CAMiLEON, in all of which he played a significant role.

Email: crusbrid@staffmail.ed.ac.uk

Bill Simpson, Librarian and Director of the John Rylands Library, University of Manchester

Bill Simpson was educated at the universities of Liverpool and Aberdeen, where he studied Ancient Near Eastern Studies. He began his career with posts at the universities of Durham and Manchester, before becoming University Librarian at the University of Surrey in 1985. In 1990 he moved to the University of London as University Librarian, and took up the same post at Trinity College Dublin in 1994. Bill became Director of the John Rylands Library and University Librarian of the Victoria University of Manchester in September 2002. Bill serves on a wide range of professional bodies, including being a Director of the Consortium of University Research Libraries, a Trustee of the People's History Museum and a Curator of Oxford University Library Services. He has previously chaired the Council of National and University Librarians, the Standing Committee on Legal Deposit and the National Preservation Office and has served on a range of British Library and international advisory bodies. He has published both professionally and academically, and was awarded the Jubilee Medal of Charles University Prague in 1998 for his work in promoting academic and library links with the Czech Republic.

Email: Bill.Simpson@manchester.ac.uk

Simon Tanner

Simon Tanner has a Library and Information Science degree and background. He is the founding Director of King's Digital Consultancy Services (KDCS) at King's College London. KDCS provides research and consulting services specializing in the information and digital domain for the cultural, heritage and information sectors. Before joining King's, he was Senior Consultant at HEDS – the Higher Education Digitisation Service. He has also previously held IT, management, and library roles for Loughborough University (Library Systems Manager), Rolls-Royce and Associates (Head of Library Services) and IBM (UK) Laboratories (Information Officer).

Marilyn Deegan and Simon Tanner are Series Editors of the Digital Futures series for Facet Publishing, and co-authors of *Digital Futures: Strategies for the Information Age* in that series.

Email: Simon.Tanner@kcl.ac.uk

Dr Sarah Thomas, Carl A. Kroch University Librarian, Cornell University, USA

Dr Thomas was Adjunct Professor of German and Carl A. Kroch University Librarian at Cornell University since 1996, where she has been overseeing Cornell University's 20 libraries, which received the ACRL Excellence in Academic Libraries award in 2002. From 1992 to 1996 Dr Thomas worked at the Library of Congress, Washington, DC, latterly as Acting Director of the Public Service Collections. Prior to that she held cataloguing appointments at the Widener

Library, Harvard, and Johns Hopkins University. Dr Thomas has also managed library co-ordination at the Research Libraries Group in Stanford, California, and for eight years was Associate Director for Technical Services at the National Agricultural Library, Beltsville, Maryland.

Email: bodleys.librarian@bodley.ox.ac.uk

(From February 2007, Sarah Thomas is Director of the University Library Services, and Bodley's Librarian, University of Oxford).

John Tuck, Head of British Collections, British Library

John joined the British Library in 2002 from Oxford University where he was Deputy to the Director of University Library Services and to Bodley's Librarian. He has spent over twenty-four years in academic librarianship, twenty at the John Rylands University Library of Manchester and four at Oxford.

Email: John.Tuck@bl.uk

Professor Les Watson

Les Watson is a freelance educational adviser. He was previously Pro Vice-Chancellor (Learning and Information Services) at Glasgow Caledonian University. He held this post from 1999 to 2006. During this time he was responsible for Library, C&IT Services, student services, e-learning, the Caledonian Degree and work-based learning, all of which were integrated into a University-wide Learning Service. At Caledonian, he led the development of the Learning Café, REAL@Caledonian, and the award-winning Saltire Centre.

Email: admin@leswatson.com

Professor Mike Wells

Mike Wells obtained his undergraduate and doctorate degrees at the University of Cambridge (the latter working on EDSAC II) and was appointed to the post of Lecturer in the Electronic Computing Laboratory in the University of Leeds in 1961. He became Director of Technical Services in 1968, with promotion to Professor in 1969, followed by appointment as Director of the Laboratory in 1969. He was one of the first UK Computing Service Directors to become an invited member of the Computer Board for Universities and Research Councils, and served from 1972 to 1976. During this time he took part in studies of emergent academic networks, notably ARPANET in the USA. He was one of the earliest advocates of a national academic network, and talks he gave in the 1970s inspired others with the potential value of networked computers. As a development of these interests, from 1983 to 1988 he took the part-time post of national Director of Networking to lead the Joint Network Team and the Network Executive in building the JANET network, which linked together all UK Universities. This work put the UK in a leading position as the possessor of a means by which academics all over the country could communicate and exchange digital information.

Email: eclmikew@leeds.ac.uk

Editors

Professor Rae Earnshaw, Pro Vice-Chancellor (Strategic Systems Development), University of Bradford

Professor Rae Earnshaw is Professor of Electronic Imaging and Media Communications at the University of Bradford, UK. Formerly at the University of Leeds, he has been a Visiting Professor at Illinois Institute of Technology, Chicago, USA, Northwestern Polytechnical University, China, George Washington University, Washington DC, USA, and the Swiss Federal Institute of Technology. His current research interests centre on mixed reality and technology platforms for cultural and arts creative expression. The objective is to develop generic platforms and tools for facilitating creative expression, accessing artistic and cultural material, and developing new forms of communication and interaction between humans and information spaces. He has authored and edited 33 books on computer graphics, visualization, multimedia, design, and virtual reality, and published 140 papers in these areas.

Email: R.A.Earnshaw@bradford.ac.uk

Professor John Vince DSc, FBCS, CEng

Prof John Vince was appointed Chief Scientist of Thomson Training Simulation in 1992. In 1995 he was appointed Professor of Digital Media at the National Centre for Computer Animation at Bournemouth University, and in 1999 he was made Head of Academic Group for Computer Animation. He has written and edited 29 books on computer graphics, computer animation and virtual reality.

Email: John.A.Vince@btinternet.com

Introduction

Rae Earnshaw

Earliest Libraries

Clay tablets have been used to keep records from the earliest times. However, they were used for archives rather than libraries and consisted mainly of administrative records. Private and personal libraries containing books first appeared in Greece in the 5th century BC. The Royal Library of Alexandria was founded in the 3rd century BC and was reputedly the largest library in the world. It was linked to a museum, or research centre, and appeared to be primarily devoted to editing Greek texts on papyrus scrolls. The library was initially organized by Demetrius Phalereus who wrote about history, rhetoric, and literary criticism, and was a student of Aristotle.

One of the most important libraries in Persia established in the 7th century was that associated with the Academy of Gundisaphur, which offered training in medicine, philosophy, theology and science. It was the most important medical centre of the ancient world during the 6th and 7th centuries. In the 8th century Iranians and Arabs imported the skill of paper-making from China, and by the 9th century, public libraries started to appear in many Islamic cities, although they were later destroyed by invaders. However, the contents of the texts were copied by Christian monks and were added to texts from Roman, Greek, and Byzantine works. Library design at the time reflected the labour intensive process of hand-copying of texts and the need to keep them secure. Thus librarians chained books to lecterns or shelves. Today Radio Frequency Identification (RFID) can be used if we wish to know where a book is located.

The first public libraries in the west were established under the Roman Empire and readers could access scrolls and works in Latin and Greek. Between AD 500 and 1000, starting with Monte Cassino in AD 529, monasteries became the focus for projects involving the writing and copying of books. They were centres of intellectual discussion and education and welcomed priests who came to study and learn. Some of these eventually developed into Universities.

Printing Press

In 1455, Johann Gutenberg used movable type, oil-based ink, and a wooden printing press to produce the first printed book. It was instrumental in the developing Renaissance, and later assisted in the scientific revolution a hundred years later. The printing press led on to the mass production of books, broadsheets, newspapers, and media in general. A book provided an irreducible deposit of information that could be read, reviewed, criticized, as well as providing the basis for the development of its ideas into further volumes. A book also carried with it the idea of context – the set of historical circumstances giving rise to its production, as well as the knowledge to which its author had gained access.

Computers

The first computers can be traced back to the late 1940s and were very successful in automating numerical calculations on data. It was this automation which started the information revolution. However, it wasn't until the development of the early consumer computers in the late 1970s and early 1980s that sufficient processing power became generally available and, more importantly, the software to allow the easy manipulation of text. Decreasing costs of memory soon enabled large amounts of text to be stored and processed, and also the inclusion of pictures with equal facility. This provided the environment for the first electronic book. It was also significant that because the text was held electronically, it could be searched electronically. This facilitated the automatic creation of indexes as well as allowing the reader to search the text for any words or phrases they wanted.

The Internet

Although the foundations of the Internet can be traced back to the development of networking concepts at the Defense Advanced Research Projects Agency (DARPA) in 1962, the implications of networked connections for mass use did not come to the fore until the development in 1989 of the World Wide Web – an Internet-based hypermedia initiative for global information sharing. It was the linking of information via the Internet that provided the opportunity for direct access from any point on the network to any other point. This was the key development that initiated the information revolution because it enabled any information placed on the World Wide Web to be accessed by anyone else. It therefore allowed documents to include embedded hyperlinks, digital pictures, and digital videos which transformed linear documents into a hierarchy of information of different types in different physical locations. Using the search tools referred to earlier allowed particular pieces of information in documents to be located from a user anywhere on the Internet. This process has been automated to a high level of sophistication by search engines. Further developments in this area are taking place both to provide more digitized content and to increase the sophistication of the search techniques.

Digital Futures

The development of the Internet provided the framework for linking information and people. Asia has the largest number of Internet users (400m) compared to Europe (300m) and North America (200m) as at the start of 2007. However, in Asia this is only 10% of the population of 3.7bn, whereas in Europe it is 40% of 800m, and in North America it is 70% of 300m. The greatest potential for further growth is in Asia. The total number of global users is 1bn which represents 17% of the total world population of 6.5bn.

The term "Information Superhighway" conveys the picture of millions of bits/sec being transported around global networks. However, the key concepts are connectivity and access, not just for business and commercial reasons, but also for social and recreational activities.

Convergence

The convergence of IT, telecommunications and media is bringing about a revolution in the way information is collected, stored and accessed. There are three principal reasons why this is happening – reducing cost, increasing quality, and increasing bandwidth. Moore's Law results in ever-decreasing costs of processing, storage, and transmission. Digital information preserves content accuracy (e.g. digital television) in a way other systems do not. High bandwidth transmission from one place to another on the planet is now possible. Information is ubiquitous and globally accessible, and can be held and accessed just as easily on a global network as on a local personal computer or in a local library. Distinctions between local and global are fading as the centre of function and access moves from the physical location to the virtual address.

Net Generation

The net generation has come of age and their influence is more pervasive in shaping the design of learning spaces and the provision of current and future information and IT services in many schools, colleges, and Universities. Learning spaces in some institutions have been redesigned to meet these new needs and requirements. The concept of a Third Place has been developed that is neither work nor play but is a combination of the two. A Joint Information Systems Committee (JISC) study on "Designing Spaces for Effective Learning"[1] sets out some of the possibilities.

Location

There is now more location-independent working with mobile devices. There is probably more of this to come as it is in principle more eco-friendly, since it usually involves less travelling to places to obtain information. Location independence also implies greater flexibility for the user, and normally access to digital information is 24 hours a day 7 days a week, and is therefore not limited to the opening times of a traditional library.

Intelligence

Devices are increasingly intelligent and network-ready. User interfaces are becoming more adaptable and flexible, and can be tailored to particular application domains. Digital intelligence is becoming seamless and invisible, enabling more attention to be paid to the content and the user's interaction with it. This revolution is having effects on the development and organization of information and artefact repositories such as libraries, museums, and exhibitions, and the way in which physical and digital aspects are mediated to users. Service providers are in an increasingly competitive market place where the interface to the user is increasingly important.

Environments

Improved toolkits with online audio and video assistance enable the digital environment to be a productive place for the user to study and access information. However, it is generally acknowledged that the readability of information on display screens is usually less than that of printed books or journals, at least for extended periods. It is not a matter of a simple comparison of text on a screen with that on a printed page. Developments in the area of hypertext have enabled electronic documents to refer directly to others *in situ*; thus a document viewed on a screen is more likely to be a hierarchy of documents. Where the computer has a network connection, this is from a global database of information. Books are linear, not hierarchical.

Digitization

Mass digitization projects are bringing traditional library materials online, with consequent changes to the infrastructure of libraries and the role of librarians. One such project is being led by Google and is digitizing older printed books with no copyright restrictions. Currently the company has ten agreements in place, including the libraries of Harvard University, Stanford University, New York Public, and the University of Oxford.

The Open Content Alliance, sponsored by the Internet Archive and Yahoo!, is digitizing works after seeking permission of the copyright holder, in contrast to Google who assume fair use unless explicitly told not to copy by the copyright holder.

A large number of digital libraries now exist, alongside traditional libraries.

Push versus Pull

Pull services are gaining market share because they are centred on the user and deliver added value; push services may decline. Books and libraries have been typically push services, and publishers are primarily interested in the economics of book production if they are a company with shareholders. With the rise of the Internet, users decide which information they wish to look at and then drill down if an area is of particular interest. Thus service providers seek to provide information which pulls users in. Attractive pull services are often quickly acquired by larger commercial organizations because of their content and existing user base. The open access approach implies a shift from supply-led to demand-led information provision.

Follett Report

A review of library and related provision in higher education in the UK was commissioned in 1992 and reported on at the end of 1993[2]. It was chaired by Sir Brian Follett and the primary aim of the group that was set up was to review:

- the implications of the growth in undergraduate student numbers for library services
- the role of libraries in support of research, given the increasing number of periodicals and specialist books, and their increase in price
- the developments in information technology and the implications for libraries.

It was the first general review of library provision since a report in 1967 by the Committee on Libraries established by the University Grants Committee in 1963.

The Follett Report noted the shift that was starting from libraries as containers of information to information access. It was recognized that it was no longer possible for any single library to contain all the resources required. Shortfalls in space for libraries and materials were noted and urgent action was recommended, given the importance of libraries to the delivery of teaching and research. The

Funding Councils accepted the Follett Report's findings and a sum of £10 million was made available in 1995 for building work in libraries related directly to student numbers. It was also recommended that the Funding Councils should jointly invest £20 million over three years in support of a series of development projects designed to further the use of IT in a number of areas. These included access and interfaces to national networks (e.g. the Joint Academic Network – JANET), navigational tools, electronic document storage and delivery, electronic journals, databases and datasets, library management systems, library automation, institutional information strategies, and training. The exploitation of IT was regarded as essential in creating the effective library of the future.

Post Follett

Have the developments recommended by the Follett been achieved? The answer is yes, to a large degree. Library space and information access assumed a new priority in University planning and resourcing. Building work extended libraries and provided new facilities for users and more space for archives. The total of £140 million funding was a relatively small amount and with institutions required to contribute two thirds of the funding, it still needed a significant commitment from the institution. However, it did pump prime the provision of expansion space and did act as a catalyst for later building projects. After the three year funding period arising out the Follett Report, the expansion programmes continued due to the new impetus from increased student numbers and the requirements of new technologies.

One key thrust of the Follett Report was to increase the support for research. This has been accomplished by a variety of initiatives including access to e-resources, the provision of datasets funded by JISC, and national access schemes via the Society of College, National and University Libraries (SCONUL). An example of the latter is SCONUL Research Extra – a passport to the libraries of over 150 participating higher education institutions.

A further successful outcome of the Follett Report was the collaboration over IT developments for the future. Key issues such as copyright, liaison with publishers, and access to electronic journals and databases have benefited from collaboration and negotiation at national level. Resources have been obtained at reduced rates and the community has benefited by working together. The Consortium of Research Libraries in the UK (CURL) has sought to increase access to distributed resources (electronic and print) to all users. The principle of sharing resources and expertise has clearly benefited the local, national and international research community, and is a model for the academic community to follow. It is unfortunate that the current drivers at national level to greater selectivity in research funding and greater autonomy in curricula discourages collaboration on the academic content in UK Universities at a time when there is major collaboration on service infrastructures and access to quality national and global repositories. Such competition is fundamentally divisive and is not in the best interests of UK academia as a whole.

Electronic journals are available from libraries and access is usually provided to all staff and students via campus networks to their desk top or laptop using their username and password. This access is therefore location-independent and is effectively global. A number of projects have been sponsored by the Joint Information Systems Committee (JISC) to prototype IT developments and provide new user services, and in general these have had a significant impact on the development of library services. Institutions are required by the Funding Councils to have a defined Information Strategy, and the senior person for this should take a leading role in the management of the institution. The objective of this was to provide an institutional framework that would ensure proper oversight of the area and a sustainable future.

The use of electronic documents in libraries and increasing access to other libraries and resources via national networks (e.g. JANET) resulted in a degree of overlap between the traditional library and the Computer Centre. In same cases, institutions have merged these services with one overall head. It is an example of converged services and appears to work well, although historically the cultures of the staff have been different (e.g. the former with collections of materials and the latter with the development and support of systems). In recent years these services have been extended in some institutions to include learning support services in general. Some institutions have de-merged library and IT services and strengthened the link between the library and e-learning provision. Other institutions have taken the opportunity to provide new kinds of learning environments that are user-configurable to some degree (e.g. the University of Warwick Learning Grid and the Saltire Centre at Glasgow Caledonian University).

Areas where Follett recommendations have not been so successful were in staffing and the Fielden Report on Human Resource Management in Academic Libraries. However, developments have been taken forward by SCONUL. Management training for senior librarians was seen as a key issue and this has been addressed by the provision of the Leadership Foundation. In addition, SCONUL was successful in supporting the development of a leadership course for second tier library staff. SCONUL was also involved in the development of a set of performance indicators to measure quality and impact as well as quantity. Librarians have also been involved in the Quality Assurance Agency's audit process.

The Power of Interaction with Information

Information technology is also being utilized in the context of cultural and arts creative expression. This utilizes IT tools and techniques supplemented by video and projection technologies, and tangible and ubiquitous sensors or interaction devices. The latter enables the creative process to be accomplished in a more natural and intuitive manner than current interfaces allow. This will facilitate the development of generic platforms and tools for facilitating creative expression, accessing artistic and cultural material, and developing new forms of communication and interaction between humans and media spaces. Applications include creative work in media production, exploitation of cultural assets, new kinds of contemporary design, facilitating arts and performance, and developing new kinds of museums, which move from passive repositories of collections and artefacts to dynamic and interactive centres of activity and debate. Archives and information are not just seen as content, but also as medium – capable of reinvention, reinterpretation, and recommunication. This has implications for content creation, human/computer interaction, display techniques, and also the next generation of educational and learning environments which can be tuned to human needs and requirements.

Digital Media

The increasing power of computers, speed of networks, and the reducing cost of memory has enabled multimedia information to be handled as readily as numbers or text. One frame of an animation 1,000 by 700 pixels requires 700 kbyte of storage. For 30 frames per sec and 24-bit colour this would need 500 Mbyte. For a 5 minute animation this would require 150 Gbyte (not to mention backups, various revisions etc). Digital cinemas can receive films via the network and save the production costs of traditional film reproduction – typically $5 million for the world-wide release of a movie.

The Digital Media Alliance, Florida, defines digital media as *"the creative convergence of digital arts, science, technology and business for human expression, communication, social interaction and education"*. Many traditional media companies now generate their content in digital form for distribution via CD, DVD, or the Internet. Marketing strategies for content increasingly utilize multiple media channels to hit different markets simultaneously. New media forms such as wikis, blogs, podcasts, and the distribution of user-generated content (e.g. YouTube) are all changing the nature of information and how it is stored, accessed, and distributed. Filtering, accreditation, and synthesis of content are created through new hierarchies of peers and information affinity groups on the Internet.

A digital library is a repository where a significant proportion of the assets are in digital form. They are indexed and searchable via electronic means, which is an advantage over paper-based information. When the library is networked, it can provide local and remote access with equal facility.

Remediation

New technology is regarded by some as an intrusion into the more classical world of information and value which will brings its own new kinds of technological values to replace existing aesthetic and cultural ones. In other words, a divorce will be created between the new world and the old world. It can equally be argued that new media achieve their cultural significance by refashioning earlier approaches[3]. Earlier examples of this are photography refashioning painting, film refashioning stage production, and television refashioning films and radio.

Challenges for Libraries

Information is no longer exclusively library-centric but is also network-centric. The centre of gravity has moved from information provision to information access. Online search (via engines such as Google) is replacing physical search. Mass digitization projects of library collections are accelerating this trend.

Recent discussions have centred round not just *converged* services but also *shared* services. A digitized library does not have to be on an institution's campus any more. National and international networks ensure seamless ubiquity of access. Thus service providers can be anywhere in the global village – bandwidth, distance and time are no longer the primary issues. Librarians who were formerly holders of specialist collections and advisers to users who visited the library are now moving to roles which reflect the increasing accessibility of information.

There are changing patterns of learning, teaching and scholarship – for example in the way information is used and deployed, the ways in which learning is facilitated and measured, and the timescales involved. New genres of scholarly work (e.g. Perseus) exploit the digital library environment to evolve interactions through time, space, and language. Automated analysis of data in publications is now possible. Discipline mark-up languages are available.

Combining the best of both worlds – the traditional library and the online search – to meet the developing requirements of users is a key challenge for the future.

This Volume

The changes that digital convergence is bringing about are substantial and are also likely to be long-lasting. This volume presents key aspects in this rapidly moving field in the areas of libraries, and information sciences, and technology – from international experts who are leaders in their fields.

This book contains contributions outlining the developments in libraries and information access both pre- and post-Follett by many of those who were, and are, closely involved in leading libraries and IT developments (including networking).

Dr Reg Carr

Reg Carr's 36-year professional career in academic libraries, has included 30 years in some of the UK's largest university research libraries (Manchester,

Cambridge, Leeds, and Oxford). He has occupied a position of influence and leadership in the developments and innovations in academic research libraries. He was University Librarian Keeper of the Brotherton Collection in the University of Leeds from 1986 until 1997 when he became Director of University Library Services and Bodley's Librarian in the University of Oxford in 1997. He retired in December 2006. He was Secretary of CURL and Chairman of SCONUL and was a member of JISC and Chairman of the JISC sub-committee responsible for overseeing both the influential eLib programme and the development of the Distributed National Electronic Resource. He was on the Board of the international Research Libraries Group from 1997 to 2003. In 2000 he was appointed as an external member of the Board of Overseers' Visiting Committee for the Harvard University Library, and from 2001 to 2005 he was Vice-Chairman of the Digital Preservation Coalition.

The last ten years has been a pivotal decade. There have been technology challenges associated with ensuring that users are able to get information in digital form at the point of need. Management challenges have included how to optimally organize service delivery across physically separate subject libraries within organizations. Estates challenges have included how to provide further space for archives.

This volume reflects the influence that Reg Carr has had upon the field of libraries and information systems, and the contributions from the authors are made in his honour. Readers are also referred to the book published by Reg Carr in 2007[4].

References

1. http://www.jisc.ac.uk/uploaded_documents/JISClearningspaces.pdf
2. http://www.ukoln.ac.uk/services/papers/follett/report/
3. Bolter, J. D. and Grusin, R. (1999) *Remediation: Understanding New Media*. MIT Press, Massachusetts.
4. Carr, R. P. (2007) *The Academic Research Library in a Decade of Change*. Chandos Publishing, Oxford.

PART 1

The Organization and Delivery of Digital Information

1

From "Boutique" to Mass Digitization: the Google Library Project at Oxford[1]

Ronald Milne

1.1 Introduction

Sir Thomas Bodley, in founding his Library in Oxford in 1602, intended it to be not just for the University of Oxford, but also for what he called the "Republic of Letters". By this he meant that the library's collections should be open to all who had need of them. This ethos is one that has held good for four centuries, and of which Oxford is proud. The Bodleian's doors are open to the intellectually curious, whether they have an academic affiliation or not. Indeed, it is notable that 60% of the Bodleian's registered readers are not members of the University of Oxford.

From the start, Bodley intended his library to be one of the great libraries of the world. He encouraged his "very great store of honourable friends" to give money and books to support his project. The Bodleian acquired the legal deposit privilege in 1610, the first library in the UK to do so, and today it the oldest extant legal deposit library in the world. With a stock of over 8 million items, built up by legal deposit, purchase and gift, Oxford is fortunate in possessing in the Bodleian what is the richest array of manuscript and print collections of any university library in the world.

Over the centuries very many scholars have travelled to Oxford to use the Bodleian's collections, while those unable to make the journey, or unable to stay for long, have used microfilms and transparencies as surrogates to aid them in their studies. Recently, the advent of the Internet and the ability to digitize large quantities of text and images, and make them available over the Web, has transformed ways of working.

1.2 A Brief Outline History of Digitization at Oxford

Oxford has been involved in digitization projects since 1993, when through the sponsorship of Toyota City, the Bodleian undertook a project focusing on motor car ephemera in the library's John Johnson Collection, supplemented by images of other forms of transport. The images were produced by means of Kodak's Photo-CD technology: the original items were photographed onto 35 mm slides, and scanned onto Photo-CD discs. These were then processed to convert the images to compressed JPEG and GIF images at various resolutions.

The technology has, of course, moved on since then and the University has undertaken a host of other digitization activities in the interim. These include the Early Manuscripts at Oxford University project funded through the joint higher education funding councils' Specialized Research Collections in the Humanities initiative.[2] It created high-resolution digital images, which were scanned directly from the original manuscripts. Over eighty manuscripts dating from the 9th to 19th centuries were selected as major treasures from their respective Oxford libraries, to create access to material where the original might otherwise be too fragile to handle.

Other projects include the Broadside Ballads project (also funded under the Specialized Research Collections in the Humanities initiative), the creation of archive quality digital images of political and satirical prints and trades and professions prints from the John Johnson collection under the JISC Image Digitization Initiative (JIDI)[3] and, more recently, the digitization of the Shikshapatri, funded by the New Opportunities Fund (now the Big Lottery Fund).[4] The Shikshapatri, a fragile Sanskrit manuscript, written by Shree Swaminarayan, founder of Swaminarayan Hinduism, outlines moral and spiritual codes for everyday life.

In 2000, recognizing the opportunities for enhancing access through digitization, the Andrew W. Mellon Foundation gave generous help in establishing the Oxford Digital Library (ODL). The Foundation funded the essential infrastructure of the ODL and supported a range of digital projects based on core research material from Oxford's library holdings. It aimed to promote scholarly effort with relevance to research and teaching by digitizing, delivering and enhancing the University's major library holdings. A grant programme for projects was managed by the Oxford Digital Library in collaboration with an editorial board, comprising scholars and librarians from within and outside Oxford. Examples of the great variety of material digitized under the grant programme include political cartoons from the period of the French Revolution and Napoleonic wars from the Bodleian's Curzon Collection, and Sibthorpe and Smith's *Flora Graeca* (1806–1840) illustrated by Ferdinand Bauer. That project undertook the digitization not only of the printed volumes, but also the original hand-coloured drawings from which the printed engravings were made.

Consistent with the policy of making its collections as accessible as possible, Oxford has also been a major participant in commercially funded projects such as Early English Books Online (EEBO)[5] and Eighteenth Century Collections Online (ECCO).[6]

1.3 A Move from "Boutique" to Mass Digitization

The projects described above, and others like them undertaken in Oxford and elsewhere, have generally focused on a particular subject area or genre. This has been for good reasons on the one hand funding has been strictly limited and, on the other, it has seemed to make good sense to concentrate, in an academic environment, on projects that are of immediate interest to scholars. A lot of excellent work has been done, and if one had an observation to make it would merely be to remark that most of the work has been done piecemeal, without much reference to digitization work going on elsewhere. Without wishing to detract from the digitization projects that have been undertaken so far, they may largely be regarded as "boutique" activities when compared with the Google Library Project.

The Google project, in contrast, involves digitization on an industrial scale. Books are digitized *en masse* rather than cherry-picked. They are "selected" only in as far as they should be in a fit state, in conservation terms, to undergo the non-invasive Google digitization process and they should be of a format with which the Google scanning technology can currently cope.

1.4 Reg Carr and Early Contacts with Google[7]

Oxford's earliest significant library contact with Google was in late 2002 when, as a result of discussions between Reg Carr, Director of University Library Services and Bodley's Librarian, and the University's North American Development Office, Google was identified as a potential partner in the "Hybrid Library" element of Oxford University Libraries Capital Campaign. Reg Carr was introduced to Raymond Nasr (Google's Vice-President, Executive Communications) at a *Silicon Valley Comes to Oxford* seminar held at the University's Said Business School. It was during lunch and an extended tour of the Bodleian that the possibility of Bodleian–Google cooperation was raised.

Clearly, the discussion had resonance. There appeared to be an obvious alignment between the two organizations and it made perfect sense to explore possible projects and collaborative efforts. Further contact with Google followed soon after the initial meeting, with David Drummond (Google's Vice President for Strategy and Business Development) visiting Oxford in January 2003 and Reg Carr being invited to visit Google a month later, in February 2003, to coincide with a scheduled Research Libraries Group meeting in Mountain View.

While visiting Google at Mountain View, Reg Carr met with a number of senior members of Google staff and discussed ways of developing Google access to information sources "hidden" in the Deep Web and beyond the Web. Evidently, Google already had an emerging ambition to expose much more material to its

Web crawlers and to digitize and index it, and the talk was of an "offline content project". This has proved to be a rough prototype of what eventually became known to the world as Google Book Search.

During the same visit, Reg Carr presented a paper on seamless access to research resources which discussed possible Google/Oxford synergies, and he urged Google to have conversations with major research libraries, such as the Bodleian, about ways of providing Google Search access to research library materials, both electronic and non-electronic, as a means of enhancing the quality of search results. It was agreed that Google's long-term mission and Oxford's aim of digitizing and making its material available over the Web were well-matched, and it was proposed that discussions should continue.

During the next few months discussions about a library-related project continued by e-mail. Reg Carr travelled to Mountain View again in November 2003, together with a member of staff from the University's North American Development Office, for more focused discussions on the exact nature of Oxford libraries/Google collaboration. Work with publishers and initial discussions with "a number of leading research libraries" was alluded to. Agreement was reached that "the Google team" would visit Oxford as early as possible in January to view the set-up at the Bodleian, to progress the matter and, more specifically, to firm up on the detail. The Oxford visit to Mountain View concluded with a tour of Google's experimental in-house digitization operation.

In mid-January 2004 a four-man Google team visited Oxford for a full-day discussion with senior library staff who might be involved in any future project. The team also toured the Bodleian. Agreement was reached that Google and Oxford would pursue an agreement whereby Google would set up a digitization operation in Oxford to create digital copies of public domain materials for mutual use and benefit.

Between February and December 2004 there were frequent exchanges of drafts of the agreement, discussion documents and points for negotiation. Reg Carr continued to have oversight of the negotiation process while the author and the University's Director of Legal Services became more intensively involved in the fine detail of the discussions. The most senior officers of the University gave their support to the project and approval to proceed was given by the University Council.

1.5 The Google Library Project

Who is taking part in the Project? The libraries of Harvard, Stanford, Michigan and Oxford universities and the New York Public Library were the original partners, and became known as the "Google Five". More recently, the University of California, the University Complutense of Madrid, the University of Wisconsin Madison and the University of Virginia have signed agreements with Google. It seems likely that other libraries will become participants in due course. Millions of printed works will be digitized as a result of the project, which falls under the umbrella of the Google Book Search programme.

At Oxford we are aiming to digitize as much of our 19th century out-of-copyright material as possible, amounting to between 1 and 1.5 million volumes. The project is not limited to the Bodleian Library and we expect to draw, for example, on the collections of the Taylor Institution Library (Oxford's modern languages research library) and the Sackler Library (art history, archaeology, and classics [ancient history and literature]). Together, the scope of Oxford's 19th century material is immense and caters for a very wide range of interests. We intend to digitize printed material in every subject area and will cover all works, including books and journals which would have had no particular academic interest when acquired under legal deposit. Thus, alongside academic books and journals, we will be digitizing recreational magazines, trade literature, post office directories, railway timetables, and much more.

Isn't there a risk of duplicating what is being digitized in other libraries? The answer is "yes", but the incidence of duplication is not as great as one might expect. Analysis of data from WorldCat by Lavoie, Connaway and Dempsey has shown that, among the "Google Five", 56% of works are held uniquely by one of the Google Five libraries and that, when one compares two libraries out of the five, eight out of ten books are held uniquely.[8] Other interesting data that emerge from the analysis, particularly in light of the assertions that the Google Library Project is an example of Anglo-Saxon cultural domination, is that about 50% of the holdings of the five libraries are in languages other than English, and that over 430 different languages are represented in the libraries' joint holdings.[9]

Between the signing of the agreement with Google and the scanning operation starting, we spent much time considering logistics and refining workflows. From the start, Oxford appointed a project manager to undertake day-to-day liaison with Google, and Google had a project manager on site in Oxford over six months before scanning commenced. As part of the pre-digitization process, books are appraised to determine their suitability for scanning, with Oxford conservators having the absolute right to say that a book may not be scanned for conservation reasons. Books are transferred by van from the Library stacks to the digitization centre nearby. The Bodleian, a non-circulating library, has not barcoded its books in the past but, as it is an essential part of the pre-scanning workflow, this and associated bibliographic work is being undertaken as part of the production line process.

Results of surveys of Bodleian holdings undertaken as part of the preparatory work for the project showed that as much as 20% of 19th century holdings are wholly or partially uncut. This was an unwelcome finding if not a complete surprise, given the amount of material acquired under legal deposit. We also found that around 3% of the Bodleian's stock from that period is uncatalogued. We are addressing these two matters.

The Google digitization process captures the whole book, in as far as possible. Thus, boards are digitized as well as the text block. Frontispieces, plates and other illustrations are captured, too, although fold-out illustrations and diagrams fall outside the process at present. All pages are digitized in colour.

The agreement with Google is non-exclusive. Google retains a "Google Digital Copy" and Oxford receives an "Oxford Digital Copy". The digitized book is navigable, the entire text is searchable, and there will be a link from the Oxford catalogue to the digital copy. As the books being digitized at Oxford are in the public domain, complete copies of individual works can be made freely available over the Internet to anyone who has Web access. The costs of the infrastructure and the planning required are such that Google has agreed to host access to the Oxford copy for the time being. There are potentially many different ways in which we could make the Oxford Digital Copy available in due course. Unsurprisingly, we have already been approached by a number of individuals and organizations suggesting that we accord high priority to their area of activity!

1.6 Conclusion

What effect will mass, or large-scale, digitization projects have on the information landscape? Given the millions of books and journals that will be scanned in the course of the Google Library Project, digitization on such a scale surely represents a step-change in the dissemination of information that parallels the impact of the invention of printing from moveable type in the 15th century. In enhancing access to printed material that is not otherwise easily available, the Project has the potential to act as a transforming agent, in learning, teaching and research as well as many other activities. Will it mean the decline of traditional libraries? Anecdotal evidence would suggest that, while dissemination of the printed works will be greatly facilitated, and many who would not otherwise be able to access particular material will be satisfied with a digitized copy, others who perhaps had not intended to visit a library will be inspired to see the original. Scholars will regard their viewing on the Web of material held in the Bodleian and other libraries as valuable preparation and allow them to plan their research in Oxford and elsewhere more efficiently.

Would Sir Thomas Bodley have approved of books in his library being digitized, and on such a large scale? Without doubt he would have regarded the Google Library Project in Oxford as a natural extension of his desire to make the Bodleian's collections readily available to external readers, regardless of affiliation. The Bodleian ethos of facilitating access to all the concept of the "Republic of Letters" has found expression in the Digital Age and of that Sir Thomas would be proud.

Notes

1.   The greater part of this chapter has appeared, in substantially the same form, in Art libraries journal 31 (3) 2006, 5–10, with the title "Upholding Bodley's vision: the Google mass digitization project at Oxford". (That article is to be reprinted in a slightly revised version in Liber Quarterly 16 (2006) 3/4). The section of the present chapter headed "Reg Carr and early contacts with Google" has appeared previously in substantially the same form in Ronald

Milne, "The Google Library Project at Oxford" in William Miller and Rita M. Pellen (eds) Libraries and Google. New York: Haworth Press, 2006, 23–28. Copies available from the Haworth Document Delivery Service: 1-800-HAWORTH. E-mail address: docdelivery@ haworthpress.com.

    The author thanks ARLIS UK and Haworth Press for permission to reuse material previously published.

2.   See: http://www.hefce.ac.uk/research/initiats/Srcith/

3.   The JIDI project enabled digitization of copyright-cleared resources in a number of archival collections: See: http://www.ilrt.bris.ac.uk/jidi/.

4.   See: http://www.nof.org.uk/

5.   See: http://eebo.chadwyck.com/home/

6.   See: http://www.gale.com/EighteenthCentury/

7.   I am indebted to Reg Carr for allowing me to use his personal notes as a source for this section of the chapter. I further acknowledge as a source his contribution to the Opening Plenary Panel session of the CNI Spring 2005 Task Force Meeting, Washington DC, 4 April 2005.

8.   Lavoie, B., Connaway, L. S. and Dempsey, L. (2005) Anatomy of aggregate collections: the example of Google Print for libraries. *D-Lib Magazine,* 11(9); http://www.dlib.org/dlib/september05/lavoie/09lavoie.html.

9   *ibid.*

2

Digital Services in Academic Libraries: the Internet is Setting Benchmarks[1]

Norbert Lossau

2.1 Introduction

Academic libraries have taken on various roles over the course of their history. They are long-term guardians of knowledge, competent brokers of information and reliable guarantors of quality. In the future, a further role will gain central importance: the role of service provider[2]. The volume of holdings or the excellence of a collection will no longer constitute the strategic critical success factors. The academic library of 2007 will put the user (or customer) much more at the centre. This will no longer be implicit, in the sense of well-meaning provision by the library information professional: in the future, customer orientation will mean that all library activities will be measured by whether or not they represent a worthwhile service for the end-user. Success is defined by user acceptance.

The Internet, in developing as an authoritative cross-sectoral platform for digital services, has become a frame of reference for their design. Academic libraries can no longer ignore the general performance characteristics of Internet services: intuitive usability even for non-experts, easily comprehensible functions, strong performance, quick changes from one service to another, permanent availability, as well as the "guarantee" of a successful outcome. Some much-loved library customs and traditions will have to be very carefully considered,

---

1   The article is the English translation of the German article: "Digitale Dienstleistungen in wissenschaftlichen Bibliotheken: Das Internet setzt Maßstäbe." In: *Zeitschrift Buch und Bibliothek*, BuB, Dossier zur „Bibliothek 2007", 3, 57 (2005, 05, pp. 365–376).

2   The demand for new service strategies has also internationally been prioritized (e.g. by Andrew K. Pace, *The Ultimate Digital Library*, Chicago, ALA, 2003).

from the users' viewpoint, and measured against the service benchmark of the Internet, to see whether they are sustainable. Libraries can no longer learn only from other libraries. Success can also be achieved through the careful assessment and analysis of services from other business sectors, less in terms of content than in terms of methodology and structure.

Learning from the Internet does not, however, mean that its recipes for success should simply be copied. Libraries have their own traditional strengths, which they should creatively incorporate into new services. Examples of such strengths are the neutral evaluation of information sources, the categorization and filtering of relevant content, the concern for cost-effective access for the user, as well as the securing of long-term access to information.

Academic libraries consider themselves to be guarantors of a high-quality supply of literature for the academic community. What does the provision of information services mean today? How do we define digital services in the age of the World Wide Web? The following article attempts to answer these questions and in so doing to help orientate libraries as they set an important new course for the future.

2.2 Services and How they are Aimed at the User

Librarians in academic libraries are convinced that they are developing and delivering their services in their users' best interests. However, being user oriented has frequently meant librarians and professionals deciding for the researcher or student which literature should be used and how. This philosophy, which is stamped with didacticism, can still be seen today in the so-called Stefi study which appeared in 2001. This suggested that the users should be the ones to change, rather than the mind-set of librarians:

> In principle, there is every reason for electronic academic information services to be improved primarily in respect of intuitive navigation for users. It is important to be careful, however, when considering any measures for improving the use of electronic academic information resources in higher education, that an impression of insufficient clarity and lack of structure is not in fact an expression of a lack of systematic know-how about how to use electronic academic information resources. In any case, it is to be expected that as competence in the use of electronic academic information resources increases, so the impression of lack of structure and clarity will lessen.[3]

For a long time there has been no systematic communication between libraries and users about the form services should take. Users have either made use of the library services gratefully, come to terms with their deficiencies, or looked for

---

3   „Stefi-Studie": *Nutzung elektronischer wissenschaftlicher Information in der Hochschulausbildung.* Commissioned by the Bundesministerium für Bildung und Forschung, Projektträger Fachinformation. Produced by Rüdiger Klatt *et al.* Dortmund, August 2001, p. 14. http://www.stefi.de/download/bericht2.pdf.

alternatives. These alternatives are increasingly being found outside libraries, as can be seen by the increase in Internet search engine use. New evaluation studies on user behaviour, which in Germany have been carried out in particular by the ULB Muenster, are taking account of these trends and are delivering abundant and informative findings[4]. In the international arena, attention should be drawn to the LibQual analysis, developed by the American Association of Research Libraries (ARL)[5]. In addition to these studies, which evaluate existing services with a view to improving them, market research techniques developed in industry are also being tested. This is to enable requirements and preferences for new products to be incorporated during the planning stage[6].

As well as these planning and evaluation tools, academic libraries have another great treasure, which they have so far failed to exploit adequately: their direct proximity to users. It is possible to establish contacts in libraries in many ways, including through local subject libraries, subject specialists and information and enquiry services.

The information discovered in this way is currently being used to improve services in discrete areas in the short-term. It is astounding that these findings often do not make their way into the general strategic plan of the library.

The first step in making sure services are directed at the user is to observe and plan these services from the users' perspective. For this to work successfully, librarians must first be able to think themselves into the user's method of working. Only then will they be able to specify requirements in a meaningful way. Ideally, the users themselves should be brought into these development processes.

2.3 Users in Research, Teaching and Study

Now, more than ever before, libraries should be observing their users' working practices carefully, before drawing conclusions about which services are

---

4   Nutzungsanalyse des Systems der überregionalen Literatur- und Informations-versorgung: Part I: Informationsverhalten und Informationsbedarf der Wissenschaft. Study commissioned by the Deutsche Forschungsgemeinschaft, DFG, carried out by the ULB Münster in collaboration with infas, edited by Roswitha Poll et al., June 2003. http://www.dfg.de/forschungsfoerderung/wissenschaftliche_infrastruktur/lis/download/ssg_bericht_teil_1.pdf. The study contains a comprehensive, international bibliography of usage analyses.

5   LibQual+[TM], http://www.libqual.org/

6   ProSeBiCA (Prospektive Steuerung der Serviceangebote von wissenschaftlichen Bibliotheken mittels Conjoint-Analyse; Prospective Steerage of academic library services through Conjoint-analysis) has been a joint project of the Marketing Faculty (Prof. Decker) and the University Library at Bielefeld University, collaborating with the TU Cottbus and the Sheridan Libraries at Johns Hopkins University, Baltimore, U.S. The underlying conjoint-methodology offers various product qualities and combinations as options and is asking for preferences and the willingness to cover costs for services.

worthwhile, in addition to using direct contacts, planning tools and evaluation studies.

Since working practices themselves are subject to a higher dynamic, through the influence of the computer on work and communication processes, this has become all the more important. Only when libraries become more familiar with the current working practices of the academic community and are prepared to keep this knowledge up-to-date, can future and forward-looking library services be developed. Internet services, such as Google, eBay or music exchange markets, enjoy the success that they do because they have become expert at judging customer behaviour exactly and tuning their services precisely to certain core demands (for example to retrieve relevant information without specialist training, or to get good value for money when shopping).

The way researchers, teachers and students approach academic information varies in its complexity. Each approach is stamped by the cultures of different disciplines and is then differentiated even more by individual preferences and competencies. In theory, therefore, there is an infinite variety of individual information management practices. In order to get a handle on this it is helpful to look at some examples of main working cycles and paradigms:

2.3.1 The Formulation of Research Themes and Concepts

In this scenario, researchers gather information sources as comprehensively as possible, with the aim of stimulating new ideas but also of confirming and checking the findings they have to date. The spectrum of information sources includes quality assured specialist literature, databases, enquiries via email lists, email communication with faculty colleagues, research data and primary data, results from Internet searches and so on.

Researchers complain about the high amount of time they spend on searching and accessing information sources, as is shown by the ULB Muenster study[7]. Considering the much cited information overload, deficiencies in library search services are just as much to blame as licensing problems.

2.3.2 Structuring of Content and Exchange of Relevant Information in the Project Context

While work is being done on a project or a certain theme, all the various information sources must be kept permanently in mind. This has always been true for individuals, but increasingly it is also true within collaborative working groups, which could be in a single institution or spread over several institutions. The growing number of interdisciplinary research projects, research networks, graduate training groups and virtual institutes are evidence of this. Biologists, chemists and information scientists, for example, are working together on genetic research and are dividing up complex research themes

---

7   „Nutzungsanalyse...", loc. cit., pp. 88f.

among various institutions as separate packages of work. The project consists of a continual exchange of acquired concepts, initial research results and partial findings, allowing on-going work to progress in a complementary manner.

A central challenge for researchers is to present heterogeneous information resources from different disciplines in a content-based structure, which can be understood by all partners. Modern methods of representing knowledge make use of so-called topic maps, for example, as well as ontologies. These structures can be easily visualized, making it simpler for biologists to understand chemistry information sources, and vice versa.

While libraries do provide content-based categorizing tools, these only exist in the form of abstract classification systems and keyword schemas, which apply to particular works, not to concrete project concepts. In addition, they are only available through centralized bibliographic systems and services, and not in the decentralized working environments of researchers, as independently usable and, if necessary, modifiable tools.

2.3.3 Publishing

The publication process is currently going through a time of great change. New types of publication are emerging as a result of the introduction of additional business models (Open Access). For example, digital media (multimedia elements) is being integrated as part of the publication, and computer programmes and simulations are being included, as is digital research data (test series, statistical data, genetic sequences and so on).

In addition, publications are no longer automatically perceived as the conclusion of a piece of research. Instead they are more often interpreted as a variant of academic communication[8].

2.3.4 Summary

Methods of working with academic information are becoming differentiated to an extent which was not encountered in pre-Internet times. In the future there will be a marked customization of working environments. Academic users will want to make use of particular digital services in their own distinct combinations as and when they are needed in research or teaching groups. It will have to be possible to install services directly on individual desktops, as well as in combination with other services. A well-known example of a stand-alone service like this is the Google search box (and Google Scholar), which is easy to install locally on every desktop.

---

8   Van de Sompel, Herbert *et al.* (2004) Rethinking scholarly communication. *D-Lib Magazine*, **10**(9); http://www.dlib.org/dlib/september04/vandesompel/09vandesompel.html, doi:10.1045/september2004-vandesompel

2.4 Academic Users and General Internet Services

In library circles, discussions about the significance of the Internet are often confined to the use of academic information resources. As far as information professionals are concerned, there is soon a consensus that Internet services are of insufficient quality, and confirmation of this view is provided by relevant studies. At the same time, libraries have to concede that researchers and students are increasingly using general Internet search engines for their academic research[9].

Because of this focus on specialist Internet use, another equally relevant aspect has receded into the background: the general performance features and characteristics of Internet services. With the Internet having developed to become the uncontested central platform for digital services, and moreover with commercial services available for the academic community via the Internet, it has become high time for libraries to have a very close look at the basis for this success. Internet services have permanently changed the experiences and requirements of all users, with library clientèle clearly no exception. In order for libraries to remain competitive, these requirements must be analysed and translated into library services.

2.4.1 General Experiences and Requirements of Users

The following performance features are expected of digital services:
- easily comprehensible functions
- intuitive usability even for non-experts
- strong performance, meaning fast response times.

Beyond these generally known characteristics, it is worth looking in more depth, as follows:
- The Internet has emancipated users. They can act independently, set the time and place of their activities themselves, and can get all the information they need to prepare for their course of action themselves. Banking can be done online, insurance tariffs can be calculated anonymously for the individual, holiday trips can be planned and purchases suitably researched.
- There is an extremely low use threshold for Internet services. Basic knowledge will do for the normal or occasional user. The simplicity and intuitiveness of interfaces can act as an incentive for the spontaneous use of services.
- The amount on offer over the Internet is overwhelming. Every user has a real chance of finding something for every need: principally a guarantee of success.
- The Internet encourages a light-hearted approach to services. It is smooth running, you can navigate in an unstructured way, you don't have to think in

---

9   Cf. *Nutzungsanalyse...*, *loc. cit.*, p. 91f. (here: 71% of the respondents)

advance, and you meet with new surprises again and again. You learn new unexpected things, you can move around freely and unobserved in unknown information areas, without standing out as a layman. Even the least "sporty" user can surf the Internet.

- The Internet facilitates user communication. Newsgroups, thematic forums, chatrooms or organized online dating agencies: millions of users are now communicating online.

Forward-looking strategic planning should not, however, be limited to the adaptation of successful models. Libraries should also take the initiative and develop such models creatively around their own strengths. There is especially room for such developments to be made in areas where Internet services are weak, for example in the indexing and cataloguing of content.

2.5 Libraries and Digital Services Today

In Germany, local academic libraries as well as interregional service providers (especially head offices of library networks) already offer, in differing intensity, a multiplicity of digital services which are accessible over the Internet. In comparison with other countries, Germany can count itself among the leaders in terms of comprehensiveness and quality, alongside the USA, Great Britain, Australia, Canada, the Netherlands or the Scandinavian countries, to name just the most well-known players. Many other countries have also developed note-worthy services in individual libraries (for example, the Bibliothèque Nationale de France with its Gallica service).

Among the noteworthy services offered by German academic libraries are:

- Online library catalogues (OPACs), union catalogues, Karlsruhe virtual catalogue
- Digital libraries/information portals
- Virtual subject libraries/subject gateways, Vascoda
- Electronic Journal library (EZB, Regensburg)
- Document delivery
- Online interlibrary loan
- Full-text servers (e.g. through digitization)
- Dissertation servers
- E-learning platforms
- Virtual enquiry systems (Virtual reference desks, chat, online tutorials).

Many of these services contain a bundle of several facilities. For the North Rhine Westphalia Digital Library, these include metasearches, information about access rights, administration of personal profiles, alerting services and a shopping basket function. Local library systems make administrative lending services available as well as searches.

In the meantime some services, such as document delivery services (Subito, Jason and others) have established themselves and cater well for the demand for full-text from academic customers. Administrative services such as being able to see reservations and lending details, and to make renewals, and recently the online interlibrary loan service, have begun to enjoy great popularity. They are part of the general trend of Internet services towards self-service. Other services typical of the Internet such as virtual enquiry services are still too new for reliable judgements to be made as to how they will be accepted by users. Services such as dissertation servers and e-learning platforms, insofar as they are run by libraries at all (and not, for example, by the computing services), are closely linked to the prevailing local attitude to publishing and teaching, and are therefore to be viewed within certain basic conditions.

Core library services include the online catalogue, and now the general and specialist gateways to the digital library, which enable integrated searches across heterogeneous information sources, especially catalogues and databases. The spectrum of these services, which have been built up over the past 10–15 years, is impressive from a librarian's viewpoint.

Looking more closely at the use of precisely these services, the satisfaction of libraries has to be seen in relative terms: definitive studies over the past few years have highlighted significant deficiencies. These findings should be sufficient reason for libraries to react, but there are still further developments emerging, which demonstrate the need for action even more urgently: on the one hand, competing products from commercial providers are increasingly being offered over the Internet in this service area. These products are both free (search services such as Google Scholar and Scirus) and chargeable (searching and full-text services such as Scopus and Web of Knowledge).

On the other hand, it has emerged that specialist researchers in particular disciplines, especially science (for example high energy physics), have begun almost self-sufficiently to organize their own search strategies and increasingly also their own literature provision. They resort to library services, especially journals, during the publication process in order to verify citations, or during the academic application procedure, in order to check the spectrum of publications from applicants.

2.6 Libraries and Digital Services in the Near-Future

In the coming years libraries must make every effort to direct their services at the real needs and requirements of their customers. The strategy to take them there must be: rigorous adjustment of existing services with attention to the requirements described above, together with the building up of value-added services, which stand out above other services, including commercial services, and which can therefore lead to increased use.

2.7 Reorganization of Library Search Systems and Access to Full-Text

Among the core requirements of researchers and students are comprehensive searches for academic literature and access to the documents and data with as little expenditure of time and money as possible. These requirements are not satisfactorily met by current library services in the form of catalogues, digital libraries and (subject) gateways, as has been demonstrated by the German Research Council study on "use analysis" of services in special collection areas mentioned above.

The following areas should be taken into account:

- Comprehensive, integrated indexing and searching for information sources
- Intuitive usability of search systems
- Information services structured by subject and relevance filtering of search results
- Direct access to full-text and data.

2.7.1 Comprehensive, Integrated Indexing of Information Sources

Users are interested in asking questions about content. Historians and Sociologists, for example, want to pose socio-political questions in a historical context; biologists, medics and bioinformation scientists are searching for the mysteries of the human genome. The information portals made available by libraries no longer cover the whole spectrum of academic literature and data, leading to an increased use of Internet search engines, something that has become more pronounced since the introduction of Google Scholar as an academic search service in November 2004. This becomes of particular concern to libraries when such search services are used not only to complement other services, but exclusively. The first hints from researchers that they are moving in this direction have already been distributed across relevant mailing lists.

It is a fact that online information sources are not being taken up sufficiently through local and interregional information portals. This has not altered with the latest service offered by a national academic portal, Vascoda. Many of the traditional forms of information, such as databases, electronic journals and so on, still cannot be integrated in searches; newer forms such as pre-print and full-text servers, dissertation servers or media servers may be missing from search systems entirely.

The absence of the digital services which have been produced by the libraries themselves is especially astounding, given that for the most part they are freely accessible. The services referred to are the many hundreds of digitized collections which have been produced using public funding over the last 15 years in Germany and many other countries. The reasons why the licensed services are missing are partly financial. However a universal desideratum is for the technology of information portals and catalogues to be improved. This is optimized for searching for structured data (metadata). Full-text searching is at best an add-on.

It is imperative that the search systems behind current information portals are moved onto search engine technology, which has demonstrably proved itself in the Internet and which has been implemented successfully in the academic information sector through Scirus (Elsevier) and, most recently, Google Scholar (Google). Scirus was originally developed for electronic journals produced by the publisher Elsevier as an alternative search platform to the Science Direct server. However, today it already encompasses many other sorts of academic information, with particular emphasis on STM, and is free to use.

The latest service from Elsevier, Scopus, which is not freely available, is currently in the introductory phase. It encompasses over 14,000 electronic journals from more than 4000 academic publishers, all of which have been linked together. Both search systems are based on search engine technology, as is Google Scholar, which has been publicly and freely available as a beta version since 9 November 2004, and which has the aim of gradually making the entire body of academic literature available for searching. In the library sector the demonstrator BASE from Bielefeld University Library has successfully taken its first steps, and is currently being intensively developed further[10].

2.7.2 Intuitive Usability of Search Systems

Users perceive library search systems to be unwieldy. Simply looking at the length of the help pages shows that they are not designed for quick intuitive search queries. The difficulties begin with choosing the suitable search field. From a library viewpoint, the number of search fields is helpful, but for users it is hardly meaningful or sensible to see "originating organization", "serial keyword" and "accession number". What sort of user knows the difference between a "keyword" and a "subject term"?

Analyses of Internet search engines show that 99% of users prefer the single line search box. If a user has decided on using the library system for their query, they are normally unaware of the searching potential offered by "Boolean searches" or various "truncation options". Even library information professionals are regularly surprised by the multiplicity of combinations. However, contrary to the wide-spread belief among librarians, entering search terms is only part of the problem. The inflexibility of the display and sorting of search results (at most by author, title or year), as well as the restricted ways to refine searches, are far more significant deficiencies and are caused by the way the system is set up.

Once again, search engine technology offers models for solutions. Search engines offer various static and dynamic processes for sorting and ranking search results, which are based on current, on-the-fly analysis of the full text and data searched. Functionality such as "more on this topic", or "restrict to this

---

10   Bielefeld Academic Search Engine: http://www.base-search.net/

topic" or "Did you mean XY?" produces even more results at the click of a mouse.

2.7.3 Structuring of Information Services and Search Results by Subject and Content

From a researcher's perspective, a search should include as many information sources as possible, and at the same time deliver only the most relevant results. Academic libraries have tried to approach this balancing act pragmatically by building up virtual subject libraries. They have divided the information space into subject-based segments, taking the plan developed by the German Research Council for special collection areas as a starting point, the structures of which tend to be supplier-oriented.

Limiting the items available for searching was meant to increase the chance of subject relevance. Only sources which have been specially selected are included in searches. In contrast to this, academic search engines such as Scirus and Google Scholar offer an information spectrum that spans different subject areas and still attain surprisingly high relevance in the results because of the technologies working in the background. At the same time they are encountering, whether they like it or not, a pronounced increase in interdisciplinary research.

Focusing on the indexing of content is one of the traditional strengths of libraries. This is coming in useful in the age of the Internet, since it is in this area that traditional Internet search engines are showing clear weaknesses and are not sufficiently able to distinguish between what is relevant and what is unimportant. As more information sources are being integrated into search systems in the interests of comprehensive research, academic users are needing content filters even more pressingly. Such filters can be used in refining search results as well as in navigating across information areas (browsing).

The tools that are currently available, such as classification systems and fixed vocabulary thesauri, have to be further developed for use in search engines in the online environment. Librarians must actively participate in the development of new tools such as ontologies and topic maps in the context of the semantic web discussion. In particular, the Web Ontology Language (OWL) will be used for indexing content in the Internet in the future. The impetus for these latter concepts is currently coming from computer and information scientists.

In contrast to the indexing of content, formal description is considered less important by researchers. The reduction in the number of descriptive categories in Dublin Core is indicative of a trend which has been strengthened by the development of the metadata harvesting protocols of the open archives initiative (OAI-PMH). Libraries should react appropriately to these developments, and at the least should rethink the indexing of online information sources.

Traditional formal cataloguing according to RAK-WB rules will not be practicable, simply because of the sheer number of documents. Reduced description schemas should be used, such as Dublin Core, according to the type of information. Automatic processing to extract metadata is already being used in limited corpora, and promises to be successful, but is clearly not yet scaleable. These developments must be carefully observed. While it would be desirable to have at least one line of formal description metadata, full text indexing could also be sufficient for certain document types.

2.7.4 Direct Access to Full-Text and Data

From a user's perspective, even the best search systems lose half their value, if they can't get to the underlying documents and data at all, or only after considerable expenditure. This isn't particularly important for free content, as it can be clicked on directly. The problem lies with chargeable information sources. In the area of journals there is a certain movement to transfer the operating costs from use to production, through the Open Access model. For example, authors or libraries might be asked to pay a publication charge. It is questionable whether this model will actually catch on.

A glance at the Internet raises some doubts. High-value content from journals can be read and downloaded for a small fee, after the abstract has been read for free. The transaction is managed through a commercial agent[11]. This process also works well for music titles over the Internet. In the short or medium term, academic publishers will also have to adapt their online services. When that happens an article from the Science Direct server will no longer cost 30 Dollars, but only about 4 to 6 Euros, the same as the cost of document delivery using Subito. Turnover will be achieved through large numbers of accesses over as many and as attractive search engines as possible. Libraries should support these developments, not in the sense of a complete dissolution of the subscription systems which have been used up until now, but as a sensible complementary solution to be implemented in particular areas. Reports of libraries' initial experiences are currently being collected.

2.8 Structural Changes to Services

One of the fundamental ways in which the requirements of academic users have changed has been in the customizing of working environments, specifically of desktops as control centres for digital services. The fact that many different working methods have been adopted, as was described elsewhere, has also had serious effects on library digital services, such as online catalogues or information portals to digital libraries. These services are based on technical systems which were developed on the basis of librarians' assumptions about user behaviour. The more these assumptions differ from the reality of working practices, the greater is the probability that relevant services are no longer reaching their intended customers. This leads to the conclusion that structural changes to

---

11   The *Stiftung Warentest* consumer journal offers single articles at a rate of 0,50 cent to €2,50 and has commissioned the First Gate Click & Buy billing and accounting agency.

services and service providers are a necessity. This will be further described using information portals as an example.

2.8.1 Existing Information Portals Made More Flexible and Modular

Existing information portals are principally a result of the work librarians have put into formal description and indexing of content. The systems behind the portals were selected and constructed with the administration of this complex data in mind. The search services that are available are really add-ons. The portal systems are focused on the form and structure of metadata in their functionality and design.

Other services, such as checking local access rights (availability queries) or setting up user profiles, were hard coded into the systems. With users' requirements increasing for all services, the limitations of these systems are becoming more and more obvious, as they have to use new hard coding to integrate additional services at great cost. Knock-on effects from the systems can be observed in the portals themselves, as technical limitations restrict the possibilities for taking up new services creatively.

For this reason, there is increasing support for portal concepts which make a distinction between systems and services. This would mean, for example, that a different system, and if necessary a different service provider, could be responsible for internal data administration than the one responsible for the search services offered to users. Each system has its own strengths and weaknesses, and in an ideal situation the best system for the purpose should be used.

In the IT sector, this concept has already become accepted practice and is used successfully by system integrators in particular. In this way the North Rhine-Westphalia digital library was able to move its existing meta search onto search engine technology relatively quickly and without having to replace the entire system. With the development of web services, the technology for rebuilding portal architecture in this way is available as standard. All services observing this new W3C standard will be available in the future as the building blocks for individual compilations of services.

As the architecture of information portals is made more flexible and modular, new possibilities are opening up both for libraries as service providers and for the end-users themselves. Libraries can access a wide spectrum of services through their local information portal which they can add to and modify as and when necessary. They can also use their resources in a more targeted and effective way, because they can decide for themselves whether they would like to develop and maintain a particular service themselves or whether they would like to re-use an external service.

Instead of maintaining a diverse collection of links to different web pages, users who have set up their electronic workplace themselves can integrate services and relevant access points on their desktop and mobile terminals. For example, in the future users could install their preferred access point for searching their library information portal in the frame of their browser (similar to the Google search box). It would also be possible for this search access point to be combined with other services. For example, it could be integrated with the learning platform or perhaps with popular text editing programmes.

2.8.2 Combination of Local and External Services

This modularizing of IT systems and services opens up completely new possibilities to local libraries in creating their information portals. Of particular strategic relevance here is the question of how home-grown, locally produced services should be combined with external services. For many people in authority in libraries today, it has become abundantly clear that no single institution can produce the whole spectrum of services on its own. However, what course of action should libraries take?

Service providers from the non-academic sector have decided on a pragmatic solution and are working with service providers that specialize in the Internet. Savings banks, insurance companies, and many others seeking to have an online presence, are buying in the necessary know-how for individual services such as on-line banking or tariff calculators. Up until now libraries have been hesitant to take this approach. One reason has been that libraries do not have the same levels of funding as other service providers.

A further, more significant reason, however, has been the way in which libraries have imposed special requirements on external service providers, sometimes with good reason, sometimes less so. If, for example, an external search system has to reproduce the structure of the library catalogue 1:1, it has been given an unnecessarily high obstacle to hurdle. This area is full of concrete examples, particularly with respect to library services such as digital libraries and multimedia servers.

Libraries are also reluctant to integrate such external services, when they can be seen by users. This is for a different reason, but one which must be taken very seriously: they need to be able to justify keeping their own staff. It could occur to budget holders and resources managers to ask questions about staffing levels if services are no longer produced in-house. Aside from the fact that in certain circumstances a redistribution of personnel to, for example, the acquisitions cost centre, could be sensible, libraries in this position should go on the offensive. There are so many challenges to overcome, that other tasks have urgently to be both set and taken on. If users can be made to appreciate the relevance of new services, this ought to strengthen the argument.

Before taking on external services it is sensible to have agreement on the standards to be observed, which all the different services being combined must comply with. The technical Web Services standard has already been mentioned. With a view to the users, and taking the content as a starting point, librarians should also require standards to be met in indexing of content and access protocols. Long-term reliable access should also be a requirement, as should system stability.

Once such standards and minimum requirements have agreed upon, there is nothing standing in the way of serious scrutiny of these services. The requirements expected and established for the library's own user community should form the decisive criteria. As far as local libraries are concerned, providers of "external" services can be close at hand in the computing centre or the media centre, in other libraries outside the home institution, in head offices, service cooperatives such as Vascoda, individual virtual subject libraries, subject information centres; or they can be commercial providers such as publishing houses, search engine companies or content integrators. Nationality is important, however, because of the question of language. Services can be provided for free but can also be chargeable (not-for-profit or commercial).

Taking this as a starting point, it is possible to imagine many future scenarios for combinations of services, for example:

- Joint information services from libraries and computer centres, such as has been realized in the University of Mannheim[12].
- Combination of search services in the sense of "embedded links" through the incorporation of commercial academic search engines (Google Scholar, Scirus).
- Universities offering to support their authors through the publication process by bringing in external services (for example, DIPP/NRW, GAP).

2.9 New Digital Library Services[13]

Library services that have already been introduced will continue to be provided for the foreseeable future, although they may have altered structures, new technologies and possibly different providers. There are already new challenges ahead. For example, the new action and funding programme of the Federal Ministry for Education and Research has highlighted areas which come under the slogan "e-science and networked knowledge management". E-science is here to be interpreted as "enhanced science"[14]. The programme takes up challenges which have political support, because of the trend towards networked research and teaching in the sense of cooperative knowledge-building, independent of institution, state or subject boundaries. In information technology this development is being driven forward powerfully through Grid technology. Libraries are in demand, when it comes to linking academic literature with research data as well as (interactive) software programs (for example simulators) in both the administrative and searching areas of portal systems. In addition there are innovative ways of representing knowledge and visualizing context for academic content, for example through ontologies and topic maps. All work cycles in the academic production processes are affected by this, from

---

12 http://www.uni-mannheim.de/uni/infocenter/startseite/index.html
13 Acknowledgements go the Electronic Services group and the ProSebica project members for their detailed list of new services at academic libraries (namely Ralf Hofacker, Bettina Koeper, Susanne Riedel, Erik Senst and Sebastian Wolf).
14 The e-Science-funding programme of the BMBF had been opened on 9 November 2004 (http://www.pt-it.de/in/escience/).

project research and teaching to publication. Libraries are well qualified to take on an active role in this area in the future. They already have international networks at their disposal and are open-minded towards cooperative working.

These ways of developing content further will mostly benefit researchers. However, there are also many services that are primarily used by students. Among these are personalized services, such as[15]:

- *My UL links*: quick links which can be put together by picking from a comprehensive selection.
- *My literature lists*: extracted from the catalogue by marking individual hits, added to a titled list and saved. These lists contain bibliographic information about the title and can be converted into current bibliographies and/or exported into bibliographic management tools.
- *My news and information*: current information which can be freely selected, such as, for example, library notices, news stories, stock market charts, weather etc.

Virtual enquiry and advice systems have arrived in Europe from the US and are increasingly being provided by libraries. The most well-known is the QuestionPoint system, developed by the Library of Congress (Public Service Collections Directorate) and the OCLC Online Computer Library Center in Dublin, Ohio. At the current time over 1000 libraries are taking part. In Germany these include the University Library in Frankfurt/Main and the State and University Library of Goettingen: an impressive example of a cooperative service being provided[16].

Examples of how mobile and new Internet services are being transferred to the library sector are searching and lending services becoming accessible over mobile terminals and the dissemination of library notices via RSS-feed (Really Simple Syndication). In Germany, RSS-feeds, which can be read either using a feed-reader or directly in some browsers or email clients, are being offered by Tübingen university library and the library of TU Harburg, for example[17].

There are no limits to the service ideas libraries could exploit. What, for example, is to be said against libraries cooperatively constructing thematic, academic Wikis, which every librarian and academic can contribute to according to their own interests and competencies? Why should libraries not be able to construct distributed and, if necessary, grid-based, search indexes? What about a peer-to-peer network for quality assured academic publications, provided as an open platform for authors by librarians?

---

15 Further services can be found on the following library web sites: http://www.hsu-bibliothek.de/mylibrary/, http://mylibrary.cornell.edu/MyLibrary/Main.

16 Questionpoint: http://www.questionpoint.org/; UB Frankfurt/Main: http://www.ub.uni-frankfurt.de/questionpoint/question.htm; SUB Göttingen: http://www.sub.uni-goettingen.de/0_fragen.html.

17 http://www.uni-tuebingen.de/pol/bibmenu.htm, http://www.tub.tu-harburg.de/1.html. An overview about RSS-Feeds offered by libraries can be found at: http://www.lisfeeds.com/.

What works in the Internet for music titles, should in principle also be practicable for academic articles. Libraries could provide authors with the appropriate software, which can be installed on every desktop with an exe file. In principle, the effectiveness and scalability of the predominantly centrally constructed services must be examined against the background of e-science and the Grid.

Normalized keyword thesauri are already being created cooperatively. Why should this not be possible for many other services? As a network the Internet offers a useable model particularly suitable for federalized Germany. In the future, libraries could be among the forerunners developing relevant practical applications.

2.10 Building Blocks for the Future Development of Local Services

The strategic plan for a University Library could contain the following building blocks.

2.10.1 Joint Production of a Service Catalogue by Skilled Senior Library Management Staff in Close Cooperation with Employees

The catalogue is intended for users and the end result should not be a list of all bibliographic library activities such as selection, acquisition and cataloguing. Rather, it should contain the products which the user is interested in, for example, the literature on offer in the local subject library. Senior library management staff and employees must work together to find a new understanding of services, though observation and analysis from the users' perspective.

One possible scenario could be setting up a steering group consisting of senior management and employees, who in turn coordinate and steer individual working groups on particular topics. This form of organization was considered suitable for the purpose by Bielefeld University Library. In this manner it has involved a total of around 50 employees in the process, about 30 per cent of the total work force. At the moment a small editorial team is working on about 200 product sheets about all the library services which have been produced by the working groups.

The work on the service catalogue may then form the basis for a further step, which may have knock-on effects on internal business processes. It will be necessary to establish priorities for future services and their organization, and this can lead to the modification of existing roles and to the reassigning of resources. While under the direction of senior management, this step should also be taken jointly with employees.

2.10.2 Carrying Out a Prospective Analysis of Customer Needs Using Market Research Tools

Conjoint analysis is a method used in economics for researching consumer behaviour, and is currently being tested for the library sector as a pilot project at Bielefeld University Library sponsored by the German Research Council. It is a suitable means for comparing and bringing together the wishes and ideas of customers and the service catalogue as created by the library as service provider in the early planning stages. The final results of the project will be published at the beginning of 2006.

2.10.3 Analysis of Local Resources and Deciding on Areas of Emphasis

Internal factors should be taken into account when working on the service cata-logue, as well as creating public descriptions of content for the users. The best catalogue in the world is of no help at all if it can't be finished because of finan-cial reasons. Additional funding cannot be expected to cover continuous opera-tion. The costs of new or altered services must therefore be covered through altering emphases in job descriptions and reassigning resources.

2.10.4 Further Development of Senior Library Management and Employees

Both senior management and all employees must not allow themselves to forget that it is acceptance by academics and students that justifies the library's exis-tence at the end of the day. All decisions and measures taken on the strategic and operational level should be continually analysed as to whether they really represent added value from a user's perspective. This change in mind-set is hard to learn through vocational training. It must be lived out over a long period of time by employees following the example set by senior management. Senior library management will also need to foster a culture of innovation within the library, by valuing creativity and spontaneity and harnessing them construc-tively and not by simply checking to see whether suggestions match current business practices and responsibilities.

In the future, employees will have to be more intensively deployed for various services. Individuals themselves are usually prepared for this and their profes-sional skills should be developed through vocational training opportunities. The flexibility of the work force will place middle management under increased organizational demands, and if necessary they should also be supported through training.

2.10.5 Integration of External Service Providers

Focusing on services instead of internal work areas and business practices allows external service providers to be used, without users necessarily having to be aware of it. In the future, billing processes for pay-per-view or digital services such as RSS-Feed will be able to be integrated in the same way as external search engines or literature suppliers for special acquisition areas.

2.11 Conclusion and Outlook

The way researchers and students go about working with academic information has fundamentally changed with the coming of the Internet. What has remained unchanged is their basic need for comprehensive, fast, and, where possible, free or at least good value access to literature and data. To achieve this, the libraries of 2007 are switching their present research systems over to modern search engine technology. They are combining local services with external products, which could come from individual libraries, an improved Vascoda service (an interdisciplinary Internet portal for academic information in Germany), or from commercial search engines, which we know today as Google Scholar and Scirus. In doing so, libraries are strengthening their efforts to develop intelligent filtering of information content, and are working closely together with the academic community to do so.

Today's Digital Services no longer *cater* for the user, they place services *at their disposal*. Researchers and students decide for themselves, which service they wish to use and in which form, whether it be by using a combination of services via a central service portal or by using single services which are individually installed on a desktop or pocket PC. The library guarantees the quality of these services, takes care of them, and is ready with advice when needed.

The way academic libraries develop their services in the future will no longer be governed solely by a librarian's traditional understanding of use. Rather, they will take into account the general development of Internet-based services. They will adapt worthwhile basic models and combine them with special qualities appropriate to the way researchers and students work.

Inter-library cooperation must be reorganized nationally and internationally by 2007. Instead of centralized portals and a collection of local one-stop-shops offering comprehensive information services, there is a need for integration and networking of services. This can be provided interregionally, nationally and even internationally. For Germany a first step would be the creation of a "Yellow Pages" to describe services in the area of academic information. The primary target audience would be libraries and other providers of academic information services.

A central hub would be possible, for example using Vascoda, the Digital Library Forum or the Kompetenznetzwerk für Bibliotheken (an organization with responsibility for library statistics, international cooperation and standardization). However it would be preferable to create a platform cooperatively which would be maintained in a decentralized way, much like wikis and weblogs. The only thing needed would be to define certain standards. The services described could be provided free of charge or for a fee, depending on whether or not they were developed using public funds. The Internet has introduced concepts such as "powered by XY" or "provided by ABC". These can be made use of creatively by libraries. A local library can then produce a service catalogue targeted at its current clientele, and can then decide whether it will develop services of its own or whether it will take on external services.

The German Research Council has for many years supported the system of interregional literature provision through special collection areas. The academic libraries of 2007 have the opportunity to construct a modern, flexible and decentralized system of service provision. This would be in keeping with the federal character of the Republic of Germany, the basic structure of the World Wide Web, and, very recently, the requirements of technical grid systems. A fundamental rethinking is required on the part of those responsible in individual libraries, interregional centres and funding organizations. This can only be achieved, if we stop focussing on traditional service-concepts, which place the provider at the heart of our strategies. The concept of user-centred services is becoming more than a slogan: it is opening up the prospect of fundamentally new structures for library services even on a national level.

3

The Early Years of the United Kingdom Joint Academic Network (JANET)

Mike Wells

3.1 Introduction

This is a personal account of the way in which the United Kingdom's Joint Academic Network (JANET) came into being. The account is loosely historic, but at some points I have stepped out of a simple time-line approach in order to use that most powerful of tools, hindsight, in order to put a gloss on events. I would not like it to be thought that I was the only, or even the principal actor in the formation of JANET. Many others played at least as large a role as myself, and many others continue to do so.

3.2 The Computer Board

3.2.1 Early Days

The Computer Board, or to give its full title, the Computer Board for Universities and Research Councils, was created in 1966. It was brought into existence to ease some of the problems that were confronting the universities and research councils in their attempts to fund the provision of computing resources. In 1966, computers meant "mainframe" computers. Computers then were physically large. Leeds University's first computer, a Ferranti Pegasus, filled the nave of the non-conformist chapel in which it was housed and its second computer, an English Electric KDF9, filled the Sunday School room at the rear of the chapel. Computers then were also expensive. The KDF9 as originally installed in 1962 cost about £250,000. For comparison in 1963 I bought a three bed-roomed detached house, in a decent suburb of Leeds, for £4,000. That says almost as much about the movements in university salaries as it does about the changes in prices of houses and of computers. More to the point, an expenditure of this order was comparable with the university's annual equipment grant. It was clearly very difficult for a university to fund the acquisition of a computer, and having once purchased the machine, the subsequent recurrent costs for maintenance, operating staff and user support staff were a heavy burden.

A report by Professor Brian Flowers (1966) led to the creation of the Computer Board, which first met in September 1966. Its remit was to make recommendations to the Secretary of State for the provision and support of computers in universities, and to advise research councils on their proposals for computers, excluding computers "provided solely and essentially for the purpose of specific research projects". The difference between the Board's role in respect of universities, where it advised the Secretary of State as to how money should be invested, and the research councils, where it advised the Councils on their proposals is highly significant. The *de facto* situation was that the Board was able to assign funds to universities for the purchase of equipment and for at least some part of the costs of maintenance, operation and support. In general, provided that the Board's advice did not run counter to Government policy, and fitted the overall financial envelope of the funds assigned, Secretaries of State would accept it. The Board was also required to ensure that equipment supplied was used and operated effectively. The Board's role with respect to Councils was rather different, in that it did not provide funds for initial purchase, and it was not responsible for ensuring that equipment was effectively used. I do not imply by this that research council computers were not effectively used, but the control was exercised by the councils rather than the Board. A brief account of the Board's work can be found in Verdon and Wells (1995)

It is worth considering the different approaches to provision of funds that would have underlain the decision making of the Computer Board and the several research councils. It must be clearly understood that the Board was not a part of the University Grants Committee. However their general approaches were rather similar. In essence the UGC, and the Board, each approached funding issues on the basis that its role was to ensure that minimum standards were reached and maintained; they were concerned to achieve a level playing field, by filling in any perceived inadequacies. In contrast, each research council, quite rightly, saw its role as seeking out and supporting the work of centres of excellence. Then, as now, the best research work being undertaken often relied heavily on the provision of adequate computing resources, and as a consequence the research councils concentrated their funding on providing computing resources for what they judged to be their best projects. There was thus an inbuilt tension between the work of the Board, which was attempting to remedy inadequacies in provision, an activity which of necessity directs some funds towards those sites where the level of computing provision was weakest, and the research councils which were attempting to improve still further the computing provision for those workers and projects which were already well provided. This difference reflected into the whole approach to cooperation between separate universities in meeting their computing needs. In the 1960s, computing was in effect always done on mainframes, and in what was then termed "batch" mode.

The individual user would submit her job to the Computer Centre, usually by walking across campus with a deck of cards or a reel of paper tape. Computer operators would run the job on the computer and sometime later the user would collect her results. The whole process might easily take several days. This meant that it was quite feasible to think of the computer being remote from the user, possibly not even on the same campus.

3.2.2 Grosch's Law: Regional Computer Centres

In general terms, the power of mainframe computers increased rapidly with its capital cost, a fact summarized by "Grosch's Law", which asserted that the power of the computer increased as the square of its cost. In these circumstances, it made good sense for two or more sites (i.e. universities) to pool their resources on funding one large system, rather than several smaller ones. There was, of course, a down side; each university could advance compelling why it should be the one to house the only computer. Between 1966, when the Board first came into existence, and the early 1970s, several regional computer centres were established. They were based in one of the larger universities in a geographical region, and were required by the Board to offer services to workers at other universities in that region. Users submitted their work in a variety of ways. Some users simply travelled to the Regional centre; some universities offered a courier service; some used a "remote workstation". At that time a workstation consisted of input devices (paper tape reader or punched card reader) and output devices (paper tape punch, card punch or printer) which were connected via some form of interface unit to a data link to the regional centre. These data links were invariably operated over telephone circuits leased from the GPO, for the very simple reason that the GPO at that time had a monopoly in the provision of such circuits. These point to point links between regional centres and their clients in other universities gradually evolved into simple networks.

Over this same period, the research councils, driven by exactly the same economic imperatives were also developing similar networks. Each research council system was primarily intended for that council's own purposes, and was usually located at one of that council's laboratories. Each research council's computers served two communities, one based in the council's own sites, and consisting in essence of that councils own staff, and a second community of that council's grant holders based in universities. In some cases a research council which had a large enough group of grant holders in a university department would fund the provision of a mainframe computer to meet the needs of that group, and might require that group to provide remote access computing facilities to grant holders in other departments or at other universities. It was therefore possible that a university could have several workstations, one connecting to its Regional Computer Centre, and another or even several others, connecting to remote main frames located at research council sites.

There was an important addition to this range of systems. In 1964 the Atlas Computer Laboratory was established, adjacent to the National Institute for

Research in Nuclear Science (NIRNS) at Chilton south of Oxford. This housed an ICL Atlas computer, at that time among the most powerful computers available in the world, which was specifically designated to provide access to computing resources to anyone in the university or research council sector who could demonstrate a sufficiently good case. It was almost axiomatic that some of those bidding for time on the Atlas would also be holders of research council grants, but that was not a prerequisite. The Atlas computer was later to become a benchmark standard for assessing the power of a computer system.

3.3 The Network Reports of 1973 and 1975

I was appointed as a member of the Computer Board in 1972. Shortly after I joined the Board, a study group visited universities and research establishments in the United States and Canada. Naturally, the sites visited included some of the most prestigious and active, from which it was clear that the group might learn how to do things properly. It also visited some of the less prestigious and less active sites, from which it was hoped that the group might gain insight as to what should be avoided. For obvious reasons I name no names, but I can still recall the difficulties the leader of the group had in explaining to some sites why we had chosen them to visit. However, two site visits were particularly important, for all the right reasons. One was to the "Triangle Universities Computer Centre" (TUCC) in North Carolina. TUCC was the primary provider of computing resources to three more or less equally large universities, any one of which might reasonably expect to justify its own computer centre. Instead, they had opted to cooperate, and use a single larger centre, which was jointly managed by the three universities. The second was to the "ARPANET" project in Washington. The US military's Advanced Research Project Agency, ARPA, had set up a unit to develop a network system which was independent of any manufacturers hardware or software, and which would be scaleable in size and resilient against the failure of any one part of the network. At that time ARPANET was in its infancy. It had a very small number of connected sites, and an even smaller number of switching centres. But it was clear that it would grow.

One point which all of us on the study group noted was the very different approach to funding of tertiary education. Universities in Canada and the US drew nearly all their income from student fees and endowment income. Naturally, each university guarded its funds jealously. In the UK we had a highly centralized approach. This has disadvantages, but my personal belief is that these drawbacks are a small price to pay for the advantages. In particular I am convinced that the UK would not have been able to make such rapid progress in exploiting networks if the funding regime had been different.

On the study group's return, the Board felt that it was making good progress in establishing various forms of cooperative provision of computing resources, but that there was merit in further consideration as to how, if at all, it should proceed in establishing any form of network. In 1973 a working party, chaired by myself, was set up to seek out what was the current level of network provision, and to advise on any future actions. The working party's report met at best with rather muted support, and a certain amount of outright hostility. One of the main criticisms was that the report did not clearly define the aims of any network development that the Board might undertake. Accordingly I was asked to chair a second working party, whose terms of reference were:

1. to examine the foreseeable requirements of universities for access to remote computing facilities, to assess the traffic involved, and the costs of alternative strategies for meeting these requirements

2. to review current UK progress in computer-to-computer networks, particularly those involving the universities and the research councils

3. to consider whether there were any management problems requiring detailed examination.

3.3.1 UK Academic Networks in 1975

The working party's first act was to survey the existing provision. The results showed that there were star networks operated by Board funded regional computer centres in London, Manchester and Edinburgh and a further mesh network for the South-West universities. Networks connected universities and research council sites to Atlas and to the SRC computers at the Rutherford Appleton laboratory and Daresbury, and to the NERC computers at Swindon and Bidston. In addition to these academic networks, there were networks based on the proprietary protocols associated with various manufacturers, most noticeably IBM and DEC. There were also point to point links operating between pairs of sites. The total annual cost of networking provision was summarized as:

Rental of GPO lines and modems	£240K
Support staff	£385K
Maintenance charges	£300K
Other charges	~£85K

Note that these were annual charges. There was an additional annual expenditure, estimated at £350K, on hardware procurement. This was a total annual spend by universities and research councils on networking in the order of £1M, at a time when the Board's annual grant was just under £10M. The survey also showed that there was frequent overlap between provision by the Board and the research councils, with parallel leased lines running between two sites. Two quite distinct types of network were being developed. There were wide area networks, used to transmit data between sites. In addition, individual universities and research council establishments were introducing local area networks which connected users on a single site to one or more mainframe systems, allowing users to submit jobs and collect results, and to move files of data between systems. In many cases a sites local area network was also connected to the wide area network.

This fact finding was a reasonably straightforward response to the second of the terms of reference. However, it proved much more difficult to address the first of the terms of reference. It became clear to the working party that it would be difficult to forecast the overall demand for network connections, either in terms of which pairs of sites would wish to be connected, or how much traffic would flow between any pair of sites. The reason lay in the way users responded to the provision of network access. It is self-evident that where there is no network access users would make no use of networks. However, provision made for one, identifiable, purpose, would promptly be exploited by users for some other, totally unforeseen, purpose. In part the situation was made more difficult to forecast because of the emergence of intra-site networks, which served to move data across a university campus or research council site. These were usually initially developed to allow workers on that site to connect to their local computing resources, but were then used to provide onwards connections to facilities at other sites. Much of the traffic on the campus network was aligned on the provision of access to interactive computing. When a user submitted work to a large, remote facility, she would usually be prepared to wait some hours for the results to be returned; with interactive computing, the user expected to receive her results within a matter of seconds, or at most a few minutes. From these simple beginnings, there was gradually emerging traffic which passed not between a user at one site, and a facility at another, but between a user at one site and a user at another. Traffic in which the user is present for the duration of the whole of the interaction with the remote system, and person-to-person traffic both put a new type of demand on the network. Equipment does not mind if responses are slow. People do. This puts a premium on having networks which can not only move large volumes of traffic, but can also move small volumes in a short time, measured at most as a few seconds. It seemed to the working party that the only sensible course would be to provide a network which would allow any site to connect to any other, and which could adapt to the differing needs of users, and then let nature take its course. Paradoxically, it was believed that such a completely general purpose provision, which could be upgraded as demand arose, would in the long term be more effective than attempting to arrive at detailed predictions of the flow between each pair of sites, and provide a network configured to meet that need.

On the third term of reference, as to whether there were any management problems requiring detailed examination, the report was fairly guarded. In fact, I was quite clear in my own mind that the main problem areas would not be technical, but would lie precisely in the details of how the community could resolve the issues of who should determine policy as regards funding, setting of objectives, and generally controlling a shared resource which would be central to the work of a large fraction of the research and teaching community.

In contrast with the first report this second report was well received. Quite what produced this change in response is difficult to say, since there was little real difference between what the two reports said. The most important recommendations emerging from the second working party were that the Board and the research councils should strengthen their collaboration in the provision of networking facilities, and together set up a small full-time unit to coordinate network developments, and that Board should allocate 3% of its annual hardware expenditure on the provision of network facilities.

3.4 A Technical Digression

I have tried to avoid being overly technical, but to make some of what follows easier to follow I have to clarify some terms relating to networking in general, and to computer networking in particular.

3.4.1 Switching

A connection simply carries data from one location to another. There is no necessity to specify the destination of the data, or the route it should follow to get there. A connection which can carry traffic in only one direction, is known as a simplex link. A connection which can carry traffic in both directions simultaneously is known as a duplex link.

The situation becomes more complicated as soon as there are more than two locations involved. One approach is to install a separate link between every pair of locations. For n locations this will require $n \times (n - 1)$ simplex connections, or half that number of duplex connections. An alternative is to connect each location to a single central point, and for data to flow by passing to the central point, and then from the centre to its destination. This requires only n duplex connections, or twice that number of simplex connections, but has created a requirement for a new type of unit, a "switch" which can pass incoming data from one link to the outgoing link which leads to the final destination. In addition, we have created a need for an extra type of information, which defines where the data is to be sent. A further alternative is to have each location to connected to one (or more) of several switching units, and to provide interconnections between the switching units. Data now passes from a location to a switch; if the destination is also connected to that switch, the data can pass to its final destination; if the destination is not connected to the first switch it must be passed on to other switches until one is found which is connected to the final destination.

The second group of terms relates to the way in which a network manages the details of the switching process. The terms are

1. Circuit switching
2. Message switching
3. Packet switching.

In a circuit switching network, the transfer of data from source to destination takes place in two quite distinct phases. The first phase establishes the route which data will follow between source and destination, via one or more switches, and establishes a circuit, a complete connection between source and destination. In the second phase data passes from the source to the destination via this circuit. In most cases there is a third phase, which comes after the completion of the data transfer, during which the circuit is cleared, and any resources used in by the circuit are freed. This is the model that was, and still is, used for telephone speech traffic.

In a message switching network, the data to be transferred from the source, in the form of a complete message, is prefixed with an address which defines the destination, and the message-plus-address is passed from the source to the network. The address is used to route the complete message across the network, which does not retain any information about the route the message takes. This is the model that is used for telegraph traffic, and is now used for text messages for mobile phones.

In a packet switching network, data is transferred across the network in small packets. The address of the destination is appended to each packet as it is transmitted from the source. The switch(es) in the network use this address to determine a route for the packet of data to its destination, and this is done afresh for every packet which is submitted for transmission. In the majority of cases, the data to be transmitted will not fit in to a single packet, and the total transmission takes the form of several packets, which may well take differing routes across the network before arriving at their destination. It is this form of switching which forms the basis of most current networks. A packet switching network can operate in a "connectionless" mode, in which the route for each packet is determined afresh. A packet switching network can also operate in a "connection-oriented" mode; when a user wishes to transfer data, the network first creates a connection, known as a "virtual circuit", between the source and the destination, and then all subsequent packets of traffic flow along this virtual circuit. Paradoxically, nearly all speech traffic is now carried on connectionless packet switching networks, but the telephone user sees a connection oriented service.

The benefits of packet switching are in scalability and resilience against failure. As a network grows, and more locations are added, new sites can simply be connected to their nearest switch. If a switch becomes overloaded, it is a relatively simple matter to add another switch, or to replace a switch by a more powerful one. If the underlying physical network becomes overloaded, extra links can be added. Because of the way in which switches cooperate to route packets, there is very little to be done by way of administration. If a switch, or a network connection, fails the remaining switches and connections will continue to operate; if each locations is connected to more than one switch, and if each switch is connected to several other switches, it is perfectly possible for the failure of a single switch or connection to leave the entire network still fully connected.

3.4.2 Protocols and Network Architecture

When designing a network it is essential to break down the software which is needed to allow information to be transmitted between programs running in separate locations into manageable units. This breakdown takes two forms, into interfaces and protocols. The software at each location is treated conceptually as a number of layers, each of which offers services to the layer "above" it, implementing these services using the services offered to it by the layer "below" it. Breaking the software down in this way allows the "higher" layers to be shielded from the details of how the services it provides are implemented by the "lower" layers. The highest layer deals directly with users' applications, while the lowest layer, sometimes called the "physical" layer, deals directly with the hardware forming the transmission system. The detailed description of the ways in which a higher layer can request services from a lower layer, and of the lower layers responses to these requests, define the "interface" between a pair of adjacent layers. The complete set of layers is frequently referred to as a "stack", not to be confused with the stack which forms part of the internal register set of many computers.

As well as this flow of data up and down between the separate layers at each location, there is a conceptual flow of information between layers at the same level at the two ends of the data link. Again there is a detailed description of what types of exchange can take place between corresponding layers at the two ends of the link, and this set of conventions is referred to as the "protocol" for that layer. In fact, there is no direct exchange of information between the corresponding layers. Rather, each layer passes information down, via the appropriate interfaces into the successive layers below it at one end until the information reaches the physical layer, where it is transferred across the data link, then up through the interfaces, finally reaching the corresponding layer at the far end.

At first sight this looks to be a very cumbersome way of proceeding. It has one huge advantage. Provided that the interfaces between layers and the protocols across layers are preserved, it is possible to replace any implementation of a layer with a completely different one, for example replacing a link running over a copper cable with one running over an optical fibre, without changing any other part of the implementation.

In practice, it is normal to separate the protocol stack, with the lower layers implemented on a small front end computer. At the same time, these lower layers, but only the lower layers, will be implemented on the computers that act as switches within the network.

3.4.3 Network Reliability

All equipment is liable to fail. The reliability of a unit can be measured in several ways. One way looks at how long the unit runs before it fails, and how long it then takes to bring it back into service. Both of these are essentially statistical measures, and are respectively known as the "mean time between failures" (MTBF) and the "mean time to repair" (MTTR). The quantity

$$1 - (MTTR/MTBF)$$

gives a measure of the fraction of time for which the unit is usable. It is often called the availability, and expressed as a percentage. So a unit which on average runs for 1000 hours between failures, and is then repaired in 3 hours would have an availability of 99.7%.

It is often possible to design a system in such a way that unreliable units can be combined to give improved overall availability. For example, we might have a situation in which the user can make use of either one of two units, each with an

MTBF of 100 hours, an MTTR of 1 hour, and an availability of 99%. There is a 1% chance that when it is being used this first unit will fail. We arrange that if the unit that is being used fails, the failure is detected by the system, and the work is automatically transferred to the other unit. This second unit has a 99% probability that it is working, and the overall probability of both units having failed is 1% of 1%, or 1 in 10,000.

It is of course also possible to design a system in such a way that reliable units are combined to give reduced overall availability. This will arise if the user requires both units to be working at the same time. In the case of the two units above, each has a 99% probability of working, but if they must both be working the overall availability falls to 98%.

A large network contains switches used to route traffic, and lines to carry the traffic between switches. We can connect each site (or switch) to more than one switch; this will allow the site (or switch) to continue working if one of the lines, or one of the switches, fails. There are of course costs. The obvious one is the cost of the extra lines and switches. Less obvious is the cost of rerouting traffic in the event of a failure, since this requires software that is capable of detecting the failure, and then automatically carrying out the rerouting. Connectionless protocols have this property by default, as each packet is routed afresh.

It is important when discussing system reliability to realize that the perception of users may be very different from that of those running the system. Users are, quite rightly, concerned with their own work. If the part(s) of the system that they are using keeps breaking down they will view it as unreliable. If the breakdowns that occur affect only a small subset of users, those running the system, who think in terms of overall reliability, may well assert that the system is reliable. From their limited perspectives, both are right.

3.5 The Network Unit

The recommendations outlined at the end of Section 3.3 were accepted more or less in their entirety, and in 1976 the Board established the Network Unit. This unit was small, just three people. The head of the unit was Mervyn Williams, of the GPO, and the two other members were Dr (now Professor) Roland Rosner and Dr Chris Morris. They were active in work on protocol development, and in encouraging others to become involved in this work. This work was in some sense constrained by pressure to develop protocols which were aligned on those promulgated by the CCITT. The Comité Consultatif International Téléphonique et Télégraphique is the international body which lays down standards for telephony and telegraphy. It is, by its very nature, dominated by commercial bodies which rely on charging to raise revenue, and this in turn led to many of its proposals for protocols being connection oriented. The members of the Network Unit worked tirelessly at identifying needs, and produced two detailed reports. The first was not well received, but the second in late 1978 was accepted by the Board, and many of its proposals were implemented. Two new units, headed by Roland Rosner, were established, the Joint Network Team (JNT) and the Network Executive. The Executive would be primarily concerned with the installation and operation of a national network to serve the entire university and research council community, while the JNT would continue to act as an advisory body, continuing the work on network architecture and protocols. There was a general expectation that the backbone of any such network would be provided and operated by the GPO. There was no agreement as to how to fund such a national network, although there was strong pressure from some quarters in favour of meeting the costs by charging users.

3.5.1 The Manning Unjamming

Between 1979 and 1982 the user community was demanding more and more network provision, but still with no agreement on funding. As the 1975 working party had believed, the issue was not one of technology, but of funding and control. The situation was finally unjammed by a bold move on the part of Dr Geoff Manning, of the Science and Engineering Research Council (SERC), the successor body to the SRC. He proposed that the entire costs, capital and recurrent, of any national network should be met by the Computer Board, and that the JNT/NE should own and operate the network on behalf of the universities and research councils. At the same time each of the research councils would separately transfer any networking equipment which was providing inter-site connections to the Network Executive. At first sight it might appear that the research councils had the better of this deal, but in fact they would hand over a considerable investment on equipment, and give up their control over what was by now an essential part of their work, and there was a deal of resistance to these proposals among research council funded workers. It says much for Geoff Manning's powers of persuasion that he was able to persuade the Computer Board to pay the whole costs, while also persuading the research councils to give up direct control of "their" networks. In the event, the SERC and NERC participated wholeheartedly. The AFRC remained rather independent, and continued for some time to operate separately. The MRC, most of whose workers were located in university departments, had always relied on their host universities for network provision.

The staff of the JNT and the NE could not be direct employees of the Board. Curiously, although the Board commanded a budget of millions of pounds, it was not a legal person, and could not make a contract. It was decided that the two units would continue to be employees of SRC, and would remain based at the ATLAS centre. This in itself gave rise to suspicions in some (university) quarters that there was a bias towards the research councils.

Early in 1982 I took on the role of Director of what would become the national academic network. One of my first tasks was to reach a final clarification of the role of the GPO, with which the JNT had been in discussion for many months. The GPO had recently established its own packet switching service, PSS, and it was suggested that this should form the backbone of the academic network. The GPO was approached with a proposal that the academic community might become a bulk customer of PSS, in exchange for a discounted price. The response from the GPO was disappointing. The GPO claimed that as the monopoly supplier of the service, it could not offer different prices to different classes of customer, and the Board would have to pay at the standard rates. A back of the envelope calculation suggested that from the outset the annual cost of implementing the backbone in this way would consume all the Board's yearly budget for networking. This raised a problem. If the GPO could not meet the community's needs, then the community would have perforce to build and operate its own network. The legal position of the research council networks was tolerably secure, as each research council could argue that it was a single organization, and that any of its grant holders in university sites who had access to their wide area network was in some sense a member of that organization. The Computer Board itself was not a legal person, and so it was not possible to use the Board as an overarching body. There was no way in which separate universities would be able to argue that they were part of a single organization, and thus any national network would infringe the GPO monoploy. The GPO was in fact extremely helpful over this issue, and I was able to have several helpful discussions with some of its officers who dealt with regulatory issues. The GPO's main concern was to have no infringement of their monopoly position in respect of voice traffic in the UK, not least because voice traffic at that time produced far more revenue than data traffic. We were able to reach an informal agreement, that provided there was no attempt to divert voice traffic on to the academic network, then the GPO would not initiate any form of action. It was also agreed that the Network Executive might be able to claim that it was acting as a Crown Agent in offering data services to third parties. The only ways by which a person can formally become a Crown Agent is either by an order in Council, or by the person successfully using the claim that he is acting as a Crown Agent as a defence in a court action. Fortunately, no action was ever initiated, and the subsequent privatization of the GPO data transmission services that followed the creation of British Telecom meant that no one from the Network Executive has ever faced the courts.

3.5.2 Coloured Books

From its inception the Network Unit and later the JNT had been active in the development of protocols. This work had been based on the CCITT X-25 protocol, a connection-oriented protocol, which was favoured by CCITT because it was thought that such protocols made charging for network services easier. There was also pressure from UK government to develop home grown networking products. By the early 1980s the UK academic community had developed a complete suite of connection oriented protocols. Each protocol was defined by a document with a different coloured cover, and eventually the complete set of protocols became known as the "coloured books". The Board used its control over the university sectors capital expenditure on computing equipment as a means of forcing manufacturers to provide implementations of these protocols. In practice, the manufacturers often met this requirement by placing a contract for the development of any necessary protocols with the university to which it was selling a computer system. These protocols were to be freely available to the academic community.

This situation should be compared with the availability of the connectionless protocols which were favoured by the ARPA community. Any US computer manufacturer wishing to sell to an ARPA funded project was required to provide implementations of these protocols. A protocol is like any other piece of software in the sense that once it has been written and tested, the marginal cost of making another copy is effectively zero. As a result, most US suppliers made the complete protocol stack available at no cost to customers. Naturally at that price, they found plenty of willing buyers.

3.6 The National Academic Network

In 1982 the Network Executive began the task of coordinating the various separate academic networks, each using slightly different protocol stacks running on different sets of hardware. The Executive inherited a total of ten switching centres; three from universities, Bath, Belfast, Cambridge; three from Board funded regional computer centres Edinburgh (ERCC), London (ULCC) and Manchester (UMRCC); two from the SERC, Atlas (sited at the Rutherford Laboratory) and Daresbury; and two from the NERC, Bidston and Swindon. With the exception of the switch at Bath, the network switches were found at sites such as regional computer centres or research council central sites, which had large mainframe systems. This made good sense. By definition, these were sites at which large amounts of data would be entering and leaving the network. They were also sites which already had in place arrangements for round the clock operation, which it was essential to have in place for the network switches. The Bath site was part of the academic network which had been established between the universities in the South West. This network was unusual in that from the outset each of the member sites had a machine from the same manufacturer, English Electric, who later became part of ICL. These machines were of course compatible with each other, and of roughly comparable power, and the network was used for load balancing between the sites rather than a means of routing work to a central site. The Belfast switch was in essence a collection point for the Northern Ireland universities wishing to route work to other parts of the UK. The Cambridge switch reflected the fact that there were a large number of research council grant holders associated with the university, and that despite the government "Buy British" policy, Cambridge and Newcastle Universities both had large IBM computers which users at other universities wished to access.

At this time network switches were very expensive in comparison with the cost of the circuits which interconnected them. This was especially so in a small country such as the UK, where the greatest distance between switches is in the order of 500 km, and some switches were only 50 km apart, as compared with ARPAnet, where inter-switch distances were typically in the order of 1,000 km. The optimal configuration for a UK academic network would probably have been in the form of one large switch, based somewhere between Leeds and Manchester. There would have been one immense drawback to this configuration; if the single central switch failed, the entire network would fail. This was an important consideration. In accordance with the Government's buy British policy, the Network Executive sourced its switches from within the UK. The only available switches were based on a GEC manufactured system. These were initially run with software written at the Atlas laboratory, but it was decided that the GEC written software should be used. The reliability of these switches was poor. We had agreed targets of a mean time of 2000 hours (approximately 3 months) between faults on the switches, and a mean repair time of 4 hours. These targets would have given an availability of 99.8%. In practice the reliability of the switches varied very widely. The best switches did achieve the target, but the worst were failing every three or four days. The hardware was quite good, but the software had frequently to be reloaded, this being the quickest way of dealing with its faults. The situation was not helped by the fact that even a small switch required as its base a system of approximately the same power as the Atlas computer. This was a major psychological barrier; part of the so-called procurement policy was an insistence that where a university's total requirement for computer power exceeded one Atlas power, then the University was limited to buying a UK manufactured system. There were those who argued that rather than using this much computer power simply to enable traffic to flow in a network, it would be more effective to use these systems to provide "real" computing to users.

The transfer of control of the separate research council and Regional Computer Centre wide area networks to the Executive took place during 1983. There was no wholesale change of staff or equipment. Rather, the Executive proceeded by placing a contract for a Network Operation Centre (NOC) with each site that ran a switch. These contracts laid down staffing levels needed to operate the NOC; the staff concerned remained as employees of the local university or research council, but the cost of employment became a charge against Computer Board funds. This had the advantage of ensuring continuity of employment for the individual staff, and safeguarded aspects such as seniority and pension rights, and reduced the loss of highly qualified staff. The Board took over the costs of equipment maintenance, and of leased lines.

3.6.1 The Formal Start of JANET

The formal transfer of equipment and the start of the single academic network took place on 1 April 1984. One of the agreed objectives of the single network was to replace the multiple funding sources of the existing networks, i.e. The Computer Board for the universities components, and the separate research council components by a single unit, funded wholly by the Board. The April 1st date was conveniently near to the start of the Treasury Financial year, and this eased the transfer. It was also easily remembered, as being All Fools' Day, in George Orwell's year. By this time the network had also acquired a name, JANET. There are conflicting views as to the origin of this name. It is, of course, a contraction of Joint Academic Network. For my part, I rather prefer the notion that it was in honour of the Network Units first secretary, Janet Charles.

JANET differed from other networks then operating in the UK in a number of respects. There were two commercial networks, the Post Office's service, PSS, and a corresponding international service, IPSS. Clearly both of these services charged for use. There were those who would have preferred to charge for the use of JANET. I, and many others, argued strongly that we could think of no better way of restricting the take-up of JANET than by charging. The dominant costs in owning and operating a network are standing charges which do not increase with use. Once the standing charges have been met the marginal costs of using the network are very small. If the charges reflect the standing costs they will appear to users as being very high, but from the perspective of the funding body, these costs must be recovered. Any charging regime will necessitate the development of software to capture usage, at a sufficiently detailed level to enable billing. This software must also incorporate adequate security mechanisms to safeguard against misuse. All of this adds non-productive software to what is already a complex product. Add to this the human effort needed to control and manage the accounting and charging system, and there is a large amount of non-productive investment. This non-productive effort acts as a powerful disincentive to users to exploit the network. Mercifully, JANET was, and largely continues to be, a non-charging network. There are exceptions, principally where JANET access is provided to an organization which is not covered by the Joint Information Systems Committee (JISC), the direct successor to the Computer Board which underwrites the costs of JANET for all higher and further education bodies. In these cases there is a fixed annual charge to the organization to meet the cost of the connection to JANET.

Other networks were owned by a single organization, for example those operated by the banks. These networks were used for a narrow range of applications, by a tightly disciplined group of specialist users. In contrast JANET, although technically owned by a single organization, the Network Executive, was answerable to a large number of organizations, in the form of fifty or so fiercely independent universities, and several equally independent research councils. The range of applications was large, and open ended; provided that the individual applications conformed to the current version of the protocols, each application could do as it wished. The number of users was also large; at that time most universities restricted access to their computer resources to members of staff and to graduate students, mostly in Science and Engineering, but this still gave a user community of many thousands. Whatever else might be said of these users, they were in no sense tightly disciplined.

The key to controlling this potentially chaotic situation was that JANET itself ended just beyond the point at which it entered a site. JANET functioned purely as a wide area network between sites, and offered almost no other services. Traffic joined JANET at a carefully defined and documented boundary between the source site and the wide area network, and left at the corresponding boundary at the destination site. Provided that the traffic conformed to the published protocols, there was no further control by JANET as to what went on at these two sites. In particular JANET offered no security against unauthorized access to a connected site's systems, control of which was entirely the responsibility of the local site. Again, this led to some difficulties in the early stages, with demands from some quarters for JANET to offer security and control of unauthorized use. The fact is that if a service can be misused across a wide area network, it can almost certainly be misused more locally. Turned inside out, this implies that unless a service is secure against being compromised locally, the operators of the service should certainly not even consider connecting it to a network. JANET was, and is, an open network, accessible with a minimum of formality to users of computer services in its constituent universities and research council sites. From time to time this led to lurid accounts in the press of people who had broken into JANET. We used to liken this to breaking and entering the A1.

JANET offered two value added services:

- access to commercial networks
- a Name Registration Service (NRS).

The charges for using PSS and IPSS contained a fixed element for the provision of a connection, and a usage related element, based on the number of packets sent. It made sound economic sense to provide a small number of access points, for use by the whole academic community, to these commercial services. It was agreed the fixed element of the charges would be met centrally, and that users should meet the usage related charges for their use of these gateways, which would therefore need to incorporate mechanisms for authorization and charging. These gateways operated as centrally managed services available to the whole community.

A large network is continuously undergoing changes both to the configuration of the network, and to the systems accessible via the network. Ensuring that all parts of the network are kept properly informed of these changes is a major administrative task. The NRS was an attempt to ease this task, by partitioning it so that each site could administer the changes it was making. At the outset there was some misunderstanding by users of the purpose of the NRS. The NRS was a means of mapping between the name attached to a service, and the address of that service. In this sense it is not unlike a telephone directory, which gives the telephone number of a subscriber. It was intended to be accessed by a machine rather than a human, and consequently showed a rather hostile interface to even an experienced user. In principal users should not need to know the addresses of services, but should be able to use service names. It took some time to persuade users of this.

3.6.2 JANET User Groups

As well as the technical activities necessary to start JANET, I took great care to establish user groups, and to ensure that these groups had real power. A wide area network has three distinct types of user. Some "users" are technical staff at each site, responsible for the operation of the local computer systems, including of course the site's local area network and its connection to JANET. In creating

JANET, we were fortunate that nearly all sites housed a computing service, with highly competent staff, who could oversee the running of the connection to JANET. Other "users" are those who simply want to use the network to access some remote facility, or more likely, to access a user at another site. Clearly there are very large numbers of these, and they are usually referred to as end-users. Usually end-users are individuals, but in some cases they are themselves a service, such as a library, which in turn might have still further users. I took the view that in this case, the end-user was still the Library, rather than the reader, since the reader's use of JANET was incidental to her work.

I wanted to create a user group which would provide a forum for discussion of JANET's progress. I insisted on having a single group, containing representatives of all classes of user, so that end-users at each site could feel that their views were not being filtered by the staff of the local computing service. As I pointed out above, users of a network can have a very different perception of its reliability from that of those running the network. This divergence can become very serious in the case of a network. The end-users at a site will take the view that the staff of the computer centre are part of the network, and will tend to hold them responsible for failures of all sorts, including those over which the local staff have no control. This can cause needless tension between the staff of the site's computer centre, and the site's users. I was anxious to ensure that all concerned were aware of this, and were kept as fully informed as possible. By and large I think the user group was successful in doing this.

Because JANET covered the whole of the UK, the user group was organized on a geographical basis, with seven regional groups; each site sent two delegates to these regional meetings, one from the computer centre, and one end-user. There were also discipline based user groups, representing High Energy Physics and later Library services. The regional and discipline based groups sent representatives forward to a national meeting, and the Chairman of this national group was an ex officio member of the Network Advisory Committee (NAC), the body established by the Board to oversee JANET. I confidently predicted that this chairman would be a member of staff of a computer centre. I am happy to say that I was totally wrong in this prediction, and the first user group chairmen were all end users, and without exception contributed greatly to the work of both the user group and the Network Advisory Committee.

The user group played a valuable role in emphasizing that JANET was not a research network, but a network for the support of research. By this I mean that the main driver for those responsible for running JANET was the provision of a reliable network, not the development of new network components. Of course there were times when in order to properly support a new end user application it would be necessary to develop new network products, but where this was done it was in response to a specific end user requirement. In general however, those who ran JANET were continually surprised by users ability to think of ingenious ways of exploiting what they were offered.

At least one member of the Executive and I made a point of attending meeting of the regional and discipline based user groups. There were nine of these groups, each meeting at least three times a year. The user groups were enormously successful. They gave end users a mechanism for making their views known to the Executive and the NAC, with a minimum of formality. They also gave the Executive and me an opportunity to involve users in decision making. This was especially valuable when it was necessary to decide between several courses of action each with advantages and drawbacks, and each achievable within the overall budget. I believe that we were able to avoid a number of mistakes by having access to such a well informed and highly motivated pool of experience. I shall always be grateful to those many users who contributed to the user group meetings.

3.6.3 Upgrading JANET

The network configuration that we inherited in 1984 was essentially the product of pulling together a number of disparate networks. Its principal advantage was that it allowed us to get a single network operating to a single set of standards up and running in a matter of a few months. However, it was manifestly not the most economic configuration. Quite simply, it had too many switches, and it was not as reliable as was wished. To improve the network it would be necessary to close down some switches, and remove some links. At the same time, the remaining switches needed to be improved, and the lines between the switches needed to be replaced by higher speed connections. It proved possible to do all of these.

From the outset the NE monitored both the reliability and the traffic levels on JANET. These measurements provided strong evidence of the need to JANET, both to improve reliability and to ease network congestion. As well as the problems with reliability outlined earlier, users, especially those performing interactive work at a remote site were experiencing unacceptable delays. Traffic on a network tends to follow a Zipf's law distribution, with a few heavy users creating most of the traffic, and a very long tail of users creating only a small part of the total load. It is also sharply periodic, with the busiest hours, typically mid morning and mid afternoon, having traffic loads ten times those of the quieter periods. If one simply measures the average traffic over twenty-four hours, a link or switch may appear to be operating at say 10% of capacity; however, this can conceal peak loads, sometimes lasting several hours, when the unit is running at peak capacity. Such a heavily loaded unit can give rise to long queues, which in turn leads to poor response times.

When JANET first started, the only sites allowed to connect were the universities and research councils. However, research council grant holders in Polytechnics were allowed access to JANET. In some cases, a link was supplied directly to the grant holder, but a steadily growing number of Polytechnics had local area networks, and in these cases it was sometimes just as easy to connect this local area network to JANET. Quite often, this was most easily achieved by installing a connection to the nearest University, and within a matter of months of the start of JANET there was agreement that all Polytechnic sites should be connected, either directly or via their nearest university. The opportunity was taken to replace the central part of JANET, which linked London and

Manchester universities, and the SERC's Rutherford and Daresbury laboratories. Much of the additional funding came as a result of proposals for major upgrading of the computing facilities at these four sites, with a consequent need for improved network access particularly for interactive work. The technical situation was also improving, in two senses.

The formation of British Telecom (BT), had led to improved availability of higher data rate connections. This reflected a change in the way these links were supplied. Until this time, the links were provided by using a modem to connect to what was essentially a speech (analogue) circuit. Now, BT were prepared to allow direct access to the digital circuits which had were used to carry traffic between its exchanges. This gave the public access to digital "Kilostream" and "Megastream" circuits with bit rates up to 64 Kbps and 2 Mbps respectively, much higher than the 9.6 Kbps and 48 Kbps with which JANET started. BT also had equipment which allowed a single Megastream circuit to be treated as a number of separately configurable 64 Kbps circuits, and by using this the NE were able to create what was effectively a fully linked configuration between the four major switches at London, Manchester, Rutherford and Daresbury. In parallel with this, GEC were able to offer higher speed units to attach to their switches, which allowed these higher line speeds to be exploited.

Welcome as they were, the improvements in hardware were accompanied by an even more welcome relaxation in the attitude towards protocols. By 1986, it was becomingly increasingly clear that the connection oriented coloured book protocols were not competitive with the connectionless ARPA protocols. It is an open question whether this represented an inherent superiority in the connectionless protocols, better implementations of them, or their availability on better hardware. Whatever the reason, the UK academic community had experimented with various means of allowing the two protocol stacks to coexist. These experiments had shown that this was technically feasible, and for some five years it was hoped that JANET could operate permanently in this way. It was not until 1991 that use of the coloured books was finally phased out.

3.7 Hindsight

I promised some hindsight. By 1987 I had been in post as Director of JANET for five years; my original intention had been to stay in post for two years. There had been a number of changes in my own circumstances, and in the staffing of JANET, and I decided to step down. JANET, and the academic community at large were fortunate in securing Dr David Hartley as my successor.

One of JANET's strengths has always been the way in which it was centrally funded. From the outset, effectively all the costs of acquiring, maintaining and operating JANET were met by the Board. This eliminated at a stroke what would have been a crippling burden of designing and administering a system to recoup the costs of JANET from approximately 50 universities and five research councils which it served, plus no doubt a similarly demanding task within each institution. However, the fact that the staff of the JNT and the NE were technically civil servants employed by a research council was by this time creat-ing more problems than it solved. Accordingly, David Hartley took steps to cre-ate the United Kingdom Education and Research Network Association (UKERNA), thus removing it from the necessity to conform to civil service norms for recruitment and promotion. UKERNA was, and to this day still is, a not for profit body, which is responsible for all aspects of running JANET, under contract to the Joint Information Systems Committee (JISC), which replaced the Computer Board in 1991.

Another of JANET's strengths was that it was essentially a bearer network. Applications programs were, and still are, almost invariably developed by end-users, who are of course in the best position to judge their own needs. The policy was, and still is, to develop only those products and services which are inten-sively network oriented, and can reasonably seen as a central meeting of a wide-spread demand; examples are the formation of a unit to monitor JANET performance, and the provision of Video Conferencing services.

JANET started in 1984 serving about fifty Universities, and about ten research council sites. The exact number of end-users was not known. At that time, most universities limited access to their computing resources to staff and graduate stu-dents, usually in science or engineering, and to a small number of undergradu-ates these same disciplines. Most SERC and NERC staff were computer users. I estimate that in 1984 there were about thirty thousand end-users of JANET. With the conversion of Polytechnics into universities, and the creation of many new universities, the number of sites which have "as of right", and centrally funded, access to JANET has increased hugely. In addition, many other sites are "associ-ates", with either a direct connection to a JANET switch, or a connection to an "as of right" site which provides onwards connection to JANET. The total number of end-users is still not known, but is thought to be about eighteen million, or 30% of the UK's population! When JANET started, the links between switches ran at 48 Kbps, and the links into universities or research councils at 9,600 bps. Today, the central core of JANET, or SuperJANET, operates at 10 Gbps (a Gigabit is one thou-sand million bits) between switches, and a typical site connects at 625 Mbps. Details of the current configuration are available on the JANET web site at http://www.ja.net/. These are impressive figures for growth in scale and improvements in performance. The performance improvements come largely from improved technology, but it is important to understand that JANET has always been at the forefront in exploiting the best products, and has often been a pioneer customer. The growth in size reflects the confidence in JANET of the existing user base at any one time, and the willingness of others in the academic sector to participate. I think the Particle Physics community, and the Library sec-tor have both been especially effective in this respect.

With hindsight, we should have been much more aggressive in resisting the pressures to use the CCITT rather than the ARPA protocols, and to follow the procurement policy which restricted us to buying only UK products. I am rea-sonably sure that if at the very outset we had tried to overrule the procurement policy, we would not have been able to create JANET. I believe that had I fought harder, earlier we would have been able to migrate sooner.

There is one area in which I am sure that JANET has been hugely successful, that of breaking a big task down into a lot of small ones, and returning most of these tasks to the end user community. The JNT has always largely restricted its role to that of negotiator, bringing together interested would-be users of a new type of service with would-be suppliers, and then letting nature takes it course. Only in those rare cases where the realization of the new service implies alterations to JANET as a bearer network has there been central intervention. This has allowed the central role of JANET, as the bearer network, to be carefully insulated from the successes or failures of the hundreds of projects which JANET supports.

I would like to finish by giving my thanks to all those who have worked to make JANET the success it has undoubtedly been, and continues to be.

References

Flowers, B. (1966) *University Grants Committee, Report of a Joint Working Party on Computers for Research*, Cmnd. 2883. HMSO, London.

Verdon, F. P. and Wells, M. (1995) Computing in British Universities: The Computer Board, 1966-1991. *The Computer Journal*, **38**(10), 822–30.

JANET web site: http://www.ja.net/

PART 2

The World Library – Collaboration and Sharing of Information

4

World-Class Universities Need World-Class Libraries and Information Resources: But How Can they be Provided?

Sir Brian K. Follett

4.1 Introduction

Faculty undertaking research at the cutting edge of their subject must have access to the world's knowledge base: it is a key infrastructural requirement of a research-intensive university. The challenge is how to organize and deliver this requirement, either within a single university or jointly across, say, a nation state.

Over the last few years the most obvious trend in science journals has been their arrival on the Internet and libraries have chosen, or been forced, to outsource much of their provision onto publishers' websites. This has yet to occur on a major scale in the humanities and social sciences, or in the provision of undergraduate materials, and so the paper form still predominates but for how long is an interesting question. If I speak as a scientist, and not as a librarian (or University Rector), the electronic trends of the past few years have many virtues. The speed of access to scientific articles, as well as the efficiency of hunting for materials, has been transformed by the web. In many areas especially biomedicine the provision of powerful databases and search engines created by the NIH mean I can cover my own areas of endeavour (biological clocks; reproductive biology) thoroughly, easily and quickly with a small investment of time each week. There are downsides, of course. Few scientists browse in their libraries any more. What is more the sheer growth in overall publication means that review journals have become more important (e.g. *Trends in...*; *Annual Review of...*) whilst weekly publications like *Nature, Science* or *Naturwissenschaften*, must be read to retain a sense of what is happening more widely in science. All

55

these trends may be causing certain distortions. Only a few percent of articles submitted to *Nature* are being published so that if one submits an article the chances are that it will never be read by a research scientist but judged rapidly, and rather crudely, by the publishing team. That is negative and in some ways it lowers the esteem of such weekly publications. More broadly it reflects a trend in many countries that scientists must publish in those journals with highest impact factors.

Within the research library itself the changes have been more profound. The web has proved itself a truly disruptive technology: it brings great benefits but at the same time it threatens the traditional place of the university library at the heart of the institution. Librarians have responded flexibly to the challenges but one aspect has defeated all of them: the continuing rise in acquisition costs that outstrip underlying inflation. The traditional approach to excessive cost pressures is to adjust expenditure between activities but this has proved difficult because the traditional roles of libraries have not disappeared whatsoever, indeed they may have intensified. Perhaps we are really watching a world-wide trend whereby information resources are becoming more important within society. Put another way this information aspect of a university is growing relative to some other aspects.

At a university or supra-university level the pressures become most obvious in financial terms. So what, if anything, can be done about it?

4.2 The Increasing Importance of Universities

The last fifteen years has witnessed another trend which is quite distinct from "information resources". Across the world governments of all political persuasions are changing their views of universities and, as manufacturing wanes, nations are attempting to move up-market into higher value products and services. This is placing universities in a far more central position within society than they have experienced previously. They are being viewed not only as the key generator of highly trained persons but through their research as a major stimulus for new "knowledge-based" industries. For example, in the UK there is now a significant focus upon patents and spin-out companies emerging from the universities, primarily in science and technology but increasingly also in the creative and service industries. In summary the opportunities for our universities have become much greater but because most remain heavily dependent upon the taxpayer for resources they are watched by government and also attract the critical gaze of the media and of the public. We are adjusting but it is not proving an entirely comfortable experience!

One consequence in some countries (but not yet all by any means) is that governments have driven through changes aimed at improving the competitiveness of their universities both between themselves (the market economy for research and teaching resources) and internationally. Experience shows that these changes are not universally welcomed by the universities, or their faculty, but the available evidence but points strongly to the fact that the advantages of some competition greatly outweigh the disadvantages. This has occurred most obviously in the quantity and quality of research outputs (e.g. the UK's so-called research assessment exercises every few years, the less frequent analyses of research-doctorate programs in the USA, and the research analyses being undertaken by the DFG in Germany), in the greater financial independence of institutions (at Warwick University in 1980 the proportion of funding coming as state grant was 90%, now it is 22% and the turnover is twice as large in real terms), and in a university's ability to attract higher quality undergraduates and graduate students (including those from abroad). I do believe that it has been this kind of evidence which has persuaded governments to invest more heavily in their universities. They see them as agile and responsive organizations with a focus upon the "customer" (student, research contractor) rather than upon themselves. In the past year alone the UK government has introduced three more changes in the university system: firstly a ten-year financial strategy to strengthen the science and technology base (defined broadly as *Gesellschaft*), secondly providing proper overheads for research grants and contracts ("full economic cost provisions"), and thirdly a significant increases in undergraduate tuition fees (from ca. 1800 to 4500 Euro per annum). These are intended (a) to put university research and teaching on a sustainable economic basis and (b) to drive up the quality of both teaching and research. This is the backdrop to considering libraries which, in my view, constitute one of the key infrastructure requirements in any leading university. The UK government's strategy arises in part from arguments about the future basis of the economy but without doubt it is backed up by growing statistical evidence (King, 2004) that some nations are performing significantly more strongly than others in a range of scientific and technological disciplines, and that the UK does rather well out of such analyses. In Switzerland, King's data should be even more valuable in any debates with its governments: Switzerland's S&T productivity (citations per paper normalized across academic disciplines) is ranked first (1st Switzerland; 2nd USA; 3rd Denmark; 4th UK; 5th Netherlands; 6th Germany, etc.).

Slowly but surely all these changes are leading to a greater differentiation between universities. This trend is encapsulated in national "league tables" of universities (e.g. US News and World Report each autumn, the (London) *Times* in May of each year) which are widely read, much criticized within universities and followed avidly! This "league table mentality" has been taken one step further recently with attempts to compare universities between countries (e.g. Shanghai Jiao Tong University; The Times Higher Education) *and to the growing conviction that a country must have a number of "world-class universities" if it is to be at the cutting edge in the new "knowledge economy."* The most recent example of a nation responding to these pressures is Germany where in 2006 a serious competition has taken place for major extra funding in certain universities. As someone privileged to play a minor role in this "excellence initiative" I can vouch for its intensity and its importance to the competing universities.

On this basis the USA can relax. It dominates the lists with 28 of the "top 50" (55%). That comes as no surprise (even given the rather English-language dominance of the tables). But in some ways what is most interesting are the other nation states with more than one university in the "top 50". These are the UK

(7), Australia (3), Canada, China, Japan, and Switzerland (2 each). One of those two Swiss institutions is ETH, ranked well into the top half of the "top 50" and at position ten in the Times Higher table.

Thoughtful academics should question the precision of such league tables but we should never underrate the capacity of such analyses to be used by governments to shape policy (after all, in other spheres of life school, health, defence and industrial policies we expect evidence-based decisions).

4.3 Funding the Library

So, one can probably define those universities which are "world-class" and which must provide extremely comprehensive information resources for their future health and welfare. But can they afford such resources? The answer, I think is "yes" and "no". I only have limited data on library expenditures in major universities but the picture for Europe is not encouraging. Oxford and Cambridge spend far more than virtually any other universities (and are also favoured by the UK copyright deposit system) but the sums expended are only one-half of those at Stanford, Berkeley, Yale and Michigan. The situation is much worse for the next tier of research-intensive British universities with serious claims to be defined as "world-class" and universities such as University College London, Imperial College London, Bristol, and Manchester spend only a fraction on their libraries compared with their peers in the States. Let me enter a caveat at this point, however. There is no obvious correlation between a universities expenditure on its library and research productivity of their faculty (e.g. citations per faculty). Perhaps some enterprising librarians will demonstrate such a correlation by more sophisticated methods and thereby improve their arguments for more resources. Insofar as the UK is concerned we were puzzled by the apparent underinvestment in journals scholarly monographs not leading to a greater difference with peer universities in the States. We cannot prove our hypothesis but think that part of the explanation lies in the British Library's national collection of periodicals held at Boston Spa which allows academics rapid access to the full range of world journals, and so has allowed individual universities to spend much less than their counterparts across the Atlantic. If true here is a fine example of national endeavours "adding value" and I shall return to the issue below.

Nevertheless "the under-funding of libraries" is a perennial issue for all librarians and for the university's administration. Most of the costs in libraries are inflating at rates similar to those in the university at large (staff salaries, provisions of buildings) but without doubt there have been much faster rates in (a) the costs of S&T journals, (b) in the offering e-library provision whilst continuing to take the print version, and (c) in the requirement to mount new on line services (e.g. institutional repositories, catalogue retroconversions, online access to search engines). Yes, university libraries are genuinely underfunded.

So, what should be done? The most obvious solution would be for each university to rebalance its internal expenditure and shift more resources to the library system. My best estimate is that at Oxford and Cambridge the extra costs of handling the "hyper-inflating" items listed above (S&T journal subscriptions, new services) would require an annual increase in the materials budget for each library of about 1.5m Euros. With a university turnover of 500m Euros this is feasible and even across a decade the expenditure on libraries would rise from 6.2 to 8.5% of total costs. It could be done if the will were present and the faculty perceived the provision of superb information resources as a *primary* infrastructural requirement for the R&D base.

To be honest I suspect these arguments have not been argued through in virtually any university. Indeed, I am not optimistic that a university would willingly rebalance expenditure in favour of libraries, not least because there is a long-standing maxim that the most effective way to improve a university is to invest in more faculty and not in improving the infrastructure. As an academic, I also believed this but as Rector I would argue that universities are under capitalized and over trade, and that their best way forward is to restrict investment in people but ensure the resources exist for the individual faculty to optimize their outputs.

Is there an alternative? The most obvious is to shift a significant proportion of S&T journal costs from the library (central university) onto the researchers themselves. There are many potential models but the simplest is to make publishing another cost of research similar to the purchasing of materials (chemicals, time on a large machine, animals), of staff (postdoctoral fellows, graduate and technical assistants) and of laboratory space. If this had happened thirty years ago then I suspect many of the inflationary issues would have not run away from us so fast or for so many years. Ironically, contributing to the costs of publishing one's research results has been a peripheral factor all along. For example, page charges of many journals lower subscription costs significantly less whilst purchasing reprints has always been a highly expensive business for the researcher. I make the obvious point that if publication costs in the sciences were moved to the researcher from the librarian (and robust means adopted to circumvent the obvious difficulties) then this would have two effects. Firstly, it would lower central library expenditure significantly and secondly it would bring the customer (the researcher) much more directly in contact with the cost problems faced by librarians. One suspects that whilst the scientists are isolated from such issues ("the library is a free good paid for by others") then their involvement in the publishing debate will remain peripheral and they will not act decisively against excessive publisher (profit or not-for-profit) demands and pricing strategies, let alone wholeheartedly embrace approaches such as institutional repositories. Somehow we must involve the general mass of researchers in issues related to publication: frankly, this is not happening even when there is an active international discussion about "open access". It has caught the eyes of research grants funders (NIH, Wellcome Trust, UK Research Councils) but the debate it still peripheral from the heartland of the researchers themselves, and the Rectors themselves studiously avoid becoming involved!

The approach above would, I believe, go some way to tackling the costs of S&T journals but it may only cap that particular element of the cost structure where publishers feel they are currently able to drive a market. If I speculated about the future then I can see parallel developments in the social sciences and humanities, let alone in the widespread cry from undergraduates that "there are not enough textbooks in the library". This last is indeed true and the internet offers a clear solution but who is to pay for the textbook to be available on each student's computer?

4.4 A National Approach

Some world-class universities could doubtless solve their problems – or at least ameliorate them – but there are weaknesses:

1. Costs will probably continue to rise faster than basic inflation for at least the next couple of decades. Partly this is because the internet is leading to a society where more and more access to information resources is seen as a societal good (quantity is the thing, forget quality!). Partly it lies within our own culture of linking academic success to publication so that the real power lies not with the customer (the researcher) but with the publisher (commercial and not-for-profit) and the intermediaries (providers of search engines). No wonder, the NIH and the Wellcome Trust are moving to an open access situation.

2. For sound reasons (usually associated with undergraduate teaching) most countries have adopted a model of having many universities (ca. one per half million of population) and truly massive urban universities have not proved ideal either for teaching or for research. The result is many university libraries at the very moment in history when the technology (the Internet developed, ironically, by the public sector and universities) means that one server can supply the entire world with information from a given journal. This inversion lies at the very heart of the librarian's dilemma and is why cooperation and deep collaboration between universities is essential, not a luxury to be argued about! The researcher simply wants information and is not terribly interested in where it comes from. They like the provision of materials at their desk-top from electronic sources: it is efficient, customer friendly and delivers information rapidly, particularly because they are not paying for the service directly.

3. The vast proportion of a nation's universities are not in the world-class league and capable one way or another of supplying their information needs. Since I believe that the health of a nation's research depends as much upon them as on the leading universities then what can be done to help them provide information resources.

4. Finally, let me mention the great national libraries. In most countries these are funded separately from university libraries and have grown up with a somewhat different culture. Yet we know that over one-half of the activity in the British Library is the provision of resources for research. This may have as its public focus the great reading rooms but the library also subscribes to a vast range of journals: far more than any other library in the UK. A number

of us in the British Library and the UK university system do not think that the current arrangements are ideal for either party in this electronic age.

4.5 The Research Information Network

It was these concerns which dominated discussion within the so-called "UK Research Libraries Support Group". In particular we were all struck by the lack of a national strategic view over what were the really major issues on "information resources". Individual projects abound in the UK but do they add up to a coherent approach and represent the best value for investing what are scarce resources? We have funded dozens of individual electronic projects in Britain and new developments spring up regularly (e.g. Digital Curation Centre at the University of Edinburgh funded by JISC). We have many library associations discussing and planning their own cooperation. We have funded national developments to tackle access to research libraries. Whilst without doubt this demonstrates willingness in the UK to cooperate and be at the forefront of library developments it lacks coherence and an overarching national strategy which determines priorities.

As a result our single major recommendation was to create a Research Information Network (RIN) with the objective of stimulating much stronger collaboration between libraries and in a number of areas, providing a national resource. This is not by any means a novel idea because librarians have a rich history of collaborating for the common good. Let me give three instances where major improvements have taken place because of collaboration. The Document Supply Centre of the British Library was established in the bleak years after World War II and grew into an important service for all universities. OCLC in Dublin, Ohio is a not-for-profit cooperative providing cataloguing and search facilities to thousands of research libraries. SuperJanet is the UK's academic network and is paid for centrally by top-slicing the public funds given by the government to support the universities. It keeps the UK network at the leading edge and is remarkably sound value for money.

The RIN was established in 2004. The initial key players are the universities and their government funding bodies, the British Library, the Office of Science and Technology which supports the government's Research Councils, and the national libraries in Wales and Scotland. Personally I would like to see the Wellcome Trust, as a great medical charity, on the governing body too. The office is located within the British Library.

The central theme in the RIN is "collaboration and cooperation" and the actions are focused upon "doing those things together that are best done together and *not* doing those things together that are best done separately". Put more formally the RIN will have three aims:

- To determine a national strategy and priorities. This strategy should be led by the priorities of the professional researchers (as is happening, for example, in the e-science programme run by the UK Research Councils). This strategy will cover much more than the electronic world.

- To develop a programme of work and raise the funding. This is important because the RIN must under no circumstances evolve into a talking shop: to survive it has to improve services and practice, and for this to be recognized by librarians and researchers. *To avoid the trap of it being dominated by small groups with particular agendas the RIN must surely focus upon a very small number of big issues.*
- To play an advocacy role nationally and internationally. In the former case to ensure that the case for research information resources is argued at the highest levels of government and becomes a far more overt plank of national research strategy. In the latter case to work within the EU and across the world since the issues are identical and one can envisage benefits from a cooperative of national RINs.

4.6 The RIN's Immediate Tasks

The types of task where joint working could offer advantages are not too difficult to discern:

- **Access:** Research in UK universities is moving inexorably to consolidation around a small number of major centres. It is perceived as being the only way in which the country can assemble sufficient critical mass to become competitive with the best. But, as mentioned above, it is important we maximize access for all professional researchers and the current investment to ensure openness of all our leading libraries is critical.
- **Electronic research collections:** This lies at the heart of the new library. Once back runs of journals have been digitized and are held in secure repositories (not with the publishers) then we could dispense entirely with paper and simply keep a number of sets on a national basis. When will this occur: the British Library suspects 2010–2012. I need not list the obvious questions but these surely need resolving on a national if not a supranational scale. Looking forward there are questions relating to access to electronic journals in a highly commercial world. One thing is certain the RIN needs to take further the issues involved in national site licencing.
- **Humanities and electronic research collections:** The focus of this chapter is on S&T but in many ways one of the most exciting possibilities is opening up humanities archives so they are available worldwide. Already there have been some important successes, sometimes led by commercial interests (English Books Online), but developments are eclectic and a means of identifying clear national priorities is lacking.
- **Discovery tools – catalogues, search engines:** The lack of national catalogues in some countries (including the UK) beggars belief and the reasons offered for why they are not necessary would draw admiration form a legal mind. The RIN needs to investigate this matter once again and decide whether or not it is a sufficient priority. Perhaps even more important is the issue of search engines which are sometimes quite excellent (most areas of biomedicine courtesy of the NIH, many other disciplines with a long history of sophisti-

cated aggregators, e.g. chemistry) but more broadly are not perceived as such. At this point I entered www.scholar.google.com and sought papers published by myself between 1970 and 2005. The answers arrived within two seconds, a remarkable phenomenon. Yet, the list is an incomplete one and could never be used as a basis for uncovering what I (or presumably anyone else) have published on bird photoperiodism and seasonal breeding. It is building true intelligence into these search engines which might constitute the greatest challenge. Here one surmises commercial entities have the finance, drive and capacity to create markets and already alongside Google there is Scopus from Reed-Elsevier and Web of Science.

- **Collaboration in collection management:** In theory this should be relatively noncontentious since the financial advantages and the enhanced coverage are quantifiable. Yet in many ways this encapsulates the cultural challenge of getting the universities to act together, particularly in a competitive era. It is all too easy to offer arguments about "university autonomy", "competition between universities" or "academic resistance" (see "Barriers to Resource Sharing among Higher Education Libraries" available at http://www.rslp.ac.uk/circs/). If I wished to choose one of my own priorities for the RIN then this might be it because we cannot seek significant new public cash for libraries without being willing to tackle collaboration in collection management constructively, rapidly and on a significant scale. These issues spill over into the field of "national reference collections" and "lender of last resort".

- **Scholarly communication:** This is a most active issue with the protagonists arguing their cases persuasively. If the Wellcome Trust and the NIH can insist upon materials being available within months of publication on a public access database then the situation may change dramatically and by the time this article is published we may know the answer. My colleague Stevan Harnad at Southampton who is highly active in the debate about Open Access offered me a summary of the current situation. He stressed that Open Access (which is the objective) is the ultimate objective, i.e. immediate, permanent, free, online access to the 2.5 million articles published in the world's 24,000 peer-reviewed journals. He believes the key lies with the authors who effectively have two choices. The first is to publish in a journal which offers open access and may, or may not, recover its costs through charging the researcher to publish (the researcher pays model referred to earlier): the gold road to open access. The second is to self-archive a supplementary version of the article in a toll-free repository, organized either by the authors' institutions or on a discipline basis: the green road to open access. Harnad observes that the gold road may be better but publishers are in no hurry to convert to a researcher pays model. Hence, at the moment, the green road has more attractions because the vast majority of journals (92%) have already given their authors the green light to self-archive their own articles. A self-archiving mandate from grant awarding bodies around the world would ensure the creation of institutional repositories and the rapid development of OAI-compliant harvesters so that in effect all articles would be located in one global virtual archive, seamlessly searchable and accessible.

- "Leadership": Let me end with the issue of leadership. My own involvement in library matters over the years has been very much as the amateur and an enthusiastic supporter of libraries and librarians. That is now coming to an end because of other commitments but I do believe the library system needs to cultivate friends in high places. I do not think that we have been successful enough in getting our key messages across to those who determine national research policy. Information provision is one of the most important infrastructural requirements of a research culture and yet, largely by inaction, countries could lose that provision. It will not disappear quickly or equally in all academic disciplines but slowly as the system becomes ever more commercialized for profit then the risks increase.

Reference

King, D. A. (2004) The Scientific Impact of Nations. *Nature*, **430**, 311–16.

5

The International Dimensions of Digital Science and Scholarship: Aspirations of the British Library in Serving the International Scientific and Scholarly Communities

Lynne Brindley

5.1 Introduction

This chapter describes recent activity and strategy of the British Library as we endeavour to serve the global scholarly community, equally recognizes the need to balance the traditional with the new and in doing so "redefine" what is a great research library in the 21st century. There is no doubt that the digital revolution has transformed the landscape we all operate within; bringing us closer together and presenting new opportunities and new challenges in the process.

5.2 Context

Research is internationally competitive and our best universities jockey for the best research talent at all levels and in all disciplines. Arguably what has made research libraries great in the past will not alone make them great in the digital environment of today and the rapidly evolving information context in this early part of the 21st century. We see a picture of ever more rapid innovation, mostly happening outside libraries and driven from the commercial sector; a picture of confusion and contradiction in the range of business models that are emerging and being experimented with; and new demands from discerning and empowered users. Such a challenge is an exciting opportunity for LIS to play new roles and define a new future. There is, in any case, no choice but to change, and change quickly if we wish to remain relevant for the future. The challenge for libraries in the 21st century, as now only one part of a great diversity of alternatives, is to find new ways to add value and remain relevant in this rapidly changing, confusing and competitive environment. While the distant future for libraries is not clear, it is timely for libraries to challenge some historic assumptions and ask some fundamental strategic questions.

Technology is turning on its head our assumptions about our value; it is challenging the roles of all accepted players; and it is enabling increasingly promiscuous users with different and higher needs to have a much wider choice to fit their digital lifestyles. To help unpick some of the opportunities and methodologies emerging for international scholarship in the digital world, we will examine some specific projects being undertaken at the British Library and identify broader lessons and wider possibilities for us all as we look ahead.

5.3 British Library: International Profile and Activities

The British Library is located in a global, multi-cultural city, with a mission and funding to make a major contribution to the national economy and to the social and cultural enrichment of Britain's citizens. Our strap-line is "the world's knowledge" and our vision states that "we exist for anyone who wants to do research – for academic, personal or commercial purposes". It was the aim of Sir Anthony Panizzi – Principal Librarian of the British Museum Library from 1856–1866 – to make it the "second best library in the world" – second, that is, only to the combined national libraries of each country. His policy was:

> "to bring together from all quarters the useful, the elegant, and the curious literature of every language; to unite with the best English library in England or the world [i.e.the BML], the best Russian library out of Russia, the best German out of Germany... and so with every language from Italian to Icelandic from Polish to Portuguese..."

In the modern age, the breadth of Panizzi's vision has particular resonance. The British Library, along with the UK's other great national institutions, plays a vital role as a "neutral space" in which the UK can build and strengthen wider international, diplomatic relations.

Our readers come from around the world and the top fifteen countries of origin for readers are: 8 from Europe, the US, Canada, Israel, Australia, India China and Japan. Approximately half our web visitors, researchers and library professionals, access our site from overseas, a similar pattern to that of users of the online catalogue. Usage reflects the particular historic strengths of our collections from the Middle East, Eastern Europe, South Asia and North America. We are currently assessing the results from our wide consultation on what our future content strategy should be. As the world changes we envisage strengthening our content acquisition, increasingly digital, from China, India, Anglophone Africa, and selectively South America. Each year we spend over £15 million (US$28 million) on overseas purchasing, complementing the value of our UK legal deposit of c. £12 million (US$23 million).

Our professional and scholarly co-operation has a strong international flavour. This is true of our exhibitions, our exhibition loans, representation on international professional, technical and standards bodies, conference attendance and presentations, and official visits both to and from the BL. We have memoranda of agreement with a number of national libraries, with a particular focus at present on:

China – where the memorandum identifies the broad scope for future collaboration between our two institutions and builds on contacts of long standing conducted on an informal basis which have worked well for the benefit of both institutions and their users including recent collaboration together on the International Dunhuang Project.

South Africa – where our focus has been on knowledge transfer – including conservation, legal deposit, governance, and strategy – and where we know there is a "multiplier effect" deriving from the NLSA's leadership role in Africa.

The National Library of Iraq – where we have sought to assist both on reconstruction of the collections and also on the development of networks of professional support for the Director of the Iraq National Library and Archives.

We run a major international Endangered Archives Programme, with funding from the Lisbet Rausing Charitable Fund, to assist researchers and repositories to rescue archives under threat and make them available to wider communities of interest, while retaining them in the region of origin. Copies are deposited at the British Library for use by scholars worldwide. The first 18 awards made in 2005 were distributed as follows:

8 to Asian programmes

4 to African programmes

3 to South American programmes

2 to Australasian programmes

1 to Middle Eastern programmes.

From the preservation of rare periodicals in Mongolia to a pilot in Liberia to preserve and open up the presidential and national archives; from the salvage and preservation of rare music in Yunnan, China, to identifying the potential corpus of a Mapuche collection in Chile – the endangered archive programme is a significant demonstration of the benefits to international scholarship of international collaboration.

Within Europe, where of course multi-lingual issues figure strongly, TEL (The European Library) is growing in importance and the British Library is playing a central role in its development and further forthcoming EU investment in digital library developments. TEL became an operational portal service in 2004 giving researcher and "informed citizen" access to 15 European national library collections and is now fast-tracking the new EU member states (seven at present) into membership. The eventual target is 45 European national libraries in membership. Membership commits each participant to maintaining the basic user interface in "their vernacular" through the TEL Language Working Group and participants are encouraged to provide metadata in their own language, English and any others they can. Multilingual searching is being explored through MACS and DELOS and has been raised as an issue with Google.

5.4 International Digital Scholarship Projects

The following description covers two of our current high profile digital scholarship projects, which exemplify the potential to contribute, through collaborative activity, to changing the shape of scholarly and research activity. Both involve the digital re-uniting of physically dispersed material across continents and libraries: both have political sensitivities and involve activities well beyond simple digitization.

5.4.1 The Codex Siniaticus

The Codex Siniaticus is the oldest surviving bible, produced in the middle of the fourth century, and an extremely important landmark in the history of the book. The Codex was preserved for many centuries at the Monastery of Saint Catherine but now just over half of the original book survives, dispersed between the Monastery, the British Library, Leipzig University Library and the National Library of Russia in St Petersburg. Due to the extreme age and fragility of the Codex, none of the holders of the different portions is able to allow access to the manuscript, beyond display in a glass case. We are now undertaking, with St Catherine, the other holders of the manuscript and leading international scholars, a major project to reproduce the entire Codex in digital form, employing cutting edge technology and advanced scholarship to achieve a virtual re-unification of the different manuscript parts. Biblical scholars in Germany and the UK are leading a new transcription of the text; multi-spectral imaging is likely to enable differentiation of different scribes and correctors of the manuscript and therefore potentially challenge the dating and accepted interpretations of biblical history; an internationally distributed TV documentary, high-quality facsimile, conference and collection of scholarly essays and exhibition are all planned.

5.4.2 The International Dunhuang Project

The International Dunhuang Project has been running for over ten years and represents collaboration between the British Library and libraries in China, Russia, Japan and France. It focuses around the manuscripts, paintings, textiles and other artefacts dating from 100BC–AD1200 found in the Library Cave at Dunhuang and at numerous other ancient Silk Road cities in the late 19th/early 20th century. The material was dispersed to museum and library collections worldwide, making access for scholars difficult. Priority has been given to conservation and cataloguing work, but digitizing the manuscripts began in 1997 with the aim of bringing together collections in virtual space. In this way, Silk Road material is becoming increasingly available to scholars and the general public alike. The IDP has created an essential scholarly resource with local centres in London, Beijing, St Petersburg, Kyoto and Berlin, with Chinese, Russian, German and Japanese versions of the website being maintained locally as well.

5.5 Mass Digitization Projects

These, perhaps, are two extraordinary examples of the art of the possible to change the face of scholarship in the digital age. But there are many more examples from the BL and from across the world.

At the other end of the spectrum are initiatives to create an enormous critical mass of materials for research and scholarship. Gale's international programme to digitize all pre-1800 texts in English, Early English Books Online is facilitating new research. With funding from the NSF and working with the University of California, Riverside, we have digitized our 18th century newspapers and will make them available online; with funding from the UK government's Joint Information Systems Committee we are digitizing our 19th century newspapers. We are working with Microsoft on digitizing out of copyright books and are starting with 19th century English novels, a corpus which is likely to surface new leads for researchers on material long-neglected in the print world. OCR and online searching will facilitate new kinds of research, previously impossible.

As should be expected while we redefine ourselves in the digital age and develop new and more effective patterns of international working, there will be political issues which we need to consider and tease out. For example, Jean-Noel Jeanneney of the French National Library has raised concerns about Google's potential influence on global culture; that the creation of an immense database of content from the United States will taint the future generation's interpretation of history and culture, as more people rely on the Internet to learn about the world. In an article in Le Monde entitled "When Google Challenges Europe," he warned of "the risk of a crushing domination by America in the definition of how future generations conceive of the world." While welcoming the BL's joint digitization programme with Microsoft – since in his view it diminished the risk of a Google monopoly – nevertheless he saw the BL/Microsoft deal as an act of "anglo-saxon solidarity" with a big American enterprise and, as such, counter to the close co-operation with the European national libraries who are working towards the development of the European digital library.

Our view at the BL is that it is plain we must adopt a portfolio approach to digitization, with a range of publicly and privately-funded initiatives. Thus we remain committed to CENL, TEL and other European initiatives, and to working collaboratively with other libraries in Europe, as well as to similar initiatives in North America.

These examples have been used – from the iconic to the large scale; from externally funded public good projects to commercially funded, subscription based programmes; from BL focussed to globally collaborative projects – to indicate the potential contribution our great libraries have to richly enhance and change the face of humanities research and scholarship

Are there general lessons and points to make? Almost certainly as libraries we can and should do more together to promote and create greater awareness of what is available for scholars already. Almost certainly we are only at the beginnings of trans-border digital join-up of relevant parts of our collections. There is certainly a lot more scope to engage at a discipline level internationally on what projects might really make the most impact on scholarship of the 21st century and a question for discussion is how we might better do this, despite the differences in mission, funding, governance and national priorities?

5.6 Responding to the Needs of Researchers in the Main Disciplinary Areas: Science, Technology, Medicine, Social Sciences, Arts and Humanities

What has been covered so far would appear to offer profound and growing opportunities in the digital space to play an increasingly critical role in underpinning 21st century research in the humanities. But what is equally clear is that there are very different trends in the different disciplinary areas that are suggesting different roles in STM and social sciences. This is strongly recognized in Redefining the Library, the British Library strategy 2005–2008 and our proposition in each broad area is different. To some extent this is recognized in the programme of this meeting which has later sessions on Science in the Public Interest and Copyright and Creativity in international scholarship, both implying advocacy and leadership roles for research libraries.

In STM we have a critical role to play in the digital preservation of the record of science, and we are working closely with the Koninklijke Bibliotheek (the National Library of the Netherlands) who are leading the European task force on Permanent Access to the Records of Science. We are also working closely with peer bodies in Government and quasi-Governmental bodies in the context of the UK's 10 year science strategy on the development of a route map for e-infrastructure for research. We have a clear mandate to engage with the new forms of publishing and particularly with the open access and subject repository movement, in the development of tools for virtual communities, and to ensure join up with data repositories and the creators of e-science. There is a quite clearly a role for the national library vis-à-vis questions of quality assurance in the web environment, in navigation, and in facilitating seamless access across repositories. In terms of the BL's role of supporting innovation we have a particular responsibility to ensure support for those small and medium enterprises which do not have the same access to rich and deep collections of digital science as do researchers with well-funded university libraries. As a national library we also have responsibilities relating to the public's understanding of science and its engagement with major issues. Arguably there are different forms of international engagement, focussed more on technology partnerships and collaboration both with public and private sector partners, e.g. bioinformatics institutes, research funders, data repositories, digital library and digital preservation experts.

In the social sciences the BL strategy is explicitly one of collaboration, particularly at national level to ensure greater join-up and exploitation of resources which are often difficult to find – so called grey literature and its migration to the Web environment. We are also key dataset providers and archives but again our aspirations are largely UK focussed. Our strategic approach to opening up our rich resources to social science scholars is to develop small teams of disciplinary experts to expand our relationships with key partners and ensure long term join up of digital preservation efforts.

5.7 Reaching out to Scientists and Scholars to Advise on the British Library's Agenda

The British Library does of course have a range of formal and informal mechanisms to connect it to scholars. As has already been mentioned, its international relationships with libraries and international professional bodies, and with those engaged in digital library developments is already extensive. Being a national library, rather than a research library with a focussed university constituency, however, makes direct connection with scholars a more complex business.

Our formal mechanisms include an Advisory Council which has representatives of major disciplines who as part of their role assist us in reaching out to and networking with discipline experts. We engage directly with UK Research Councils (who fund much of UK research activity and are discipline based), and the Wellcome Trust, and with the major learned and scholarly societies, such as the Royal Society and the British Academy. Through these contacts we are enabled to reach groups of academics in different disciplines and can tap both formally and informally into their expertise. In addition we work jointly on projects with a number of universities and their academics.

In a significant development this spring, Library was awarded "Academic Analogue status" by the Arts and Humanities Research Council (AHRC). This means that the Library is now eligible to apply to all of the AHRC's responsive-mode schemes, where previously bids had to be led by higher education institutions. With this no longer the case, the Library can tailor future bids directly to its own strategic requirements, while continuing our emphasis on partnership and collaboration with other academic bodies. The Library is working towards achieving similar Academic Analogue status with the Economic and Social Research Council to take forward similar benefits in the social sciences. The concept of the British Library as analogue has huge possibilities for the way in which we can take forward and support scholarship.

At the British Library our direct scholarly engagement is primarily with the UK base of scholars, even though we recognize that the international community is the recipient and beneficiary of much of the resulting endeavour. In a recent wide-ranging report on UK-USA research collaboration and strengthening transatlantic research partnership, undertaken by Sir Gareth Roberts, encouragement has been given to the Library of Congress and the British Library to work ever more closely together to facilitate such relationships, particularly through better coordination and systematic digitization of primary and secondary resources of interest to the humanities and social sciences, and through exchange of scholars. Initial priority is likely to be given to our respective archives of newspapers and sound recordings. This newly emerging bi-lateral model might offer a practical model of to make tangible progress.

5.8 Reflections for Discussion

For the essential question for all of us is how can research libraries be most responsive to the international dimensions of scholarship when contributing to the creation and support of international digital resources? What broader lessons can we take from the experience and activities of the BL?

The first observation would be that we are all at very early stages of recognizing the potential to support international digital scholarship. Our projects are exciting, ground-breaking in some cases, but also feeling their way, in terms of what can make a real difference to the highest quality research activity. A first step might well be the creation of greater international awareness of what is available, better mechanisms for feedback on the usefulness to scholars of what has been created and suggestions for future priorities

Second, we need to recognize that research libraries are going to play very different roles depending on the needs and behaviours of different disciplines. Most of our international digital scholarship work has been focussed so far on the humanities and the opportunities afforded by opening up legacy collections, joining up dispersed collections through digital scholarship projects. Our roles in support of STM and social sciences are likely to take on very different manifestations.

Third, most of our relationships with scholars and researchers are institutionally or perhaps at best nationally joined up. Of increasing importance is the joining up of relationships with other resource providers – data services, software developers, other cultural bodies, such as archives and museums. How do we prioritize these possibilities and which will have the most impact on the quality of global research? How practical is the joining up, particularly given differences in mission, funding, governance and national priorities? What is the realistic balance between planning and opportunism?

Fourth, international efforts in digital library developments and digital preservation are well underway and our task professionally is to ensure that we share best technical and professional practice to ensure that we do not re-invent wheels, that our particular efforts contribute most appropriately to these enormous global challenges and that inter-operability is sought.

In conclusion, without boundaries of physical space, the hegemony of institutions is disrupted. The very concept of institution is downplayed in the digital world – with beneficial effect – making institutions less formidable and enabling cross-institutional study. Indeed, so far as our users are concerned, institutions are entirely irrelevant in the digital world. Our convergent interests are around a shared network space – and yet historically we have focused our efforts within our own institutional and national domains. There are opportunities for joining up our thinking about digital scholarship internationally that will significantly benefit users and require us to think much more creatively, outside our institutional and national boundaries.

As a practical starting point, two particular areas come to mind where the ball is already rolling and where there is potential for global impact if we can co-ordinate our efforts effectively: the digitization of 19th century printed books via the Google Library Project and the digitization of newspapers where we are making a substantial commitment through a £2m publicly-funded programme to deliver 2 million digitized pages of 19th Century newspapers (in addition to the 1 million pages of 18th century newspapers we have already digitized under the separate Burney newspapers project. Working together across international and institutional boundaries to develop a critical mass of digitized material could provide the necessary key for expanding our roles in the digital world. Not only would the end product be of immense scholarly value, accessible to all via the web, but in the process we would begin to untangle some of the procedural, cultural and regulatory difficulties inherent with the new possibilities digital has given us.

For instinctively – researchers, scholars, libraries, internet surfers alike – we sense the potential digital gives us to make the world's knowledge available to all – wherever in the world it is physically held. Our challenge is how to make this a reality. We need to be listening to our users to ensure we meet their needs. We need to be developing new skills and technologies to deliver added value to our scholarly communities – and sharing that good practice. We need to recognize the difficulties in international collaboration and work together to surmount them.

6

CURL – Research Libraries in the British Isles

Peter Fox

6.1 Introduction

In 1982 informal discussions took place between Dr Fred Ratcliffe, Librarian of the University of Cambridge, and Douglas Foskett, Goldsmiths Librarian, University of London, about the need for the sharing of machine-readable records between the major research libraries of the United Kingdom. Those discussions were extended to involve representatives of other libraries, and in the following year the Consortium of University Research Libraries (CURL) was born. At that time, and for a number of years to follow, CURL was a fairly informal grouping of the seven largest university libraries in the country (Cambridge, Edinburgh, Glasgow, Leeds, London, Manchester and Oxford). The libraries had come together to "explore the possibilities of closer co-operation, particularly, but not exclusively in the use of automation", and it was the development and maintenance of the catalogue database that occupied most of the energies of CURL until the beginning of the 1990s. The early history of the organization, the reasons for its establishment, and a description of activities in its first decade is given in Ratcliffe and Foskett (1989).

Today, almost a quarter of a century after its foundation, CURL has become a very different animal. It has grown from seven to 29 members; its agenda is a very much broader one; its role and influence have expanded immensely. From being viewed with some suspicion as a club for the elite and (as one wit described it, rather unkindly but not entirely without justification) as the "Consortium for Unusually Rich Lunches", CURL has become a major force in academic librarianship, not just in the British Isles but on the world stage, with an agenda that seeks to promote its collections and expertise for the benefit of scholarship as a whole, regardless of whether that scholarship resides in its member institutions or, indeed, in these islands.

6.2 History of CURL

The history of CURL for at least the first decade of its existence was largely the history of the database and, despite the efforts of a number of its members, chiefly Henry Heaney, Librarian of the University of Glasgow, to extend the activities of the organization to encompass other areas where the major research libraries had common interests, the problems of maintaining and funding an ever-growing database dominated CURL's agenda. A number of factors led to the creation of a climate in which a change could take place, with the database continuing to underpin many of CURL's activities but no longer demanding all its attention. Those factors included the successful bid to JISC (the Joint Information Services Committee of the higher education funding councils) for funding to support and develop the database, the growth in CURL's membership, consortial membership of the Research Libraries Group (RLG), and the appointment of full-time CURL staff.

Undoubtedly the most significant single innovation that enabled the organization to develop its agenda was the appointment in 1997 of a full-time Executive Secretary. A full-time officer with the responsibility of managing the database had been appointed in 1995 and the Database Officer has remained an essential role within CURL ever since. However, CURL had been established as an informal grouping, and that remained its hallmark until 1997, with the running of the consortium regarded as a part-time activity. The original Chairman and Secretary were Dennis Cox, Librarian of the University of Leeds, and Douglas Foskett respectively, both of whom remained in office after retirement from their full-time jobs. They stood down in 1991 and were succeeded as Chairman by Brenda Moon, Librarian of the University of Edinburgh, and as Secretary by Reg Carr, Cox's successor at Leeds.

Although a part-time Assistant Secretary had been appointed at Leeds, the running of CURL essentially devolved upon its secretary between 1991 and 1997 – an enormous and sometimes unreasonable demand upon someone who was also running a major university library. It is a tribute to Reg Carr's ability and sheer hard work that CURL and Leeds both flourished during that period. During the same period, CURL doubled in size from its original seven members and became a company limited by guarantee, with formal articles of association and charitable status. By 1996, however, it was clear that the organization had become too large and the demands and expectations of its members too diverse for this part-time administration to continue to operate effectively.

In 1997 Clare Jenkins was appointed as CURL's first full-time Executive Secretary and a CURL office was established in the British Library of Political and Economic Science at the London School of Economics. At the same time, the management committee was replaced by a new Board of directors, with Peter Fox, Librarian of the University of Cambridge, as its first Chairman. The structure of the organization has remained essentially the same since then, with the only change being the move of the CURL office, first to the University of Glasgow, and then, in 2002, to the University of Birmingham.

6.3 CURL's First Strategic Plan

CURL's first formally-articulated strategic plan, for the period 1997–2000, consciously sought to expand the range of activities that the organization would undertake, and placed responsibility for implementation in the hands of three steering groups, each chaired by a member of the Board. The key areas of activity were: resource description and discovery, access to CURL resources and resource management. The plan has been revised several times since it was formulated, but much of CURL's work can still be accommodated within those three strands, though with different emphases and with the addition of some new areas that could not have been envisaged in the mid 1990s.

"Resource description and discovery" was an extension of CURL's original *raison d'être*, the database of catalogue records. The database was growing rapidly and was a major source of cataloguing data, not just for CURL libraries but for non-CURL members as well. COPAC, its online catalogue, had become a standard tool, heavily used both within the UK higher education community and outside it and had become "*a major international showcase for the resources of United Kingdom academic libraries*" (Field, 1999, 140). In 1998 JISC confirmed that COPAC should become a core element of its national dataset service, MIDAS, based at the University of Manchester. Both COPAC and its underlying database have now become effectively a UK national union catalogue, especially with the addition of the British Library's database, and at the time of writing (2006) the CURL database contains almost 50 million records.

Retrospective conversion – the transfer of records from card and printed catalogues into online form – became a growing priority as users increasingly expected to be able to find records for books via online databases. In 1999 CURL successfully bid for over £500,000 from the higher education funding councils' Research Support Libraries Programme (RSLP) to automate or create original records for 19th-century pamphlets held in 15 member libraries and two non-CURL institutions. The project was completed in 2002, with almost 180,000 records added to COPAC and made freely accessible to anyone.

The need to carry out further retrospective conversion remains a live issue today for many libraries, and after lengthy discussion with the Heritage Lottery Fund (HLF), CURL launched the Britain in Print Project as a pilot in 2003. It is now in its second phase, which will run until 2007. Supported by the HLF, and led by the University of Edinburgh, the project will create electronic records for all 40,000 pre-1700 British books in the ten participating libraries and will deliver these though a web-based catalogue. By the end of the project around 42,000 new online catalogue records will have been created. The project will also produce online learning materials targeted at schools and drawing on the resources represented by these records.

The demand for online access to catalogue records is not confined to those for printed materials. In 1999, JISC awarded funding to CURL and the universities of Liverpool and Manchester to develop a Higher Education Archives Hub. Fifteen universities provided content for the pilot project, most of it collection-level descriptions but some in the form of full finding aids. By 2001 the pilot had become a service, and the Archives Hub now provides a single point of access to almost 20,000 descriptions of archives held in over 150 UK institutions, forming part of the national archives network. The service continues to be a CURL-supported activity, with the database hosted at the University of Manchester and systems development work undertaken at the University of Liverpool.

The second of the three main strands in the 1997–2000 strategic plan was "access to resources". In 1996 CURL had undertaken an initiative to draw attention to the riches in the collections of its members by publishing a *Guide to the research collections of member libraries*, which provided a subject-based overview of the collections of the then 13 CURL libraries (Pickering, 1996). Each library was also encouraged to bring to the attention of its users the availability of the resources of the other CURL libraries via their guides for readers, web links, etc. The consortium itself sought "to develop enhanced access, for research purposes, to CURL's combined information resources through physical and virtual access and through document delivery" (Thomson, 1999, 144). A group was established to investigate the feasibility of an inter-library-loan service based on the records in COPAC. This was the first of several, so far abortive, attempts by CURL to set up inter-library-loans and document-supply services based on the holdings of its members.

The third strand was "resource management". Initial activities included work to map collection strengths, to promote the formulation by member libraries of collection-development policies, and to develop the deeper collaboration known as "collaborative collection management", which was one of the strands of the RSLP programme (Naylor, 1999). One of that programme's projects, COCOREES (COllaborative COllection management project for Russian and East European Studies), led by the University of Oxford, ran from 1999 to 2002, with a membership of 12 partner libraries, most of them CURL members. The CURL Board felt that the project's experience might enable it to serve as a test-bed and demonstration platform for further collaborative collection management initiatives and in 2002 a newly scoped project, CURL-CoFoR, (Collaboration For Research) began. This has now become an established service offering researchers in Russian and East European Studies a nationwide database of library collections and journal holdings in the UK.

Within the context of resource management, CURL's approach to the issue of preservation of the collections of member libraries was a good example of how the consortium recognized a need but also realized that, rather than try to do everything itself, it could achieve more through the development of strategic alliances and support for other bodies. In 1995 it had been agreed that CURL would become one of the group of institutions providing funding for the National Preservation Office (NPO), and the CURL Board took the view that, rather than duplicate the work of the NPO it would work with that organization by bringing to its attention projects that it felt were important for the research library community and by supporting the NPO in carrying them out.

In the area of digital archiving, however, CURL recognized that it had expertise within its member libraries that enabled it to play a leading role in research into this new and rapidly developing area, and was successful in obtaining funding from JISC for the CEDARS project (CURL Exemplars in Digital ARchiveS). The project, which ran from 1998 to 2002, was a joint one between the universities of Cambridge, Leeds and Oxford. Its principal objective was to explore digital preservation issues and, by the time its funding came to an end, it had become a world leader, publishing important guidance documents on digital preservation strategies, distributed digital archiving, preservation metadata, digital collection management and intellectual-property issues. in the development of standards for metadata (http://www.leeds.ac.uk/cedars).

The link with the National Preservation Office represented one of a number of strategic alliances, the most important of which was that with the Research Libraries Group (RLG). The activities of RLG were felt to be particularly relevant to CURL's needs and all CURL members were required also to become RLG members; this requirement was rescinded only in 2006 with the incorporation of RLG into OCLC. RLG had extensive experience in digital information management, preservation and conservation, and resource sharing, as well as offering access to the RLIN database of members' holdings for public access) and record retrieval and access to other databases that are significant for research. The attachment to the UK of an RLG staff member from 1996 to 2002 proved extremely valuable for CURL, and staff members from CURL libraries benefited from attending RLG symposia and meetings, and from placements in RLG member libraries in the United States. The election in 1999 of Reg Carr to chair the RLG Board demonstrated clearly the position of influence that CURL and its member librarians had achieved within an organization that, from being predominantly North American in outlook and membership, had become more overtly international in approach.

6.4 CAUL

The development of strategic alliances was not limited to links with North America. In 1999 the librarians of ten CURL libraries participated in a study tour organized by CAUL, the Council of Australian University Librarians, which included visits to CAUL institutions in Brisbane, Melbourne, Canberra and Sydney. A number of issues emerged which influenced CURL's future strategic thinking, particularly the Australian approach to resource sharing, the possibility of global collaboration with "like" communities of research institutions, as well as a number of initiatives in curriculum development, which were subsequently pursued on a bilateral basis between CURL and CAUL members. The return visit from CAUL members to the UK took place in 2000 and this allowed the discussions that had started the previous year to continue.

6.5 SCONUL

Closer to home, the relationship between CURL and SCONUL (Society of College, National and University Libraries) – a potentially divisive one for academic libraries in these islands – has been remarkably smooth. All CURL members are also members of SCONUL and officers of the two organizations meet regularly to review the most effective approach to issues of concern. It has been agreed that SCONUL would in general take the lead in playing a national role in the case of issues that affected other academic libraries as much as CURL members. Typical of these are copyright, health libraries, and access issues. In more specialized areas, such as preservation, CURL assumes the leading role.

6.6 Wolfson Foundation

The importance of the CURL members within the UK's research library scene was recognized in 1996 by the award from the Wolfson Foundation of £450,000 to nine CURL libraries to allow them to establish Wolfson Technology Resource Centres. The initial grant was followed by similar grants to the four new members which had missed the first round of bidding. In 2005 the Foundation again agreed to provide £6–10 million over a period of three to five years to assist CURL member libraries in improving access to, and long-term preservation of, their collections.

6.7 SPARC

Following a strategic review in 2000, the topic "scholarly communications" was added to the portfolio of activities, and a number of initiatives were undertaken to encourage more effective dissemination of the research output of universities. CURL joined SPARC, the Scholarly Publishing and Academic Resources Coalition, an alliance of universities, research libraries and other organizations established to address the problems of the current scholarly communication system. In 2001 CURL, in association with LIBER (Ligue des Bibliothèques Européenes de Recherche) and a number of other European partners, established SPARC Europe, which co-operates closely with the US parent organization. CURL also organized advocacy events in 14 member institutions, at which the spiralling costs of journals, e-print archives and other alternative publishing methods such as open-access, were debated.

6.8 SHERPA

In 2002 CURL part-funded the SHERPA project (Securing a Hybrid Environment for Research Preservation and Access), hosted by the University of Nottingham as part of the JISC FAIR (Focus on Access to Institutional Repositories) Programme. SHERPA, which forms an important strand of the CURL advocacy campaign on scholarly communication, has encouraged the development of openly accessible institutional digital repositories of research output in a number of member libraries.

Also in 2002, the British Library and the national libraries of Scotland and Wales, that had been associate members of CURL, became full members, and the organization dropped "university" from its title, becoming the Consortium of Research Libraries in the British Isles.

6.9 British Library

Greater use of electronic journals, especially by scientists, has resulted in a decline in usage of some printed materials such as scientific journals, and this, together with the growing pressure on storage space in research libraries, led CURL and the British Library to commission a study in early 2005 to investigate different possible approaches to the storage of printed materials in UK research libraries, particularly those in higher education. The study established that there was a shortage of storage space and recommended that a collaborative approach, the creation of a "UK research reserve", would be in the best interests of all stakeholders. A joint CURL/British Library working party was established to explore the feasibility of such a development and in November 2006 the joint group was successful in obtaining funding from the higher education funding councils to support an "early adopters" scheme to test the business model, carry out advocacy work and develop guidelines to assist libraries in collection-management decisions in respect of low-use materials. This project is an early example of collaboration with the newly-established Research Libraries Network, now the Research Information Network, which looks set to be a major feature of CURL activities in the future.

6.10 JISC

When CURL was established in 1982, one of the principal factors that made it distinctive was the importance of the collections of its member libraries. As we move into an increasingly digital age, the significance of those collections has, if anything, increased, as users expect to have access to the holdings of the world's great libraries via the Internet. An indication of this came with the announcement by JISC in late 2006 that it would be providing funding to meet the costs of digitizing the full content of the 19th-century pamphlets in CURL libraries whose catalogue records had been automated with an RSLP grant between 1999 and 2002.

6.11 Conclusion

For many libraries a move into a more or less totally digital future is a serious possibility. The research libraries in membership of CURL have to embrace that digital future, whilst at the same time ensuring that they provide for the stewardship of their collections in traditional print and manuscript form. The organization's vision in 2006 is to use the combined resources, both traditional and digital, of its member institutions to help build the distributed and hybrid research library of the future. It foresees a time when researchers, wherever they are in the world and whatever their discipline, will be able to identify resources in any format from their desktop, have access to an increasing range of electronic resources, both born-digital and digitized, have physical access to manuscripts or printed items that have not been digitized and cannot be moved, and have other printed items from outside their own institutions delivered to them efficiently (http://www.curl.ac.uk/about/vision.htm). This is a vision that the founders of CURL, 25 years ago, would have found hard to conceive, but it is entirely consistent with their view that the contents of the CURL libraries were a resource for the world. What they achieved by using automation to make catalogue records more widely accessible, their successors are now doing by providing access to the full contents of their collections.

Acknowledgements

This is a substantially revised version of an article from New Review of Academic Librarianship (Fox, 1999) and is published with permission. The author is indebted to Clare Jenkins and Robin Green for reading and commenting on a draft.

References

Field, C. D. (1999) CURL and resource description and discovery. *New Review of Academic Librarianship*, 5, 125–42.

Fox, P. (1999) CURL: past, present and future. *New Review of Academic Librarianship*, 5, 115–23.

Naylor, B. (1999) CURL – resource management. *New Review of Academic Librarianship*, 5, 149–57.

Pickering, O. (1996) *Consortium of University Research Libraries: a Guide to the Research Collections of Member Libraries*. CURL, Leeds.

Ratcliffe, F. W. and Foskett, D. J. (1989) The Consortium of University Research Libraries (CURL): a new co-operative venture in the United Kingdom. *British Journal of Academic Librarianship*, 4, 1–18.

Thomson, F. M. (1999) Access to resources. *New Review of Academic Librarianship*, 5, 143–8.

PART 3

Cultural and Strategic Implications of Digital Convergence for Libraries

7

For Better or Worse: Change and Development in Academic Libraries, 1970–2006

Bill Simpson

7.1 Introduction

It has been fashionable among librarians to view the changes that have occurred over the past thirty years or so from the particular standpoint of digital technology and its impact primarily on how we deliver information to our users. This is probably unavoidable and even right given the effect that technological developments have had on almost everything that libraries do. Technological change has been fundamental, in fact, to many of the wider changes in the culture of libraries that I discuss in this article but other changes in management styles, relationships with staff and expectations among users, to name but a few, stem from wider developments in society to which I shall also refer. Considered alongside technological change these other developments help demonstrate how fundamental a shift has taken place in a generation.

There is scope for much more detailed study and discussion of the issues I have raised in this short contribution and it may still be too early to attempt a complete assessment of all the changes that have taken place over the past thirty years or so. Those that were externally driven by changing social attitudes, customer expectations and the digital revolution were probably inevitable and recent innovations in university management suggest that more will follow. It would be interesting to know how much difference individual librarians or librarians as a group have made, not to the changes themselves but to how successfully they were introduced. In other words, could we have done it better?

7.2 Style Matters

When I began my own career as an Assistant Librarian in Durham University Library in 1969 my immediate line manager, the redoubtable and eccentric Keeper of Oriental Books, invariably addressed me as Simpson. If he called me Mr Simpson I knew I was in trouble and I have no doubt that he did not even know my Christian name. He cheerfully smoked his pipe and cigarettes indiscriminately in the Library, sometimes setting fire to himself in the process whilst managing somehow not to burn the place down. A brilliant if slightly unhinged polymath he had built the Oriental Collections from scratch after the Second World War, working closely with academic colleagues who regarded him with a mixture of awe for his knowledge and astonishment at the range and scope of his eccentricities, on which it would be unkind to dwell. He combined vast erudition, total disregard for his appearance, wild mood swings and fluctuations in behaviour and a paranoid distrust of the staff who reported to him. He would have been considered unemployable today, yet he achieved vastly more than many more reasonable people who carried on with their quiet, industrious lives.

My brief sketch of my first boss illustrates, even allowing for the fact that he was considered eccentric in the late 60s and early 70s, a number of very significant changes over the past thirty years in how libraries are managed and run. The formality of addressing male staff by their surnames and females always as Miss or Mrs has long gone, though I experienced a kind of coelacanth version of it in the University of London Library in the early 1990s before introducing some long overdue changes there myself. Smoking in working areas of the Library had been prohibited at Manchester some time before I moved there from Durham in 1973, an early harbinger of a much wider social change that was to follow. Collection development is now guided by written policies rather than emanating from small cabals of librarians and academics acting opportunistically and often on the basis of inspired guesswork as to what would be of lasting significance. Personal appearance and hygiene are taken very seriously and any member of staff found wanting in this area will soon be told to clean up their act. Above all, psychological aberrations would not be tolerated by users or colleagues.

The world of librarianship that we now inhabit is, in its social norms and mores, ostensibly more relaxed and friendly than that of thirty or so years ago but, paradoxically, it is also less tolerant, more prescriptive and more circumscribed. It is, though, I am sure, a better world for younger colleagues, who are protected by the "restrictions" to which I have referred, from the eccentricities and wild mood swings among managers from which I and other young staff sometimes suffered early in our careers. Those who regret the demise of the "characters" are inclined to forget that, whilst providing excellent spectator sport for others, those characters were often hell to work for!

7.3 And the Substance

The academic library of 1970 was entirely print based and its activities were highly labour intensive, with inordinate effort going into the creation of locally produced catalogue records on cards or slips of paper so that each individual library system more or less replicated what others were doing across the world. The assiduous checking of each entry by supervisors or cataloguing team leaders was followed by the filing of entries into banks of drawers or rows of sheaf binders according to strict rules. Circulation services were entirely manual, with loan records kept in duplicate or triplicate by borrower, author and/or classification number. The boxes containing these records (the "charge") occupied large amounts of space and when, as occasionally happened, one was dropped and its contents spilled out pandemonium ensued. Document supply in those pre-BL days involved separate agencies such as the National Central Library, National Lending Library for Science and Technology, regional bureaux and a certain amount of inspired guesswork, with or without the use of BUCOP and other aids. All of this, with the total dependence on print meant that libraries had an air of permanence, both in their physical appearance and in the range and nature of the activities that went on within them. As a result I was able to say on the completion of the James Ussher Library at Trinity College Dublin, where I was Librarian until 2002, that the Ussher bore less resemblance in structure and function to the Berkeley Library that was completed in 1967 than the Berkeley did to the Old Library, completed in 1731. The information revolution of the 70s onward meant that the solid, monumental and inflexible buildings of old had given way to buildings designed to be light, airy, environmentally acceptable and highly flexible in structure and function.

The ongoing shift from print to e-publishing was preceded by a shift from manual to largely automated library management systems as the card catalogue gradually gave way to the OPAC, more or less seamlessly in retrospect but, to those of us who lived through the transition, with much debate and a certain amount of angst at the time. The records were being stored electronically but were still produced locally, taking such inspiration as we could from the National Union Catalog, the British Museum's GK3 and other such "Guides to the perplexed" (with apologies to Maimonides) as we could find. Was our cataloguing better for being home grown and the product of so much intellectual effort for what many would regard as so little return? It is hard to know and the answer is probably "sometimes" but what is not in doubt is that the combination of subject and cataloguing responsibilities for a particular discipline meant that subject librarians had a much better knowledge of their stock than is usually the case today when, apart from creating the order request, the subject librarian may have no further contact with the stock for which (s)he is responsible. Modern cataloguing practices are infinitely more cost-effective than those of a generation ago but result in a less joined-up approach to collection development in individual subject areas.

While there can be no doubt that the advent of BLDSC and other document supply services such as RLG's SHARES have totally transformed the face of interlending and document supply and produced a vastly improved service to users who need material from other libraries, it is debatable whether the majority of those borrowing and returning their own library's books in today's heavily automated environment receive a significantly better service than their predecessors of thirty or more years ago. Automated systems have enabled libraries to manage their lending services more effectively and facilities such as on-line or automated telephone renewals are a boon to readers who cannot visit the library physically, but the chief gain brought by the automation of lending services is that is has enabled us to cope with greatly increased numbers of users as higher education has expanded without significantly increasing our staffing levels. The improvement has been in efficiency rather than quality of service and, with the advent of self-issue machines in recent years libraries have become more like banks as transactions increasingly take place without human interaction.

The revolution brought about by the advent of sophisticated library management systems has brought very real gains for users who can access catalogues remotely, reserve or renew books on-line or request documents from BLDSC in the knowledge that they will have them almost as quickly as if they were in their own library. It has brought huge gains in library efficiency in the face of the very rapid expansion of higher education in recent years but these gains have to be expressed in terms of the additional staff we have not added to our workforce rather than in reduced staff numbers. What seems to have been lost in the process is much of the interaction between staff and users and the empathy that developed as a result of this. Combined with the fact that, for many academics in particular, the library now comes to them electronically so that they do not have to visit it physically, this change in relationships has thrown up a whole new series of challenges for academic libraries and librarians.

7.4 The Ecstasy of e-

Much has been written on the transformation brought about in information provision by the advent of e-publishing, whether in relation to the content, its metadata, licensing and copyright issues, or in more recent times, alternative publishing and long term preservation models. Much less time has been devoted to the associated issues, which are vital to librarians and the future of libraries, of perceptions and expectations of our roles. As long ago as 1990 the then Vice-Chancellor of the University of London assured me, as the newly appointed University Librarian there, that electronic journals would solve libraries' financial problems "in the next two or three years". They hadn't done so by 1992–3 and they still haven't done so now but that did not prevent my being asked by one of the University's Vice-Presidents at a recent operational performance review of the JRUL in Manchester "what savings are being made as a result of your heavy investment in e-resources?" Of course we can answer such questions with reference to savings in processing costs, storage and preservation but this isn't what those who control our funding have in mind and the myth that "electronic = cheap = less spent on acquisitions" is so curiously persistent that it seems to be in danger of becoming one of Richard Dawkins's "memes".

The idea that electronic information is much cheaper than print is combined in the minds of many academics, particularly those in science, medicine and engineering, with the view that libraries are no longer required "because I can get everything I need on my computer and have no need of a library". I have lost count of the number of occasions on which, over the past few years, I have either been told categorically that, except for Special Collections, there won't be any libraries in ten years time or asked "Do you think there's any future for libraries?" This attitude is based on both ignorance as academics confuse the computing infrastructure with the content ("the pipes with the gas") and a self-centredness which takes no account of the needs either of students, for whom the library is much more than a purveyor of information, or of academics in areas such as the humanities for whom instant, up-to-the-minute on-line information is not the absolute boon that it is for those working in SME.

The twin dangers for librarians are that if we dispute the assertions of our imminent demise we are regarded as Luddites desperately clinging on to the familiar to protect our jobs, but if we do not we lose the argument by default, even though the weight of evidence is on our side. It is always uncomfortable to argue with a body of received wisdom such as that which has become the new orthodoxy in the SME community and one risks ridicule in doing so, but it is a risk we must take, whilst demonstrating by the quality of service that we provide in all media that we are in reality giving a lead in the information revolution rather than resisting it. I would like to think that the massive e-resources that we provide in Manchester would make us immune to any suggestions of being reactionary but this isn't always so and, alongside the questions about how much money we save by substituting electronic for print publications, we are under considerable space pressure as capital planning exercises assume that the physical library will shrink. It can be helpful when researchers in the humanities protest loudly that multi-volume works on which they depend have been moved from open access to closed storage!

If I have dealt with the issue of perceptions of the impact of the e-revolution on library costs and services at some length it is because it represents a profound shift among most academics in a single generation from viewing the library as central to their work ("The Library is the heart of the University" as Vice-Chancellors used once to proclaim like a mantra) to viewing it as, at best, peripheral and, at worst, irrelevant. To some extent we may have contributed to this perception ourselves as we have pushed the e-aspects of our work at the expense of almost everything else that we do over the past twenty years or so. It may also have been inevitable given that a huge and irreversible revolution has occurred and we may currently be in the antithesis stage of Hegelian dialectic, with the ultimate synthesis in the form of full acceptance by academics of the hybrid library as the norm for the future yet to come. Either way, the world of 2006 is far less stable and certain than that of 1970 for university libraries and I suspect that our successors will have to navigate through much choppier waters than those which contributors to this volume will have experienced – rough though some of ours have seemed at the time.

7.5 Power to the People?

If the internal governance of libraries was autocratic in the early 70s, with relatively little interaction beyond the strictly necessary between senior management and more junior colleagues, so was the relationship between libraries and their users, with the possible exception of those senior academics, not necessarily members of the Library Committee, who had the ear of the Librarian or were otherwise able, by way of a combination of perceived power and ruthlessness, to intimidate him (and it was almost invariably a "him" at the time). There were those such as Nance McAulay at Durham who sought to move away from autocratic management with the introduction of staff meetings at which colleagues were encouraged to express their views freely and openly and I well recall such meetings in the "dungeon" at Place Green, where the stuffiness of the heating system on cold winter afternoons was more than compensated for by the opportunity of engaging in tentative debate with the Librarian herself. Such openness was, though, exceptional at the time and it was another decade or more before management styles became overtly more participative and, to a degree, democratic.

To my knowledge no systematic study has been made of the impact of the glut of early retirements of senior librarians and their replacement by younger colleagues, who had been at university in the 60s, in the mid 1980s. Those of us who fell into this younger group of successors were "baby boomers" who had not known the unquestioning discipline of military service and, though we had mostly been at grammar schools in the late 50s and early 60s, this experience had been overlain by that of the social revolution that the mid to late 60s brought. Having lost much of our own unquestioning respect for authority figures we were hardly likely to try to become such figures to others – and would probably have felt ridiculous if we had attempted to do so. We were undoubtedly part of a wider process which included the disappearance of the culture of deference but, wittingly or unwittingly, those of us who became chief librarians twenty or so years ago ushered in a culture in which, if all people cannot be equal in pay and status, we can at least treat each other with equal respect and courtesy irrespective of relative places in a hierarchy.

The relationship between libraries and users has undergone a similar process of change but for a different reason. The abolition of grants followed by the introduction of tuition fees has transformed readers/users into customers who are buying a service and will no longer accept whatever is on offer without complaint. The result is that library opening hours increasingly reflect what readers want rather than the convenience of staff and, as universities conduct satisfaction surveys of libraries and other activities, we are regularly required to address perceived shortcomings of provision, whether of the insatiable demand for extra copies of undergraduate textbooks or in the provision of information in electronic form even when it is not yet available electronically. If the relaxation of management styles in the 80s is to be reversed in the future it will be because managers themselves now have less freedom to manage as they would wish because they themselves are obliged to respond to an emerging culture of constant assessment and monitoring.

It is paradoxical that the desire of university managers to control libraries and make them more accountable has gone hand in hand in many institutions with the abolition of library committees. For all their faults and inadequacies such committees were a valuable sounding board and source of advice from representatives of the academic community and it will be interesting to see how successful the trend away from representative committees to executive authority, subject to more formal and ongoing performance measurement and review, will be in delivering effective library provision. It gives power to far more people, each of whom can have a say in the regular satisfaction surveys, but it is power without responsibility that can be exercised thoughtlessly as one ticks boxes on a questionnaire rather than the genuine influence that can be built up over an extended relationship through membership of a committee or other governing or representative group. Some changes may not be for the better!

7.6 Jeux sans Frontières

The world has expanded dramatically beyond the walls of our own libraries during the last thirty years to an extent that would have startled our predecessors for whom SCONUL, with its multifarious sub-committees and working groups and, for the more adventurous, occasional forays abroad to IFLA, would have been the norm. Possibly, as with more democratic and relaxed internal management structures, academic librarians have simply followed unconsciously society's wider developments as people have embraced foreign travel as a normal part of life. Just as the Algarve, Umbria and Florida have replaced their homely British counterparts we librarians have fled halls of residence in UK campus universities in favour of LIBER meetings in St Petersburg, RLG meetings in Los Angeles and CURL visits to Australia. We have, in fact, become much less insular and more globally aware and this wider awareness and enhanced international co-operation has been fostered also by the advent of email and, more recently, international recruitment to senior library posts in the UK. It had long been a tradition for British librarians to become directors of Commonwealth university libraries, but the relatively recent arrivals of Helen Hayes and Sue McKnight from Australia at Edinburgh and Nottingham Trent respectively, with the imminent arrival of Sarah Thomas from the USA as Reg Carr's successor at Oxford, mark a sea change as our profession moves from being a one-way process of Brits going overseas to a truly global recruitment market. This is an exciting development which promises to challenge and broaden our thinking in the UK if, and it is a big "if", academic librarianship does not become so bland and uniform that, apart from levels of resource, it is impossible to distinguish one country from another. I personally look forward to the appointment of chief librarians from non-English speaking countries to senior posts in academic research libraries in Britain, though I fear that linguistic shortcomings mean that it will be much longer before the reverse happens more than very exceptionally.

As academic librarianship has, at least at the research level, become globalized, it has also segregated itself within the UK into "research" and, for want of a better tem, "less research" oriented libraries with the advent of CURL alongside SCONUL (strictly the old SCONUL and COPOL, both of which were still in existence when CURL was founded in 1983). This was probably an inevitable development in view of the growth of SCONUL into a very broad church but was not the reason for CURL's foundation, which occurred when SCONUL had not much more than fifty members. When founded CURL had a specific remit and agenda that could not be delivered by SCONUL but it has grown into a wider organization with a much more general but research-focused mission. It has undoubtedly weakened SCONUL as it has become usually the primary external focus of directors of research libraries, including the national libraries, at SCONUL's expense but recent co-operative initiatives between the two bodies in areas such as the joint CURL-SCONUL-e-Research Group bode well for the future. In any case, though the advent of CURL may have wounded SCONUL, the wound was never likely to be fatal as long as SCONUL remains the primary consultative body for academic libraries. It is noteworthy that, even if levels of participation have diminished, no CURL member has ever resigned from SCONUL.

The horizons of some academic librarians have broadened also as some libraries have been converged with their universities' computing services (and, occasionally, more besides) to create new super-directorates of information services. Others' horizons may have been foreshortened as they have found themselves reporting to the former head of computing services or even to an entirely new information "supremo" to whom both the librarian and head of computing report. In the best case scenario, where the librarian has emerged as the head of a converged service, (s)he has found the involvement with RUGIT and related bodies a challenge and a stimulus. Not all examples of convergence have worked and some universities have reluctantly accepted this failure and de-converged but it is to the credit of librarians that convergence has generally worked well when led by the library.

Senior librarians today have travelled more, participated more widely beyond our home institutions and countries and undertaken a wider variety of activities than our predecessors. Whether the benefits we believe we have delivered to our users as a result of this are real or would have followed inevitably from technological advances is hard to judge and something that, in retrospect, we cannot know but, as with society as a whole, our becoming less insular and introverted has almost certainly delivered real if less tangible benefits to our institutions.

7.7 Sed Quis Custodiet Ipsos Custodes?

But who will guard the guards? Whether we apply it to senior managers or to all staff the question is one that is now repeatedly implied by the plethora of personal and organizational performance reviews, health and safety, equality and diversity and other similar requirements for compliance that are imposed upon us. Viewed negatively such requirements distract us from our core tasks of providing high quality services and contributing to national and international developments which will provide future enhancements to those services. It is easy to become frustrated and irritated by the demands for compliance with deadlines, often imposed by management consultants who have no other function but to manage such activities across the institution. On reflection, however, such requirements can have real benefits if we see the stricter regimes to which we must now conform as enabling rather than threatening and disruptive mechanisms. There is nothing wrong with demanding proof that the highest possible standards of service and best use of resources are being maintained by library management and the focus provided by the annual operational performance review is much sharper than any general and sometimes fairly superficial oversight provided by many traditional library committees. The important factor is that such review should be used positively and not as an opportunity for an annual round of library-bashing (or, for that matter, bashing of any other university activity) unless it is deserved. Here Vice-Chancellors and others who chair such review committees need to consider carefully the balance between carrot and stick in the approach they take.

At the personal level the opportunities presented by performance and development review, if used well, are enormous. The plethora of courses, training and mentoring schemes that can be offered to staff vastly exceeds anything that was available even a decade ago and fitting staff to the right channel for meeting their needs is one of the gains that PDR offers. If I recall correctly, the only outside training I received in the four years of my first job in an academic library was a one day course in basic photocopier maintenance. My staff at Manchester now have a vast array of training opportunities available through NOWAL and other external providers, as well as the courses offered by the University itself. As far as training is concerned the world is truly a better place! And if our staff are better trained than we were we can at least hope that they will, in time, become better university librarians than we have managed to be.

8

Combining the Best of Both Worlds: the Hybrid Library

David Baker

8.1 Introduction

Reg Carr was one of the first people to use the term "hybrid library", but also to advocate, implement and define it:

> "The dominant user view of a library is of a physical place. But libraries are services which provide organized access to the intellectual record, wherever it resides, whether in physical places or in scattered digital information spaces. The "hybrid" library of the future will be a managed combination of physical and virtual collections and information resources."[1]

He saw the hybrid library as:

> "one of the most potentially valuable things to emerge from the LIS [library and information services] world in the 1990s...; and... one of [the] greatest challenges for the opening decade of this new millennium",

not least as a way of managing

> "all our massive and growing collections of traditional and digital materials in a coherent way, for the benefit of our users, by harnessing and exploiting the new technologies in appropriate ways."

This chapter seeks to review the development of the hybrid library to date, to explore the issues associated with the implementation and management of the concept, and to consider future trends and developments in the field.

---

1   http://www.bodley.ox.ac.uk/librarian/malibu2001/malibu2001.htm

8.2 What is a Hybrid Library?

A hybrid library is here defined as an organizational entity that brings together a wide range of academic assets including metadata, catalogues, primary source materials, learning objects, datasets, digital repositories and physical resources in a structured and managed way. The library is a place to search for these assets, to discover their existence, to locate them and then, if required, receive them. Hybrid libraries are not necessarily be linked to a single physical space or a single organization, though many have grown and will continue to grow out of a physical entity or entities. The common denominator in a hybrid library, as opposed to a purely digital library, is that it has one or more physical bases, collections and services as well as digitally-based ones. The primarily physical elements of hybrid libraries are themselves increasingly areas encompassing a set of resources, facilities and services in which digital/web-based, as well as more traditional research and learning, can take place. But they will increasingly be just one part of a much larger organizational whole that places greatest value on maximum access whether in terms of timeframe or type. At the same time, "traditional" libraries, or traditional elements of primarily digital libraries, where Information and Communications Technology (ICT) is applied to the management of hard copies, their organization, access and delivery, will continue because digitization is not feasible, justifiable nor wanted or needed (Burnhill and Law, 2005), or a digital version could be generated on demand. In addition, there is currently a massive backlog of printed work that must somehow be linked to or turned into digital material.

8.3 Recent History

The United Kingdom Higher Education (UKHE) is a complex and varied sector, yet today there is a pervasive common denominator: the use of ICT to support teaching, research, managerial activities and the delivery of academic support services (Joint Information Systems Committee [JISC], 1995; Higher Education Funding Council for England [HEFCE], 1997). Until recently, there was a single "dominant design" in LIS – that of hard copy storage, access and delivery. However, as described elsewhere (Baker, 2004), by the early 1990s, the UKHE LIS sector had got to that final

> "specific pattern stage of innovation ... [where it was] vulnerable to the possibility of a revolutionary new product introduction." (Noori, 1990)

The development of Internet -based resources and services and the breakdown of the old dominant design was a "landmark" change (Kingston, 2000). On the one hand, new technology was being applied to existing markets; on the other, new markets were being tapped once new products and services were fully developed. Existing suppliers, such as traditional libraries and document delivery services (and, indeed, users) began to find it

> "difficult to adapt to environmental changes with... an ageing product." (Noori, 1990).

The Follett Report (Follett, 1993) changed the LIS landscape for ever, though developments in North America and Australia have also been significant (see, for example, Greenaway, 1997). Even before "Follett", there were the beginnings of a new, more integrated, more innovative approach to the "document delivery" elements of library provision that sought to bring all the various elements together under the control of the end-user rather than the inter-library loans librarian (Baker, 1991; Baker, 1992a; Baker, 1994a; Baker 1994b). The Electronic Libraries (e-Lib) Programme (1995–2001) that emerged from the Follett Report sought to change the way in which UKHE LIS delivered functionality, services and content to their users, with special emphasis on IT delivery. The investment was substantial (£60m) and stimulated over 100 projects (Tavistock Institute, 1998, 2000; ESYS Consulting, 2001).

There were three basic phases to e-Lib:

Phase	Description
1	The "let a hundred flowers bloom" period, with a wide range of programmes and projects being approved or commissioned in the wake of the Follett Report's recommendations. The aim was to look at the many ways in which ICT could be applied to library services to best effect.
2	This was a time of turning projects into products or services, and of ensuring a complete portfolio of activities that covered the whole spectrum of library activities. The emphasis was frequently on scalability, and on co-operative solutions.
3	This was the integrative phase, designed to bring together the various strands and initiatives, and to continue the push towards viable and coherent digitally-based services.

Though the Follett Report concentrated on the "electronic" library, there was also a widespread recognition that the rich "legacy" of print-on-paper collections could not be ignored and needed to be retro-engineered into the digital future that was being predicted and planned, if not yet implemented. Hence phase 3 began to develop the concept of the "hybrid" library, and initiated projects that would provide the best of both worlds traditional and electronic to the end user. JISC Circular 3/97 states:

> "the challenge [was] to bring together technologies ... plus the electronic products and services already in libraries, and the historical functions of our local, physical libraries, into well-organized, accessible hybrid libraries."[2]

In a 1995 Delphi study carried out for the University of East Anglia, the author suggested that:

> "many elements of traditional provision would remain alongside newer approaches. With development in e-journals, etc. researchers may become more self-sufficient and visit the library less often, but students are likely to continue to see it as a place to work and get help. Integrating print and electronic provision successfully will require careful planning, and skilled training/coaching of students to ensure that they make full use of both new and traditional media." (Baker, 2004)

---

2   http://www.ukoln.ac.uk/services/elib/papers/circulars/

Reg Carr stated that the library sector was:

> "looking to integrate new technologies into the library service array, to enable the hybrid library to extend its services beyond the existing range, and in particular to facilitate resource discovery beyond the physical limitations of the physical library, both locally and much more widely."[3]

But the development of the hybrid model was not just about a single library or collection: it was about recognizing the growing power of the Internet and the need to bring together resources regionally, nationally and even internationally as well as locally. One of the outcomes of e-Lib was thus the Distributed National Electronic Resource (DNER). Reg Carr saw the DNER as a kind of national hybrid library and one that allowed the presentation of national services in a local context.[4]

Much of what was predicted, proposed and planned in the 1990s has already come to fruition, for there have been significant changes in academic library services and more broadly in the way in which people access and use information. Further major change is almost inevitable over the next few years. The remainder of this chapter looks at the key issues and challenges facing the UKHE sector, and its librarians in particular, as the hybrid library develops further.

8.4 Content and Usage

> "The 'Library' is being de- and re-constructed, with a digital future being seen as the norm in many environments." (Baker, 2005).

The potential of the Internet offers the possibility of universal access to everything, as evinced by the DELOS vision:

> "Digital libraries should enable any citizen to access all human knowledge anytime and anywhere, in a friendly, multi-modal, efficient, and effective way, by overcoming barriers of distance, language, and culture and by using multiple Internet-connected devices."[5]

Scholarly communication now spans everything from primary data through various versions to final product in its "bound volume" state. The journal article (rather than the journal or the journal issue itself) is now the unit of e-publishing or usage in some areas, and is breaking down further into fragments of articles for student usage. The take-up of e-books is less robust at this stage, though mass digitization programmes are beginning to tip the balance and recent research (Higher Education Consultancy Group, 2006) has suggested that the potential for this form of e-publishing is now considerable.

---

3   http://www.bodley.ox.ac.uk/librarian/malibu2001/malibu2001.htm
4   http://www.jisc.ac.uk/pub99/dner_vision.html
5   http://www.delos.info/

The author argues elsewhere (Baker, 2005) that, ultimately, the shape, nature and speed of these changes in the scholarly communications process will be driven by quality assurance and integrity and peer review requirements in scholarly publication will remain a key variable in terms of future change and development. At the present time, there are still concerns about quality assurance "on-line", especially with continued and worsening "information overload" and increasingly blurred boundaries as to "publication".

> "One of the key lessons learned by the JISC through investment in a range of programmes to enhance access to research and learning resources ... is that we are operating in an environment where users interact with a variety of digital and non-digital objects. In searching for high quality ... resources in networked environments they will encounter an array of electronic records pointing to both original items, a book, manuscript or painting, and records leading to digital and increasingly born digital resources, a satellite data stream, multimedia essay, or digital art work. In all of these cases [users] will need to be confident about the quality of the information that they are accessing and have the skills of judgement and understanding in place to assess and utilize what they find..." (JISC, 2002)

There is already much useful information and evidence about user behaviour and the user psyche, thanks to studies such as EDNER (Brophy, 2004). EDNER recognized a particular challenge with regard to the phenomenon of "satisficing" or the practice of accepting less than the best in terms of search results. The best may be "the enemy of the good", but the over-immediacy of the Internet often leads to a lack of critical evaluation of search results on the part of staff as well as students. On the one hand, there is still a need to build quality and kitemark controls; on the other, the ability to find unreliable sources and evaluate them critically is seen as a vital part of study. Users need to feel in control, and in any case personalization and customization tools fit well with new approaches to learning. But personalization doesn't mean working alone, and facilitation of group work and social interaction is always likely to be a prerequisite. This is where the library as physical space remains especially valuable.

Effective, user-friendly access to libraries, their content and services, then, is of paramount importance. There is a need for ever-more intuitive and deep search tools that ensure the widest possible interlinked, interoperable and unified access to content from a range of sources, through resource-access integrations. These tools need to cope with various formats and discrete and disparate sources to allow for the maximum integration of physical and e-holdings and to offer the ability to guess implied meanings and to rationalize semantic options. In a research context, the increasing move towards personalization and customization via the Internet needs to include the ability to annotate, manipulate, and follow trains of thought from unstructured, raw data to finished product.

Research within the JISC-funded Virtual Norfolk project, for example,[6] has shown that the take-up of learning materials is significantly enhanced if individual end-users can manipulate content for their own learning and teaching

---

6   http://virtualnorfolk.uea.ac.uk/

requirements. This approach relies on the developed of fusion services capable of bringing together relevant material, arranged according to numerous different objectives or characteristics, and crucially, as determined by the user. Technology tools must therefore allow end-users to access a variety of materials and to generate customized learning or research pathways to them. Much user behaviour revolves around popular search engines, because the interfaces provided are perceived as comfortable to use with fit-for-purpose results. Neil Beagrie comments:

> "although many wider public consumer trends may seem remote to the academic sector, they do have parallels in, and provide a broader context for, developments."
> (Beagrie, 2005)

Certainly, EDNER and similar studies suggest that simplicity at the point of contact works best. Metadata becomes the key in what should be an unconsciously managed research environment: an overload of unprocessed, uncategorized data will always be disconcerting; users have increasingly high expectations of library delivery and all but the most determined won't bother if they cannot access information seamlessly, easily and properly. Tools and services are still required that will make the collection and organization processes easy without sacrificing quality control, and which will ensure effective presentation to the user by enabling the core search-discover-locate-receive functions to take place easily, efficiently and transparently. But behind the interface there must be relevant content, of whatever kind and, as already noted, the richness of our traditional library collections as for example at the Bodleian Library need to be kept to the fore, hence the long-term validity of the hybrid library concept .

8.5 Integration

The e-Lib programme's hybrid library initiative was about integration, and seamless, end-user driven access to a wide range of previously disparate resources and services the desired outcome. Digital developments offer even broader opportunities for integration between academic library and parent institution and between learning, teaching, research and scholarly activity, not least through integrated provision. In most cases, the hybrid library will bring together content and services from a range of suppliers, both commercial and non-commercial. In the hybrid and even more so the digital library, physical location is increasingly immaterial and formats are diverse, and integration needs to be underpinned by shared and common standards, interoperability and open access, with all initiatives using the same concepts and terminologies. There is much work and experience on which to build, both nationally and internationally, but single-point access to everything is still a long way off. The CREE project (Awre, 2005) concluded that there is a need for further investigation into both internal/external integration (including the integration of Open Archives Initiative (OAI) materials) and interoperable technology use. The ability to cross-search over a wide range of different kinds of objects and resources from a whole variety of sources and the value of it also needs more research.

There remains, too, a need for work on both institutional and subject portals, redefined and refocused in the context of overall trends and a clearer agreed position within the developing Information Environment. The CREE project (Awre, 2005) examined the use of Internet search tools in portal/non-portal environments. By developing and promoting standards for a conformant portal framework, search tools can be adapted as portlets that can sit beside each other within an institutional portal. CREE is also important for its information on behaviour. A range of variables sways users, notably: context, subject, and type of resource important in developing personalizable portals.

But the fundamental issue in terms of integration is of join-up from the start. Earlier electronic and digital library developments were cumulative – incremental and single advances that did not create innovation over the whole spectrum but were, arguably, part of a "reverse product cycle". (Barras, 1986)

> "The key point to stress with regard to the reverse product cycle is the fact that the new product or service comes at the end of the cycle rather than at the beginning. The drive for improvement begins with increments and it is the cumulative effect of improvement and innovation that leads to the discontinuity of radical change through the appearance of a new dominant design." (Baker, 2004)

Prior to e-Lib phase 3 and later, integration was often an afterthought. Hybrid libraries don't work without real integrative approaches. Given that current work in one area (as for example content creation) will spread into other areas, it is of paramount importance that integration is at the heart of future library development. The emphasis should be on innovative integration from the point of view of the user rather than the service provision, with long-term market research from the start. (Baker, 2005)

8.6 Engagement and Embeddedness

There appears to be a good deal of "sign up" to the concept of the hybrid library and its implementation, but "on-the-ground" reality suggests that realizing this vision is not so straightforward. Experience from the FAIR project[7] and the conclusions of EDNER (Brophy, 2004), for example, show that the wealth of information already available in digital form is underutilized, let alone material in hard-copy format. Inevitably, institutions will need to be convinced of the worth and benefit of new developments; yet ultimately, local implementation and exploitation of library tools, assets and services will be the key to sector-wide success. There are still many cultural issues to be addressed before optimum utilization is achieved even though, as Reg Carr put it, the hybrid library projects that were at the heart of e-Lib phase 3 aimed to:

---

7   http://www.jisc.ac.uk/index.cfm?name=programme_fair

"address the ... human resource implications and issues, such as staff training and development for the enhancement of key skills [together with] ...institutional take-up of ...models as they were developed, as evidence of their long-term value. "8

Many current strategies and policies talk of "widest possible access", albeit "within publishing constraints", which could be significant. The ability to offer widespread access to material is dependent on managing access rights, further developing tools, middleware, and links back to local collections and catalogues virtual or otherwise. The strategic rhetoric is supportive of working together, but collaboration will work best only where there is both enlightened self-interest between institutions, subjects and areas and a high degree of trust in relation to security, integrity, authenticity and quality in particular. But

"it is important to bear in mind that it is not only users of electronic services and resources who are going through a process of cultural change in exploring new ways of accessing and using resources. Providers of services of interest to learning and research both commercial and publicly funded are clearly also helping to mould and shape this new environment. These stakeholders have a real and vested interest in ensuring that the information and resources they provide can be accessed through and integrated with national frameworks." (JISC, 2002)

Even within the library community, there are political and cultural issues that tend to encourage the setting up of barriers. These militate against the kinds of collaboration and co-operation that are required if end-users really are to have seamless access to what (at the provider end) are a whole series of distributed and disparate sets of resources.

"Growth in genuinely collaborative collection management would probably be the best indicator of deep resource sharing. However, we are doubtful that change can be brought about in this are if any initiative is left as voluntary, and recommend that the RSLG and the funding bodies consider the case for central action and associated incentives." (Schofield *et al.*, 2001)

8.7 Economics

We remain short of economic models that will help us to plan strategically the management of the future hybrid library . White and Davies (2001) comment that:

"The advantages of electronic access and/or the opportunities for extending access to a wider range of titles is gained at significant cost either in cash terms or as a proportional increase in spend. We all know too well that library budgets are not infinitely elastic and priorities regarding materials and other inputs have to be established. Whether such strategies are desirable, or can be afforded still remain questions to be addressed by individual institutions... The entire issue of information and document access will continue to exercise managers on a range

---

8   http://www.bodley.ox.ac.uk/librarian/malibu2001/malibu2001.htm

of issues – strategic, financial, technical, and operational. The opportunities and choices grow as do the challenges and difficulties of decision-making."

This position is reinforced by Schofield (2001):

"under current arrangements it is generally impossible for libraries to share ... resources on any other basis than by aggregating the existing spend, so there are no economies of scale to be enjoyed. There are potential savings to be had from institutions collaborating to form a bigger virtual customer, but there is also a cost in terms of staff time required to manage the process. An objective evaluation of the costs and benefits of different forms of procurement arrangement would be helpful."

Financial considerations underpin the realization of visions and strategies and will be a key determinant of direction as well as success. Funding stakeholder rhetoric[9] within HE is about strong and sustainable business. Benefits are as important as outcomes: user economics based on a philosophy of free access at point of use wherever possible require services perceived as high value for money by those who fund them. New economic models need to be developed for the hybrid library, in the context of present and future digital and related developments in order to ensure cost-effectiveness and best return on investment. Do we have a true understanding of the economics of hybrid library provision, including the cost-benefits and implications of long-term sustainability and the most economic models for subsidiarity between local, regional and national activity? Cost-effectiveness and measurable returns on investment for institutions and users are crucial. Economic models still need to be developed for the hybrid library in order to ensure cost-effectiveness and best return on investment. A key performance indicator will be the extent to which productivity in learning, teaching and research and the sector's ability to deal with the increasing pressure on resources notably through resource sharing are increased.

8.8 Summary

"The more things change, the more they can never be the same." (Veaner, 1982). The academic library world has been transformed beyond all recognition during Reg Carr's career, and he must take significant credit for being one of those who led the way. There is no turning back: indeed, the pace of change quickens, and the challenge of managing that change is arguably the key element of the hybrid library future. The hybrid approach will continue, as he has consistently argued, to be the central element in future library development for many years to come, even though the shape, nature and level of "hybridity" will change over time. There remain significant challenges to the realization of the vision described earlier in this chapter, but the work done by JISC in particular has already ensured that there is a very firm base on which to build in what

---

9   See, for example: http://www.hefce.ac.uk/; http://www.shefc.ac.uk/; http://hefcw.ac.uk/; http://www.lsc.gov.uk/; http://www.deni.gov.uk/

is now a global hybrid library environment. There may be more landmark change on the way, but it is hard to conceive of any more exciting period than that encompassing the last fifteen years and the majority of Reg Carr's working life as a senior leading professional in the field.

References and further reading

Awre, C. (2005) *The CREE Project: Evaluating Contextual Use of Internet Search Tools.* http:// www.hull.ac.uk/esig/cree/downloads/CREEASSIGNationarticle.pdf

Baker, D. (1991) From inter-library loan to document delivery. *Assignation: ASLIB Social Sciences Information Group Newsletter*, **8**, 24–6.

Baker, D. (1992a) Access versus holdings policy with special reference to the University of East Anglia. *Interlending and Document Supply*, **20**(4), 131–7.

Baker, D. (1992b) Resource allocation in university libraries. *Journal of Documentation*, **48**, 1–19.

Baker, D. (1994a) Document delivery: the UEA experience. *Computers in Libraries International 1994: Proceedings of the 8th Annual Conference.* Meckler, London.

Baker, D. (1994b) Document delivery: the UEA experience. *Vine*, **95**, 12–15.

Baker, D. (1998) The multimedia librarian in the twenty-first century: the viewpoint of a university librarian. *Librarian Career Development*, **6**(10), 3–10.

Baker, D. (1999) *The Future of Information Services at the University of East Anglia: the Final Report of the Delphi Project.* Unpublished paper.

Baker, D. (2002) Document delivery: breaking the mould. *Interlending and Document Supply*, **30**(4), 171–7.

Baker, D. (2003) Document delivery: a new paradigm? *Interlending and Document Supply*, **31**(2), 104–10.

Baker, D. (2004) *The Strategic Management of Technology: a Guide for Library and Information Services.* Chandos, Oxford.

Baker, D. (2005) Digital library futures: a UK HE and FE perspective. *Interlending and Document Supply*, **34**(1), 4–8.

Barras, R. (1986) Towards a theory of innovation in services. *Research Policy*, **15**, 161–73.

Beagrie, N. (2005) Plenty of room at the bottom? Personal digital libraries and collections. *D-Lib Magazine*, June. http://www.dlib.org/dlib/june05/06contents.html

Brophy P. *et al.* (2004) *EDNER: Final Report.* CERLIM (Centre for Research in Library and Information Management), Manchester.

Burnhill, P. and Law, D. (2005) SUNCAT rising: UK Serials Union Catalogue to assist document access. *Interlending and Document Supply*, **33**(4), 203–7.

Dearing, R. (1997) *Report of the National Committee of Enquiry into Higher Education.* The Funding Councils, London.

ESYS Consulting (2001) *Summative Evaluation of Phase 3 of the Elib Initiative: Final Report Summary.* ESYS Consulting, London.

Follett, B. (1993) *Joint Funding Councils' Libraries Review Group Report.* The Funding Councils, London.

Greenaway, J. (1997) *The Coordinated Interlibrary Loan Administration Project [CILLA]: Final Report & Recommendations of the Feasibility Study.* AVCC, Canberra.

Higher Education Consultancy Group (2006) *A Feasibility Study on the Acquisition of e-Books by HE Libraries and the Role of JISC: Final Report.* Unpublished.

Higher Education Funding Council For England (1997) *Information Technology Assisted Teaching and Learning in Higher Education.* Higher Education Funding Council for England, London.

Joint Information Systems Committee (1995) *Guidelines on the Production of an Information Strategy.* Joint Information Systems Committee, Bristol.

Joint Information Systems Committee (2001) *The Distributed National Electronic Resource.* Joint Information Systems Committee, Bristol.

Joint Information Systems Committee (2002) *Circular 1/02: Focus on Access to Institutional Resources Programme.* Joint Information Systems Committee, Bristol.

Joint Information Systems Committee (2002) *Information Environment: Development Strategy, 2001-2005.* Joint Information Systems Committee, London.

Kingston, W. (2000) Antibiotics, invention and innovation. *Research Policy,* **29**, 679-710.

Noori, H. (1990) *Managing the Dynamics of New Technology : Issues in Manufacturing Management.* Prentice Hall, New Jersey.

Schofield, A. *et al.* (2001) Barriers to resource sharing among higher education libraries: a report to the Research Support Libraries Programme (RSLP). *The New Review Of Academic Librarianship,* **7**, 101-210.

Tavistock Institute (1998) *Electronic Libraries Programme: Synthesis of 1997 Project Annual Reports.* Tavistock Institute, London.

Tavistock Institute (2000) *1999 Synthesis of e-Lib Annual Reports: Phase 2 and Phase 3.* Tavistock Institute, London.

Veaner, A. B. (1982) Continuity or discontinuity – a persistent personnel issue in academic librarianship. *Advances In Library Administration and Organization,* **1**, 1-20.

White, S. and Davies, J. E. (2001) *Economic Evaluation Model of National Electronic Site Licence Initiative (NESLI) Deals* (LISU Occasional Paper; 28). Library and Information Statistics Unit, Loughborough.

9

Beyond the Hybrid Library: Libraries in a Web 2.0 World

Derek Law

9.1 Introduction

In a recent talk, Reg Carr commented:

> "Almost 20 years ago, I published *An Introduction to University Library Administration*, with Jimmy Thompson, the Librarian of Reading University; and I was inordinately proud of that book, which for a few years at least became a standard library school text. But re-reading the book today is like drifting through the galleries of an ancient museum: it bears virtually no relationship to the book which I would write if I were writing it now. It describes, quite literally, another world that is dead and gone. The writer L. P. Hartley put it perfectly when he said that 'The past is a foreign country': they did things differently there. And the biggest change that I detect between then and now is the radical change of culture that has come about in our environment in the last ten years." (Carr, 2006)

It was the same Jimmy Thompson who had memorably, but wrongly, predicted the end of libraries in the face of computers, in his book of the same title, he concluded that:

> "The Librarians and Libraries that do not accept the change will inevitably be victims of the evolution. For the dinosaurs it will indeed be the end." (Thompson, 1982)

He also quoted Fred Lancaster:

> "We are already very close to the day in which a great science Library could exist in a space less than 10 feet square." (Lancaster, 1978).

That day has arrived. But what we may look back and see is that it was Thompson's timing rather than his premise which was wrong. Library literature over the last decade has tended to focus on how we should respond to or use technology. It has tended to focus on what users want from those technologies rather than wondering whether users have changed. Even supporters of libraries would have to conclude that neither the academy nor academic librarians have a crisp notion of where academic libraries fit in the emerging 21st century information panoply. Increasingly libraries seem to resemble "Miss Havisham", dressed in their wedding pomp and finery but living in an empty house waiting for the lover who will never come. The concept of the hybrid library has been a useful way station in developing our thinking on the future path of libraries, but it is an already dated concept which assumes evolutionary rather than revolutionary change.

Although there is growing evidence of the need for a fundamental rethink of the role and place of libraries, most of such debate takes place on the electronic lists, journals and blogs which all too few librarians read. (Peters, 2006) Traditionalists reach for the comfort blanket of the library as place and for the precedents of history. The library as place has been invested with a virtuous glow which paints it as the last remaining substantial social space in universities; as the last remaining public place of trust in society, in the case of public libraries a place where young children can be left in the care of story-telling strangers while parents shop. The fireside myths of library history tell of a resolute four thousand year journey through change: from the oral tradition through the great library of Ashurbanipal with its tablets of stone to papyri then the monastic scriptoria. Then we moved on to Gutenberg and the printed word and further development into sound and film collections. The profession comforts itself that throughout these four thousand years we have often been buffeted by the great waves of change, but never yet capsized. Librarians are adept at finding comforting statistics showing that the slumbering power of libraries remains real. A recent report from OCLC (OCLC, 2003) recorded that:

- there are five times as many library cards as Amazon users
- there are more libraries than McDonald's outlets in the USA
- one person in six in the world is a registered library user
- there are over one million libraries and over 700,000 librarians worldwide.

However true those figures are, they do not matter if they represent the past and ignore the fact that there has been a fundamental shift in both users and the content they seek.

9.2 The New Users

The worry for librarians in the Web 2.0 world should be not that technology is changing rapidly, but that a generational change is affecting users in quite fundamental ways.

> "It is now clear that as a result of this ubiquitous environment and the sheer volume of their interaction with it, today's students think and process information fundamentally differently from their predecessors." (Prensky, 2001)

Prensky developed the concept of digital natives to describe individuals who have grown up in an entirely internet world.

It is worth considering their characteristics and assumptions. The Beloit Mindset List (Beloit College, 2006) sets out to define this group in soundbites and notes some of the attributes of new college students:

- "Ctrl + Alt + Del" is as basic as "ABC."
- They have never been able to find the "return" key.
- Computers have always fit in their backpacks.
- Stores have always had scanners at the checkout.
- They have always had a PIN number.
- Convenience trumps quality.
- They don't remember when "cut and paste" involved scissors.

It is easy to forget that today's twenty-one year olds spring entirely from a digital world. John Naughton pithily described this in the *Observer* (Naughton, 2006). For today's twenty-one year olds born in 1985 the Internet was two years old which was the same year as Nintendo launched "Super Mario Brothers", the first blockbuster game. As they went to school, Tim Berners-Lee was busy inventing the World Wide Web, which emerged as a phenomenon as they moved into secondary school. The Palm Pilot was launched at the same time. Also at that time, pay-as-you-go mobile phone tariffs arrived, enabling teenagers to have phones. Napster and Blogger.com were launched in 1999, just when they were doing GCSEs. The iPod and the early social networking services appeared in 2002, when they were doing A-levels. Skype launched in 2003, just as they were heading for university, and YouTube launched in 2005, as they were heading towards graduation.

And what do these digital natives expect?

- Choices
- Selectivity
- Personalization
- Instant gratification
- Cheap, fast, and good
- Mobile anytime anywhere technology.

As a consequence, 73% of college students reported using the Internet more than the library. (Hong, 2006)

Holliday and Lee (2004) undertook studies which confirmed this and discovered the following about the digital natives:

- They expect research to be easy and feel they can be independent in the process.
- They do not seek help from librarians and only occasionally from professors or peers.
- When they can't find what they need, they give up and assume that the information cannot be found.
- Students often stop after their initial searches thinking they have completed the research process and fail to choose a particular focus.

- Access to full text articles seems to have changed students' cognitive behavior. Instead of having to read through material at the library, they can now download material at their desks. They do not have to take notes or read through them to develop themes and ideas, an activity central to a focused research project.
- Electronic articles enable cutting and pasting, possibly leading to increased plagiarism.

And so we have a growing group of users for whom the library is at best a secondary resource and where library usage statistics are maintained and bolstered by the provision of network connectivity rather than book collection quality.

9.3 Content

The nature of content has also progressively changed while libraries have not. The nineteenth and much of the twentieth century can be defined in terms of words, whether spoken or written. Short phrases can encapsulate major events. No explanation is required for "Let them eat cake", "the thin red line", "Custer's last stand", "Dr Livingstone I presume", "Never in the field of human conflict has so much been owed by so many to so few" or even the formula "$e = mc^2$". Conversely the last fifty or so years can be defined almost entirely in images: film of the burning airship Hindenburg; the Dunkirk beaches; the mushroom cloud of an atomic bomb, the assassination of JFK; Neil Armstrong stepping on the moon; the beauty of fractal images; the obscenity of the aircraft crashing into the Twin Towers. Digital natives expect image content, hence the huge success of Youtube and Flickr. This shift in medium has largely passed libraries by although the JISC has made noble attempts to address the issue in the face of a supine constituency.

Frighteningly but perhaps aptly, Prensky describes this:

> "It seems to me that after the digital 'singularity' there are now *two kinds* of content: 'Legacy' content (to borrow the computer term for old systems) and 'Future' content 'Legacy' content includes reading, writing, arithmetic, logical thinking, understanding the writings and ideas of the past, etc. all of our 'traditional' curriculum. It is of course still important, but it is from a different era. Some of it (such as logical thinking) will continue to be important, but some (perhaps like Euclidean geometry) will become less so, as did Latin and Greek. 'Future' content is to a large extent, not surprisingly, digital and technological. But while it includes software, hardware, robotics, nanotechnology, genomics, etc. *it also includes the ethics, politics, sociology, languages and other things that go with them.*" (Prensky, 2001)

Digital content is also changing from the concept of "authoritative" as embodied in the printed word, to user created and often image based. 57% of online teenagers create content for the internet on social spaces such as Myspace, Youtube and Flickr. 62% of content viewed by online users under the age of 21 is generated by someone they know (Hong, 2006). And user created need not mean poorer. The user created films of the Indian Ocean tsunami or the bombing of the London Underground are every bit as valuable as historic documents as any written record of previous events. But community based written content can also have validity. Wikipedia (Wikipedia, 2006) is a free encyclopaedia and a wonderful community based resource. Jordanhill Railway Station in Glasgow has the distinction of becoming the one millionth entry on Wikipedia. The entry was begun on 1st March 2006 with a single sentence. Within 24 hours it had been edited 400 times and expanded to become an entry that prints out as five pages. There is no such entry in *Encyclopaedia Britannica,* which is barely 10% of the size at 120,000 entries. Wikipedia is currently the 17th most popular site on the Internet at 14,000 hits a second. And much more up to date than *Britannica.* The first entry on the 2006 Israeli-Lebanon conflict appeared on the wiki within six hours of the capture of the two Israeli soldiers by Hezbollah. The argument rages as to accuracy and whether a thousand amateur administrators can provide adequate quality control or as Jorge Cauz, president of the *Encyclopaedia Britannica* recently put it, "Wikipaedia is to the Encyclopaedia Britannica as American Idol is to the Julliard [*sic*] School" (McGinty, 2006). This comment seems to miss the point entirely.

The prevalence of "good enough" information is shaking up the commercial content industry in ways that remain unresolved. However what we can see is the emergence of large aggregators of data meeting current user need as compared to libraries aggregating data against historic assumptions.

9.4 The Research Process

Taking these elements together leads inexorably to a change in the research process itself. It is a commonplace that the Internet has internationalized research. Papers now appear with literally hundreds of joint authors, while research data, debate and papers are shared across the Internet in real time. The growth of digital natives and user developed content then combine to create a concept which can best be defined as aliteracy. It should not be confused with illiteracy or even dumbing down, but reflects the growth of a constituency which can function perfectly effectively without reading, or books or libraries. Clever and well informed people no longer find libraries essential and there is growing evidence of two parallel worlds on-web and off-web. It is at least conceptually possible to acquire a PhD without reading anything, at least in science and technology. The student engages in tearoom discussion where most information transfer has always taken place formulates a hypothesis, writes software, runs computer controlled experimental equipment and uses more software to analyse the results. The literature review which is always an element of the doctorate requires cut and paste skills, not reading skills. Even that will not require library access for long. The Google Library project plans to digitize some thirty-six million volumes over the next few years, (Milne, 2006). Who will then need even a large university library? The aliterate hive mind ignores the off-web in favour of the big gravitational hubs of the Internet and these are increasingly the places where other people build systems and services on top of the hubs.

The underlying issue for libraries is not an overload of information but a shortage of attention for the abundance of information. This is as true of research as teaching, where we increasingly want to gather create and share. We are only just beginning to understand how data flows through the research process from research bids and bid management to human resource management and research outcomes. Instead of the historic position where users adapted their workflow to the library, visiting us at fixed times, now we have to adapt to their workflow.

9.5 Social Systems as Competitors to Libraries

So if we are not to be left high and dry we need to develop a Libraries 2.0 to match Web 2.0 and that in turn will be dependent on our ability to focus on and determine the needs of the new user and not the technologies which they have currently adopted. These Web 2.0 spaces form big hubs where users congregate and on which services can be built.

The big upsurge in social networking services is based on blogs, wikis, Instant messaging and other tools which are creating new spaces where services are being built, spaces which are quite foreign to libraries. YouTube acquired twenty million users a month in eighteen months and they watch one hundred million video clips a day. YouTube has now been taken over by Google in a perfect example of aggregation. MySpace has one hundred million users and the number is growing by 240,000 a day, while Google receives one billion requests a day. (Naughton, 2006).

Unlike social-networking sites such as LinkedIn and Friendster, which concentrate on developing relationships, social sites such as del.icio.us, 43Things and Flickr focus their attention on organizing data. Users organize their own or other's data in the public sphere and the social, or community, aspects arise from there as users share and seek out like-minded individuals. And if even classification is under threat, what is left?

These services are described on their own websites in simple jargon free attractive ways. For example,

> "del.icio.us is a social bookmarking website the primary use of del.icio.us is to store your bookmarks online, which allows you to access the same bookmarks from any computer and add bookmarks from anywhere, too. On del.icio.us, you can use tags to organize and remember your bookmarks, which is a much more flexible system than folders. You can also use del.icio.us to see the interesting links that your friends and other people bookmark, and share links with them in return. You can even browse and search del.icio.us to discover the cool and useful bookmarks that everyone else has saved which is made easy with tags."

> "Yahoo Answers launched on December 8th 2005. The service allows any Yahoo user to ask any question and get answers and advice from other Yahoo users. The

community picks the "best" answer, and everything is archived for search." Within five months a user posted the ten millionth answer.

"The Semantic Web is about two things. It is about common formats for interchange of data, where on the original Web we only had interchange of documents. Also it is about language for recording how the data relates to real world objects. That allows a person, or a machine, to start off in one database, and then move through an unending set of databases which are connected not by wires but by being about the same thing."

"Wikipedia describes how folksonomies develop in Internet-mediated social environments, users can discover (generally) who created a given folksonomy tag, and see the other tags that this person created. In this way, folksonomy users often discover the tag sets of another user who tends to interpret and tag content in a way that makes sense to them. The result, often, is an immediate and rewarding gain in the user's capacity to find related content. Part of the appeal of folksonomy is its inherent subversiveness: faced with the dreadful performance of the search tools that Web sites typically provide, folksonomies can be seen as a rejection of the search engine status quo in favor of tools that are both created by the community and beneficial to the community." (Google, 2006)

And as to place, most Starbuck's cafés provide superior wireless internet access to most libraries.

It is then easy to tabulate where digital natives go to meet their information needs instead of the library:

Traditional library activity	Web 2.0 world
Cataloguing	Automated metadata, del.icio.us
Classification	Folksonomies and the semantic web
Acquisitions	eBay, PayPal, Amazon and Abebooks
Reference	Yahoo Answers and Wikipedia
Preservation	Digital Archives and repositories
User Instruction	Chatrooms
Working space	Bedroom and Starbucks with a laptop
Collections	YouTube, Flickr, Institutional Repositories, Open Access
Professional judgement	The wisdom of crowds

9.6 Future Library Services

But libraries are great survivors and there are areas where the profession can claim to have relevant skills. Ironically these are best seen as developments and rebranding of traditional skills.

If it is possible to redefine the library in such terms, there are three key areas which will be the core of such a library service:

Traditional library	Web 2.0 world	Library 2.0 world
Cataloguing	Automated metadata, del.icio.us	Metadata
Classification	Folksonomies and the semantic web	Locally provided and relevant folksonomy
Acquisitions	eBay, PayPal, Amazon and Abebooks	E-archives, e-data and quality assurance
Reference	Yahoo Answers and Wikipedia	Branded links to trusted resources
Preservation	Digital archives and repositories	Institutional repository
User instruction	Chatrooms	Moderate chatroom
Working space	Bedroom and Starbucks with a laptop	Wired campus and 24-hour workspace
Collections	YouTube, Flickr, institutional repositories, open access	Aggregation of unique content with other libraries
Professional judgement	The wisdom of crowds	Teaching retrieval skills

The first lies in content acquisition. One way of looking at this comes through the so-called long tail proposed by Chris Anderson (2006) as a way of describing the niche markets and small businesses developing around the big hubs such as Google, Yahoo and Amazon. But if new as a concept it is not new as a practice.

> "Libraries were into long tails before long tails were cool. Any library stocking more than a few thousand titles (i.e. the vast majority of libraries) knows all about the long tail. In fact, most large libraries have collections that extend far beyond the utmost limits of the longest tail. In other words, many items in their collections have not been used since added. Perhaps some libraries, in an effort to boost circulation statistics, have focused too much on the 'heady' end of their collections. Rather than cater to the clamorers for [Dean] Koontz, perhaps libraries should cultivate more long-tail usage. If the long-tail phenomenon is here to stay, perhaps the 80/20 rule (that 20 percent of the collection accounts for 80 percent of the use) will become increasingly suspect." (Peters, 2006)

It is very easy to describe library services and systems in terms of this long tail economy. We have developed systems for resource sharing, supported by shared and standardized cataloguing, messaging and delivery services and reciprocal access. It is accustomed to depending on others for services through a commonly created infrastructure. It is broadly possible to identify and borrow a copy of any book, in any language, from any country published in the last fifty years. However more recent library activity has tended to disregard this notion of building shared systems, so that in the UK there is no truly national union catalogue and a quite fragmented resource sharing infrastructure. We have forgotten the lessons of the past and need to rediscover the importance of aggregation. But the first building block will be an understanding of how we create, build and collect electronic collections locally.

When tens of millions of books are directly available through Google, what will libraries have to offer? It has arguably been the case that library collections were built for the future user not the current user, certainly in the humanities and historically based disciplines. It was also the case that and probably still is the case that research libraries collect more non-commercial items than commercial items. Archives, ephemera, local publications, government publications and so on are all acquired. It is a major failure of the present generation of librarians not to have engaged with collection policy for born digital material. There is no real debate on what should be collected and by whom and as a result valuable material is already being lost. Not just electronic mail, but increasingly the wikis, blogs, text messages, video clips and photographs never mind the research data, electronic maps and electronically plotted chemical structures which will form the historical documents of the future are simply ignored. Our successors will rightly blame us for this. An easy answer is that Libraries 2.0 should collect the born digital material which will give us brand differentiation. The same is true of all the intellectual output of our universities. The Institutional repository is an activity and space which librarians are ideally equipped to manage. We can see some elements of this future – although not yet with born digital material in such deep archives as the immensely rich Valley of the Shadow pulling together resources from a range of media, on the American Civil War. As was always the case, in the text-based age it will be our special collections and archives of electronic materials which will give libraries both purpose and brand differentiation. To follow the argument to its conclusion we should then accept Dempsey's (2006) premise that it is the aggregation of these resources that will turn libraries into a major gravitational hub where any salvation must lie.

Having created the content, its preservation is another obvious activity. Research libraries have the great advantage of not being commercial activities. They have the luxury of storing material which may not be needed for decades. Commercial companies are, of course, driven by the need to make a profit. The technical issues around digital preservation remain uncertain but the lack of understanding and preparedness is all to clear. It revealed that fewer than 20% of UK organizations surveyed have a strategy in place to deal with the risk of either loss or degradation to their digital resources. This was despite a very high level of awareness of the risks and potential economic penalties. The survey further revealed that the loss of digital data is a commonplace and indeed is seen as a routine hazard by some with over 70% of respondents saying data had been lost in their organization. Awareness of the consequential risks is high, with 87% recognizing that corporate memory or key cultural material could be lost and some 60% saying that their organization could lose out financially. In 52% of the organizations surveyed there was management commitment to digital preservation but only 18% had a strategy in place.

The third area of need is in user instruction in information management skills. We can lament the fact that a Boolean gene to improve searching does not exist, or we can get to grips with search engines. There is little value in bemoaning the inadequacy of either users or the search engines they use. Libraries need to work with the grain of Google and help users understand how to maximize its effectiveness. Simply exposing users to Google Scholar as an alternative to Google would make a difference. At least some librarians are beginning to recognize the need to explore how they can take advantage of Google to assist users (Cathcart, 2006).

9.7 Beyond the Hybrid Library

Twenty years or so on, Carr has joined Thompson in the ranks of those who worry about the end of libraries.

> "The ultimate warning note, however, is contained in a recent North American article which picks up many of the issues addressed here and which identifies many of the 'disconnects' between the services our academic libraries currently provide and the wants of the so-called 'Net Generation' now coming into early adulthood: 'Finding the right way to achieve balance between traditional values and the expectations and habits of the wired generations will determine whether libraries remain relevant in the social, educational and personal contexts of the Information Age' (Thomas & McDonald, 2006). In the final analysis, it is possible that 'What users want' may always remain something of a mirage (or at least a moving target). But one thing is certain: failure to take it properly into account would be sure to leave the academic library high and dry in the desert of lost opportunities." (Carr, 2006a)

But if we look at the key skills of librarians and information professionals, they remain as vital as ever. Selection, storage and (user) support remain the basic attributes of a library in the Web 2.0 environment. And Ranganathan's requirement for the right information to the right user at the right time remains pithily apt. In an environment with too much information, saving the time of the reader is what will ensure our continuing relevance.

But the library has no right to any of these three areas. The question is not so much what follows the hybrid library as whether, standing on the edge of the abyss, we have the self-confidence to make a great leap forward into (web) space.

References

Anderson, C. (2006) *The Long Tail: How Endless Choice Is Creating Unlimited Demand.* Random House, London.

Beloit College (2006) *Mindset Lists.* http://www.beloit.edu/~pubaff/mindset/. Viewed on 5 November 2006.

Carr, R. (2006) The role of the JISC in changing the research library and information culture in the United Kingdom. *JISC/CNI Conference,* York.

Carr, R. (2006a) What users want: an academic 'hybrid' library perspective. *Ariadne,* 46. Originating URL: http://www.ariadne.ac.uk/issue46/carr/intro.html

Cathcart, R. and Roberts, A. (2006) Evaluating Google Scholar as a tool for information literacy. In: *Libraries and Google* (ed. W. Miller). Haworth Press, Binghamton, NY.

DPC (2006) *Mind the Gap: Assessing Digital Preservation Needs in the UK.* Digital Preservation Coalition.

Google (2006) These quotations all come from a Google search conducted on 5 November 2006 using the site names. They are then simply cut and pasted to illustrate the point being made.

Holliday, W. and Qin, L. (2004) Understanding the millennials: updating our knowledge about students. *Reference Services Review,* **32**(4), 346–66.

Hong, M. (2006) *Content in the Emerging World of Digital Natives.* http://www.stuntdubl.com/2006/09/25/matt-hong/. Viewed on 5 November 2006.

Lancaster, F. W. (1978) *Towards Paperless Information Systems.* Academic Press, New York.

McGinty, S. (2006) Online Amateurs beginning to put 'Britannica' under pressure. *The Scotsman*, 1 August, p. 27.

Milne, R. (2006) The Google Library Project at Oxford. In *Libraries and Google* (ed. W. Miller). Haworth Press, Binghamton, NY.

Naughton, J. (2006) It's the 'digital natives' versus the 'immigrants' as kids go to work. *The Observer*, 1 October.

OCLC (2003) *Libraries: How they Stack Up*. OCLC, Dublin.

Peters, T. (2006) The long tail wags the dog. *ALA Techsource*, 7 July. http://www.techsource. ala.org/blog/2006/07/the-long-tail-wags-the-dog.html is an excellent example of such a blog.

Prensky, M. (2001) Digital natives, digital immigrants. *On the Horizon*, 9(5), October.

Thomas, C. F. and McDonald, R. H. (2006) *Millennial Net Value(s): Disconnects between Libraries and the Information Mindset*. http://dscholarship.lib.fsu.edu/general/4. Viewed on 5 November.

Thompson, J. (1982) *The End of Libraries*. Bingley, London.

Thompson, J. and Carr, R. (1987) *An Introduction to University Library Administration*, 4th edn. Bingley, London.

Wikipedia: http://www.wikipedia.org/

10

Libraries and Open Access: the Implications of Open-Access Publishing and Dissemination for Libraries in Higher Education Institutions

Stephen Pinfield

10.1 Introduction

This chapter discusses the consequences of open-access (OA) publishing and dissemination for libraries in higher education institutions (HEIs). To date, this topic has not received much coverage in the professional literature, despite the fact that a number of librarians have been leading advocates of OA. One explanation of this might be that librarians have been so focused on OA as a perceived answer to the "serials crisis" that they have not looked beyond that at the long-term implications of OA for libraries. Another possible explanation is that librarians have habitually taken a wider view of information issues (wider that is than just that of the library as an organization) and have therefore concentrated on the benefits of OA for the research community in general rather than on the consequences for libraries in particular. Whatever the explanation (there is probably some truth in both of the above for the library profession as a whole), it is certainly the case that a number of issues associated with the relationship between OA and libraries require further consideration. Key questions (which are addressed in this chapter) include:

- How might OA help information provision?
- What changes to library services will arise from OA developments (particularly if OA becomes widespread)?

- How do these changes fit in with wider changes affecting the future role of libraries?
- How can libraries and librarians help to address key practical issues associated with the implementation of OA (particularly transition issues)?

By addressing these issues, it is hoped that this paper and other similar studies will give rise to more discussion of this strategically significant area for libraries.

This chapter will look at OA from the perspective of HE libraries and will make four key points:

1. Open access has the potential to bring benefits to the research community in particular and society in general by improving information provision.
2. If there is widespread open access to research content, there will be less need for library-based activity at the institution level, and more need for information management activity at the supra-institutional or national level.
3. Institutional libraries will, however, continue to have an important role to play in areas such as managing purchased or licensed content, curating institutional digital assets, and providing support in the use of content for teaching and research.
4. Libraries are well-placed to work with stakeholders within their institutions and beyond to help resolve current challenges associated with the implementation of OA policies and practices.

Each of these points will be discussed in turn, but first some remarks on the phenomenon of open access itself.

10.2 "Open Access"

"Open access" is normally defined as a situation where content is made available freely, immediately and without restriction. The content may then be used and re-used without restrictive copyright and permission barriers. A classic definition of open access is contained in the Budapest Open Access Initiative (2002) statement:

> "The literature that should be freely accessible online is that which scholars give to the world without expectation of payment. Primarily, this category encompasses their peer-reviewed journal articles, but it also includes any unreviewed preprints that they might wish to put online for comment or to alert colleagues to important research findings. There are many degrees and kinds of wider and easier access to this literature. By "open access" to this literature, we mean its free availability on the public internet, permitting any users to read, download, copy, distribute, print, search, or link to the full texts of these articles, crawl them for indexing, pass them as data to software, or use them for any other lawful purpose, without financial, legal, or technical barriers other than those inseparable from gaining access to the internet itself."

This definition covers what Peter Suber (2004) identifies as the two main components of OA: firstly, overcoming "price barriers" and secondly, overcoming "permission barriers". The removal of the price barriers allows the content to be freely accessed in full by all comers. The removal of permission barriers allows the material to be re-used "for all legitimate scholarly purposes".

In practical terms, OA is normally thought to be achievable via two routes: OA journals and OA repositories. OA journals are normally very much like traditional subscription journals in terms of content and presentation. They often contain peer-reviewed, edited articles that are presented in periodical parts. However, they are usually funded in different ways, typically either by sponsorship or by publication charges. A publication charge is normally paid before publication by the author (or more accurately via the author by their institution or funder), and the article is then made available on OA. One recent variant of this business model (the so-called "hybrid" model) allows authors to pay an OA fee to a publisher who will then make a particular paper in a subscription journal available on OA.

OA repositories on the other hand do not require a new business model, although some have suggested that as more content is made available in them new ways of paying for the production of the content will emerge. Repositories can be set up by subject communities, institutions, or other stakeholders, to collect material which (in the case of research outputs) is usually formally published elsewhere. A repository will contain electronic copies of journal articles (so-called "eprints"), either in a form before they have been refereed ("preprints") or after ("postprints"). Repositories can also house other content including data, conference proceedings, and learning objects. Repositories are usually set up using international standards which mean they can interoperate; effectively creating a global network of interlinked repositories.

10.3 Benefits of OA

The benefits of OA have been described in detail elsewhere (for example, Jacobs, 2006). Comments will be confined here to some key points closely associated with library work: dissemination, impact, use, and economics.

Firstly, dissemination. A key point here is that OA deepens "narrowcasting" and widens "broadcasting". It is often observed that the primary aim of researchers when they publish their results is "narrowcasting": to communicate their findings to a small specialized group of fellow researchers working in the same subject area (see Rowlands, Nicholas and Huntingdon, 2004, 1). These researchers are in a position to read, build on, and cite publications within the field. Bearing in mind the narrowcasting imperative, some have questioned whether OA is necessary. The implication is that research output only has to reach a narrow audience and that it usually does so. However, as librarians know, it is not the case that researchers have access to all of the literature in their field they require. Perhaps the most common request from researchers to their institutional library is for more journal subscriptions. The fact that publishers are continually marketing old and new journals to academics and librarians demonstrates that publishers themselves do not believe that researchers have access to all the content they need. Even narrowcasting then is not working in the current system. OA has the potential to improve the penetration of narrowcasting.

It will also widen broadcasting. OA will widen the dissemination of research output both within and outside the research community. Within the research community, OA material is more likely to reach scholars across different disciplinary boundaries (where the library may not previously have been able to justify a subscription). Outside the research community, OA content is more likely to reach audiences in the health and social care sector (to inform clinical practice), and the commercial sector (to improve knowledge transfer) and beyond. These two specific examples (healthcare and private industry) are ones of where widening the audience of research publications could bring significant benefits.

This leads to a second key issue to be discussed here: impact. Researchers write for impact. Impact is normally measured in terms of citations. Studies demonstrate that across various disciplines work made available on OA is cited more than work made available through other means (see Lawrence, 2001; Antelman, 2004; Harnad and Brody, 2004). Such empirical evidence can be used to demonstrate to researchers that it is in their interests to disseminate their work via OA routes. Since their status and esteem within their subject community relate closely to the impact they make, it is important for academics to maximize the impact made by their work.

However, the idea of "impact" should perhaps also be seen in wider terms. From a public policy point of view, governments fund research in order to make an impact (in the broadest sense of the term) on the economy and society. One key element of this is knowledge transfer from research institutions to industry. Making the research literature available more easily to the commercial sector has enormous potential to improve knowledge transfer. Measuring this, however, is difficult far more difficult than measuring citations. Nevertheless this should not stop people trying to get at evidence in this area. Houghton, Steele and Sheehan (2006) have provided some impressive early data demonstrating the economic value of increasing access to research outputs.

Evidence of this sort may help to counter the idea of the so-called "free-rider problem". This is the idea that making research output available on OA leads to a loss of income for publishers (and therefore the economy as a whole) from commercial consumers of the information, such as pharmaceutical or biotechnology companies. Such a loss would indeed represent a shift in the way publishing was funded as a consequence of OA. However, when it is understood that one of the key reasons the government sponsors research in the first place is to enable knowledge transfer and to promote innovation, then the "free-rider problem" comes to look increasingly like the "knowledge-transfer success". This potential success remains to be analysed and quantified. More work is required in this area.

The third key benefit of OA moves beyond issues of dissemination (narrow or broad casting) and impact (narrowly or broadly defined) to the issue of use.

Open access is not just about access but also about use. Gaining access is a necessary prerequisite to doing useful things with the content. For example, OA facilitates more effective search and retrieval of content, using technologies associated with the Open Archives Initiative (OAI). It also facilitates more sophisticated processing and analysis of content. This may often involve non-human processing, what Clifford Lynch (2006) has called "open computation". The content may be analysed or mined in various ways described by Lynch so that existing research may be accelerated and new avenues for research created. Access barriers associated with the traditional publishing system make such activities difficult if not impossible. Once again, more work is needed in this area but the potential benefits of these activities are clear.

A final point on the benefits of OA relates to the potential it has to correct a dysfunctional market. The recent independent studies of the journal publishing market have concluded that it is not working optimally because of structural problems. This was the conclusion of the UK House of Commons Science and Technology Committee in 2004 (House of Commons, 2004), and the European Commission sponsored study in 2006 (European Commission, 2006). The problems are based on the nature of the product itself the journal. The fact that journals are collections of unique content means that each journal title is its own "mini monopoly": the content cannot be easily substituted with an alternative title (Houghton, 2005, 170–171). Once a journal has established itself in its subject area, it increasingly becomes a "must have" title, making demand for it relatively price inelastic. In other words, if the price is raised, people will still buy it. The fact that the consumers of the content (researchers) are not normally the purchasers helps to exacerbate the problem, since price signals do not operate as they would in most markets. Journal publishers have been able regularly to impose price rises way above inflation because of these features of the market, creating a situation where prices paid by customers are considerably above costs of production.

With potentially high profit margins available, the market has concentrated to become dominated by five or six major commercial companies. Furthermore, it is clear that the journal market is very unusual in that suppliers of established products can in fact increase their market share by *raising* their prices. In most markets a supplier increases market share by lowering the price, by improving the product or by increasing their marketing. However, in the academic journals market publishers can increase their market share by raising their prices because of the situation of their primary customers (libraries). Libraries work with relatively fixed budgets, increases over retail price inflation are unusual. If the journal publisher raises the price of a "must have" journal, librarians have to cancel other titles in order to continue to a subscription to the "must have" title. The publisher thereby increases market share.

These features of the market are magnified by the "Big Deal" electronic packages of journal titles. Most Big Deals are purchased as a whole with little flexibility to select or cancel individual titles. The attraction of the Big Deal for subscribers is that it gives them immediate access to more content. Publishers are able to provide more content in a context where marginal costs (costs over and above the fixed costs associated with producing the first copy of the content) are very low. In fact it is in their interests to offer as much content in their package as possible to make it more attractive to buy and less easy to cancel. In this way it is very easy for some of the large Big Deals to become "must have" *packages* and for subscribers to find themselves locked in. If the package price goes up by more than inflation, librarians are now beginning to find themselves in a position where they may have to cancel other packages or groups of titles to afford them. Such trends only serve to increase concentration in the market further.

OA has the potential to address some of these systemic problems in the journals market by creating more competition. This would have a major impact on libraries which have in recent years had to devote considerable resources to managing the complexities associated with journal pricing models, licensing terms and delivery mechanisms.

Benefits in the areas of dissemination, impact, use and economics have meant that library managers have tended to support OA, at least in principle. Of course, the level of enthusiasm varies but librarians have often been amongst leading advocates of OA within their institutions and beyond.

10.4 The Range of OA Material

Most of the debate about OA in the academic community has until now concentrated on a particular type (albeit a very important type) of content: journal articles. That is clear from the Budapest Open Access Initiative definition of OA above. However, in order to think about the consequences of OA for library services, it is important to include the whole range of OA material that is currently emerging. There are at least five major categories of such material:

1. Current research output: typically in the form of journal articles, book chapters and other similar quality-controlled material.
2. Grey literature: ranging from conference proceedings to reports.
3. Data: some of which may have previously been published or purchased by libraries, such as census data and other publications by government or nongovernmental organizations. Other data sets may previously have been publicly unavailable but can now be disseminated on the internet, such as large experimental data sets, some of which may be compiled collaboratively.
4. Out-of-copyright monographs: many of which are currently being retrospectively digitized as part of mass digitization projects run by organizations such as Google and Microsoft.
5. Institutional digital assets: including materials such as electronic theses, and learning objects.

Many of the materials in the above categories represent high-quality information resources which have traditionally been purchased or licensed and then managed by libraries. Libraries have also traditionally managed other information materials such as metadata resources, including bibliographic databases. It is becoming increasingly common for some of these to become available on OA as well.

The question is what would be the implications for libraries if much of this material becomes available on OA?

10.5 The Impact of OA on Libraries

Perhaps a useful way of considering the impact of OA on libraries is first to consider the role that libraries currently perform in making content available. First, in the paper-based environment, libraries in institutions carry out following processes:

- Selection of materials (title-by-title, normally including assessment of quality/authenticity, and liaison with academic staff)
- Procurement of materials (usually involving payment, budget management, etc)
- Cataloguing and classification to enable retrieval (metadata being made available to users via a public catalogue)
- Provision of additional indexes for article-level access (often themselves selected and purchased)
- Physical preparation of materials (checking, labelling, tagging, binding etc.)
- Access arrangements (including shelving of the physical item, organization of physical space and guiding users around it)
- Circulation arrangements (including lending policies, self-service facilities etc.)
- Ongoing collection management (may include relegation to stack/store)
- Support and training of users (enquiries, guides, training etc.).

For paper-based content, these functions have to be performed at an institutional level since each institution is assembling its own physical collection. Individual libraries may achieve efficiencies in parts of the workflows by, for example, buying in externally-produced catalogue records, or outsourcing the procurement or physical preparation materials. Whether carried out in-house or externally, it is the library that is responsible for providing this service for its institutional users. It is assembling a local collection of resources for them the precise nature of which will be unique to that institution.

Many of the processes carried out in a print environment have an equivalent in an electronic one where the information materials are purchased or licensed. The physical preparation and management of materials are no longer necessary, nor is the provision of circulation services. However, content still has to be selected and acquired. Often there are new processes involved, such as product trials, and new complexities, such as dealing with package pricing models. Metadata describing the resources still has to be produced or purchased and then managed. The library catalogue remains important (usually providing access to electronic as well as hardcopy resources) alongside a number of other online indexes. Access arrangements for the electronic content need to be put in place, with the library setting up organized digital spaces to mirror the physical spaces they already provide. These online portals often simplify the experience for the user by providing a single sign-on authentication process or meta-searching across various resources. All of this needs to be underpinned by user support and training. In addition, there is at least one new process involved in electronic acquisition which does not apply to print media. This is the selection of different user interface and access arrangements. In some cases the same content can be available via different routes and with different user interfaces, and these need to be assessed and selected.

As far infrastructure is concerned, the library in an online environment is now relying on institutional IT services to support its work in delivering electronic resources (as well, of course, on the services of external providers). In some institutions, library services are in fact now delivered by the same organization as IT services because of the considerable overlap in their roles.

What both these sets of processes (managing purchased print resources and managing purchased or licensed electronic resources) have in common is that they are selecting, aggregating and making available resources which are then available in a unique combination to a particular group of users. In any institution the combination of resources available to its own users will be different from those in other institutions. They will also often be accessed differently and may involve a different user experience.

Which of these processes then will need to be carried out by institutional libraries for OA material? In simple terms, very few (see Table 10.1). Particularly if OA was to become widespread, many of the functions carried out institution-by-institution in the current environment would no longer need to be duplicated in every institution for OA content. Neither the content itself nor the interface through which it is delivered would need to be selected. There would no longer be a need to acquire the content or to catalogue or classify it for a single set of institutional users. Many collection management functions would no longer be required. Local support and training would still be required but many services associated with pointing users to content would be better carried out at a higher (supra-institutional or national) level. Institutions would certainly be able to find efficiencies in these areas by eliminating unnecessary duplication if OA were to become widespread.

Of course, where there is a mixed economy of purchased, licensed and OA content it will be necessary for libraries in institutions to continue to guide their own users to all of this material via gateways such as library catalogues or institutional portal (indicated by "?" in Table 10.1). However, if OA were to become more widespread carrying out such work at an institutional level will become less necessary. Users would certainly begin to prefer global search services to locate information, as is increasingly the case even now. Libraries will more than ever need to ensure that data from their catalogues and other local search services are surfaced in the global search engines in order to ensure local content remains visible.

Table 10.1 Libraries and content services in HEIs.

	Printed material	Electronic content (purchased)	OA material
Selection of content	✓	✓	✗
Interface/access selection	✗	✓	✗
Procurement	✓	✓	✗
Cataloguing and classification/metadata	✓	✓	?
Provision of indexes	✓	✓	✗
Physical preparation	✓	✗	✗
Access arrangements	✓	✓	✗
Circulation services	✓	✗	✗
Collection management	✓	✗	✗
User support and training	✓	✓	✓

10.6 New Roles

In an environment where OA were to become widespread new roles for information professionals would, however, be created. A significant number of these would be at what Lorcan Dempsey (2006) has called the "network level" OA is one of a number of trends that seems to be pushing a good deal of significant activity to this level. Subject communities, consortia of institutions, funders, or national agencies could usefully deliver a range of services to enhance access to content. New repositories might develop at the network level, PubMed Central and UK PubMed Central are early examples of such services. However, it would be particularly useful if other services could develop at this level provided by (within the language of OAI) "Service Providers" as opposed to "Data Providers". Service Providers can provide access to a range of resources by harvesting metadata and/or content from repositories and other Data Providers and then delivering (at least some of) the following:

- metadata normalization and enhancement
- automatic indexing and classification
- structured searching
- subject-specific gateways
- format-specific gateways (for example for theses)
- text/data mining and analysis of content
- citation analysis
- qualitative assessment of content
- proactive direction to content ("if you are interested in that, you may be interested in this").

Such services would complement those of standard web search engines by providing more sophisticated search and processing functionality.

All of these types of services are in fact required now. There are still too few Service Providers, for example, delivering even simple structured search services of OAI-compliant repositories. These will no doubt develop as more content becomes available on OA. Whilst these services will be created by teams including librarians, it is unlikely that they will normally be provided by institutional libraries. Such libraries do not usually have the capacity to develop services like these, nor is there any real reason for them to do so for a single institution. Providing such services at a higher level to serve a larger number of users would be more cost-effective. A search service for a particular subject community across different institutions is an obvious potential example of a useful service.

However, librarians based in institutions are likely to have the opportunity to take on new roles. One of the key roles in an OA context is to set up and deliver repositories and the collection of services associated with them. Repositories might include the range of information materials produced in the institution, including research papers, data, reports, theses and learning objects. Consideration needs to be given at an institutional level to a range of technical, process and policy issues in setting up repositories serving local users (see Jones *et al.*, 2005).

Libraries are ideally placed to take responsibility for delivering repositories in their institutions. As the role of librarians as the gatekeepers of externally-published information resources begins to shrink, their role as the guardians of internally-produced information resources has the potential to expand. Librarians are used to providing robust institution-wide services to a range of users. They have experience of working with people from different subject areas in order to support their activities and to deliver services to them. Librarians have a culture of customer service. They also have professional skills associated with the management and curation of information. Institutional repositories represent an opportunity to extend these skills into a new area on behalf of the institution.

However, repositories not only represent an opportunity but also a challenge to the library profession. As well as seeing repositories as opportunities for exercising information management skills and vehicles for achieving content dissemination, it is essential that repository managers set up services that further the strategic objectives of their institution. Repositories can be used to generate management intelligence for the institution and help to inform the development of research strategy. They can also be a vehicle for knowledge transfer and commercial liaison. The information profession has to ensure that its members are equipped to engage in the wide-ranging discussion associated with the general processes of the creation of research and teaching outputs as well as in the specific area of information management.

One of the specific functions of information management that will continue to be important is preservation. Libraries have traditionally had this role in a print environment and it is likely to continue in an electronic one. OA materials will need to be built into emerging strategies for digital preservation. Apart from the technical challenges, no clear organizational workflow or funding models for digital preservation have yet emerged. It is unclear whether or how institutions, national libraries, commercial organizations, or other agencies will be involved in digital preservation activity. However, it is probable that all of these stakeholders will have some involvement. Some initial work has been done in this area, but a great deal remains to be done. In particular, the whole question of digital preservation needs to move from a largely theoretical or proof-of-concept stage to a practical production level stage. New roles will probably develop for institutional libraries as it does so.

Institutional libraries also have the potential to develop new or enhanced services to local users in supporting the use of content in research and teaching. Services might include sourcing, manipulating or digitizing content on-demand for users. Particular areas of expertise, such as knowledge of intellectual property rights, will be essential here. Advising users on IPR in relation to their own content or that of others is required. This is especially important in complex areas where content can be easily made up of different components from different rights holders were different permissions are applicable; something which is becoming increasingly common.

Another practical on-demand service which might be developed at an institutional level is print-on-demand. If an increasing number of monographs are available online, dealing with the issue of how they can be read will become a priority. If the reader wishes to work on a text extensively, current screen technology may not make this comfortable or convenient. Of course, the technology may change in the five to ten years it will take for OA monographs to become very important. However, the problem is already real for purchased electronic books. In fact, the expansion of the e-book market has undoubtedly be a held up by this technological limitation, as well as the lack of a clear business model for the sale of in-copyright books in digital format. Librarians could help to address this for local users by providing services to print out e-books where copyright allows (which would be the case for OA books).

It is possible that the delivery of such a service could prompt a rethinking of the whole approach to storage of out-of-copyright monographs. Rather than multiple libraries storing duplicate copies of the same book, "just in case" (with all the costs that involves), it may be more cost-effective for libraries to digitize the item and store it in digital form and then agree to provide a print-out when required, "just in time". There would then be no need to store the physical item. A costed life-cycle analysis would need to be carried out comparing storage, preservation, and delivery of physical items against electronic ones in order to inform decisions. The prejudice that librarians often have that digital preservation is very expensive needs to be balanced against the fact that physical preservation (when costed out properly) is also expensive (see Rusbridge, 2006).

Another practical service that it has been suggested could be provided by libraries in on OA world is administering payment of publication or OA charges. Libraries have teams of staff who currently administer periodical acquisitions and might redeploy them in this way. In some institutions libraries have already taken on this role in a small-scale way. The Wellcome Trust have provided funds to a number of institutions to pay publication charges for its grant holders, and in some cases this money is being managed by the library. It is arguable that libraries would be in a good position to take on this role especially if the market developed such that funds were not paid on a per-article basis but as a series of larger-scale pre-payments, effectively being institutional accounts with the publishers. This is already possible with OA publishers such as BioMed Central. It is even conceivable that in a market such as this subscription agents would morph to become intermediaries in the process. However, assuming a role like this has its downside for libraries. Libraries might be put in the difficult position of having to ration the available funds, making decisions about who could and could not publish, and where they could publish. More work needs to be done on how such a situation could be managed within institutions.

10.7 The Future of Libraries

These changes to the role of the library as a result of OA will, of course, contribute to some wider changes that are occurring for libraries and librarians. A few brief comments on this bigger picture should perhaps be made here in order to locate OA developments within their wider context from a library point of view. Over the last decade libraries have had to radically reinvent themselves with the burgeoning of electronic information. If anything, this is likely to continue. In the next decade the prospect of electronic information replacing print, rather than just coexisting with it, is likely to become more and more likely. The role of the library will need to continue to change.

Jerry D. Campbell (2006) has identified seven key roles that he feels libraries will (or have the potential to) carry out in the future:

- Providing quality learning spaces
- Creating metadata
- Offering virtual reference services
- Teaching information literacy
- Choosing resources and managing licences
- Collecting and digitizing archival materials
- Maintaining digital repositories.

It is a little surprising that Campbell does not identify preservation (hardcopy or digital) as a future role of the library, although "collecting and digitizing archival materials" and "maintaining digital repositories" imply this. The last three roles he does mention take the traditional role of libraries as collectors of content into new areas. This role encompasses material which will continue to be purchased and licensed; material of this sort will certainly continue to be important for the foreseeable future. Apart from in-copyright monographs, a great deal of value-added quality content will continue to be available only to purchasers. Even if much of the research literature is OA, a hybrid OA-subscription environment will undoubtedly continue to be the norm for the information landscape as a whole. In addition, libraries will continue to collect, preserve and make available rare or unique material. Such content will remain the raw material of research. Finally, the management of institutional content in digital repositories is likely to become important in ways already discussed.

Three of the remaining four roles (metadata creation, reference services and training) are all about facilitating and supporting access to content. This activity is likely to continue to be important, although the place of the institutional library in this work is likely to change, particularly in the area of metadata creation (as above). Characterizing the support role as "reference services" and "training" is perhaps a little restrictive. Libraries have the potential to deliver more proactive services than this implies, services that will need to be provided in a physical as well as a virtual world.

The first role that Campbell mentions continues a long established practice of the library providing physical spaces. The ways in which the spaces are conceived is changing rapidly but the fundamental provision remains important. This and all of the roles discussed by Campbell are opportunities to be grasped by the library profession. They are not a birthright. The library profession must take existing skills into new areas and develop new skills if it is to forge out a meaningful place for itself in the future of information provision.

10.8 Implementing OA in Institutions

Libraries and librarians have a strong record in pursuing an institution-wide mission to deliver services for a broad range of customers. Over the last 15 years in particular, libraries have also developed the role of partnering other institutional stakeholders in key developments and of themselves leading innovation. They are therefore well-placed to work with stakeholders in their institution on addressing some of the key practical and policy issues associated with the implementation of OA.

Achieving cultural change within institutions in relation to OA is a major challenge, but one which many librarians have already begun to address. The way in which this can be achieved has been discussed in detail elsewhere (for example Ashworth, Mackie and Nixon, 2004). What is clear is that it requires libraries to take on a leadership role. It involves liaison (formal and informal) at a variety of levels within the institution and can only work if librarians have a good understanding of the entire information chain (rather than just the library's role in it) and of institutional strategy (rather than just the library's part in it). It also requires a long-term commitment, since if anything has become clear in the last five years it is that achieving cultural change is perhaps the major challenge associated with OA (Pinfield, 2005).

Another practical role that librarians can play is in discussions on the introduction of institutional OA policies and procedures. This has become an urgent priority in the UK since the introduction of OA mandates by a number of research funders, some of the central research councils and the Wellcome Trust. Informing researchers of their obligations as grant holders and creating procedures to make it easy to comply are immediate challenges. Some of the arrangements suggested by research funders have the potential between them to create confusion amongst researchers who may be unsure of where to self-archive their publications, for instance. Librarians can work within their institutions to establish policies to make things as straightforward as possible for researchers. It may be possible, for example, to advise researchers to self archive all publications in their institutional repository and put in place mechanisms to ensure that relevant publications are subsequently routed (on behalf of the researcher) to any other repositories as required.

A further practical challenge currently being addressed by librarians in many institutions is the question of the management of publication or OA fees. Many librarians have taken on the role of administering special Wellcome Trust funds provided for OA fees, not because they necessarily see it as their long-term role but in order to ensure that the money is used for the purpose intended by the Wellcome. They have also worked within their institutions to ensure that other funds can be made available for non-Wellcome researchers. In the UK, the research councils have stated that publication fees can be paid from funds claimed as part of institutional "full economic cost" charges. In practical terms, what this means is that funds should be made available within institutions for researchers to use for the purposes of paying publication charges, although they can also use money from their individual direct grants (if they have them). However, there are few if any institutions where such funds are available. Because of their awareness of the issues, librarians have been leading voices in institutions ensuring that appropriate funds are identified, advertised and managed.

Librarians have also worked with stakeholders within and outside their institutions on useful experiments in the area of scholarly communication. Such work looking at policy development, creation of workable business models, and analysis of data needs to be continued in liaison with publishers and funders. In particular, libraries need to work with the stakeholders in identifying credible transition scenarios which maintain the strengths of the existing scholarly communication system but which can also lead to greater access.

10.9 Conclusion

The extent to which OA will become widespread in disseminating research output remains to be seen. It is likely that it will become more important, and possible that it will become the norm (at least in some disciplines). Changes are likely to take a decade or more to work through but the landscape is changing even now. It is difficult to predict when "tipping points" will be reached but there is a need for libraries to be flexible and agile organizations which can respond. Librarians need to consider seriously the strategic implications of OA for their profession and organizations. Their role is changing, just as the information environment is changing. OA is one factor amongst many that is helping to shape the future environment in which the information professional will operate. However, in both the short and long-term, libraries and librarians should not just let change happen around them. They need to grasp the opportunity themselves to play an important role in helping to determine what the future of publishing and information management will look like.

Acknowledgements

Thanks to Ruth Jenkins and Karen Stanton for useful comments on drafts of this paper. This chapter is based on a presentation given to the JISC Open Access Conference in Oxford in September 2006. Thanks to a number of delegates at the conference for their comments.

References

Antelman, K. (2004) Do open-access articles have a greater research impact? *College & Research Libraries*, 65(5), 372–82. E-print available at: http://eprints.rclis.org/archive/00002309/.

Ashworth, S., Mackie, M. and Nixon, W. J. (2004) The DAEDALUS Project, developing institutional repositories at Glasgow University: the story so far. *Library Review*, 53(5), 259–64. E-print available at: http://eprints.gla.ac.uk/408/.

Budapest Open Access Initiative (2002) http://www.soros.org/openaccess/read.shtml.

Campbell, J. D. (2006) Changing a cultural icon: the academic library as a virtual destination. *Educause Review*, January/February, 16–30.

Dempsey, L. (2006) Libraries and the long tail: some thoughts about libraries in a network age. *D-Lib Magazine*, 12(6). http://www.dlib.org/dlib/april06/dempsey/04dempsey.html.

European Commission (2006) *Study on the Economic and Technical Evolution of the Scientific Publication Markets in Europe*. European Commission, Directorate-General for Research. http://ec.europa.eu/research/science-society/pdf/scientific-publication-study_en.pdf.

Harnad, S. and Brody, T. (2004) Comparing the impact of open access (OA) vs. non-OA articles in the same journals. *D-Lib Magazine*, 10(6), http://www.dlib.org/dlib/june04/harnad/06harnad.html.

Houghton, J. (2005) Economics of publishing and the future of scholarly communication. In *Scholarly Publishing in an Electronic Era* (eds. G. E. Gorman and F. Rowland). International Yearbook of Library and Information Management, 2004–2005, Facet Publishing.

Houghton, J., Steele, C. and Sheehan, P. (2006) *Research Communication Costs in Australia: Emerging Opportunities and Benefits*. Department of Education, Science and Training (Australia). http://www.dest.gov.au/NR/rdonlyres/0ACB271F-EA7D-4FAF-B3F7-0381F441B175/13935/DEST_Research_Communications_Cost_Report_Sept2006.pdf.

House of Commons Science and Technology Committee (UK) (2004) *Scientific Publications: Free For All?* Tenth Report of Session 2003-04, HC 399. http://www.publications.parliament.uk/pa/cm200304/cmselect/cmsctech/399/399.pdf.

Jacobs, N. (ed.) (2006) *Open Access: Key Strategic, Technical and Economic Aspects*. Chandos Publishing, Oxford.

Jones, R., Andrew, T. and MacColl, J. (2006) *The Institutional Repository*. Chandos Publishing, Oxford.

Lawrence, S. (2001) Free online availability substantially increases a paper's impact. *Nature*, 411 (31 May), 521, and *Nature: webdebates*, http://www.nature.com/nature/debates/e-access/Articles/lawrence.html.

Lynch, C. (2006) Open computation: beyond human reader-centric views of scholarly literatures. In *Open Access: Key Strategic, Technical and Economic Aspects* (ed. N. Jacobs). Chandos Publishing, Oxford.

Pinfield, S. (2005) Self-archiving publications. In *Scholarly Publishing in an Electronic Era* (eds. G. E. Gorman and F. Rowland). International Yearbook of Library and Information Management, 2004–2005, Facet Publishing. E-print available at http://eprints.nottingham.ac.uk/archive/00000142/.

Rowlands, I., Nicholas, D. and Huntingdon, P. (2004) *Scholarly Communication in the Digital Environment: What Do Authors Want? Findings of an International Survey of Author Opinion: Project Report*. CIBER: Centre for Information Behaviour and the Evaluation of Research,

Department of Information Science, City University. http://www.ucl.ac.uk/ciber/ciber-pa-report.pdf.

Rusbridge, C. (2006) Excuse me... some digital preservation fallacies? *Ariadne* (46), http://www.ariadne.ac.uk/issue46/rusbridge/.

Suber, P. (2004) Praising progress, preserving precision. *SPARC Open Access Newsletter* (77), http://www.earlham.edu/~peters/fos/newsletter/09-02-04.htm.

PART 4

Shaking the Foundations – Librarianship in Transition

11

Scholarship and Libraries: Collectors and Collections

Fred Ratcliffe

11.1 Introduction

It is over thirty years since I published an article on *Professional Librarianship and the University Library*[1] in a Festschrift marking the retirement of Joan Gladstone of Newcastle upon Tyne University Library. My theme was hardly topical: of the ten other articles five dealt with the application of computers to librarianship and a sixth demonstrated how their use made new assessments of literature possible. Professional journals were awash with the subject, in the words of C. J. Hunt[1]: "the literature of computerized library systems is now immense". Miss Gladstone herself, in her 1955 *Marginal punched cards as an order record*[2], had already, if indirectly, pointed to the potential of computer applications in library administration.

11.2 Early Application of Computers to Libraries

During my time as Deputy University Librarian in Newcastle the interest of the then modest University Computing Department was focussed on the applications of computers to libraries. Cox of the Department and J. D. Dews published "The Newcastle File Handling System"[3]. The editor of the Festschrift, Alan Jeffreys, was the author of "UK Marc Project" and "The Conversion of the Catalogue into Machine Readable Form". Computer typesetting was beginning to

---

1   *Evaluating the performance of a computerized library system: the acquisitions system in Manchester University Library.* pp. 58–71.
2   *Libri*, 5(4), 1955, pp. 365–9.
3   N. S. M. Cox and M. W. Grose (eds.) (1967) *Organisation and Handling of Bibliographic Records by Computer*, pp.1–27. Oriel Press.

disturb the jobbing printers in Newcastle. The newly established National Lending Library of Science and Technology had become fully operational in 1962 and was flexing its muscles "just down the road" at Boston Spa. The foreword to the Festschrift, however, eschewed any reference to computers: it was a "labour of love", written by that genial University Librarian, Dr W. S. Mitchell. He was just about as far removed from the computer and its applications to libraries as it was possible to be. His heart was in books, in particular historical bindings, and he saw computing as a further tiresome intrusion of technology into his book world, at best another adjunct to administration, which he discharged efficiently but always with an air of distinct disdain.

11.3 Professional Librarianship

My essay, written within a few years of the Library Association's Centenary, discussed the development of professional librarianship in the context of that traditionally practised by the academic, parish and private libraries, where scholars without library training or library qualifications were still frequently to be found in charge. Recruitment of graduate staff, also "untrained", to such libraries, was a bitter bone of professional contention. The essay also recalled that the illustrious journal, The Library, had been for its first ten years the recognized "organ of the Library Association of the United Kingdom", until it spawned the Library Association Record to accommodate the reports of "professional" activities. Such accounts were beginning to sit uncomfortably alongside articles devoted to pure bibliographical scholarship. In retrospect this marked the makings of a dichotomy in librarianship, the emergence of the "professional librarian" and library science alongside the scholar librarian, sometimes referred to as the "Black letter" men, which lasted for the greater part of a century.

In the years which have elapsed since writing that essay, higher education in all sectors has witnessed dramatic changes. Whilst many could have been foreseen, their extent and importance could hardly have been predicted and nowhere more than in universities and their libraries. Today it is impossible to overstate the impact, which they made: "revolutionary" seems not too strong a term to describe them. The 21 new universities founded following the Robbins Report[4] in 1963 proved to be almost a token increase compared with the growth to 148 following the disappearance of "the binary divide" in Higher Education. The number of undergraduates in UK universities grew from 517,000 to 811,000 between 1988/9 and 1992/3 as part of a politically inspired, if unrealistic desire to see at least fifty per cent of the nation's youth at university. If for this reason alone libraries in universities had to change and, in the light of their hitherto gradual growth, change quickly. Former Polytechnics and Colleges of Higher Education, empowered previously to trade in degrees only *via* the CNAA, were now universities endowed with degree giving powers and many diplomas and certificates acquired undergraduate status. Along with the Open University

---

4   Robbins Committee (1963) *Report on Higher Education*. London, HMSO.

they played a significant part in transforming the library profession for the first time into a largely graduate and united one. Almost coincidentally librarianship assumed the mantel of a "discipline", fit for the awarding of first degrees on the pattern long established in the USA, although not with universal approval. WL Saunders[5] of Sheffield, formerly the university's Deputy Librarian and a distinguished pioneer among the new ranks of library or information science professors, expressed real doubts about its suitability for undergraduate courses, and they were not at that time introduced in Sheffield.

11.4 Use of Information Technology

Among those many developments since the end of World War II, and certainly the most significant, was the introduction and ever increasing use of information technology. The Parry, Dainton and Atkinson Reports of 1967, 1969 and 1976[6] made little or no reference to it: they were concerned about library stock, book provision, and means of spreading the "jam" via interlibrary loans, cooperation and the like. In the quarter century following Parry, during which the British Library was founded (1972), the advances in the new technology seemed never ending and its impact on the storage and transmission of information increasingly determined much in library life. Not surprisingly, the next important report on libraries, the Follett Report[7], addressed many of the problems of the university library world in this context. It sought to protect traditional library values and practices whilst explaining and promoting the use of the new technology. CURL was established as a Cambridge initiative to take advantage of these technological advances. Almost inevitably, extensive use of IT, an increasing dependence on it, led in some institutions to "convergence", the amalgamation of library and computing services, described by the John Fielden Consultancy as "the main driver of change in the organization of the library services in the UK and the USA"[8].

In the course of so much change it would be easy to believe that information technology, information retrieval, electronic access to databanks, desktop publishing, the emphasis on new media and the like had displaced such traditional ingredients of academic librarianship as collection building, book selection, bibliography, conservation. After all, the use of such innovatory techniques was by no means limited to the new institutions, essential to them as they were. The

---

5   W. L. Saunders (1968) The library school in the university setting. In *Library Education: an International Survey* (ed. L. E. Bone). University of Illinois.

6   University Grants Committee (1967) *Report of the Committee on Libraries* (The Parry Report). London, HMSO, and (1976) *Report on Capital Provision for University Libraries* (The Atkinson Report). London.

7   Joint Funding Councils' Libraries Review Group (1993) *Report* (The Follett Report). London, JFC.

8   *The Fielden Report on Human Resource Management* was issued by the John Fielden Consultancy shortly after the Follett Report.

old established university libraries were equally, inevitably deeply involved in them so that the concept of "holding and access libraries" was a reality long before the Follett Report gave it a name. Library staff in the course of becoming "computer literate" became Information Officers and Library Schools explored new titles to reflect these changes. As for the library's traditional roles, these developments came in no way at their expense, rather as an enhancement of them, and the latent store of scholarship in university libraries benefited enormously from these new means of exploitation.

11.5 Collections

Academic libraries, certainly the older ones, have traditionally been associated with great collections, great collectors and their librarians. A good library was held to be one where unique collections were held and large stocks accumulated, hence the reputation of the deposit libraries. A good librarian was one who built on and maintained these collections. It is only in comparatively recent times, the post WWII years, that access in academic libraries, now the hallmark of good library services, has been accorded the same sort of priority as acquisition, or rated as of equal importance. Today, the good librarian is expected to be as much at home with the use of information tools as with the collections in the library, even in the deepest depths of Special Collections Departments. The highly sophisticated forms of information retrieval now common in accessing remote databases have become of particular importance in the use of such collections as they find their way into online accessible form.

In such a situation it is worth considering how far the assumptions about "great collections, great collectors and their librarians" are still valid; how far their presence is still an essential ingredient of the good academic library? How much "extra" can they bring to a library which in effect has the resources of the entire scholarly world at its electronic fingertips, equally accessible to scholars and librarians alike? Over some fifty years involvement with academic libraries, acquiring and exploiting many such collections, it seems reasonable to ask how important or useful such collecting has been and is. Some were the work of a bibliophile or scholar collector, a few the creation of a "black letter" librarian, others the archive "spun off" by a business or an institution. In the copyright deposit or academic library such initiatives stand out among the large amorphous collections accumulated under the Copyright Act or formed in the pursuit of teaching and research subject provision. They reflect the personality of the collector who formed them, the identity of the institution which preserved them, with a wider dimension than that of the subject itself. It is possible to identify subjects at undergraduate and research level from a library's stock, through the presence of core books of a syllabus and multiple copies. Amidst these, *collections* are distinguished by their comprehensiveness and scholarly detail, even by the esoteric and trivial.

Although an aspirant book collector from my mid-teens, it was the introduction to the catalogue of the Christie Collection as an undergraduate at

Manchester University sixty years ago, which opened my eyes to the scholarly value and importance of systematic, disciplined collecting. In his introduction to his catalogue[9] Christie wrote:

"Although some of the volumes are what are called 'Collector's books', yet the Collection as a whole will be found to have a uniform aim and a principle of unity pervading it. It has been formed with a view of illustrating and enabling its owner to study the Renaissance, and especially the classical Renaissance of Italy and France, and it will be found that the greater number of the volumes bear upon this subject, and more particularly upon certain departments, and the lives, labours and works of a certain number of scholars upon whose lives and labours I had at one time hoped to write something... I believe that no other library... contains a more nearly complete collection, and I indulge the hope that some time, perhaps in the course of the next century, some student may feel interest in these scholars – veritable 'oubliés et dedaignés' – and may find these collections available for making their dry bones live."

The result is a monument to inspired collecting, both in its scholarly purpose and bibliographical completeness, presenting the classical Renaissance through the hard literary evidence left behind.

Christie's collection became the gold standard against which I sought to measure those which I set out to acquire for the libraries in which I worked. Only those superb collections in the Rylands, such as the Crawford or Spencer collections, later to be merged with those of the University Library, were superior to it and that only because of their greater dimensions and the money and professional help which went into forming them. They were to use current jargon, Christie libraries "writ large". Nevertheless, the Christie Collection enriched the then still new University of Manchester immeasurably and although a number of other fine collections also came to the library in the nineteenth century, none displayed the same degree of bibliographical single-mindedness, acumen and flair found in the Christie Collection. Regrettably, the exemplary unity characterizing the Collection was badly damaged in the sale of so-called "duplicates" by the university library in the eighties.

Christie's approach was clearly appreciated by my predecessor as University Librarian, Dr Moses Tyson, although the opportunities for acquiring whole collections which arose during his librarianship (1935–65) were few and far between. A medieval historian, sometime Keeper of Western Manuscripts in the Rylands, he was an "out and out" bookman. Despite the constraints imposed by WWII during the early years of his librarianship, by the end of his career in Manchester he had established an enviable reputation among his contemporaries as a collection builder. He secured acquisition funds which were in a different league from those of other university librarians and he used them not only to provide generous cover for the curricula, but also to develop the existing

---

9   *Catalogue of the Christie Collection Comprising the Printed Books and Manuscripts Bequeathed to the Library of the University of Manchester by... Richard Copley Christie.* Compiled under the direction of C. W. E. Leigh. Manchester University Press, 1915, pp. ix–xi.

strengths in Special Collections, *par excellence* the History of Science Collection. He united the rare science books in the Departmental, Museum and Medical libraries with those of the University Library to form the core of a History of Science collection. He then systematically pursued "desiderata" on a scale, which soon brought him to the notice of the book trade and, until his retirement, bought vigorously, often, if pressed for library funds, out of his own money. His last coup was the acquisition of the Partington History of Science Library, formed by Professor J. R. Partington. A Manchester graduate and sometime university teacher, in retirement an emeritus professor of London University, he had been courted assiduously by Tyson over the years. The books arrived during my first week as University Librarian. Tyson had in effect created a Collection on the History of Science of unique importance in the provinces by the end of his career.

His recruitment of staff reflected his "black letter" approach and was different from many of his contemporaries. He brought in first class graduates with research qualifications wherever possible in the course of which he pioneered academic salaries for library graduate staff. The cataloguing room at times resembled a bibliographical hothouse. Libraries in his view were the stuff of scholarship and needed scholars to administer them. He upset the Library Association by advertising for such staff and describing its qualifications as "desirable but not essential". The Library Association was not at that time the grown-up body it has later become. If such recruits went off to academic posts – a frequent criticism of his policy by "professional" librarians – he saw them go as library missionaries in an academic jungle and they went with his blessing, three at least to occupy chairs in the years to come. For much of his career his was a lone voice in the "professional" library world, that of a "wild card", but, in the University of Manchester, a very powerful one, being of senior professorial status and among other things, University Reader in Palaeography and Dean of the Faculty of Arts.

Seven years in that environment marked me for my library life and determined the shape of my career. A would-be book collector, I relished the role of institutional book collector, which is open to the university librarian. It is not possible to avoid the administrative chores endemic to most senior academic posts but, though depriving me of daily close contact with individual books, they put me into the "dream" position of determining acquisition policies, in particular in regard to rare books, manuscripts and archives. They also brought the rare privilege of meeting collectors and discussing their collections, often in the setting of their homes and libraries, usually with the aim of acquiring them. No university library can afford the scholarly expertise, time or money, which the collector brings to his collecting so that to acquire them by gift or by purchase is to add significantly to the university's scholarly treasury, frequently opening up new seams of academic gold. It is not just the books, which are acquired, it is also the scholarship which went into forming them into a collection.

By way of illustration, only a representative sample of the many transactions successfully concluded can be cited here. The first, chronologically, has to be the Pybus Collection, now in the University Library of Newcastle upon Tyne. I was introduced to F. C. Pybus, Emeritus Professor of Surgery, a few months after my arrival there. He was one of a number of serious book collectors in the Newcastle medical fraternity and by far the most distinguished. He had learned from the Librarian that his new Deputy "collected books'and invited me to view his collection at his home. It was far beyond my expectations, disciplined in the manner of the Christie Collection but with the crucial advantage of being able to discuss it with the collector. During a long bachelor life he had endeavoured to acquire all the major books of historic importance in the field of medicine in the first edition, later ones if more important, along with medical manuscripts, prints, portraits and archival items. He rarely strayed outside his chosen field, except, as he once admitted, to buy the occasional work with a fine binding to transfer to a "tired" contemporary medical book! His initial objective had been to collect all the works of William Harvey but he soon extended his sights. Items such as Harvey's own copy of his *De generatione animalium,* 1651, with three pages of notes in Harvey's own hand, or a manuscript copy of John of Arderne's *De arte phisicale et de cirurgia,* ca. AD1380, say all that needs to be said about the quality of the collection.

Endowed with a genuine photographic mind, he had an almost exhaustive knowledge of the History of Medicine, its literature and bibliography, whilst being for much of his working life the premier surgeon in the North East. His original intention was to leave his collection to the Royal College of Surgeons but he changed his mind following two successful exhibitions from his collection mounted in the University Library, which to his gratification received much press interest. Later, he allowed me to transfer the whole of his collection, including pictures, prints, engravings, letters and shelving, to the University Library, and to draft a document detailing conditions relating to his gift. The many hours spent with this great collector, who was little known nationally as such, extended significantly my bibliographic boundaries, as I witnessed the finer points of bibliography transformed into fact. For the university, which was already strong in the field of medicine and its literature, the acquisition was of major practical importance and was put to use immediately in a series of History of Medicine lectures and exhibitions. Newcastle acquired not only a splendid collection of rare and valuable materials uniquely tailored to illustrate the History of Medicine but also a highly disciplined contribution to medical scholarship.

The Pybus Collection was still much in my mind on moving to Manchester not least because of the arrival of the Partington collection. Although a *fait accompli,* it involved me briefly with the donor and endorsed my institutional collecting instincts. It comprised some fifteen hundred volumes illustrating the history of Science, many of great rarity, in the specific field of chemistry, and unlikely to turn up often in booksellers' catalogues. Such collections often reflect a lifetime's commitment and offer opportunities which are unlikely to come twice. The purchase of the Ferguson Collection of early printed books illustrated this admirably. F. S. Ferguson, sometime President of the Bibliographical Society and a founder editor of the *Short-Title Catalogue of Books printed in Britain before 1640* used his specialized knowledge to collect items of bibliographical significance and rarity. Such items seldom appeared even individually in sales catalogues at the time let alone as whole collections. The acquisition was of unusual importance as the product of a mind steeped in the subject and proved especially interesting since the library had been a sub-scriber to the two microfilm sets *English Books printed before 1640* and *1640–1700* since their inception. The Ferguson books showed clearly that there is more to a publication than the text since the hard copy provided a wealth of additional scholarly information not conveyed by the film. It also demonstrated again that there are few real duplicates among early printings. Its purchase alerted many booksellers and others wishing to dispose of materials that offers made to the University of Manchester Library, whether by gift or sale , would receive serious consideration. The library eventually had the chance of "first refusal" of much highly desirable material.

Among these was an archive, which the Professor of Modern History described as "historical gold". I was invited by Field-Marshal Sir Claude Auckinleck to visit his home in Beccles to inspect his personal papers covering the period 1938–47. He was concerned that they should go to a "non-Establishment" insti-tution with a good reputation in the teaching of history. They covered crucial periods of World War II, including the campaigns in Norway, Iraq, the Middle East Burma and India, and comprised many official reports, messages and cor-respondence with leading contemporary statesmen and soldiers. They were of particular interest for the insights they gave into the North African campaign, into partition in the Indian subcontinent and the role of the Indian Army. As a result of this donation six generals serving with Auchinleck also offered their papers, among them those of Major-General Dorman Smith, a colourful figure in the military, whose papers were especially relevant to the first battle of Alamein. The donations were important in a University where Spenser Wilkinson, later Chichele Professor of Military History in Oxford, had founded and presided over the Manchester Tactical Society in the nineteenth century and complemented significant holdings both in the library and the still inde-pendent John Rylands. The donation also brought Auchinleck to Manchester where at a conference organized by the University and Western Command, though in his mid-eighties, he made an outstanding contribution to the debate on the necessity of war for maintaining the peace. These military papers were quickly exploited by the History Department and underlined how valuable a part collection building could play in supporting and promoting subjects taught and researched in the university.

11.6 Space Requirements

The acquisition of the Auchinleck and other military papers was time consuming but hardly space consuming which was important in an already overcrowded library. That was not true of many acquisitions that followed and my staff did not hesitate to comment on the "folly" (as they saw it) of my acquisition policy. It was a time when Manchester itself seemed to be in a constant state of redevelopment and many institutions in the city were faced with storage or financial problems. When I was invited to speak with the directors of The Guardian to discuss accepting the huge archive of The Manchester Guardian and Evening News I was faced with a dilemma. The library already had an acute accommodation problem, which I had regularly brought to the attention of the university, so that any suggestion of securing such a huge amount of archival material flew in the face of reason. It occupied some 7,000 sq ft, probably more than some university faculties. Nevertheless, it was undeniably a tremendously important archive, immensely rich in research potential, which, if it had to leave the newspaper, should certainly be retained in Manchester. It included books, rare periodicals, newspaper files, archive material of all kinds, and correspondence by such as C. P. Scott, A. P. Wadsworth, W. P. Crozier and leading statesmen or figures of national importance. The association of the university with the Manchester Guardian dated back to its foundation: both found their origins in Nonconformity.

There was a degree of urgency in that the archive was housed in a disused mill in the Salford area, which was scheduled for demolition, and there was no possibility of accommodating even a fraction of the archive in the *Guardian's* new quarters in Deansgate. Having first convinced the Library Committee of the desirability of securing such a valuable collection, I approached the Vice Chancellor, Bursar and Director of Building Services, all essentially local men, who needed no persuading as to the importance and special relevance of the collection. Indeed, the Vice Chancellor himself suggested as a temporary measure the use of "redundant" university buildings intended ultimately for redevelopment. The fact that the *Guardian* directors wished to donate the collection rather than deposit it was crucial in the discussions. In the event, among the many properties acquired by the university in the process of rapid expansion in the area was a primary school a short distance from the library. It was easily adapted for shelving and offered an excellent solution with an office for library staff and potential users. When I last visited the university, the archive was still in the same accommodation, which had been adopted over a quarter of a century as part of the university library.

The merger of the John Rylands and University Libraries was formally completed in July 1972 and was of such importance as to be recognized by the change of name to the John Rylands University Library of Manchester. The John Rylands owed much to the acumen of Mrs Rylands in building its collections. She recruited E. G. Duff, the dedicated bibliophile and collector, to catalogue her new library, and appointed Henry Guppy as co-librarian with Duff for the first year, then as sole librarian until his retirement. Her purchase of the Spenser, Crawford and other collections, each the product of inspired, richly funded collecting, has often been described. These discrete collections illustrate over and again the theme of this essay. The transfer to the Rylands Building of all the library's special collections followed: aimed not only to take advantage of the greater security but also of the scholarly environment integral to Basil Champneys'[10] original design. Its style and quality complemented its contents and reflected their special character by segregating them from the day to day

---

10 Basil Champneys, architect, 1842–1935, well known for his buildings in Oxford and Cambridge.

working materials of a university library. Only the *Guardian* Archive, in its own building on the campus, was to remain until extensions to the Rylands Building could be secured.

Before the building of the library extensions began in 1976, four "redundant", buildings were used as stores by the library so that the space offered in the Rylands Building was particularly timely. The Unitarian College transferred all its valuable historical holdings to the library – books, letters, diaries and papers concerning the history of the Unitarian Church, and its famous collection on the History of Dissent. From the Hartley Victoria Methodist College in Manchester came the Hobill Collection of Methodism, formed originally by G. A. K. Hobill and strong in Wesleyana, Primitive Methodism and the Methodist New Connexion. This acquisition and the existing strengths of the library in the subject played a crucial part in the later decision of the Methodist Conference to transfer the entire Methodist Archives and Research Centre, books, manuscripts and artefacts, from its home in City Road, London, to the library. It contained an extensive collection of correspondence, diaries, account books and papers of the early Methodists and notably of the Wesley family. On the printed side it included eighteenth and nineteenth century material, much of it very rare, a unique repository in this country for Methodist scholarship, comprising well over 100,000 items. The pre-1800 publications from the Northern Congregational College followed: it included eleven incunables, much dissenting material from such as Richard Baxter and John Owen, its archives and the Thomas Raffles Collection. These with the many other collections relating to Dissent which were acquired, such as those of the Northern Baptist College, identified the library as a centre for its literature and historical materials, peculiarly appropriate to a University which counted so many Dissenters among its founding fathers. When such fine collections come together in one place, to a large extent complementing each other, their scholarly research potential is multiplied out of all proportion to the individual component parts.

This must be a *sine qua non* in collection building exercises, a basic element in a library's acquisition policy. The acquisition of the Tabley House library and muniments hardly conformed to this principle. It was purchased from the university when disinvestment in South Africa, a student *cause célèbre* at the time, led the university to reinvest at home and the Tabley House Estate in Cheshire was one of the assets acquired. To defray part of the cost and pay for restoration of the roof, the university decided to sell the library, which, thanks to its accessions budget, the university library could well afford to buy. Although it contained many books from the early sixteenth to the eighteenth century there were few truly outstanding items among the c.5,000 it comprised, but about 450, including an indifferent copy of the First Folio and a set of the *Naturalist's Miscellany*, were deemed of sufficient importance to move immediately to the Rylands Building. The collection itself, however, taken as an entity, was of peculiar interest as the untouched personal library of the Leicester-Warrens and Barons de Tabley. It was in no sense a grand collection but it mirrored the reading habits of one minor aristocratic family over three centuries. Binding had been generally carried out locally and with a few exceptions the only provenance in the collection was that of the house and the immediate surrounding area. Unlike many of the libraries in country houses, it had a "lived in" look, it was more than furniture lining the walls.

11.7 Resourcing

The Librarian's Reports of those fifteen years in Manchester record extraordinary expansion of stock through donation, deposit and purchase of which only the merest fraction can be mentioned here. The frequent cases made to the Senate and Council for increased funding bore fruit and resulted in a generous accessions budget which was supported by many successful applications to external grant giving sources[11]. As a result few opportunities had to be declined on grounds of shortage of funds, much more likely for reasons of duplication. Such an occasion occurred shortly after the purchase of the fine eighteenth century library of Robert Shackleton, Bodley's Librarian, which complemented splendidly the already rich existing holdings of French literature in the library. A friend of long standing, he had great affection for the Rylands, the first academic library he had ever used as a seventeen year old living in Todmorden, (now in Greater Manchester). He wanted an element of donation to mark the sale and his books (minus his Montesquieu collection which he donated to the Bodleian) came at a price well below their market value. Soon afterwards, his Cambridge collector friend, Ralph Leigh, Professor of French and Fellow of Trinity College, Cambridge, visited me to discuss sale of his Rousseau Collection. He had also formed a large library of eighteenth century French books, uniquely important for its Rousseau materials but with much other contemporary European material too. Desirable as the Rousseau items were the extent of duplication among the non-Rousseau materials could not justify purchase.

Within days of moving to Cambridge University Library (CUL) Leigh approached me again, more in hope than certainty. The duplication of Rousseau and other materials was significantly less in CUL than in Manchester much to my surprise. The asking price, reached on the basis of "willing buyer, willing seller", also proved to be lower and far below any catalogue price. To conclude the purchase, being so new in post, I spoke with the Secretary General of the Faculties who was horrified by the proposal, which was "unique in his experience", and by the cost. Nevertheless, the books came to the library, as a named collection, and soon proved to be the first of many such acquisitions. My reputation as an institutional book collector was re-established and the library's purchasing power and the continued assistance of external grant giving bodies never failed to accommodate such acquisitions thereafter. These were fully described to the library syndicate but the cost was normally only disclosed to the chairman. I had learned long ago in Manchester that committee members had difficulty in swallowing significant expenditure of this kind, particularly if

---

11   e.g. The National Heritage Memorial Fund, The V&A Purchase Grant Fund, The Friends of the National Libraries.

their background lay in the Humanities. Fortunately the chairman was also a book collector and shared my positive attitude to acquisitions.

The pattern of collection building in Manchester was repeated on a much larger scale on the wider canvas offered by Cambridge. Negotiations with Sir Geoffrey Keynes, the renowned bibliophile, to acquire his library began almost immediately. It comprised a number of separate collections from which CUL had hoped to purchase such items as it could afford. It was clear on viewing the library that it was of great importance both for its manuscript and various specialized printed book collections, which extended from early printings down to the present day. It had been assembled with all the expert knowledge of a gifted bookman and despite the formidable expenditure involved I proposed we buy the lot. Sir Geoffrey was at first sceptical but by anticipating death duties, it was agreed with his solicitor that a large part of the purchase price could be absorbed *in lieu*: the remainder was paid with the help of significant grants from external sources and by spreading payment over two years. Shortly afterwards, the Hunter-Macalpine library on the history of psychiatry, some 7,000 volumes from the sixteenth century onwards, was purchased. Together with the medical books in the Keynes library, an important History of Medicine Collection, the product of years of committed collecting by medical bibliophiles, was created in CUL. Both collections became available at the height of financial uncertainty and only considerable leeway in meeting payments allowed the library time to raise the money. As if to compound the financial difficulties, the Harold Forster Collection of 18th century English verse was also offered and acquired with the help of the largest grant ever made by the Friends of the National Libraries at that time. It contained many real rarities and remedied some rather surprising omissions, given that CUL is a copyright library. Other donations and purchases followed on a scale hardly imaginable in Manchester. Fortunately, among the much larger number of library staff there were bookmen prepared to assist in securing them. Even so, dealing with collectors and collections took up much time during my Cambridge librarianship.

The situation in Cambridge was uncannily similar to the one I inherited in Manchester. The library had serious accommodation difficulties, which were to plague my time in CUL as they had in Manchester. Similarly, there were frequent periods of severe economic constraint in the university sector with all the consequent infighting within universities to secure appropriate funding, which was inevitably reflected in their libraries. Balancing the budget was at times a frustrating exercise with much juggling of funds and deferring of payments. Only the presence of the library's own direct works department, a unique Cambridge facility in the university library world, made the position more tolerable as it adapted almost every conceivable area to meet the library's shelving needs. When the huge collection of *Daily Mirror* press cuttings were offered, a resource of enormous potential for the modern historian, it could not realistically be refused and had to be housed by the works department in the roof space until suitable accommodation and appropriate staff resources became available. There were no convenient redundant buildings on the campus as there had been in Manchester to house the *Guardian*. At the same time the consolidation of the Medical, Scientific Periodicals and Law libraries as dependent parts of the university library was taking place, anticipating the growth of the Dependent Library concept in different departments in the years ahead. In the context of the national responsibilities of a copyright deposit library, collection building assumed a very different, more demanding perspective.

The pattern of collecting activities remained much as it had been in Manchester though on a larger scale. There, in the early seventies, I had been approached by the Bible Society in London seeking deposit of their huge collections on "permanent loan", but unexpected improvements in its situation prevented it from happening. These turned out to be short lived. In Cambridge I was contacted again by the Director and this time the deposit actually took place. Its acquisition made a major impact on the rare books department, softened to some extent by the Bible Society staff, which came with it, initially funded by the Society. The immediate result was that, combined with extensive existing holdings, the library became one of the world's leading centres for the study of the Bible. The seventeenth century Lambeth book cases, originally made to house the Lambeth Library[12] but for long lying dismantled in store, were restored specifically to house the collection, which was of such importance as to be formally reopened by the Chancellor of the University, HRH the Duke of Edinburgh.

11.8 Further Institutional Collections

Over the following years a number of institutional collections followed either on permanent loan or by purchase. The expression "permanent loan" was first defined in Manchester after a deposit, which had been in the John Rylands for some twenty years, was peremptorily "repossessed" and sold in the London auction rooms, without redress for the library of any kind. I devised a formula for agreements between depositors and the library which aimed to dissuade "owners" from removing such collections in the future. The deposit of the Greenwich Observatory Archives brought the papers of all Astronomers Royal together under one roof and both sides of the correspondence of many distinguished scientists. The archives of the Vickers Company and its subsidiaries, which at been at the heart of national events for over a century, came boxed and indexed under the guidance of their Honorary Company Archivist. The immensely important and extensive Library of the Royal Commonwealth Society (RCS) was purchased, necessitating the raising of £3 million: its successful transfer was celebrated by a visit to the Society of Princess Margaret. It complemented the Rosenthal Collection, formed by South Africa's leading historian Eric Rosenthal. This traced in depth that country's controversial history and was so important that a major South African State University Library opposed its removal from South Africa. The Hanson Collection of Rare

---

12 The Lambeth Library was reclaimed by Archbishop William Juxon in 1660 and replaced by the library of Richard Holdsworth, Master of Emannual, in 1664. See J. C. T. Oates (1986) *Cambridge University Library: a History, etc.*, pp. 247–67. Cambridge University Press, Cambridge.

Books acquired from the Cruising Association might seem an unlikely acquisition but it comprised very many scarce maritime items and filled a distinct gap in the library's holdings. It attracted a large grant from the National Heritage Memorial Fund, a seal of endorsement in the eyes of many library syndics.

The Leigh collection proved to be the forerunner of many named collections formed by scholar collectors acquired during the next fourteen years. They were all distinguished by the same single-minded, disciplined approach to collecting, the hallmark of the true collector. The collections made by two former Deputy Librarians, F. J. Norton and J. C. T. Oates, are of special interest in that an unusually high degree of bibliographical expertise acquired through spending their professional lives in CUL went into the collecting. Norton's books included a glossed thirteenth century Apocalypse and eight incunables, but were especially notable for the many rare items printed in Spain and Portugal from 1501–1520. A distinguished Hispanist, his services to Spanish bibliography were recognized by the award of the Grand Cross of the Order of Alfonso X El Sabio. Oates's collection of editions of Laurence Sterne was easily the most important one of Sterniana outside Shandy Hall. It was formed with an eye to the Library's own notable holdings of Sterne and was, therefore, a specially pertinent addition to the impressive holdings in the university library.

During my penultimate year as university librarian I was approached by Mr Peregrine Churchill, a nephew of Sir Winston and the last surviving family member of his trustees, about the sale to Churchill College of the Churchill papers, which were already on deposit there. He was anxious to recruit me in persuading the Government to buy them for the College, thereby ensuring a permanent home for them. This caused a great deal of critical comment in the media under the delusion that they belonged to the Nation and were not the family's to sell, when in fact they were the responsibility of Sir Winston's Trustees. The sum suggested by Mr Peregrine Churchill was half the Sotheby's estimate, which itself was considerably below offers received from America. It was an unnecessarily contentious issue, in which I became reluctantly involved and was only settled by Mr Churchill's threat to withdraw the papers from Cambridge and seek export to a USA buyer. The government recognized belatedly that the threat was real and foresaw the public outrage, which export would have stirred. Mr Peregrine Churchill did not benefit personally from the sale.

The inclusion of a title in any collection is often a good guide to its value, identifying the work of a collector. The Popish Plot Collection, which appeared in a London salesroom, comprised over 1,400 Broadsides and Pamphlets dating from 1660 to 1695, among which some two hundred items appeared to be unique. Formed more or less contemporaneously with their publication by a well-informed man of affairs, they were arranged and indexed in thirteen volumes. They make a powerful impact even three centuries later. The American based bookseller, Brett-Smith, gave the library offer of "first refusal" on a collection of Restoration Drama, the result of some fifty years collecting by father and son. Despite the copyright deposit privilege, the library's holdings were surprisingly "patchy" and the bookseller, an expatriate Englishman, put an affordable asking price on the collection in the hope that it would find a permanent home in England. Both these purchases aimed to remedy deficiencies in the library's holdings in important subject areas. Two further opportunities to harness the potential of scholarly collecting came up in the purchase of the Waddleton and Harley Mason books. Mr Norman Waddleton, an Emmanuel man, formed a collection of Illustrated Colour books over some thirty years at the extraordinary rate of nine or ten volumes a day. It was probably one of the richest and certainly largest collections of its kind in private hands and Mr Waddleton intended to continue collecting with a view to donating all succeeding purchases to the library. Soon afterwards the opportunity to purchase the Dr John Harley Mason collection of rare aquatint books occurred. A Corpus Christi Fellow and friend, he like Mr Waddleton sold the books at well below market prices on a "willing buyer, willing seller basis". A distinguished academic chemist, Harley Mason was also an "authority" on aquatints, which he had collected during his university career. Together, almost overnight, these two collections established the library as an important centre for the illustrated book.

The library's reputation as an institutional collector prompted many offers of collections. The readiness to acquire collections by donation or purchase also persuaded members of the university to bring to my notice material in their subject field, which might otherwise have gone elsewhere. The library's rewarding contact with the well-known German author and political activist, Stephan Heym, came about through the good offices of a member of staff in the German Department. The author was in the University to receive an Honorary Degree and, after inspecting the university library, was introduced to me. The library impressed him, in particular its practice of naming collections after their donors and preserving them as self contained units within the special collections. It became clear that he was interested in bequeathing to a library his own archives, which were highly sensitive politically and also important in modern German literature archive. He was particularly anxious that they should survive intact and believed that only in England would his work be free from censorship. His controversial career began in pre-war Germany as a Jewish fugitive and, following service in the American army, continued in the USA during the McCarthy era. He then returned to Germany, first as a very prickly resident in the DDR, afterwards as a vigilant critic of the government of the united Germany, all of which made his concern for the preservation of his papers and library highly credible. Discussing his papers and career both in Cambridge and Berlin was an enjoyable and rewarding experience.

It is possible only to hint at the many collections, which came to Cambridge during my fourteen years as librarian, on a much grander scale inevitably than in Manchester. The much longer history of CUL, the many great names and events associated with the university down into modern times, and its international standing ensured that it must be so. The purpose of this paper is not, however, to compare library holdings but to demonstrate how the work of collectors, great and small, contributes significantly to the sum of scholarship in any library and how important to bibliographical scholarship such collections are. The Parker Library of Corpus Christi College Cambridge exemplifies this to perfection. If I had ever had doubts about the importance of collectors and collections in the annals of librarianship, my "honorary" retirement job as the Fellow Librarian of the College would have dispelled them. The first Archbishop of Canterbury to serve Elizabeth I was the modest Matthew Parker[13], a "reformer" with a small "r", who nevertheless quietly ensured the survival of Cranmer's Reformation. He might also claim to be England's first serious collector. His famous collection of manuscripts rescued as much as possible from the fast disappearing monastic and religious institutional libraries. It contains about a quarter of known O.E. texts and other early manuscripts of the very greatest importance preserving vital information about the Nation's history, which in the tempestuous times during which he lived could very easily have been lost. His own extensive collection of documents, papers and letters relating to the Reformation, a signally significant record of his own times, were also meticulously preserved. He was no less diligent in preserving his large working library, which provides an almost unique glimpse of the sixteenth century scholar at work. All collectors are concerned about the future of their collection and he proposed severe penalties for the College were anything to disappear through "indolent neglect"! This unique collection also contains books, which even in Parker's day would be seen as "collectables".

Special collections require special conditions and high among these must be the quality of staff. Dr Tyson influenced me not just in the building of collections: he also convinced me that scholarly collections need scholarly librarians to curate and exploit them, to administer them and direct the institutions which house them. Before the expansion of the university system, opportunities for him to pursue this aspect of his librarianship were limited but whenever they occurred, he opted to appoint highly qualified scholars. As a product of his recruitment policy, I sought to implement it wherever possible in the much larger and more flexible employment field of my day. Whereas I was probably the only member of Tyson's graduate staff during his thirty years as university librarian to pursue preferment in another library, the opportunities for staff to move during my librarianship were legion, as so many more academic libraries were created. As a result many of the young scholars appointed by me during my librarianship secured senior posts in the university library field.

11.9 Conclusions

Although I cannot claim to have appointed C. J. Hunt, Fred Friend, Toby Bainton and John Arfield to their first university library posts I claim them among the many who have worked with me and have gone on to become university librarians. Bill Simpson, now occupying the position I once held, indeed created, in Manchester, qualifies in much the same way and jokingly suggested recently that I should consider publishing all my "references", copies of which still clutter up my files. Among those who started their professional lives with me as

---

13   For a brief recent assessment of his life and work, see F. W. Ratcliffe, *But I See Men be Men (Matthew Parker – Master Builder and Corpus Man)*. A paper read before the 877th Meeting of the Sette of Odd Volumes, etc. Cambridge, Priv. Pr. Fieldfare Press, 2005.

library assistants are J. M. Lancaster and Dr J. A. Henshall, who both rose from the ranks in Manchester University Library, to become university librarians. Dr I. Lovecey, Dr Thomas Kabdebo, Dr Clive Field, Jonathon Tuck, Dr Paul Ayris, Dr J. T. D. Hall and Dr R. P. Carr all began their library careers as assistant librarians in libraries where I was the librarian. Both John Hall and Reg Carr had the doubtful privilege of working with me twice, first as raw recruits in Manchester, then as my deputies in Cambridge, which says much for their stamina. This chapter celebrates the achievements of all my former colleagues but in particular those of Reg Carr.

When is a Librarian not a Librarian?

Frederick Friend

12.1 Introduction

When Reg Carr began his career the role of a university librarian was reasonably clear. Admittedly the profession suffered then as it does now from poor public understanding of what a librarian does, but within a university many members of the academic community held library staff in respect and had clear ideas of what they expected from them. It is very unlikely that the academics who appointed Reg Carr to his first job would have expected his last role as a librarian to be that of a fund-raiser. This was the time of university growth in the 1960s, when taxpayer money was poured into universities in abundance and the task of a librarian was to spend money, not to acquire it. Likewise, in respect of my own career, which began in Manchester University Library around the same time as Reg's career, nobody would have expected that my career would end in a role known mysteriously as "scholarly communication". What has scholarly communication to do with libraries? Has a librarian ceased to be a librarian when they become a fund-raiser or a scholarly communication consultant?

12.2 Learning Priorities in Manchester University Library

There were and are many types of jobs available within a library, and a librarian's job description (usually verbal with only a general written statement in the 1960s) would vary according to their role and according to their position in what at that time was a fairly rigid hierarchy. Despite the rigid hierarchy there were opportunities for young librarians to gain a wide variety of experience in different roles, provided that they had the encouragement of the chief librarian. Separate staff-rooms for academic-related and clerical staff were one mark of hierarchical distinction in some libraries. Two key features of a successful future career were available to be experienced in the situation at Manchester.

The first was the opportunity to gain managerial experience in one of the small departmental libraries, and the second was the understanding of the importance of acquiring academically-rich special collections of rare books and manuscripts. Such collections make a huge difference to the value of a university library to the research community. Dr. Ratcliffe acquired many important collections during his time at Manchester, and it was very instructive for a young librarian to watch this process. Maybe this role will become less important in the internet age, when digitized manuscripts and books can be accessed from anywhere in the world, but the understanding of the research process which directed the acquisition of physical collections will still be important in the acquisition of virtual collections. Collecting the right "stuff" always has been and always will be a vital skill for a librarian to acquire. (The use of the word "stuff" to describe the variety of content needed in an academic library to feed the research process is attributed to Joseph Scott, Librarian of University College London, 1954–1982).

Work in Manchester University Library in the 1960s illustrated the expectations library users have from library services. University staff expected to come to the library building and to find the books journals and manuscripts they needed for their research on the library shelves. The role of the library staff was to acquire by purchase or donation the materials academic staff needed, to know enough about different academic subjects to be able to answer subject-related enquiries with a minimum of explanation by the reader, and to enable as many as possible of the items the reader needed to be taken to the reader's office for as long as possible. If a dispute arose between a member of library staff and a member of academic staff it would generally be about some restriction placed upon the removal of a book from the library, a petty restriction to the reader but part of the custodial role for a librarian. In the days before electronic formats, the custodial role was very strong in the minds of librarians. Many books were stolen from libraries, and library staff were very aware of the number of occasions a reader looked for a book on the library shelves and found it was missing. If this happened frequently a library would acquire a bad reputation and its service to readers current and future would be diminished.

For students, university library staff performed a more prosaic role, essentially to have a high proportion of the books on a student's reading list waiting on the library shelves in time for the student to complete her or his essay on the last minute before the deadline. Once student numbers rose after World War 2 this expectation posed the challenge of purchasing multiple copies of student textbooks, a challenge which required library staff to liaise closely with lecturers and obtain copies of reading lists in time for the books to be purchased and made available on the library shelves. The high turnover of books used by undergraduates also involved a librarian in decisions on loan periods and sanctions for the non-return of books on time. While there was a case for very lengthy loan periods for items required by researchers, undergraduate services demanded loan periods measured in days if not hours, combined with strict rules for non-return on time. Problems arose when an item required by undergraduates was borrowed by a member of academic staff, sometimes for their own use and sometimes to loan out unofficially to their own group of students.

It could be a daunting task for a young librarian to telephone a senior member of academic staff to request the return of a book required by an undergraduate. In many university libraries fines were paid by students but not by members of academic staff, and a wise librarian would direct the income from fines into the purchase of more undergraduate textbooks. Many day-to-day situations tested a librarian's commitment to service.

In some aspects administrative tidiness formed the best service a librarian could provide to library users. Keeping the books in good order on the shelves was a skill all library staff were taught from their first day in a library, and although many books went missing, it was usually when readers rather than librarians returned a book to the wrong place on the shelves – or at least that is a librarian's view! Accuracy in record-keeping was also vital. In the days before libraries had computers, a card could easily be mis-filed in the catalogue (causing a reader to think that a book was not in stock) or an issue slip could be mis-filed (causing the issue desk staff to think that a book was not on loan when it was). Cataloguing was one of the mysteries which a librarian learned and which marked out a "professional" librarian from one of the library's "clerical" staff. There was much that was pretentious about this system, but its benefit was in imparting the vital importance of accuracy in library services, an academic discipline rather like learning Latin at school. Many is the catalogue card young librarians were asked to re-type by Manchester University Library's Chief Cataloguer because of the mis-spelling of an author's name or the title of a book. Accuracy in typing was not a skill young librarians expected to need when they started work in a library but acquiring that skill did none of us any harm. Cataloguing was not without its lighter moments, as when at least one future library director mischievously joined in placing a card for a book written by a model involved in the Profumo sex scandal of the 1960s into the catalogue of Manchester University Library's grand academic collections. Despite such youthful rebelliousness we learned a respect for the value of an accurate catalogue which is as important for digital catalogues as it was for card catalogues.

Both Reg Carr and I spent some time in Manchester's departmental libraries. This was a vital learning experience in which we could make mistakes without causing disruption to the services in the two largest libraries. In my case I remember ordering tables that were too large for the Social Sciences Library. In my zeal to fit in as many reader places as possible (this was a time of expansion in student numbers) I left so little space around the perimeter of the room that readers had to squeeze their way around the walls to reach a seat, an elementary mistake which made me much more careful in library planning later in my career. Whether Reg Carr made any such mistakes I do not know, but I am sure that experience at Manchester set a good course for his career as for mine.

12.3 Traditional Career Paths

The key to a successful career at the time was to move from one large research library to another large research library, staying long enough in one position to make an impact upon library services but not so long as to become stale. The hierarchical structure of most academic libraries at the time allowed a progression from Assistant Librarian to Sub-Librarian to Deputy Librarian to Librarian, but competition for promotion was strong and acquiring the right experience on the way was vital. Computers were beginning to appear in libraries for functions such as borrowing records or cataloguing, so gaining experience in evaluating different automated systems and installing them became part of librarian's portfolio of expertise. There were also more mundane aspects of library automation to experience, as for example in the Brotherton Library at Leeds when the borrowing ticket reader jammed and had to be re-started with a gentle thump to the mechanism – a skill not taught at a school of librarianship.

12.4 The Librarian's Responsibilities

All of the experience gained in various academic libraries was preparing us (although we did not realize it at the time) for the big day when we would be appointed to our first post of "Librarian" (as a "Library Director" was called until the 1990s). Although accumulating experience on the way was vital in making a success of the responsibility of being in charge, nothing could prepare us for the awareness that "the buck stops here" when decisions were being made on the future of library services. No new library director is left short of advice from members of her or his staff on what changes should be made, and there is a general expectation that changes will be made. A "honeymoon period" generally allows time for a new library director to look and to listen, to form their own assessment of the situation, but the first two or three big decisions set the tone for the incumbency. It is very difficult to back-track or to change directions set in the first year in charge. In my first post as Librarian the priority was to introduce automation into the cataloguing system, and staff had to be persuaded to accept the OCLC system which was new to the UK at the time and which did not permit cataloguing to start until 3 p.m. because of the time difference with the United States. Risky though this decision may appear to have been, the OCLC cataloguing system is still used at the University of Essex (with normal working hours). In one sense earlier experience is preparation for such decisions, in learning what the priorities need to be, but in another sense nothing can prepare anybody for the responsibility.

Dealing with staffing issues also takes on a new dimension once "the buck stops here". An awareness of employment legislation becomes vital, again something for which a course at a school of librarianship is no preparation. The University of Essex had a tradition of student militancy which fed through into awareness of the rights of members of university staff. When discussing changes to the duties of one group of staff, they even asked for a student leader to be present at the discussions. I accepted that request but it illustrates the delicacy with which a library director has to handle staffing situations. Libraries are team organizations. Listening to work colleagues, meeting their legitimate concerns, and motivating the team to work together in the interests of library users is a vital feature of a successful library service. The librarian needs to able to find the right combination of openness, firmness and fairness in order to make a success of relationships with work colleagues. This aspect of being a librarian is not something to be learned from a textbook but is part of the person himself or herself.

A library director has to look and to listen to what is happening *outside* the library as much as to what is happening *inside* the library. Understanding what the institution's priorities are is vital for library development. A library director's diary is often full of meetings of university committees. The Library Committee is usually the formal body for determining library strategy, but a wise library director will already have picked up the right messages from conversations in the Senior Common Room. At times the messages may appear simplistic, such as "open the library for longer hours", and the library director may be tempted to reply with the problems, such as "security may be threatened". The maxim "don't bring me problems, bring me solutions" is, however, very important for a library director to bear in mind. At times academic colleagues do not understand the complexities of managing a large library, but their priorities are to be accepted and implemented if at all possible. In my experience the most difficult users to listen to are students. They may be represented on a library committee but librarians often lack the more informal contact with students they have with academic staff. For many library directors, meetings outside the university have always been vital in enabling internal issues to be placed in the context of national and international developments. It surprises some to know how frequently a library director may travel. Reg Carr's contribution to national and international librarianship through bodies like JISC, CURL and RLG has been huge.

12.5 Changing Roles?

In recent years the librarian's role at the Bodleian has been that of a fund-raiser, and this is a role which would not normally be thought of as the role of a librarian. The role does, however, have its roots in the fundamental rationale for libraries and for librarians. A library exists to meet the information needs of its users. In order to meet those needs, adequate funds are needed for buildings, for staff, for collections, and for equipment. A library director needs to be skilled in fund-raising whether those funds come from within the university or from donors outside. All library directors have to make a case for the library's budget, to persuade a university finance committee to allocate funds to the library when there are many other competing claims. Even when a library is funded adequately by a university, external funds are often needed to support special collections or special projects, for example when rare books are digitized to preserve the content. In the situation faced by a few libraries such as the Bodleian, external fund-raising acquires a higher priority than it would for an average university library, but fund-raising is a feature of modern librarianship.

Likewise today's librarians cannot ignore the importance of scholarly communication issues. The rise in journal prices well above inflation for many years has changed libraries' collection development policies, reducing the number of monographs purchased and concentrating journal purchasing into a small number of "big deals". The systemic problems of which high price rises are a symptom have to be a concern of the library community as well as of the wider academic community. It is not for a librarian to tell an academic author how to disseminate their work, but it is a legitimate role for a librarian to make an author aware of the consequences of decisions that an author makes, for example the consequences for library users of restrictions resulting when an author signs away all rights to a publisher. Reg Carr's time as Chair of JISC's Scholarly Communication Group has been a time of increasing awareness of the importance of such issues for the provision of information to university staff and students.

12.6 Conclusions

Weaving through all the new aspects of a librarian's role, the traditional threads of service to library users and being part of an academic community can still be recognized. A library is a service organization. Changes are happening in the way library services are provided – and even more radical changes are to come – but the service priorities my generation learned are still relevant. Likewise the awareness of being part of an academic community that was such a feature of library life in Manchester and other major universities is still vital if a good service is to be provided to a librarian's user community. Some of us may no longer be recognizable as librarians according to the public perception of what a librarian is and does, but however much our roles change we remain librarians at heart.

PART 5

New Dimensions of Information Provision: Restructuring, Innovation, and Integration

13

From Integration to Web Archiving

John Tuck

13.1 Introduction

The consumer review appendix of *Review for JISC of Core Resource Discovery Services* (Grayson and Gomersall, 2006, 52) shows that researchers want immediate and easy access to information.

> "Many potential users have extremely limited awareness of the bibliographic services that are available to them... Reliance on Google is widespread... Almost all users have very limited searching skills... Even when using Google, many have never got beyond entering a single term... Many users give up easily... Academic users tend to expect immediate access to any useful documents that they find".

This need for immediate information gratification was not the case when I first met Reg Carr in 1975. Googlization was far from my thoughts when, as a naive first-year research student, I entered the cataloguing room of the John Rylands University Library of Manchester, and asked to speak to the expert in French studies. This was Reg, who spent considerable time guiding me in the direction of relevant research tools for the study of French verse romances of the thirteenth century.

Three years later, this time in possession of a job as an assistant librarian, I walked into the same cataloguing room. Reg had moved on. I was able to build on his work in developing the collections and making them accessible to the next cohort of University of Manchester students of French, encouraging them in their early days of library catalogues and research. Tools of the trade at that time were not web browsers, pdfs or HTML but razor blades (used by assistant librarians to erase and allow corrections to be made to individual letters typed on to five- by three-inch catalogue cards), multilith masters and typewriter ribbons.

Twenty-eight years later, I was struck by an extract from a letter to the editor of the *Oxford Magazine* (Evans, 2006).

"The repeatedly-delayed Internal Audit *Report on the Library Depository Project at Osney Mead: Review of the Business Case* was made available on the internal web in August 2006, but no URL has been published in the *Gazette,* nor has the document itself. This does not really seem like reporting back to Congregation, as Congregation expected when it gave conditional permission for its land to be used for the new Depository under Statute XVI, A,4: "Recognizing the importance of the proposed book depository for the future delivery of library services in the University, and noting that there will be further reports to Congregation as later stages of the libraries' estates strategy are planned in detail, Congregation approves the allocation of the site at Osney Mead for the purpose of developing an automated depository for Oxford University Library Services." (http://www.ox. ac.uk/gazette/2005-6/weekly/220905/agen.htm#15Ref) (6 October 2005)".

Beautifully crafted letters of this type, frequently published in the *Oxford Magazine,* and often relating to library provision, reminded me of the four and three quarter years (from 1998 to 2002) I spent supporting Reg, as he guided Oxford libraries through the choppy waters to integration and the establishment of Oxford University Library Services (OULS) in February 2000. For a full account of integration and the process leading to it, see Moran (2005, 262–94).

During this eventful period, Reg taught me much more than a grasp of research tools for French studies. He conveyed the essential qualities of patience, perseverance, determination and resilience in the face of any challenge. French literature was never far away, however. In amongst the papers and reports on the desk of Bodley's Librarian were odd copies of *Cahiers Octave Mirbeau* and Reg Carr, *Anarchism in France: the case of Octave Mirbeau.* A year or two after leaving Oxford, I opened up a copy of *Sac au dos,* a short story by Mirbeau, which, through its title, took me back to an observation Reg made to me just before I left. "John, when you move on, you will put down one heavy rucksack, and pick up another". And this is what happened as I moved from integration at Oxford to web archiving at the British Library.

13.2 Web Archiving

Wikipedia (15 November 2006) states that:

"Web archiving is the process of collecting the Web or particular portions of the Web and ensuring the collection is preserved in an archive, such as an archive site, for future researchers, historians, and the public. Due to the massive size of the Web, web archivists typically employ web crawlers for automated collection. The largest web archiving organization is the Internet Archive which strives to maintain an archive of the entire Web. National libraries, national archives and various consortia of organizations are also involved in archiving culturally important Web content".

The history of web archiving in the British Library goes back to 2001 and a proof of concept pilot called domain.uk. Here an attempt was made to test the feasibility of harvesting a small number of UK websites (up to 100) on the basis of permissions having been granted by the website owners. The pilot proved successful and led to the establishment of a full web archiving programme, now firmly embedded in the British Library's strategy.

The Library's long-term vision for web archiving is that by 2016:

- there should be an extensive and accurate archive of the UK domain and the archive should be periodically augmented by further snapshots of the entire domain
- websites gathered automatically should be supplemented by more focused collection of areas of specific interest to the British Library
- the archive should form part of a much larger archive of the entire web
- the Library will work with partners throughout the world to ensure that researchers can access the world's web archives in a consistent and seamless way
- in accordance with legal deposit legislation, material gathered from the web should be stored and be accessible for future generations of researchers.

As a step in this direction the Library's current web archiving programme has three main strands: an underpinning collection development policy, work with the UK Web Archiving Consortium (UKWAC) and international developments managed through the International Internet Preservation Consortium (IIPC).

As a legal deposit library with a collecting remit for the UK, the British Library has a responsibility to acquire, preserve and make accessible the UK national published archive. Its British collections represent the collective memory of the nation by retaining for posterity the intellectual and creative output of British publishing. In addition to material acquired through legal deposit, the Library purchases and provides access to research-level material around the world and appropriate unpublished material in different formats. The collecting responsibility extends to UK non-print material, currently collected on a voluntary basis, but in the future to be covered by the provisions of the Legal Deposit Libraries Act 2003.

13.3 Web Archiving Policy

It is within this context that the British Library has defined its web archiving collection development policy which can be summarized as follows, and full details of which can be found at http://www.bl.uk/collections/britirish/britishandirish.html:

> "The British Library will collect sites selectively from the UK web space by prioritizing the archiving of sites of research value across the spectrum of knowledge. In addition, the Library will archive a selection of sites which are representative of British cultural heritage in all its diversity across the regions. It will also archive a small number of sites which demonstrate web innovation. Once effective methodology is determined, the Library will also adopt a comprehensive strategy by taking periodic snapshots of the entire UK web presence".

Included within the sites of cultural value category is a thematic strand where the focus is on collecting websites around key events of national life including topical events where there is likely to be frequent change of content and a significant risk of transient appearance on the web.

13.4 Challenges and Benefits

The complexity and scale of web archiving present challenges which need to be shared and worked through collaboratively. It is for this reason that UKWAC was established in October 2003. UKWAC comprises the British Library (lead partner), JISC (Joint Information Systems Committee), The National Archives, the National Library of Scotland, the National Library of Wales, and the Wellcome Library. It was set up with the objective of archiving and making accessible selected websites within the framework of a two-year pilot project and to share the costs and experiences of achieving that objective. These initial aims have been achieved and an open and freely accessible single portal to the web archive collections of the six partner institutions can now be accessed at www.webarchive.org.uk

The archive went live on 9 May 2005 and makes available more than 1600 different UK web sites, collected on a rights-cleared basis and all accessible free of charge to anyone on the web.

The content reflects the different collection development policies of the six partners and includes a number of thematic collections which reflect either events considered to be of topical importance or cultural significance. Among these are collections relating to the 2005 UK general election (93 sites), the 2004 Tsunami disaster (23 sites), the 7 July 2005 Terrorist attacks on London (49 sites) and sites relating to Women's issues (117 sites).

Some brief words about two of these collections help illustrate the different challenges and benefits which derive from collaborative working. Three UKWAC partners (the British Library, the National Library of Wales and the National Library of Scotland) were involved in collecting the 2005 UK General Election sites. The very brief window of opportunity for capturing sites during and shortly before the election campaign meant that only a representative sample could be archived. The challenge was to identify, evaluate and select sites as early as possible in the campaign to allow sufficient time to get obtain permission to archive and to gather the sites before they disappeared after the election. The labour-intensive nature of the permissions process resulted in a success rate of about 30% of the sample of 300 sites.

A further complexity was provided by the technical challenges facing the libraries. The web archiving teams had to put in place new procedures and workarounds as the high level of collaborative activity exposed some technical limitations of the PANDAS software which underpins the UKWAC web archiving system.

13.5 Joint Initiatives

The archiving of women's issues sites was a joint initiative between the British Library and the Women's Library, where the British Library took responsibility for the technical issues and the selection of sites was shared between the two libraries. The aim was a simple one: to create a new resource for future researchers and to ensure that valuable information currently on the web about women is not lost. The project started in autumn 2005 with the goal of archiving 100 relevant sites over a six-month period. Selection of sites was coordinated, each library focusing on particular categories such as: sites with research content, women's organizations and campaigns, personal sites of women, women's e-zines and blogs, etc. The permissions success rate was again low, approximately 30%, but by Spring 2006 the target of 100 sites had been reached. The sites are visited every six months and a further harvest made.

Work continues on other collection strands including Avian and pandemic influenza, the Olympics 2012 and Countryside issues. It is felt that the building up of collection-based resources will be particularly significant for researchers in the future, in particular in view of the ephemeral nature of much of the content gathered.

The work of UKWAC has demonstrated a low level of successful permissions to archive from website owners and has thereby raised real concerns about the viability and sustainability of web archiving on a voluntary rights-cleared basis. The percentage of permissions granted as a proportion of permissions sought ranges from just above 26% for the British Library, to approximately 39% for both the National Library of Wales and the National Library of Scotland, and 45% for the Wellcome Trust Library. Outright refusals have been less than 1%, the remainder comprising non responses.

13.6 Regulation

Some analysis has been carried out on why web sites may choose not to respond. This revealed the following possible factors: the legalistic nature of the permissions request, multiple and collective rightsholders of website material and the understandable reluctance to give clearance for third-party content on a site, the perception by rightsholders that their site may not be relevant or even worthy of archiving and a range of more administrative reasons such as requests sent to the wrong address as rightsholders are sometimes difficult to identify, lack of resource to respond, low priority given to the request, deletion of unfamiliar requests as spam, etc.

The situation demonstrates the need for early Regulation to enable secondary legislation to be put in place to allow legal deposit libraries to harvest relevant UK sites without having to seek permissions from website owners. The work on preparing for Regulations is being carried out by the Legal Deposit Advisory Panel, an advisory non-departmental public body set up to advise the Secretary of State on the necessary requirements and wording of Regulations which will make this possible. The Panel has been looking closely at the work of UKWAC and is fully aware of the labour-intensive nature of the permissions work and low returns as well as of the risk of loss of material on the web as sites edit, delete or revise their content. It is hoped that there will be a rapid path for Regulation, but even if this process is accelerated the statutory impact assessment and consultation processes suggest that it is unlikely that any secondary legislation will come into force before 2008.

13.7 National Web Archiving Strategy

UKWAC has laid the foundations of a national web archiving strategy and a shared technical infrastructure for the UK. As well as to continue the work of collecting and making available UK web sites, the pilot project has been extended to allow UKWAC to focus on two key areas of strategic development: the future coordination of UK web archiving at national level, taking into consideration the requirements of legal deposit legislation, and the evaluation and appraisal of software, platform and tools to ensure a future shared technical infrastructure for web archiving.

The technical development work is being carried out largely under the auspices of IIPC. (Current IIPC membership comprises: Bibliothèque nationale de France, National Library of Italy – Florence, Helsinki University Library – the National Library of Finland, Royal Library – National Library of Sweden, National and University Library – Iceland, Library and Archives Canada, National Library of Norway, National Library of Australia, the British Library and the Library of Congress.

13.8 Global Exchange and Collaboration

IIPC's stated mission is to preserve and make accessible knowledge and information from the internet for generations everywhere, promoting global exchange and international relations. More specifically its goals, as defined on http://www.netpreserve.org/ are

> "to enable the collection of a rich body of Internet content from around the world to be preserved in a way that it can be archived, secured and accessed over time; to foster the development and use of common tools, techniques and standards to enable the creation of international archives; to encourage and support national libraries everywhere to address Internet archiving and preservation"

It is within the context of the development and use of common tools, techniques and standards, that the British Library is involved in two important developments: the Web Curator Tool (WCT) and the automated smart crawler.

The WCT is a joint project undertaken by the National Library of New Zealand and the British Library. It is a tool for managing the selective web harvesting process and is designed for use in libraries by non-technical users, allowing them easily to capture web content for archival purposes. It was developed during the first half of 2006, tested, and then released at http://webcurator. sourceforge.net.

The WCT supports harvest authorization, i.e getting permission to harvest web material and make it available, selection, scoping and scheduling, description, downloading the material at the appropriate time with the Heritrix web harvester, quality review to ensure the harvest worked as expected and submitting the harvest results to a digital archive.

The WCT is not a digital archive, an access tool, a cataloguing system or a document management system. What it does is to manage the range of functions performed by the web archivist by providing a consistent managed approach. The tool is currently being tested within the British Library infrastructure and linked to an access tool. This work is being carried out as a precursor to the UKWAC evaluation of tools and software to replace the existing PANDAS software.

The need for greater automation of large-scale processes, linked to avoidance of duplication and redundant effort, lies behind the smart crawler tool project being undertaken by the British Library, the Library of Congress, the Bibliothèque nationale de France and the Internet Archive. A tool is needed that will be able to collect large numbers of websites (running into millions) and which can be set up in such a way that it can prioritize the collection of certain websites over others, according to an agreed collection policy. The scope of the project, to be led by the British Library, is the development of the Heritrix crawler to give it the ability to: recognize when resources have not changed since the previous crawl, prioritize the order in which resources are visited and gathered from the internet, recognize when resources on the internet are changing more frequently and visit and harvest those resources more frequently, perform testing to ensure that the new capabilities are scalable up to at least 100 million resources and ensure that the web archiving community can take advantage of the new capabilities. Currently at the shaping stage, the project is planed for completion in late 2008.

A third initiative in which the British Library is involved is the Automated Content Access Protocol (ACAP) pilot project led by Rightscom working with a number of international publishing bodies. The aim of the project, as defined by Rightscom, is to develop and implement a technical specification which will allow the publisher of a website or any piece of content to attach extra data, in a standardized form, to specify what uses of that piece of content or of the website are permissible. This may have particular relevance to web archiving by facilitating the means of identifying the eligibility of sites to be harvested through legal deposit. It has the added advantage of being a project where libraries, through the British Library, are working together with publishers to find an agreed technical solution to a rights management issue.

13.9 Further Issues

As these collaborative projects develop in the complex world of web archiving, the web continues to grow both in scale and technical sophistication. There are issues of territoriality to be resolved – how can the nature of the UK domain be determined from a legal deposit perspective? There are issues of size – how many UK web sites are there and how many will there be in five or ten years time? What resources, technical and financial, will be required to capture and preserve them for the future? There are a multitude of technical challenges which already make it difficult to collect certain types of web content, e.g. streaming media files, macromedia flash files, URLs controlled by JavaScript, etc.

In the words of Tim Berners-Lee, inventor of the world wide web, in the press release announcing the launch of the joint University of Southampton and MIT Web Science Research Initiative:

> "As the Web celebrates its first decade of widespread use, we still know surprisingly little about how it evolved, and we have only scratched the surface of what could be realized with deeper scientific investigation into its design, operation and impact on society".

Web archiving is a pretty heavy rucksack but it is full of interesting challenges of all types: scientific, technical, legal and operational. In his 2005 presentation to the Union League of Philadelphia (Carr, 2005), Reg Carr asks "But where do all the great libraries of the world fit into the new digital environment? Do they have a future at all?"

That they do is demonstrated by the growing cadre of library web archivists who are developing and sharing knowledge in order that researchers will have unbroken access to an almost unimaginable range and scale of web-based resources. Libraries and librarians will do more than archive the web. They will evolve to meet the changing needs of researchers of all types and they will continue to need leaders like Reg, flesh and blood people, who can manage change and who can guide the profession from Gutenberg to Google and beyond, sensitively and enthusiastically.

Acknowledgements

I would like to thank the following colleagues for their help in preparation of this paper: Stephen Green, Jennie Grimshaw, Alison Hill, Richard Price (British Library); Steve Knight, Gordon Paynter (National Library of New Zealand); Beverley Kemp (Women's Library).

Bibliography

British Library, http://www.bl.uk/collections/britirish/britishandirish.html [accessed 15 November 2006].

Carr, R. (1977) Anarchism in France: the case of Octave Mirbeau, Manchester University Press.

Carr, R. (2005) *From Gutenberg to Google: the Case of the Bodleian Library, Oxford*. Presentation to the Union League of Philadelphia, 18 October 2005. http://www.bodley.ox.ac.uk/librarian/gg2gg/gg2gg.htm [accessed 15 November 2006].

Evans, G. R. (2006) OULS again. *Oxford Magazine*, 256, 34–5.

Grayson, L. and Gomersall, A. (2006) Appendix 6 – consumer review. In *Review for JISC of Core Resource Discovery Services*: Archives Hub, Copac, SUNCAT and Zetoc, Clax, 52.

International Internet Preservation Consortium, http://www.netpreserve.org/ [accessed 15 November 2006].

Mirbeau, O. (2003) *Sac au dos, Mille et une nuits.*

Moran, B. B. (2005) Continuity and change: the integration of Oxford University's libraries. *The Library Quarterly,* **75**(3), 262–94.

Web curator tool: http://webcurator.sourceforge.net/ [accessed 15 November 2006].

UK Web Archiving Consortium, http://www.webarchive.org.uk/.

Web archiving, http://www.wikipedia.org/ [accessed 15 November 2006].

14

Not Just a Box of Books: From Repository to Service Innovator

Sarah E. Thomas and Carl A. Kroch

14.1 Introduction

A few years ago, a librarian at a major U.S. academic institution was drafting a charge for a university-wide task force that was, at the university librarian's request, examining the organizational structure of the library for potential efficiencies. Seeking to convey the complexity of the modern library, she described the role of the information professional as "knowledge manager." She was hesitant about using the phrase, suspecting that the academics who would be participating in the review might construe it as jargon. Nonetheless, in the search for something that was more expansive in capturing the breadth of services librarians provide and that got beyond the simple equation of the library with the management of physical objects, she succumbed. To her chagrin, the draft charge, reviewed by a distinguished dean, came back with the words "knowledge management" crossed out and neatly replaced by the following sentence: "The library acquires and stores books." She knew her road lay uphill.

The equation of libraries with books was underscored in the OCLC report Perceptions of Libraries and Information Resources (DeRosa, 2005) When asked to list two positive associations with the library, respondents in the OCLC survey most frequently named "Books" (18%), and when asked: "What is the first thing when you think about a library," approximately 70% named "books." Libraries have contributed to the sense that books define them by emphasizing their volume counts, with the clear implication being that the bigger the count, the more excellent the library. With the explosive growth of collections in the 1960s, library buildings constructed in the latter half of the 20th century often emphasized towers of books stacks as a defining feature. In a "damned if you do, damned if you don't" scenario, it sometimes seems that most library users think primarily of libraries as repositories for books and papers, while the larger public has already written off the warehouse function as obsolete, believing that the conversion of the world's published and printed knowledge by Google and others is more than a satisfactory substitute for libraries.

14.2 Box of Books

The massive structures of university libraries often reinforce the concept of the library as principally a "box of books." Carole Wedge, president of the centuries-old architectural firm Shepley Bulfinch, Richardson & Abbott, noted that most libraries were built as boxes to house print collections. At the same time she conceded that it was "unlikely there will be libraries without books for a long time." (Blumenthal, 2005) Large fortresses designed to hold millions of volumes efficiently, 20th-century libraries were dominated by their collections and the functions required to manage them. Thousands of square feet were dedicated to the card catalog, always located in a prominent space. Readers began their targeted searches here and made a virtue out of browsing because arcane rules and the limitations of the paper catalog so often frustrated their quest to find documents. An imperative for libraries was the adjacency of technical services staff to the card catalog, since they needed to be able to use and update this access tool to do their work. At the same time, their backroom labors were walled off from patrons, for whom the toil and expense of cataloging remained largely invisible. Circulation desks occupied the front lines, the first and last station encountered when entering and leaving the library, contributing to the idea of the library as an agent of control. The placement of library assistants or student workers at this initial point of contact often strengthened the impression of librarianship as a clerical occupation. These design features, as sensible as they were for their time, became liabilities in the Information Age. They tended to underscore a stereotypical and outdated view of libraries. Libraries were about storing and checking out books, and librarians were clerks and functionaries rather than professionals.

14.3 Information Access

At the same time this misperception of libraries was taking hold in the general public and even among some in the scholarly community, destabilizing changes were taking place in academic libraries. The increasing volume of titles published throughout the world and the rising cost of purchasing them made comprehensive collections unattainable. Many libraries, in response to economic pressures, shifted to promoting access to information over ownership of books, channeling resources first into interlibrary loans and increasingly, in to electronic collections. New technologies and digital resources made feasible a new concept of the library, one in which the physical library played an expanded role, in which storage options for books increased, and in which new services emerged to complement the expectations of the Internet society.

For a time, it was fashionable in the press to portray libraries as falling into a state of decline, with headlines such as "The Deserted Library" (Carlson, 2001) or "Choosing Quick Hits Over the Card Catalog," an article about students preferring the "chaos of the Web to the drudgery of the library." (Leibovich, 2000) Such reports reflected the transition of libraries from a largely book-dominated environment to one in which books were only one of many services, and where for some library clients, those other services ascended in importance.

In bricks and mortar libraries of the early 21st century, many changes are occurring. One of the most seismic is the transfer of millions of volumes to high-density, non-browsable storage facilities located at the perimeter of campus or at some distance from the university center. Approximately one-third of Harvard University Library's fifteen million volume collection, for example, is housed in the Harvard Depository Library. Major institutions are managing their collections differently, as central locations, with few exceptions, most notably the University of Chicago, can no longer accommodate growth. More commonly, libraries now separate high use material from low use, and they supplement access to remote materials by augmenting bibliographic records with table-of-contents data when feasible. New delivery models compensate for self-service or central library access. For example, at Cornell University, when a reader needs access to a chapter in a book or an article in a journal, library staff scan the portion of the document in question (always adhering to copyright regulations), and place the digitized version on a server, emailing the requestor that he can retrieve the item at his convenience. The ease and flexibility of this service have made it a preferred option for most library users, and have led to the introduction of similar services within on-campus libraries as a means of overcoming the fragmentation of collections in unit libraries in a world in which interdisciplinary and multi-disciplinary scholarship is increasingly the norm. The Johns Hopkins University, for instance, offers scan on demand to the desktop and the "Eisenhower Express" for delivery of items from the library to departmental offices. The University of Virginia supports LEO (Library Express On-Grounds), a library-subsidized, free-to-faculty service that delivers library materials to departmental mailboxes.

Such services reflect what user surveys and other reviews of contemporary information-seeking behavior routinely document. Hundreds of libraries in the United States and abroad have used the LibQual survey instrument to collect data on service quality and to identify gaps between user perceptions of desired quality of service and the quality of service they experience at their local institution. At Cornell three library surveys conducted over the past four years have guided the library in the development of its new services and in the allocation of its resources. Although those surveyed rated the Library's services highly, often quite close to their ideal, there is room to improve in several areas. LibQual respondents consistently indicated they wanted increased access to online resources, and that they wanted to be able to locate information on their own, rather than through an intermediary. Such results argue for allocating a greater proportion of the materials budget to electronic journals and databases and to investing more in improving web access so finding library resources, both collections and expertise, is more intuitive. Another question on the survey, about where users seek information, demonstrates the increasing reliance on the web. Respondents report that their daily use of Google or another such search engine is twice as frequent as their consultation of library web pages. Although faculty use of the physical library is modest and in decline, undergraduates and grad students continue to visit libraries regularly and they seek sanctuary for quiet reading and writing as well as places where they can work together and use computers.

The LibQual results reflect aspects of differing ways various generations approach scholarship. Joan Lippincott of the Coalition for Networked Information has written and spoken extensively on the "net generation" students and the ways in which library services can best serve them. Lippincott notes that the millennials, as the cohort born in 1982 has sometimes been called, are "digital natives," never having known a world without the Internet. The Net Generation is entirely comfortable with multimedia and has a strong visual and graphical orientation. They often learn by trial and error, like advancing through levels in video games, rather than by first mastering the instruction manual or reading the guide to the library. Highly social, they frequently work in groups, mix work and play, and multitask with ease. They are informal and seek comfort and convenience. Taking into account the characteristics of NetGen students, Lippincott recommends integrating library resources within Google or other popular Internet search engines, incorporating visual cues and elements into library online services, designing services for delivering information on mobile devices, and creating physical environments that support both solitary and team-based learning styles (Lippincott 2005).

14.4 Transformation of Libraries and Librarians

As a result of changes in society and the expectations of their user communities, libraries have transformed themselves from repositories for books, organized around library functions that are meaningful to the cognoscenti but obscure to most, to service-oriented organizations that integrate physical and virtual cultures. Library buildings are changing dramatically in their use, and consequently, in appearance. Although books remain a valued, vital, and substantial element of library service, increasingly the proportion of user, staff, and collection space in central facilities is shifting, with a larger share devoted to users. Among the many new features that are becoming standard are cafés, where students and faculty alike tarry and mingle, taking advantage of wireless access, comfortable seating, and the amenity of food and drink.

At Cornell the café replaced the periodicals reading room, a sunny but desolate corner room that had experienced sharply declining usage in the last decade of the 20th century. The popularity of the café, with over 1000 customers per day, resulted in sharply increased foot traffic into the main humanities and social sciences library. Not entirely coincidentally, the library experienced a surge of 16% in the circulation of books housed within its walls. Following a relocation of the media center to the same centrally located facility, use of DVDs and other media soared as well. A new, smaller, but equally visible periodicals room, created out of a staff workroom, holds a pared-down inventory of journals, a reduction made possible by the number of titles that can now be consulted electronically. In deference to the need for quiet space, and as a counterweight to the busy humming of the café, the new periodicals room was designated a lap-top free quiet zone. At the same time, its modern incarnation enjoys the same soft upholstered leather chairs that users invariably turn to face outward along a broad swath of window, enabling students to observe the steady stream of Cornellians passing on one of the university's most active pedestrian thoroughfares. Contemporary students prize "seeing and being seen" and the structured companionship of working alongside others.

New construction in academic libraries highlights the visibility of activity within libraries, often through the use of copious glass curtains which reveal what's going on inside to those passing by and which connects those within to the larger community. In contrast to the protective concrete fortresses that shaded books in the past, modern libraries reveal a beehive of activity, with readers, students at computers, and other intellectual pursuits serving as inviting models that draw others in. As students now tend to begin their workdays later than in preceding generations and as they continue their reading and writing until the wee hours of the morning, brightly illuminated libraries serve as beacons of warmth and security on what are often otherwise darkened central campuses. Libraries have accommodated the new student lifestyle with longer hours. At Cornell and many other academic libraries, at least one library building stays open 24 hours a day several days per week. The safety of students and the challenging of staffing late night hours have been addressed at Cornell by hiring security guards from a firm that normally contracts with museums to supply gallery attendants. The library trains these individuals to provide a firm but gentle adult presence. Other major libraries, such as Engineering and the humanities and social sciences library, remain open until 2 am when the university is in session.

One of the most highly desired services is online access to information. Library now routinely offer wireless connectivity, lockers where laptops may be secured housed and recharged, loaner laptops, and vast rooms filled with computers known as "Information Commons." At Indiana University the library and the University's Information Technology Services are partnering to provide enriched computer access in 35,000 square feet located in two central library locations. Indiana describes the Information Commons as "a place for students to interact, get technology support and research assistance, attend technology or research workshops or classes and work together in groups or individually on course assignments." (http://ic.indiana.edu/)

14.5 New Services

In addition to innovative use of their physical environments, libraries are developing a host of new services, often in concert with faculty or IT operations, to meet the demand of any time, any place information and assistance. Social networking software, blogs, chat reference, and other forms of Internet-based communication are becoming common means of supporting user needs. Reference librarians are using MySpace and Facebook to become part of the communities they serve and to engage students on the territory they inhabit. They establish mobile outposts with laptops and printers in residence halls and cafeterias, as evidenced by reports of research librarians at Duke University (Dougan, 2005). They produce podcasts and infiltrate writing seminars and other classes to teach information literacy.

At Cornell new services include support to help researchers migrate data from superseded technologies to current modes of information capture and the creation of Vivo (http://vivo.library.cornell.edu/) a virtual life sciences portal that connects researchers, laboratories, tools, and bibliographic information in a flexible gateway that unifies distributed and heretofore disconnected resources at a highly decentralized university. Plans are underway to extend the concept of Vivo to other parts of the Cornell community, including international studies and the social sciences.

The Digital Consulting and Production Service, known as DCAPS (http://dcaps.library.cornell.edu/), offers an array of assistance to clients, including faculty, graduate students, visiting researchers, and other institutions. To facilitate access to distributed expertise within the library and the university, the library has created a "one-stop shopping" approach that simplifies the effort of the client in getting a response to a question that often requires multiple inputs from organizations across the university. DCAPS staff will consult with individuals or teams writing grant proposals or planning projects that have digital imaging or data management components. They respond to inquiries relating to copyright and intellectual property, working in conjunction with the Counsel's office. They provide the expertise in digitization that enable faculty to create a library of e-clips of interviews with entrepreneurs or a database of epigraphy for classical scholars. As more of the research and teaching within the university has a digital component, they support data curation, archiving, and reuse, helping work rise from ephemeral to enduring and from individually-based to community-owned.

14.6 Collaboration

A growing area of support and collaboration for librarians lies in scholarly communication. Librarians disseminate information about authors' rights, developments in open access, public policies in the information arena, and the economics of scholarly communication. Many libraries now manage institutional repositories (IR) as a service that captures, preserves, and makes accessible the intellectual output of a college or university, and they are working actively with departments and colleges to populate these databases. At Cornell there are several initiatives to support open or economical access to scholarly findings. In addition to supporting college-based repositories, such as Digital Commons @ILR (output from the College of Industrial and Labor Relations) or DSPACE, the IR for the university, the Cornell University Library has reallocated over $300,000 annually to operate arXiv.org, the e-print server that holds over 400,000 articles in physics, computer science, mathematics, and quantitative biology. Hundreds of thousands of researchers around the world depend on the arXiv for up-to-date knowledge of new developments in their field.

The Cornell University Library also supports Project Euclid, a web service that hosts almost 50 journals in mathematics and statistics, including two of the top-ranked titles in math. The initiative was originally seeded and supported by The Andrew W. Mellon Foundation, but after five years has achieved sustainability, based on a business model that relies on publisher fees and user subscriptions to the online journals. Although not all content is free at the moment of first publication, about two-thirds of the articles in Project Euclid are available to all with an Internet connection without charge.

Software developed for Project Euclid has been generalized and extended by Cornell and the Pennsylvania State University Libraries with funding from the Mellon Foundation to support online content management of journals, conference proceedings, and monographs. This software, known as DPubS, or Digital Publishing System (http://dpubs.org/) is now available as an open source product through SourgeForge.net. One of the applications for the software is to facilitate joint ventures between university presses and libraries. At Penn state, for example, the library and the press are collaborating on making available several online journals relating to the history of Pennsylvania and they have plans to develop support for other disciplines such as Romance Studies and nutrition.

Such activities require a close connection with disciplinary experts and with other entities, such as publishers, computer scientists, or information technologists. Librarians are increasingly active in reaching out to others than they have been in the past, when their central role was to build, organize, manage, and preserve physical collections for primarily local and captive audiences. Today's users are diverse and distributed, and as a result, libraries are transforming into highly interactive collaborative organizations. They use technology to integrate physical and virtual collections and services and to provide an expanding suite of convenient, customizable, and personalized information tools and products. Library facilities reflect the trend in universities and in society to cater to a variety of learning styles, and they are more frequently facilitating partnerships and collaboration by multiple academic entities, such as university presses, IT organizations, faculty, and researchers. In response to societal changes that tend to blur the distinction between work and intellectual activities, they accommodate aspects of both in their buildings. Their focus on the user and on tailoring their information products to the user's preference stands in marked contrast to an earlier, more library-centric era. And, with users choosing to consult alternative information resources such as Google, libraries are responding to the pressure of competition. They are quickening the pace of change, becoming more experimental, federating resources with other institutions to offer a stronger, more comprehensive product, and marketing their services more aggressively and in a manner that seeks to differentiate them as specialized and uniquely valuable for their defined communities.

14.7 Innovation in Services

Increasingly, the message that the library is more than a box of books is pene-trating our desired audience. As evidence of success in redefining the library as rich and relevant set of services, much more than a repository, one academic librarian recently received a call from an Ivy League swim coach. He had seen posters advertising the library inserted in the campus newspaper, and he was asking for copies to enclose in packets designed to entice recruits to select the university as their first choice. Headed "How to survive and thrive...," the poster prominently referenced the library's web site, and boldly highlighted conducive study space, all-night hours, world-class collections, caffeine, the "plugged-in" environment, help, in-library readers for writing assistance, and the library's role as a gathering place. No word yet on how many swimmers signed up, but it's certain that the image and the substance of academic libraries today is positive as libraries innovate to provide students and scholar with the information and service they need to learn and to advance knowledge.

References

Blumenthal, R. (2005) College Libraries Set Aside Books in a Digital Age. *New York Times*, 14 May. http://www.nytimes.com/2005/05/14/education/14library. html?ex=1273723200&en=594e613ac6e9a350&ei=5088 (accessed 1 January 2007).

Carlson, S. (2001) The deserted library. *The Chronicle of Higher Education*, 16 November. http:// chronicle.com/free/v48/i12/12a03501.htm (accessed 1 January 2007).

DeRosa, C. *et al.* (2005) *Perceptions of Libraries and Information Resources.* OCLC Computer Library Center, Inc.

Dougan, K. *et al.* (2005) Creating community: Duke's East Campus libraries reach out to first-year students. *Duke Library Magazine*, Spring 2005. http://magazine.lib.duke.edu/issue17/ feature1.html, (accessed 31 December 2006).

Leibovich, L. (2000) Choosing quick hits over the card catalog. *New York Times*, 10 August, p. 1.

Lippincott, J. K. (2005) Net generation students and libraries. In *Educating the Net Generation* (eds. D. G. Oblinger and J. L. Oblinger), EDUCAUSE. http://www.educause.edu/ir/ library/pdf/ERM0523.pdf (accessed 1 January 2007).

15

Learning Enhancement through Strategic Project Partnership

Mary Heaney

15.1 Introduction

In 1996, the University of Wolverhampton appointed a Director of Learning Centres to lead the development of its library into a dynamic learning support service offering a range of environments for self-directed and peer group learning and to enhance the information environment supporting a community of 23,000 students and over 2,500 staff in the UK and overseas.

The process involved a hearts and minds change of expectations among academic staff about the contribution to expect from librarians and learning support staff in curriculum development, planning, validation and review and the development of both physical and e-learning environments. It involved investment in and re-skilling of staff, particularly in the areas of IT and media support, and incorporating learning skills development staff into the service. Staff achievement in the change agenda can be observed from the level of use of the campus-based centres and the associated "learn anywhere, work anywhere" services, on and off-campus, physically and virtually, by students and staff.

The University is a former polytechnic situated in the English West Midlands in an area of historically low aspiration and attainment at the compulsory educational level. Within this context the institutional priority is to enable and encourage individuals to realize their full potential and to achieve academic excellence through a flexible, innovative and vocationally focused curriculum.

A significant element in the development of the service over the past 6 years has been a range of activities nested with the institutional Learning and Teaching Strategy.

The 1999–2002 Learning and Teaching Strategy prioritized "Growing a learning community". It focused on supporting the development of a population of knowledgeable staff who act as champions for improvement in the quality of student learning.

To support this priority, staff from academic schools and learner-focused services were invited to submit proposals for innovation and research projects aimed at improving student learning. The criteria for proposals, and associated evaluation strategies, were set by an institutional working group. Proposals from the learning centres were reviewed and endorsed by the centres' Learning and Teaching Group. In autumn 2000, funding was allocated to 2 learning centre staff to conduct separate yet related projects in the area of information skills development.

15.2 Information Skills Development Projects

The first project (Ordidge, 2001) examined the impact of desktop IT on the empowerment of learners through information skills teaching. It evaluated Wolverhampton practice against national and international information skills models. Within the institution, it examined practice between liaison librarians working with different academic schools, and in some cases involving focused partnership with academic colleagues. In one school, information skills development was becoming embedded in the VLE (virtual learning environment) and the module had become a compulsory element of the course. As a result of the review of external practice the seven headline skills developed by the SCONUL Advisory Committee on Information Literacy (SCONUL, 1999) were adopted as the future model for Wolverhampton. The SCONUL recommendation for collaboration across academic, library and staff development colleagues was closely aligned to the agenda supported by the profile of the project as part of the Learning and Teaching Strategy. The project led to a West Midlands conference supported by the Universities Colleges and Research Group of the then Library Association on the theme of information skills in a virtual environment.

A second project (Pritchard, 2001), started from the premise that, while information skills sessions were thought to be "a good thing" by students and academic staff, there was little evidence in professional literature at that time of formal evaluation being used to gauge the impact and worth of such sessions. The project was based on 3 groups of students across different academic schools, initially offering them standard information skills sessions supported by pre- and post-session questionnaires, and followed through in a student focus group and interviews with module tutors.

A significant increase in confidence across all 3 groups was noted in the analysis of the post-session questionnaire responses. The focus group looked at most and least useful elements of the sessions and what skills participants had subsequently applied. Feedback from the focus group highlighted variations according to subject area. Discussion with module tutors focussed on the longer-term impact of the sessions on the quality of assignments submitted. This resulted in identification of significant improvements among students who had attended the sessions as compared with those who had not. The findings of this project which investigated 3 subject areas influenced the design and delivery of subsequent sessions more widely across the learning centres.

15.3 Learning and Teaching Strategy

The 2002–2005 Learning and Teaching Strategy focused on "Managing the learning environment", to develop its quality, relevance, efficiency and effectiveness so as to enhance the educational experience. Three priorities were identified:

- Staff: to develop the intellectually responsive learning community
- Students: to develop the independent learner
- Technology-supported learning: to develop the interactive learning environment.

These priorities were conceptualized within the context of 3 major strategic themes of the Higher Education Funding Council for England (HEFCE):

- Increasing and widening participation
- Enhancing excellence in teaching and learning
- Enhancing research excellence.

To enable the achievement of this iteration of the strategy, coordination support was enhanced. The nominated Learning and Teaching Coordinators were joined by 2 colleagues in each academic school and learning support service area by a Student Support Coordinator and a Technology-Supported Learning Coordinator. In learning support areas, these roles were and continue to be held as part of a portfolio by staff with other duties.

Over the course of the 2002–2005 strategy, the learning centres were allocated resources to enable staff to deliver seven further learning and teaching projects.

The Special Educational Needs and Disability Act 2001 lent a focus for a project (Pritchard, 2002) on learning centre provision for dyslexic learners, who form a significant part of the local student population. An initial challenge for this project was to attract volunteers to participate. Consequently, a smaller than anticipated group contributed to the findings. Members of the focus group were asked to provide feedback on general services and facilities, on learning centre guides and publications, and on visual elements from skills workshops. Issues of concern for this group of learners included difficulties with classification numbers, colour and fonts, and the amount of text used in signage. In addition, colour preferences to enhance legibility of print and screen-based external and internal publications were noted. The outcome of this research has informed a range of developments and raised awareness of the impact of service design on dyslexic learners.

15.4 Managing the Learning Environment

Academic year 2002–3 saw three projects focused on the strategic theme of "Managing the learning environment".

The first (Dalziel et al., 2003) investigated student use of non-university owned PCs. The project aimed to assist in determining priorities for university investment in IT support and infrastructure, in the context of the institutional strategy for technology-supported learning. A questionnaire was used to gather information. The results, based on a relatively small response from the total student population, had to be considered with some caution. Respondents indicated a desire for accessing the university's information and IT services from home, although it is clear that at that stage in the development of e-licences there were constraints on the availability of e-resources off campus. It is interesting to note that a laptop loan service, first trialled in 2001–2, continues to be a highly popular element of the learning centre service to this day.

The 2nd project in 2002–3 (Granger, 2003) proposed the development of an active learning guide for the largest learning centre which receives an average 600,000 visits per annum. This initiative built on a pilot with a group of Computing and IT students and research from other HEIs (higher education institutions) on the development of active and cooperative learning environments. A DIY (Do It Yourself) guide was developed to enable all new students to orientate themselves at a time and pace appropriate to their preferences and learning styles, and to enable them to test their new found knowledge in a supportive environment. The guide sat alongside personal contact with liaison librarians during the "welcome" period. The compulsory nature of the original pilot had been found important and 3 additional academic schools supported the rollout and provided evaluative feedback.

The project team developed the guide in association with the university's Design Team. The finished product included a building walk through section supported by signage in the building itself. This was complemented by a "Learning Centre Challenge" section consisting of 6 activities. Students were observed to be actively engaged by these exercises, working in pairs or small groups. Staff reported an increase in direct OPAC use by students, fewer basic OPAC queries and a large increase in auto service loan uptake, evidencing the early development of a level of independence among the participating students.

A complementary project (Ordidge et al., 2003) took as its starting point some findings from the Independent Learner Profile, a university-wide survey conducted in 2001 with all new students. The survey showed that 89% of new students expressed confidence about "using libraries" in general. However only 52% indicated confidence when using library catalogues and collections. The project team reviewed OPAC support materials, both print and online, in different HEIs. Much of the guidance material was found to have been written from a distinctly service provider perspective.

The outcomes from this project were four new brief guides, each with a different student-friendly focus, which emphasized the empowerment facilities offered by the OPAC. The themes were: avoiding fines, finding/reserving material, tracking material in different formats, and access 24/7. Textual content was kept to a minimum. The guides were trialled with a small cohort of students in the largest centre and subsequently released to all 8 centres. Shelvers were asked to offer them to students observed to be needing assistance among the collections. A follow-up survey 2 months later demonstrated a high level of understanding of the guide content and confidence in finding and reserving material and in use of online borrowing services. As well as enhancing the capability of students, the project enabled smarter working for staff and freed them to focus on areas of particular need. The research stimulated the development of a further small suite of self-help guides related to reading lists, IT facilities and access for visitors.

In academic year 2003–4, two further projects were initiated as part of the "Managing the learning environment" strategy theme.

The first (Thompson *et al.*, 2004) examined how business school students use reading lists to inform their information resource selections. It was noted that previous research into reading lists had focused on operational access and collection development aspects. A questionnaire was administered to business school undergraduate and masters level students during formal teaching sessions. To augment the findings from the questionnaire, a citation analysis of anonymized sample assignments for selected modules was undertaken that compared bibliographies with reading lists for the related modules. The sample was based on modules undertaken by students who completed the questionnaire.

Summary findings from this research perhaps unsurprisingly showed that students attach more importance to reading lists as they move though from undergraduate to master's level and thankfully confirmed that they consult reading lists when selecting resources to complete assignments. Opinions were sought about the preferred reading list format. Findings on this issue were inconclusive, other than a clear indication that an A–Z format by author was unpopular.

The project highlighted areas for improvement, particularly in the quality of referencing and students' awareness of its importance. It brought to the fore issues about students' understanding of the need to select quality information resources rather than the most accessible information on the web. The outcomes were used to inform conversations with academic staff about subsequent list production, decisions about collection balance and development, referencing skills development and guides to the OPAC reading lists function.

The 2nd project (Bunford 2004) examined how students made use of IT in the largest learning centre and the impact of physical layout on the way IT is used. The purpose of the project was to assist prioritization of support for and development of the IT infrastructure. Over a period on 1 month, patterns of use across the day, night (to 0300h) and weekend were monitored along with observation of the type of IT activity being engaged in by students. Discernible differences were observed between younger and more mature students in terms of social activity, both virtual and real, and tolerance for noise from peers. At weekends, the balance of usage during the survey period tended more towards social and leisure purposes. A considerable amount of multi-tasking was evident – talking to peers, emailing, working on assignments and using chat facilities simultaneously. There appeared to be little demarcation between work and leisure. The period around the survey coincided with a significant increase in registrations by students to use wireless IT. This was expected to blur the boundaries between activities yet further. The project, and the now ubiquitous availability of wireless access across campuses, resulted in major changes to the layout of IT facilities, the creation of quiet IT zones within the area of general provision, as well as special facilities for post-graduates.

15.5 Developing a Virtual Tour

Academic year 2004–5 saw a project which complemented the DIY guide and assisted further with the orientation requirements of new students into the learning centre physical environment and associated services. The project (Hammerton and Granger, 2005) focused on developing a virtual tour of the largest centre and its resources. Multiple navigation options were enhanced with new media web features including simulations and animations to enable students to enter an interactive learning experience, either on an individual basis, or as part of a more formal element in an induction programme. This approach was expected to bring benefits to students with mobility problems, to international students who might initially be struggling with text based information and to distance learning students and those based in partner colleges. The approach was perceived to be attractive to younger students for whom the virtual environment is a known comfort zone.

The project team designed a range of user profiles to generate ideas about how different students would use the tour. Research was conducted into existing web-based tours of similar environments in the USA to assist in the design of the resource. The support of students of Interior Architectural design was sought for the development of 3D graphical representations of the centre. A self-test customizable to the degree programme an individual student was following was built into the guide.

The prototype was road-tested with a small group of students and colleagues. Both quantitative results from the self-test and verbal feedback were used to improve the interface design. Accessibility for students with special needs was tested in three sessions. One covered colour vision deficiency, one involved using the site without a mouse, and the 3rd involved using JAWS screen reader software to test the site for users with severe visual impairment. Future areas for development under consideration include customization of the formative assessment exercise for students in their 2nd and 3rd years of study, and the translation of textual information into languages other than English to support international student induction.

15.6 Enhancing the Student Experience

The 2006–2010 Learning and Teaching Strategy aims to embed the strengths of the previous strategy's focus on managing the learning environment within the mainstream operation of the University, and with an overall priority of "Enhancing the student learning experience". This iteration of the strategy builds on the award in 2004 to the University of the status of Centre for Excellence in Teaching and Learning" (CETL) under the HEFCE initiative of the same title[1]. The initiative aims to reward excellent teaching practice and to invest further in that practice so that CETLs deliver substantial benefits to students, teachers and institutions. The current strategy has 2 strategic priorities:

- To enable all our diverse students to deepen knowledge and understanding, and develop skills and personal attributes which will enrich their lives and enhance their achievement and employability
- To enable our staff to develop their learning and teaching expertise in order to enhance the student learning experience.

Supported by this current phase of the Learning and Teaching Strategy, the learning centres are embarking on an extensive virtual reference project "Assist". The overarching aim is to create a new service model for information literacy development using virtual reference software[2] in both synchronous and asynchronous modes. The project is a logical enhancement of a pre-existing "Ask a librarian" asynchronous email service. The expected benefits of the project over the period 2006–2008 include enhanced support for students and staff who chose to work off campus, and the potential to engage and to improve the learning experience of students who may prefer the anonymity of a virtual service.

This very current project is grappling with issues of balance between quality dialogue and "canned" answers to FAQs, managing the demand for telephone and "chatroom" support offered by staff supporting the "extended hours" sections of the service week, and various issues of chat etiquette including the concern to ensure that the "chat" is friendly yet purposeful. The project team is establishing a resource base within the University's Virtual Learning Environment (VLE) to support staff across the centres who are involved in the development, which was formally launched in January 2007 after a trial period in autumn 2006.

A 2nd current project, this one spanning academic year 2006–7, focuses on evaluation and embedding work on structured information literacy (IL) within the humanities, languages and social sciences. It involves forums within the VLE incorporating quizzes and online tests in a number of subject areas, systematic testing of students to evaluate their use of IL skills and the benefits perceived by

---

1   http://www.hefce.ac.uk/learning/TInits/cetl/
2   Questionpoint software

academic colleagues of student skills development in this area. The project seeks to analyse the learning effectiveness of different approaches including varying the numbers of sessions, sessions delivered to students from different backgrounds e.g. home and international.

This series of 11 projects over the period 2000 to date has enabled a range of staff in the learning centres of the University – librarians, learning technologists and other learning support colleagues – to work in influential partnership with academic staff and students. The overarching agenda has been one of embedding work to enhance the quality, relevance, effectiveness and efficiency of the learning environment into the mainstream processes and procedures of the institution, so as to enhance the lives, the educational experience and the employability of students. In the past 3 years, 6 learning centre staff have been awarded the university's post-graduate qualification in learning and teaching in HE which has enabled them formally to articulate the relationship between current theory and research and the practical context in which they work.

15.7 Conclusion

In conclusion, participation in these projects has enhanced the quality of the direct contribution learning centre staff make to achieving the University's strategic goals in relation to learning and teaching, as well as the nature of their membership of teaching teams and their contribution to curriculum and organizational development.

References

Note: the Learning and Teaching project reports are available on the University of Wolverhampton's Institutional Repository.

Bunford, N. (2004) What do they do with IT? In *Learning and Teaching Projects 2003/04*. University of Wolverhampton. http://hdl.handle.net/2436/3695

Dalziel, C., Oddy, E. and Bernardes, J. (2003) Investigation into student use of non-university owned computers. In *Learning and Teaching Projects 2002/03*. University of Wolverhampton. http://hdl.handle.net/2436/5233

Granger, J. (2003) DIY Induction: developing an active learning programme in the Harrison Learning Centre. In *Learning and Teaching Projects 2002/03*. University of Wolverhampton. http://hdl.handle.net/2436/5261

Hammerton, M. and Granger, J. (2005) A Virtual "Hello" for the Harrison Learning Centre – a web-based orientation concept. In *Learning and Teaching Projects 2004/05*. University of Wolverhampton. http://hdl.handle.net/2436/3304

Ordidge, I. (2001) Developing the Information Skills Agenda. In *Learning and Teaching Projects 2000/01*. University of Wolverhampton. http://hdl.handle.net/2436/6120

Ordidge, I. *et al.* (2003) Catalogue Shopping: the power of the OPAC. In *Learning and Teaching Projects 2002/03*. University of Wolverhampton. http://hdl.handle.net/2436/5237

Pritchard, O. (2001) The Impact of Information Skills Training on Student Learning: do we make a difference? In *Learning and Teaching Projects 2000/01*. University of Wolverhampton. http://hdl.handle.net/2436/6319

Pritchard, O. (2002) Dyslexic Learners and Learning Centre Provision: could do better? In *Learning and Teaching Projects 2001/02*. University of Wolverhampton. http://hdl.handle.net/2436/3793

SCONUL (1999) Briefing Paper: Information Skills in Higher Education. http://www.sconul.ac.uk/groups/information_literacy/papers/Seven_pillars2.pdf

Thompson, L., Mahon, C. and Thomas, L. (2004) Reading Lists: how do you eat yours? In *Learning and Teaching Projects 2003/04*. University of Wolverhampton. http://hdl.handle.net/2436/3693

16

Libraries for the 21st Century

Les Watson

16.1 The Level of Investment in Educational Buildings

Expenditure on educational buildings in these early years of the 21st century is unprecedented. For example the capital investment in school building in England in 1997 was £700 million. For each of the ten years from 2005 there will be £5.9 billion provided by the Building Schools for the Future (BSF) programme which aims to rebuild or refurbish every secondary school in England. BSF is the single biggest government investment in improving UK school buildings for over 50 years. But it is not only in schools that there are such high levels of investment, Universities in England, now in receipt of tuition fees, have increased access to capital, and those in Scotland have special funding for estates development. We are at the start of fantastic activity in new building across the education sector that will last for 10 to 15 years at least and provide an opportunity to "rebuild" our whole education system. The question is what can new buildings deliver in terms of learning futures? And more importantly what might the role of the Library be in this rebuilt future? The BSF programme focuses, quite correctly in my view, on transformation, and on environments that will inspire learners.

> "School (and University) buildings should inspire learning. They should nurture every pupil and member of staff. They should be a source of pride and a practical resource for the community."

(Building Schools for the Future: consultation on a new approach to capital investment 2003; *my italics*)

16.2 Beyond Buildings

For these new buildings to deliver on inspiration, practicality, community building and the nurturing of individuals BSF, and indeed any educational building programme, must be about more than just the buildings themselves. The BSF programme does also involve significant investment in ICT (Information and Communications Technology) and in staff development, seeking to promote a step-change in the quality of secondary school provision. The strategy for Learning Services at Glasgow Caledonian University, home of the Saltire Centre, since 2001 has also taken this approach by focusing on buildings as part of a tripartite approach to strategy along a focus on people and technology. The development of the Saltire Centre was accompanied by changes in staffing structures and the deployment of a range of technology services. The usual structures of University library service, IT service and student services were integrated into a single University Learning Service, new technologies such as wireless networking and self service online access providing information and support combine with the Saltire Centre building itself in an holistic approach to the delivery of the student experience. This strategy, which I call Synergy as it exploits the synergies between people, ICT, and the environment, is a powerful driver of change in which the sum is greater than the parts.

16.3 So Much for Strategy. What about Vision?

Strategy is the how of management but is useless unless there is a what and a why encapsulated in vision and purpose. But vision, looking into the future, presents an enormous dilemma. Innovative new buildings, the physical output of vision, do not spring fully formed from the heads of architects or their clients but are the product of a lengthy process that brings together the life experiences of all those involved in the planning process. They are also the product of our hopes beliefs and aspirations and need to be future focused. Innovative libraries are no different. Part of the dilemma is that we work in an HE sector that demands certainty in its decision making. The need to know permeates our planning – and knowing at the outset, before projects start and money is committed, is the preferred position. However the future, as we have so often witnessed in retrospect, is not known. And our ability to make our hopes and aspirations real is risky business. The rate of technological change alone is so great as to cause enormous uncertainty in our planning. Given that the life of a building project is around 3 to 4 years, with all the preparation that is needed, it's not surprising that remarkable things can happen on the journey. My first involvement with planning a "learning centre" in the 1990s was during the period of early growth of network connectivity and the rise and rise of digital information. The graph we drew then that illustrated the disappearance of paper-based information – estimated to happen around 2005 – looks totally misguided in 2007 with many library collections continuing to grow. And now in 2007 we now have radically different agenda that demands a more fundamental review of the role of the higher education library.

How will students and staff learn in the future? How will they use emerging technologies? What new technologies will there be? If we do know what learning will be like in the future (and I don't think we do) then how can we ensure that our buildings, including our libraries, do not limit the possibilities for learning? And how can we ensure that our libraries remain central to our institutions? It is impossible to know the answers to these questions –we can make informed judgements based on what we detect in the environment around us. But is this enough? It is without doubt that educational purpose should drive educational building projects, including libraries. I am also convinced that the library should be absolutely central to our learning vision. If we really do wish to develop a nation of self-motivated, self-actualized individuals then we must provide the places for developing the independent learning skills required. We intuitively know that our real learning is personal – we have to do it ourselves. An important, possibly the most important, part of our learning is that which goes on outside the classroom. It is personal "practice" that makes us successful independent learners. This personal learning does and should go on in the learning spaces in our libraries and learning centres. The University library that is not central to the learning lives of its students has enormous unrealized potential. And this central role of the library as the venue for the learner cannot be left to chance – it must be nurtured in the design of our library buildings. In the past it is library operations and not educational purpose that has driven new building design as Bennett (2005 p.11) notes:

> "The knowledge base that guides library space planning is poorly balanced, tilted heavily toward library operations and away from systematic knowledge of how students learn."

And he goes on to state that (p.23) "There is no paradigm for the library of the future because we have not yet brought what we know of student learning to bear on library design". Bennett believes that "It is by realigning libraries with institutional missions that the paradigm for the future will be found". This aligns with thinking from a different perspective taken by the Joint Information Systems Committee in their publication (2006) on spaces for effective learning in which they contend that the design of our learning spaces should be a physical representation of the institutional vision and strategy for learning. I believe that there is a potential shift here of the library from the periphery of learning to the centre of learning. This is not to say that library operations can be ignored. It is clear that any visionary new library must be fit for purpose from the day it opens – but being fit for the purpose of library operations is only part of the story. It is far more important that any new library must be fit for the unknown needs of future learners.

16.4 Embracing Uncertainty

This brings us to the real dilemma in planning innovative new buildings. We are expert at how things are today but, as mentioned above, predicting the future is always risky, the only certainty is that we don't know what it will be like. Not only is the future unknowable but we also know, as Christensen (1997) tells us that our innovations often initially perform less well than current products. This applies to innovative new buildings too. However, if we base our planning and decisions on available evidence it's unlikely that we will ever produce anything new – but decisions based on an unknown future may not measure up to current expectations. As Brand (1994) points out – all buildings are predictions – they are new formulations of our ideas, but he goes on to note that all predictions are wrong. Amidst such uncertainty we have to be prepared to take some risks – and we have to be prepared to be wrong. Sir Ken Robinson highlights that we, as adults, seem to have grown to be risk averse when in his TED talk he tells of the 6 year-old girl at the back of the class who is deeply engaged in her drawing task. This is unusual for her – more often she is not interested in the work set in class and certainly not an achiever. The teacher, intrigued by this uncharacteristic concentration, asks the girl what she is drawing. The girl replies that she is drawing a picture of god. The teacher points out to the girl that no one knows what god looks like. The girl's response – "They will in a minute" – demonstrates the confidence that children have, their willingness to take risk and their lack of any fear of being wrong. As adults we are conditioned to avoid being wrong at all costs and this negatively affects our willingness to take risks. But take risks we must. Forensic examination of data about the past, the major part of most planning strategies, will not, in my view, produce innovative solutions for the future, or help us make decisions in areas where we don't know answers. This is not to say that the past is irrelevant to our planning. It teaches us some broad lessons that, along with the weak signals in the current environment, can provide direction. However as Stilgoe (2007) points out in his article entitled "Three words we should like to hear: 'I don't know'":

> ....evidence based language mutes the voice of the expert. It accentuates the positive – what we know – and often becomes a way of justifying decisions rather than making them. The temptation for civil servants and politicians is to look past the uncertain expert to the comfortable certainties.

This denial of uncertainty is not restricted to civil servants and politicians but permeates managements. In my view it is our beliefs and values and our "vision" of what we are trying to achieve that should provide the real driver for creating new futures. We have to imagine the learning futures that we wish to create – and be prepared to be wrong. Such imaginings form the basis of a Creative World View approach to visioning proposed by George Land and Beth Jarman (1993) which they describe concisely in the following way: "....the reference point is the future, not the past. We don't need to fall back on the past for our decisions. Choices are based on alignment with our purpose and our vision for a different world."

Having a clear vision and purpose is a powerful driver and prerequisite for any educational building project aiming to innovate.

16.5 The Saltire Centre

The vision for the Saltire Centre started with imagination:

> Imagine... a world in which everyone achieves their full educational potential, where academic and vocational achievement has equal value, and where experiential learning enables everyone to continually develop their knowledge and skills throughout their life.

This is a vision that is about an education system that provides continued equality of opportunity and that values the widest possible range of achievement across academic, professional, vocational and craft activity. It is a vision that is also described, in a different way, in the following paragraph that formed part of the initial paper proposing a new building that was submitted to the University in August 2000:

> The primary aim of a Learning Centre is to support people in the process of learning. This support is extended to learners in their individual endeavours, and to the institution in its development of approaches to learning. What is being proposed for Glasgow Caledonian University is therefore **not** a new Library, **not** a Learning Resource(s) Centre, but a Learning Centre.
> Les Watson 20/8/00

In essence this short paragraph suggested to the University that we build a building that is about the process of learning and, as noted by Bennet (2005) above, one that does not focus primarily on library operations. The intention was always to provide the full range of library services and operations – but one key difference in the Saltire Centre is that it puts learning first. A second key difference is that the building is also a place for delivery of all services for students making it the physical and service heart to City Campus.

16.6 And What Sort of Learning Will it Support?

I mention above the personal nature of learning and the importance of what happens outside the classroom to enable the development of the independent lifelong learner. The Saltire Centre provides a wide range of different spaces that aim to appeal to the widest variety of learner needs. At the heart of this provision is conversational learning (see (iv) below).

16.7 A Note on ICT

It is my view that there are issues of the "personal" extending to the use of ICT. A future beckons with universal ownership of ICT in the form of some form client device that can support our activities as learners. A device that will allow us to store, edit, think, and learn. As the power of ICT advances so this possibility comes closer taking us from the dull mass access to ICT that we practice today. The result of our current approach is that in our Universities for most of the 20th Century the personal computer has been anything but personal. The investment in "labs" and libraries with row after row of workstations bookable for some arbitrary slice of time by transient users does not allow the PC to become central, embedded and natural to the learning lives of our students. Those with a deep understanding of the technology know the necessity of continuous and continued access to "their" resources on "their" machine. Just as learning is now being recognized as personal and personalized I believe that ICT should also be. The major investments in ICT in the Saltire Centre, there is more information below in (viii) on this, have been in infrastructure in the wired and wireless networks, in the IP telephony, and in the use of radio frequency identification tagging of resources. As the ownership of client devices by students expands the building, having robust infrastructure, can respond.

16.8 The Key Influences and Themes in the Building

Above I have described something of the context in which the Saltire Centre was developed. Below there is detail of the key themes that emerged during the planning and design of the building. There are many influences on any building project as the project and related conversations with interested parties take place. Sitting behind this detail is the thought expressed by Freeman (2005 p.2):

> Significantly, the library must serve as the principal building on campus where one can truly **experience** and **benefit** from the **centrality** of an institution's **intellectual community.**

Some of the key themes in respect of the type of provision, students and their learning, technologies, and design that shaped the Saltire Centre were:

(i)   Flexible open space

(ii)   A spectrum of spaces

(iii)   Our expectations of students

(iv)   A role for conversational learning

(v)   Learning as a social process

(vi)   Some characteristics of modern students

(vii)   The recognition of individual difference

(viii) The integration of IT in the building

(ix)   The importance of design

(x)   Third places.

Each of these themes which influenced the thinking during the planning of the building is discussed below.

(i) Flexible open space

The uncertainty about the future mentioned earlier is a key issue. Buildings that we build today are likely to still be in service many years from now and need to remain fit for the purposes of the day. The Saltire Centre has mainly open flexible space that allows reconfiguration to be undertaken relatively easily. This use of open flexible space is an attempt to address the uncertainty about the future of learning. The concept of pace layering (Brand 1994, Morville 2005) sees a building as a series of layers that have differing life spans. The site itself has an eternal life, whereas the building structure might last 50 to 100 years. Other layers such as the external cladding of the building or the interior walls might have a life of 20 years with internal design, decoration and furniture lasting for 5 to 10 years. In a rapidly moving world it makes sense to locate the capacity for change in those items with the potential shortest life span and avoid, if possible, creating some layers, such as internal dividing walls, that have a medium term life span and are a potential barrier to accommodating changing activities. In the Saltire Centre, as it is designed primarily around open flexible space, reconfiguration is achieved by replacement of furniture. Making this an open plan building that has its interior environments defined by its furniture, with the potential for change embedding in short life layers of the building, ensures a considerable degree of future proofing.

(ii) A spectrum of spaces

There is a natural reluctance in traditional organizations to accept open flexible space where personal cellular space has been the norm. However as outlined above the inherent flexibility offered by open plan environments enables easy reconfiguration should this be needed in the future. Rather than adopt polarized views of either open or cellular we considered the possibility of semi private space in planning the Saltire Centre. Some of the study space provided is for silent, reflective, study. This is on the top floor of the five-storey building. Whilst much of the space in the building allows and encourages conversation the "resource" wall in the atrium ensures that upper floors are separate and easily controlled environments enabling silence to be maintained on the top floor.

On other floors between the extremes of the quiet top floor and the highly interactive ground floor there is variety ensuring that somewhere there is something for everyone. Acknowledging the need for occasional privacy in what is essentially an open plan building we have used temporary structures to create semiprivate spaces. This spectrum between private and open space has received little attention in most educational building projects. The Saltire Centre provides several types of semi-private space from inflatable igloo style offices, bespoke canopies over tables that have writing surfaces on their inner faces, to utility walls that can screen off an area and provide new technology for presentations. These structures not only provide a mid way between open and cellular but also fit with the life span strategy outlined in (i) above as they are relatively and low cost and easily replaceable.

(iii) Our expectations of students

Whilst "curriculum delivery" in Universities continues to be focused largely around lectures (now supplemented with extensive online content delivery) backed up with some seminar and tutorial work, what is demanded of students focuses on activities such as group work, problem based learning, project work, and performance based assessments. For the student finding a place to undertake this interactive group work on a traditional campus is not straightforward – libraries demand silence – so no surprise then that many students end up working in the refectory without access to the information resources that they need. This observation initiated an experiment in 2001 with a Learning Café, REAL@Caledonian, in the old Library building to provide much needed interactive learning space. This was never just a café, cybercafe or internet café – it was a conscious attempt to provide a learning environment that made use of technology, had a wide variety of seating styles and was designed like an open plan office. The success of REAL@Caledonian based on observed use and feedback from users provided a firm foundation for the creation of similar space in the Saltire Centre.

(iv) A role for conversational learning

The Learning Café was developed around the concept of an environment that was for people and their learningful conversations. It was created to be that space in the Library that students could use for their group assignments, problem solving work, and projects that they are continually asked to undertake. This simple idea is based on the premise that "all learning starts with conversation" (Seely Brown and Duguid 2000). At root it is clear that we do not fully understand an idea or concept until we have tested it against the understandings of others. Conversation is the natural human way to do this and should therefore be encouraged between our students and our staff. Like Seely Brown the Nobel prize winning physicist Richard Feynman (2000) recognized the power of conversation especially when the concept is extended to the personal reflective conversations that we have with ourselves. As a kid growing up in Far Rockaway Feynman had a friend named Bernie Walker. They both had "labs" at home, and we would do various "experiments". One time, when they were discussing something at age 11 or 12 he said, "But thinking is nothing but talking to yourself inside". An important aim of the Saltire Centre is to provide a wide variety of spaces that encouraged conversations of all kinds, those that take place formally around a table perhaps under a semi private canopy, others that are informal sitting around on beanbags drinking coffee, and private reflections on the silent upper top floor of the building.

(v) Learning as a social process

John Seely Brown also believes that "learning is a remarkably social process. In truth, it occurs not as a response to teaching, but rather as a result of a social framework that fosters learning". Conversations, and the inevitable accompanying social interaction are central to the Learning Café and the Saltire Centre. This theme of the sociality of learning, which sees knowledge, or indeed intelligence, as both a social construct and a result of social interaction, is rooted in a Vygotskian social constructivist view of the world (Pass, 2004). The configuration of our public facilities as a learning commons that encourages interaction and capitalizes on the power of sociality as a source of learning also challenges our view of what "social" means on our campuses lifting it above gratuitous sociality to sociality with educational purpose. Providing an environment that is inherently a social context for the learning that takes place was a key driver of much of the space development in the Saltire Centre.

(vi) Some characteristics of modern students

Our students our members of the creative class – the majority of them will take up posts in professions with a high component of knowledge and information related work. Research into these creative class people (Florida 2000) identifies shifts in their attitudes such as the preference of creative class people for experiences as replacement for goods and services because experiences stimulate their creative faculties and enhance their creative capacities. Such creative class people according to Florida's research seek an active, experiential lifestyle. Making our buildings "an experience" is a fresh perspective that demands that we think about the look and feel in considerable detail. With the advent of the personal computer and ubiquitous connectivity we imagined that the need for place and community might reduce. Not so says Florida's research: "The death-of-place prognostications simply do not square with the countless people I have interviewed, the focus groups I've observed, and the statistical research I've done. Place and community are more critical factors than ever before... the economy itself increasingly takes form around real concentrations of people in real places"

It is clear that successful 21st century Universities will be those that relate to, and compete with, real world experiences ensuring that they remain relevant to the broadest possible section of society. The importance of thinking of our buildings as experiences cannot be underestimated. The designer Karim Rashid (2005) expresses this well in point number 43 of a 50 point manifesto: "Experience is the most important part of living, and the exchange of ideas and human contact is all there really is. Space and objects can encourage increased experiences or detract from our experiences". In the Saltire Centre these thoughts caused us to think about how we could use design (see below) to make the building an experience.

(vii) The recognition of individual difference

The spaces in which we work, live, and learn can have profound effects on how we feel, how we behave, how we perform and can affect different people differently. This is not an exact science – but spaces can also limit the possibilities of our activity restricting us to old modes of working and thinking. Importantly the learning spaces that we build have the potential not only to change the way that we work but also to play to our individual difference and preference. If we design our learning spaces with the variety that exists in our learners we will be providing the maximum opportunity for each and every learner to achieve. It is clear from research in educational psychology that we all have a wide range of facets to our personal intelligence (Gardner, 1999, 2006) and consequently are all differently intelligent. Much of the debate on Multiple Intelligence theory focuses on the number and "types" of intelligences and the nature of intelligence itself, missing the key point – the recognition of individual differences in intelligences which challenges not just our one size fits all educational system but its inherent unfairness. As Gardner points a school system that majors on teaching the same materials in the same way to all students, and even assesses all students in the same ways offers the illusion of fairness, but in his view it is not fair, except to those few students strong in the linguistic and logical domains. In seeking for all human beings that continued equality of educational opportunity that I imagined earlier an education then the education system needs to be built differently. A clear message that I perceive from Gardner's work is the existence of individual differences and the inherent variety of need exhibited by learners.

These recognized differences form a basis for the current thinking by government and others on personalization. The launch document for the BSF programme mentioned earlier states: "The key to the Government's vision is learning personalized to the needs, interests and aptitudes of individual pupils". However such personalization represents a daunting challenge summarized skilfully by West Burnham and Coates (2005): "... to what extent should the individual fit the system or the system the individual?". Can we really develop an education system that plays to the skills, abilities, capabilities and landscape of intelligences of the individual? Can we afford not to? Personalization, then, is a powerful idea not just driven by a government agenda for schools, but also by the potential of new technologies, and ideas in current educational thinking.

An education that acknowledges individual difference rather than ignores it demands a new approach to what it provides and how it provides it. In the context of learning the Saltire Centre had to have the capability to respond to this variety of need and the flexibility to respond differently at different points in the University year. For example, pre-examination pressures are likely to demand more individual study environments whereas assignment deadlines might require more peer group collaboration so not only variety but the capacity to reorient areas of the building within an academic year was important and again required flexibility. Our experience with the Learning Café and the clear need to provide a wide variety of learning space drove us to provide a multiplicity of microenvironments in the new building described by our architect, Colin Allan of Building Design Partnership, as from the monastic to the mall. Some of these have been briefly described above in the section on a spectrum of spaces. Other elements of creating different look and feel to the spaces in the building are covered below in the section on design.

(viii) The integration of IT in the building

Technology is an important strand of the tripartite approach mentioned above however despite over 30 years of the use of IT in education we have generally had limited success: A point acknowledged by Charles Clarke, former minister for education in England, in his introduction to Fulfilling the Potential – Transforming teaching and learning through ICT in schools where he states "However, the potential for real transformation [with ICT] remains largely untapped". As practitioners we are torn between an objective, target driven, performance assessment culture that reduces achievement to a single assessed dimension and our own intuitive, value driven beliefs and will to do it better. It is not surprising that initiatives such as the "implementation" of new technologies rarely achieve their aspirations as, noted by Cuban (2001) that when teachers adopt technological innovations these changes typically maintain rather than alter existing classroom practices. This clear lack of widespread progress suggests to me that we take a step back and adopt a different view that puts technology in context. The recent interest in learning space is part of this broader look and a genuine attempt to do it better. Technology, as always, is in transition – so the Saltire Centre has fixed wired desktop machines along with laptops that can be borrowed that will make use of the 54g wireless network in the building. However, in both the learning café and the Saltire Centre technology has been deployed as a to support student learning and not to dominate it. The café has 80 computers for 200 seats and the Saltire Centre has 600 for 1800 seats – approximately a 1:3 computer to seat ratio in each case. The intent here is to use the technology to connect learners (Papert 1996) rather than divide them Internet café or information commons style with one student per computer.

(ix) The importance of design

I have already mentioned the range of study space provided. Design was key to achieving this. The ground floor of the Saltire Centre, the services mall, provides 600 seats for social learning containing a café and wide range of seating from informal to formal. This "mall" is separated from the other 4 floors of the building by a resource wall so that each floor has an easily managed separate environment. The upper floors are accessed by crossing the bridges from the circulation tower into each floor. This is an example of design at the macro level that has worked very successfully to enable the creation and maintenance of separate environments within the building. However in the Saltire Centre we have also paid detailed attention to many aspects of design – the design of the building itself, the interior design, and the way in which services are offered in the building. Design has also played an important part in the development of the inflatable "igloo" spaces, canopies, and utility walls to provide semi private spaces. But it has also been taken further than this each floor has a different graphic metaphor form the busy city on the ground floor, through the first floor airport departure lounge and up the building to the silent top floor which uses a domestic living room metaphor. The behavioural consequences of these metaphors are strengthened by the use of colour in the glass walls and carpets – hot colours downstairs and cool colours upstairs.

"Design is but a language. If you have nothing to say it won't help you"
(Bang & Olufsen)

From the preceding sections it is clear that we had a lot to say in the building – design has been the tool of choice for saying it.

(x) Third places

The Saltire Centre is a building for people providing inspirational space for interaction, conversation and learning. It also provides the full range of library services and access to all of our services for students. Within the building there's a multitude of micro-environments from the busy hubbub of social interaction in the ground floor café and services mall to the silent top floor. Imaginative graphics are used to convey a different look and feel on each floor supplemented by the careful use of colour and acoustic signing to send subtle messages to users about the expected behaviour in each zone. The Saltire Centre provides an inspirational learning venue for our students, and as Richard Florida (2000) states it is a third place: "Third places are neither home nor work – the 'first two' places – but venues like coffee shops, bookstores and cafes in which we find less formal acquaintances. These comprise 'the heart of a community's social vitality' where people go for good company and lively conversation". The concept of the third place is common in the commercial sector and some the common features of third places are the opportunity for users to walk through or "mall", spectacular things to see, and purposeful engagement (Mikunda 2004). The walkways and large ground floor space, stunning public works of art, and stimulating graphics make the Saltire Centre something unusual – an educational third place.

16.9 Conclusion

The Saltire Centre clearly makes an enormous contribution to the students and staff of Glasgow Caledonian University and will continue to do so for many years to come adapting, using its inherent flexibility, to meet needs as they change. The building acknowledges current educational thinking on the social nature of learning, the importance of conversational learning, and individual difference by providing a range of flexible study space and access to technology. And it goes beyond this aiming to be that essential "third place" in the lives of those who visit it becoming an essential part of the lifestyle of the emerging creative class, making learning vitally experiential. A question that I am often asked is "How does it support research?" From the descriptions above it is clear that the building is highly focused on the support of learning and consequently – in my view – cannot fail to support research and researchers as all learning is research (at the personal level) and all research is learning.

The planning and design of the Saltire Centre did involve high levels of risk taking. Many of the ideas in the building were untried and untested but its users and visitors and professional judges all give positive reports. However, to be clear, it is not a blue print for the 21st century University library but it is an excellent example of a building that works in its setting, that has some great ideas, and that can inform all of our library provision in higher education.

Further Information

Les Watson's website is at http://www.leswatson.net/

References

Bennett, S. (2005) *Righting the Balance, Library as Place: Rethinking Roles, Rethinking Space.* Council on Library and Information Resources (February), 10–24.

Brand, S. (1994) *How Buildings Learn – What Happens After They're Built.* Penguin.

Christensen, C. M. (1997) *The Innovator's Dilemma.* Harvard Business School Press.

Cuban, L. (2001) *Oversold and Underused: Computers in the Classroom.* Harvard University Press.

Department for Education and Skills (UK) (2005) *Building Schools for the Future.* http://www.bsf.gov.uk/

Feynman, R. P. (2000) *The Pleasure of Finding Things Out.* Penguin, London.

Florida, R. (2000) *The Rise of the Creative Class: And How It's Transforming Work, Leisure, Community and Everyday Life.* Basic Books, New York.

Freeman, G. T. (2005) The library as place: changes in learning patterns, collections, technology and use. *Library as Place: Rethinking Roles, Rethinking Space, Council on Library and Information Resources* (February), 1–9.

Gardner, H. (1999) *Intelligence Reframed: Multiple Intelligences for the 21st Century.* Basic Books, New York.

Gardner, H. (2006) *The Development and Education of the Mind.* Routledge, London.

Joint Information Systems Committee (JISC) (UK) (2006) *Designing Spaces for Effective Learning.* Joint Information Systems Committee.

Land, G. and Jarman, B. (1993) *Breakpoint and Beyond Mastering the Future – Today,* Harper Business.

Mikunda, C. (2004) *Brand Lands, Hot Spots and Cool Spaces: Welcome to the Third Place and the Total Marketing Experience.* Kogan Page, London.

Morville, P. (2005) *Ambient Findability.* O'Reilly, California.

Papert, S. (1996) *The Connected Family: Bridging the Digital Generation Gap.* Longstreet Press.

Pass, S. (2004) *Parallel Paths to Constructivism: Jean Piaget and Lev Vygotsky.* Information Age Publishing.

Rashid, K. (2005) *Karimanifesto.* http://www.karimrashid.com/

Robinson, K. (2007) *TED Talk.* http://www.ted.com/tedtalks/tedtalksplayer.cfm?key=ken_robinson

Seely Brown, J. and Duguid, P. (2000) *The Social Life of Information.* Harvard Business School Press.

Stilgoe, S. (2007) Three words we should like to hear: "I don't know". *Times Higher Education Supplement,* 19 April, 12.

West Burnham, J. and Coates, M. (2005) *Personalizing Learning: Transforming Education for Every Child.* Network Educational Press Ltd.

PART 6

Preserving the Content – The Physical and the Digital

17

Tomorrow, and Tomorrow, and Tomorrow: Poor Players on the Digital Curation Stage[1]

Chris Rusbridge

> To-morrow, and to-morrow, and to-morrow,
> Creeps in this petty pace from day to day,
> To the last syllable of recorded time;
> And all our yesterdays have lighted fools
> The way to dusty death.
> Out, out, brief candle!
> Life's but a walking shadow; a poor player,
> That struts and frets his hour upon the stage,
> And then is heard no more: it is a tale
> Told by an idiot, full of sound and fury,
> Signifying nothing.
>
> Shakespeare: *Macbeth*

This quotation in its true context is a cry of despair. But divorcing from the context, and reading somewhat metaphorically, the relevance of many of its resounding phrases to digital curation and preservation can be imagined. We look forward to the last syllable of *recorded* time, not just to the end of time. We look to our yesterdays, and perhaps the information that was lighted to a dusty death. We think about the poor players who strut and fret to make information available into the future, and then are heard no more (the silence of the librarian?). We see our tales reduced to sound and fury; not meaningful digital documents, but sequences of empty data points, signifying nothing.

---

1 Based on a Distinguished Visitor presentation with this title given at OCLC headquarters, Dublin Ohio on 26 October 2006.

17.1 Introduction

In this chapter, I will argue that there are non-obvious choices to be made about the "poor players" who manage data. In particular, the role of the librarian in this is not clear.

Reg Carr (Carr, 2004) attempted to persuade his CURL colleagues at a meeting in Dublin that they should address the emerging importance of data collections head on. His efforts were accepted with enthusiasm by some, resisted by others. There were good reasons for both positions, but I argue that the latter in particular is a temporary phenomenon, strongly linked to budget constraints and to the current transitional phase of librarianship from "mostly physical" to "nearly all digital".

Paul Courant, economist and ex-provost of Michigan, pointed out to a JISC/NDIIPP meeting in May 2006 that, particularly in the context of library budgets and the need to curate data: "There's plenty of money for anything. There just isn't plenty of money for EVERYTHING!" Casting one's mind sufficiently far into the future, it is clear that the trend to digital is irreversible (unless the world as we know it crashes and burns), and hence in a comparatively short time, digital data as well as digital documents will become primary stuff for libraries, and the resources will adapt accordingly. Meanwhile, awkward decisions are needed, on whether to be pioneers, early adopters or late followers!

But whether they want it or not, what *should* be the role of librarians towards data? To answer this, we need to understand a bit more about data curation.

17.2 Data Curation

In his closing remarks to the 2005 International Digital Curation Conference in Bath, Cliff Lynch drew 3 views of digital curation from an extended audience-participative discussion:

- Curation as a finite process, with handover to preservation at its end point
- Curation as a whole life process, with evolving objects, and
- Curation as managing a growing, living collection.

Librarians are most comfortable with the last of these, currently in the physical world of books and physical information objects. Building a collection against a collection policy to meet the needs of a defined community; this is home territory for librarians (and archivists, and museum curators). It extends easily enough into the digital library world, as well.

Librarians have also grappled with the first of these concepts. The idea of working on a digital resource, preparing it for preservation, chimes well with scholarly traditions.

But the idea of the changing, evolving resource, is in some ways an uncomfortable one, and not just for librarians. Nevertheless, this is the basis for much of the emerging science of today. As an example of these issues, think of curating and preserving the UK's Ordnance Survey National Map Database, OS MasterMap (http://www.ordnancesurvey.co.uk/oswebsite/products/osmastermap/). Clearly a very different proposition from preserving the 1st to 7th editions of the map sheets, the most common response is to attempt an annual snapshot, although quite what this means and how it could be used (without large amounts of supporting proprietary software) is unclear.

For the Digital Curation Centre, curation is not simply preservation. It is "maintaining and adding value to a trusted body of digital information for current and future use". Emphasizing the present as well as the future, we seek to ensure that those critical early steps are taken that will allow future preservation, and that current information will still be usable even as time extends indefinitely.

Lynch further pointed out that curation has a strong link with stewardship. It:

- Includes resource management
- Includes access and presentation
- Includes active care
- Involves long time, and thus
- Includes preservation.

Curation is clearly domain-dependent. There are significant domain-dependent issues relating to size, numbers of objects, complexity of objects, interventions needed, ethical and legal implications, policies, practices and incentives.

The DCC takes a broad view of digital curation. Whilst not exclusively data-oriented, we predominantly focus on data resources for science and scholarship. We are concerned with:

- The sustainability of the resource
- The creation or appraisal, selection, acquisition and ingest of the resource
- Growth, development of and changes to the resource
- Making the resource available ("publishing" it)
- Access management and other controls on the resource, and the ethical and legal basis of these controls
- The ability to use, combine, re-combine, inter-operate, process, annotate, discuss and review the resource through time (some of which processes will in turn contribute to the development of the resource)
- Linkage, context and metadata relating to the resource
- Maintaining authenticity, integrity, provenance and computational lineage information relating to the resource
- Maintaining the meaning of the resource despite technology change and concept drift in the outside world
- Preserving the resource, including preserving access to past states of a changing resource
- De-selection and deliberate and/or accidental destruction of the resource
- All of this, over potentially extended time periods, although timescales could also be comparatively short or medium term

- Recognizing the impacts of finite budgets and potential future policy changes, and
- Paying attention to the education, training and development of the people to support this.

17.2.1 A Curation Example

As an example of the power of data-oriented science, take the case of an early test of the "National Virtual Observatory" concept in the US. Astronomers turn images of the sky at various wavelengths into databases of objects detected by analysing those images. All these objects are well described in spatial terms, and furnished with extensive contextual metadata derived in part from their origins in particular instruments. By combining and cross-searching databases derived from the Sloan Digital Sky Survey (SDSS) with those from the Two Micron Astronomical Sky Survey (TWOMASS), astronomers quickly made a discovery. The Johns Hopkins (Hopkins, 2003) press release states:

> "Scientists working to create the NVO, an online portal for astronomical research unifying dozens of large astronomical databases, confirmed discovery of [a] new brown dwarf recently. The star emerged from a computerized search of information on millions of astronomical objects in two separate astronomical databases. Thanks to an NVO prototype, that search, formerly an endeavor requiring weeks or months of human attention, took approximately two minutes."

There are many more examples, from the Human Genome project to the satellite surveys that give us baselines for global warming, and beyond. It is a simple assertion that data are beginning to assume a role in the scientific and scholarly world similar to that of text. An article can tell you about a discovery; a database can let you test certain aspects of the theory or experimental process supporting that discovery. Verifiability is the basis of science.

17.3 Who Are the Curation Players?

Given this critical importance, how can we assure the continued curation of data? Or in the context of this article, what is the librarian's role in data curation? Whose job is it anyway? Who are the "poor players" in data curation?

Perhaps not complete, here is a classification of data curators:

- Individuals, using their hard disks, or perhaps networked drives
- Departments or groups
- Institutions, perhaps in the shape of their libraries
- Communities of institutions, either formal (as consortia), or informal (as in the case of the LOCKSS[2] system)
- Disciplines

---

2   Lots Of Copies Keep Stuff Safe, a distributed service founded at Stanford University.

- Publishers
- National services, perhaps national libraries or archives, or national data services, and/or
- Other 3rd party services.

17.3.1 Individuals

James M. Caruthers, a professor of chemical engineering at Purdue University has claimed "Small Science will produce 2–3 times more data than Big Science, but is much more at risk" (Carlson 2006). Big Science results from large collaborative exercises; the sharing implied results in better-defined data formats and access protocols, and often formal support for data sharing in proposals. But Small Science, in the labs of individual Principal Investigators usually results in data managed by their Research Assistants, or even PhD students. The data are often on individual or at best shared drives. They will often not even be adequately backed up. The individuals concerned are intimately involved in the scientific work; they know so much that they do not feel a need to write down: they know too much, and are too busy, to create good metadata or documentation. At best some time after the PI has moved attention on to a successor project, at worst when a staff member leaves and the accounts are deactivated and then deleted, these data will simply disappear; they have no tomorrow. This case is both most common and most worrying!

17.3.2 Groups or departments

In many cases, group or department curation efforts will be of similar standard, with similar risks, to the work of individuals. However, there are some beacons shining out. Take for example, the eCrystals data resource (http://ecrystals.chem.soton.ac.uk/) curated by the National Crystallography Service at Southampton. Informed by the eBank projects (http://www.ukoln.ac.uk/projects/ebank-uk/), and lately the Repository for the Laboratory (R4L) project (http://r4l.eprints.org/about.html), they are attempting to capture automatically both process-oriented but essentially private data, and also publicly available crystal structures resulting from their analyses. In R4L, they aim to capture key metadata as part of their workflow. For example, health and safety considerations require them to plan their work out well in advance; this information provides a useful source of data, as does capture of environmental information, and even the staff present in the lab at any time. Their final results are made available in the industry-standard CIF format. They are supported by their library, and are trying to extend their repository to form a federation. Even so, it is not yet clear how they relate to many other significant activities in the field taking slightly different approaches, including the American ReciprocalNet effort, and the French Crystallography Online Database (COD), or even IUCr mentioned below. Nevertheless, with the level of domain knowledge and service commitment displayed, the medium term tomorrow of this collection seems assured.

17.3.3 Institutional and Library

While the eCrystals repository is identifiably separate from the Southampton Institutional Repository and linked to the Crystallography group, the DSpace @ Cambridge repository is clearly institutional, a collaboration between the Library and Computing Service at Cambridge University. It contains many collections, including Archaeology, Manuscripts, Learning objects etc. But the largest collection by far, with some 250,000 digital objects deposited so far, is the World-Wide Molecular Matrix (http://www.dspace.cam.ac.uk/handle/1810/724) including structures of small molecules encoded in Chemical Markup Language (CML). This is definitely an institutional repository, but this part is definitely a chemical collection. The Library applies no chemical skills in curating this collection, relying exclusively on the considerable enthusiasm of its depositor, Peter Murray Rust. The collection is isolated from other chemical collections, and the repository provides no (non-generic) services that are particularly relevant to chemistry.

There are some who hold that institutional repositories such as this have no valuable place in the data world, arguing that domain science knowledge is essential to adequately curate science data (Lawrence 2005). However, institutional repositories do have two major advantages over discipline-based repositories: their institutional resource base is driven by their institution's continuing interest in disclosing its research, and their association with major institutional collecting organizations like the library tends to give them a stronger tomorrow. In this case, Cambridge has made a strong commitment to its repository, so the future of the repository and the collection in its current form is reasonably assured.

Comparatively few other libraries can claim any significant data holdings in their institutional repositories. The OpenDOAR service (http://www.opendoar.org/) listed 5 in the UK at a recent visit. The library role then is not yet nationally significant, and there is little sign of curation repositories appearing on an institutional basis anywhere other than in libraries. Given the issues about Small Science, however, perhaps librarians should be looking at increasing their involvement.

17.3.4 Community Services

If one institution can do reasonably well, can a community service supporting many institutions do better? One interesting example is the California Digital Library. Set up by the Regents of the University of California, and located in the Office of the President, CDL provides digital services to the constituent university libraries. These services include the UC Libraries Digital Preservation Repository Service (http://www.cdlib.org/inside/projects/preservation/dpr/). It does appear to be from a document rather than data tradition, and like UK libraries, has a passive role in relation to the collections preserved; either the individual libraries or more likely the research groups and staff they serve (two or more steps removed) provide the curation skills, and CDL provides preservation. Nevertheless, their tomorrow is reasonably well assured.

LOCKSS (http://www.lockss.org/) provides a completely different example of a community service. In this case the community is much more like an Open Source community: a self-selected group of collectors using open software on cheap commodity computing boxes gathers web-like objects (for which the collectors have the required rights) into a cache, continually checks their integrity against other boxes, and makes them available to their community should the original disappear[3]. LOCKSS is also rooted in a document tradition (libraries collecting eJournals), but is being increasingly applied in other contexts. However, there is intrinsically little domain knowledge in a system such as LOCKSS. Nevertheless, it is potentially a very valuable model because of its high redundancy, low cost, high reliability and high attack resistance; these are properties that it is difficult to replicate in larger scale systems. Consequently, a LOCKSS system of peers configured to capture data could also have a strong tomorrow.

17.3.5 Disciplines

Of the examples above, only the group example had the active involvement of domain scientists in the curation of their data. The "doubters" of institutional repositories claim that discipline-based repositories have the major advantage of that active involvement. As the National Science Board report on Long-Lived Digital Data Collections (NSB 2005) suggests, they also act in "community-proxy" roles, particularly when it comes to defining data and metadata standards. Here are a few examples:

- Archaeology in the UK is served by AHDS Archaeology (formerly ADS). Staffed by archaeologist curators, they understand complex issues such as the legal opportunities and requirements provided for archaeological finds discovered during building and civil engineering development processes. They have a strong relationship with their community and their peers, being located within an academic archaeology department. As an example, see their digital resource on Roman Amphorae (Keay, 2005), AHDS Archaeology does appear to relate solely to the UK (in their immediate stakeholder group, rather than archaeological scope), and internationally the scene appears rather fragmented. Their "tomorrow" is supported by a combination of funding sources, including deposit fees and research council grants.

- As mentioned above, Astronomy is an example of Big Science that is organizing itself around systems of Virtual Observatories. This is part of a major international effort. Astronomy requires very expensive, shared large facilities (it is definitely Big Science), and is used to collaborating internationally, and to sharing data. The VOs are well integrated into their community, who understand that they are essential to generate certain types of new scientific knowledge. Because they can clearly be seen as another Large Facility (a tele-

---

3   This picture is slightly complicated by the LOCKSS Alliance, a subscription-based membership organization whose fees sustain the Stanford LOCKSS team for software development and the activities including publisher negotiations associated with acquiring the rights and technical capabilities to preserve new content.

scope into the past, perhaps), their tomorrow is well assured by community commitment.

- Atmospheric Science, like most of the environmental sciences, clearly understands the value of past observations (which cannot be repeated), and hence the value of curating today's and tomorrow's observations. The Director of the British Atmospheric Data Centre (BADC), which is funded by NERC, is a strong believer in the necessity of having domain scientists as curators (Lawrence, 2005); he also acts on his belief in exercising a strong community-proxy role. Internationally, atmospheric science seems well served with repositories, but perhaps they are more fragmented than one might expect (although the NERC Data Grid is trying to unify a few of them). Their tomorrow is mostly dependent on grant funding, but with a strong commitment to the need to support such activities from its funder.

- High Energy Physics is another example of Big Science (indeed, flexing its muscles as Biggest Science!). The Large Hadron Collider is building tiers of data stores in many different countries to handle the floods of data that will emerge once it becomes operational.

- Pharmacology is interesting. In particular, the International Union of Pharmacology (IUPHAR) has a database of pharmacological receptors. It is attempting to build academic credit for the contributors to this database, and as such is taking steps to introduce quite fine-grained data citations (Buneman, 2006). Funding of the database is extremely limited, which certainly acts against an assured tomorrow, particularly if curation requires significant database investment.

- The Social Sciences, both in the UK and the US, have long and mature histories of data curation. Both ESDS (http://www.esds.ac.uk/) in the UK and ICPSR (http://www.icpsr.umich.edu/) in the US are staffed by Social Science curators; they are alert to opportunities, able to appraise material offered, and have a strong relationship to their disciplines, where acceptance for deposit can be seen as a badge of merit. In the case of IPCSR, with their broad mix of funding streams, tomorrow is fairly well assured. In the case of ESDS, with more limited funding streams (primarily ESRC and JISC) there may appear to be more risk. However, ESDS is certainly viewed as one of the jewels in the ESRC portfolio, so their tomorrow is also pretty strong.

These examples, some more successful than others, show that discipline-based curation services can work, and do have advantages. However, disciplines are hard to define, and fracture almost as soon as defined. The successful examples above do not represent the full breadth of the discipline base; in fact they are exceptions rather than the rule. ESRC can see a need for one curation service covering all of the economic and social sciences in the UK, but NERC funds 7 just within the environmental sciences. It is not clear that anyone in the UK funds any curation service covering engineering data, despite the obvious long-lived compliance requirements. There are around 800 databases world-wide of relevance to nucleic medicine (Bateman 2006), of which maybe 100 are supported by the European Bio-Informatics Institute. It is a very patchy picture, and one where directors of discipline-oriented curation services are perpetually chasing funding, and live in fear of those dreaded words: "policy change".

17.3.6 Publishers

Sometimes publishers have close connections with their disciplines. While some publishers are distrusted as rapacious, whose possible moves towards data collection would be seen as yet more attempts to gain exclusive rights for profit, others can be seen as having a strong and trusted role. One such is the International Union of Crystallographers (IUCr), which publishes Acta Crystallographica in various parts. IUCr, working with their community, defined the Crystallographic Information Framework (CIF, http://www.iucr.org/iucr-top/cif/) that allows crystallographic information to be shared, and has made deposit of validated structure information a pre-requisite for publication of articles or structures in their journals. They provide services that allow CIF files to be checked for various quality parameters. They are also pioneers in the use of Digital Object Identifiers for data objects. Their combination publishing and membership business model is probably secure for tomorrow, although all publishing business models are under threat right now.

While publisher mandates for deposit can be powerful drivers (as can funder mandates such as the Wellcome Trust's) it is clear that many publishers would be viewed with extreme suspicion if they tried the same approach. Perhaps the key here is IUCr's close identification with its discipline.

17.3.7 National Bodies

What about national bodies? The British Library is undertaking a serious development programme for its Digital Object Management system, motivated by its upcoming non-print legal deposit powers and responsibilities. However, it is oriented towards "cultural heritage", broadly interpreted, and does not claim much data or science domain expertise. While the BL will no doubt accept data (e.g. the National Mapping Database referred to above), they are not natural data curators.

The National Archive has set up the National Digital Archive of Datasets (NDAD, www.ndad.nationalarchives.gov.uk) at the University of London Computing Centre, to be a specialist archive for government datasets. NDAD understand the complex government regulations, dynamics and requirements, and are technology specialists, understanding databases very well. Although some of their datasets have significant science value, NDAD is not staffed by domain scientists, and they remain subject generalists. Tomorrow, there is every likelihood that the operation will pass back in-house to TNA, who will, however, have a long-term interest in sustaining it as part of its statutory duties.

In the US there is a variety of national bodies with a discipline science responsibility. NASA and NOAA are two examples making serious data available for public and scientific use. In these organizations, domain scientists do curate the data, and sometimes with massive budgets. However, they tend to be subject to the current political context, which can lead to continuity problems (policy change again!), and are often subject to "un-funded mandates" (legal requirements to carry out responsibilities without the means to do so). The political context places these organizations continually in some jeopardy.

17.3.8 Third Parties

What about 3rd party organizations? The first two worth mentioning could also be classed as community-based, perhaps. OCLC runs a digital preservation service (http://www.oclc.org/digitalarchive/about/), on a demand-driven basis, agnostic as to content. Its tomorrow is based on belief in a business case; it is unlikely to be paying its way at this stage. Portico (http://www.portico.org/) is a preservation service set up (essentially) by Mellon, with subscription funding from universities and publishers, to preserve eJournals. It too has no data or domain science expertise, and is highly dependent on those publisher preservation rights agreements. The funding mix and the power of Mellon (which cannot afford to see this venture fail) probably means its tomorrow is secure.

Finally, we should think about the role of real for-profit 3rd parties, such as Iron Mountain (http://www.ironmountain.com/digital/erecords/archives.asp). Records management IS a curation problem, and any company that can make a successful business from electronic records management is very likely to seek to branch out into other forms of curation. They may have no science expertise, but they may have self-belief, ambition and large reserves that will allow them to buy in the skills they need to secure a market. Their tomorrow, however, may be very dependent on the viability (quarter by quarter) of their business plans[4], competition, take-over, the stock market, interest and exchange rates... We should be concerned at their forthcoming roles, but only in the sense of taking opportunities aware of the risks.

17.4 Moving Things to the Network Level

Lorcan Dempsey (Dempsey, 2006) often talks about "moving things to the network level". It is clear from the above that institutions have some fundamental sustainability advantages, but lack the critical mass of domain science involvement in curation, or fragment it when they can sustain it. Disciplines do exist at the network level, and have huge advantages for data curation in being able to direct domain expertise to the curation task. But sustainability is always an issue for disciplines (and many network level services), and many if not most disciplines have never even got to the point where sustainability has to be confronted!

---

4   For example, at time of writing it appeared that an email curation service, Cryoserver, may have gone into liquidation, with uncertain effects on its clients (Williams, 2006).

Can we combine the institution and the discipline to achieve network effects with institution components? The much-touted Web 2.0 effects are achieved by cunning combinations of mass appeal, highly scalable centralized services, and some "power of crowds" synergies from the participation of many individuals. It is difficult to see how this will work in the academic sector, at least at scales that will attract venture capital (although there are a few examples, such as Connotea, www.connotea.org). However, perhaps there is some way of putting together disciplinary segments of institutional repositories to achieve network-level effects? It is not clear how (or if) this can be done, but we should be trying!

17.5 Conclusions

At the beginning, I asked what should be the role of librarians in data curation. There is as yet no clear answer, and certainly no simple answer. But for now, librarians SHOULD be continuing to take data ever more seriously, thinking about the relationship between publications and the data on which they are based, and working with their discipline colleagues where opportunities arise. Capturing ANY valuable data is never a wasted opportunity.

Yesterday, Reg Carr took leadership positions in CURL, RLG and JISC, supporting efforts such as these. Tomorrow, we hope his successors will be as visionary.

Bibliography

Bateman, A. (2006) Editorial. *Nucl. Acids Res.*, **34**(suppl. 1), D1.

Buneman, P. (2006) How to cite curated databases and how to make them citable. *Proceedings of the Conference on Scientific and Statistical Database Management.*

Carlson, S. (2006). Lost in a sea of science data: librarians are called in to archive huge amounts of information, but cultural and financial barriers stand in the way. *The Chronicle of Higher Education*, **52**, 35.

Carr, R. (2004) *The Challenge of e-Science for Research Libraries*. From http://www.bodley.ox.ac.uk/librarian/escience/escience.htm.

Dempsey, L. (2006). Libraries and the long tail: some thoughts about libraries in a network age. *D-Lib Magazine*, **12**(4).

Hopkins (2003) Virtual observatory prototype produces surprise discovery. *Headlines @ Hopkins.* From http://www.jhu.edu/news_info/news/home03/mar03/nvo.html.

Keay, S. (2005) Roman Amphorae: a digital resource. *AHDS Archaeology.*

Lawrence, B. (2005) Function creep and institutional repositories. *Bryan's Blog.* From http://home.badc.rl.ac.uk/lawrence/blog/2005/03/31/function_creep_and_institutional_repositories.

NSB (2005) *Long-Lived Digital Data Collections: Enabling Research and Education in the 21st Century*. National Science Board Report. National Science Foundation.

Williams, C. (2006) Email archiver melts away. *Channel Register.*

18

Some Key Issues in Digital Preservation[1]

Marilyn Deegan and Simon Tanner

18.1 Introducing the Digital Domain

The digital birth of cultural content and conversion of analogue originals into bits and bytes has opened new vistas and extended horizons in every direction, providing access and opportunities for new audiences, enlightenment, entertainment and education in ways unimaginable a mere 15 years ago. Digital libraries have a major function to enhance our appreciation or engagement with culture and often lead the way in this new digital domain we find ourselves immersed within. The underlying information and communication technologies are still generally referred to as "new" or "high" technologies – they remain highly visible, and have not yet, despite their pervasiveness, become part of the natural infrastructure of society.

The need to deliver cultural resources, especially from major cultural organizations such as museums or national libraries, has become an imperative closely associated with the core mission of these organizations to educate and elucidate, to promote and disseminate and to preserve culture. These attempts to reach out to new audiences and to refresh current audiences are major driving factors behind many digitization programmes and the shift towards digital repositories. The justifications for delivering cultural resources digitally can rarely made on purely financial grounds as the fiscal returns on investment are relatively small, but the returns for culture, education and prestige are high (Tanner, 2004).

---

1   An earlier version of this piece was published in *Digital Preservation*, edited by Marilyn Deegan and Simon Tanner (Facet). It is reproduced here with the permission of the publishers.

18.2 Preservation and the Impact of Nature, Politics and War

Preservation is the continuous process of creating and maintaining the best environment possible for the storage and/or use of an artefact to prevent damage or degradation and to enable it to live as long a lifetime as possible. It has sub-activities, such as conservation and restoration, which involve specific treatments to an artefact to stabilize and preserve it for the future, or to restore it to a state of former glory. One of the key responsibilities held by libraries, museums, and other memory organizations is that of preserving culture. This may be preserving the record of a way of life or the very roots of a culture, its language, literature, music, and traditions. Digital libraries play an important role in preserving culture and in connecting people with their national and regional identities. This work is essential to support the very foundations of our civilization, which is based upon our ability to pass information and knowledge, whether technical or cultural, from one generation to the next.

Recorded information and knowledge resources are at constant risk from natural disaster and human mediated destruction. "As Thomas Jefferson well knew with his family fire, there are few more irreparable property losses than vanished books. Nature, politics, and war have always been the mortal enemies of written works" (Coleman, 2006). The loss of archives includes examples such as the Catholic University of Louvain, Belgium, which burned down in both 1914 and 1940 due to wartime bombing, destroying 230,000 books, 800 of them incunabula printed before the year 1500, and 900 manuscripts. Most recently, the Asian Tsunami, the New Orleans disaster accompanying Hurricane Katrina and the South Asia Earthquake have all had an impact on a number of museums, libraries, and archives as well as the people of many countries, affecting not just lives but cultural memories (ICOM Disaster Relief for Museums). In the 1970s, the Khmer Rouge regime in Cambodia decimated cultural institutions throughout the country. They threw books from the National Library into the street and burnt them. Less than 20 percent of the library survived and the damage to Cambodia's rich cultural heritage remains an open and unhealed wound. In the last 150 years, a new danger has threatened: the "'slow fires' of acidic paper" (Kenney, 1996), which has necessitated the large-scale microfilming of millions of pages of documents over many decades in order that the content is not lost. Many digital reformatting initiatives grew out of earlier microfilming projects, lighting the "'fast fires' of digital obsolescence" (Kenney, 1996).

Culture is at constant risk and the digital domain may exacerbate this risk by maintaining resources in formats that have problems for long term storage and retrieval. But the digital library itself is a powerful tool for holding back the tide of cultural diffusion and loss. Digital libraries are often the key tool by which citizens can engage with their own history, culture, and language whilst also being of enormous value in restoring cultural artefacts to public view where the original is lost or too fragile for normal display.

Materials published on the web may derive from professional sources such as publishers or libraries, with analogue versions also available elsewhere which will continue to be available even after they disappear from digital view, but what of other kinds of digital documents? In the past, ephemera such as playbills, advertisements, menus, theatre tickets, broadsheets etc. have survived, albeit sometimes rather haphazardly, and are now collected, stored, conserved and valued as vital witnesses to political, economic, social, and private aspects of the past. Today, these artefacts appear on the web for a matter of days, to disappear from view as if they had never existed. There are, too, many government documents, records, and other official papers which only ever have a digital form: what is being done about these?

We must differentiate between digital preservation (which is about ensuring full access and continued usability of data and digital information), and preservation through digitization (which allows for greater physical security of physical analogue originals). Strategically it becomes self-evident that to reduce the stress upon the valued original, the data created must last as long as possible. Thus processes and intentions for preservation must be decided early in the digital lifecycle to ensure that repeating the digitization directly from the original is reduced or hopefully eradicated.

18.3 The Scale of the Digital Preservation Problem

Civilized society depends on the quality of its knowledge of its own past, and a falsification of that past, whether deliberate or accidental, damages the society. The Soviet Union is a prime example of a society which rewrote its history regularly to reflect the prevailing political mores, destroying valuable evidence along the way (Preserving Digital Information, 1996, 1). Lack of care in preserving our digital past and present will certainly ensure that we will have an impoverished digital future.

We now face a new threat in the form of digital obsolescence. "Not brittle papyrus and crumbling mortar is the most severe threat to our cultural heritage today, but, as Mary Feeney (Feeney, 1999), expressed it, "the death of the digit." This "death of the digit" is related primarily to two factors:

- First, technology develops ever more rapidly, reducing the time before a particular technology becomes obsolete.
- And secondly, unlike their analogue counterparts, digital resources are much more "unstable" with the effect that the integrity and authenticity of digital cultural resources is corrupted." (Geser and Mulrenin, 2002)

Digital preservation of cultural resources faces a number of challenges:

- Preserving the data stream's integrity
- Preserving the means to interpret the data stream
- Preserving the means by which the resource is experienced.

Digital data is in danger, not because it is inherently fragile or flawed, but because there is a continually accelerating rate of replication, adaptation and redundancy of hardware, software and data formats and standards which may mean that the bit stream may not be readable, interpretable or usable long into the future. All data is stored as a code and therefore requires an element of decoding before it is recognizable and usable in a computing environment, even if open data standards are used. For most people the bit stream for a word processing document, for example, would be totally unintelligible without the suitable computer applications, software, and operating system environments to interpret and repackage the data into a readable form. We take this automatic decoding for granted until we try to read a word processing file from 10 years ago and find that none of our current systems or software have any idea what the bit stream means without significant coaching or expert help.

The longer the data is left unattended, its data coding unrecorded, the faster systems will become obsolete and the expertise to recognize and decode that specific type of bit stream will become unavailable. Data could be lost forever, unrecoverable without effort that will probably not be cost-effective. There is a direct analogy with the decipherment of ancient scripts where the knowledge of the language used and the system of coding of the written scripts is lost and must be recreated from scraps of knowledge, intuition, research and other language fragments that may be stems of the ancient script. The linguistic bridge to the past built upon the decipherment of hieroglyphics or Linear B are very highly valued for the historical information we now have about those societies and cultures of up to 3,000 years ago. These decipherments were often life works for the people who succeeded and were preceded by centuries of hard worked failure. In the case of Linear A the battle continues (see Singh, 1999). As described by Maurice Pope,

> Decipherments are by far the most glamorous achievements of scholarship. There is a touch of magic about unknown writing, especially when it comes from the remote past, and a corresponding glory is bound to attach itself to the person who first solves its mystery. (Pope, 1975)

The challenge for our digital future is to not perpetuate a scenario of data loss and poor records that have dogged our progress over the last 25 years. Otherwise, in just 50 years from now the human record of the early 21st century may be unreadable, and its decipherment an expensive and intellectually challenging feat way beyond the achievements of the great codebreakers of the 20th.

18.3.1 Disposal of Originals and Their Replacement by Surrogates

A highly disputed area in libraries is the deaccessioning of print originals and their replacement by digital or analogue surrogates. The most controversial questions here arise when actual disposal of originals is proposed. Sometimes, there is no real choice to be made: for instance, the Department of Preservation and Collection Maintenance at Cornell University recommends that for brittle books, a printed photocopy surrogate is created on archival paper, and the original then discarded (see http://www.library.cornell.edu/preservation/operations/brittlebooks.html). This is done using a digital scanning process, and therefore digital images are also available. The Cornell Brittle Books Project also experimented with Computer Output to Microform technologies to create preservation microfilm copies of the books. The content is therefore safe for the long term. Cornell has become a world leader in digital reformatting and preservation, and runs many courses and workshops on the topic (see http://www.library.cornell.edu/preservation/training/index.html).

The decision to discard originals by libraries and archives is never taken lightly, but over time materials do have to be discarded for reasons of space and cost. This is not a new issue: repositories have always discarded materials to make way for new items. In the past, materials were sometimes reused. Vellum, for instance, was so costly that it was scraped down and reused which has paradoxically allowed the recovery of materials that were not actually supposed to survive. The Digital Image Archive of Medieval Music for instance (DIAMM see http://www.diamm.ac.uk/), has recovered music from fifteenth-century fragments of vellum that had been used for other purposes, for instance as binding reinforcements for non-musical sources. Vellum is so durable that it was possible to recover readings, despite damage by water, dirt, rats, glue, or the effects of being stuck down to a wooden board for 600 years or more, and some hitherto unknown pieces of medieval music have been discovered in this way (Craig-McFeely and Deegan, 2005).

If some economical means of preserving access to the content can be found, this is often done. This process is part of the responsible stewardship of cultural materials by librarians and archivists, but there are times when these issues become matters of public concern. In the second half of 2000, for instance, there was mounting controversy in Britain and the USA about the jettisoning by major libraries of some of their historic newspaper collections. These collections were all preserved on microfilm, but the disposal of originals caused an outcry in the press. Major libraries such as the Library of Congress in the USA and the British Library in the UK have been microfilming newspapers for many decades in order to preserve the historical record rather then the objects, but the critics of the disposal policy advanced many arguments for the retention of the paper copies. As a society, we are wedded to objects rather than surrogates, even if this causes expensive problems, and some of the objections to the disposal were romantic rather than rational.

18.4 Why Data Needs Preservation

18.4.1 The Nature of Data

Data is at risk because it is recorded on a transient medium, in a specified file format, and it needs a transient coding scheme (a programming language) to interpret it. Another problem is that digital data can be highly complex, and meaning derived from data can depend as much on how individual data objects are linked as on what those objects are. Of course, written documents are also highly complex objects, but their structure does not need to be comprehended for their preservation, only for their interpretation. Over time, knowledge of how to interpret documents can be lost, but this can usually be recreated, as their textual and physical characteristics are explicit. Their decipherment generally needs only human faculties. Digital documents differ from analogue, too, in that they are not inextricably bound to their "containers", and therefore preserving them is not necessarily a matter of preserving containers as it is in the analogue world.

18.4.2 The Complexity of Digital Data

The complexity of digital data will not be apparent to the readers and users of the future if the creators of the present have not made them explicit. An innovative, multimedia DVD derives as much of its meaning from links between digital objects as from the informational content of those objects themselves. Complex digital objects, too, need complex programs to run them, and these programs are constantly in flux, with new versions appearing frequently. If the DVD has been produced by a publisher with today's market in mind rather than tomorrow's users, then documentation of the links and the methods used to create them might not be a priority: the objective is sales, not preservation. After all, some publishers may not even want the products preserved for too long, as they will want to produce new versions, updates, etc. which they can sell again and again. The library which purchases, delivers, then tries to preserve that DVD could have a very expensive task, especially as in order to maintain market advantage, many publishers have very different interfaces, encoding schemes and media structures. Librarians can be faced with thousands of products in hundreds of formats: a difficult and expensive enough situation for providing access to them, a disastrous one for their preservation. Now that copyright libraries are facing the responsibility of accepting non-print materials, these questions are critical for them.

18.4.3 How Is Digital Data to Be Preserved?

There are two key issues for data preservation, which surprisingly have little to do with preserving the original bit stream:

- Preserving the physical media on which the bit stream is recorded
- Preserving the means of interpreting, reading, and utilizing the bit stream.

Given that the bit stream is merely a very long series of binary codes, the preservation of the physical media should maintain its integrity over time. However, being able to read, use, or interpret that bit stream may become increasingly difficult as systems evolve, adapt and eventually become redundant, so presenting a fog through which the bit stream becomes unusable.

18.4.4 Why the Urgency?

Digital data does not have a long enough natural lifetime for us to wait for better media to come along. The life of data written even to optical media, such as CD-ROM or DVD, may be measured in years rather than decades. Finding machinery to read the bit stream might become tricky within a few years, very hard after a decade and require some very serious computer archaeology after 15 to 20 years. As yet data storage has not found its stability equivalent of paper or microfilm, but the evolution of the technology may be around the next corner. The storage of data started with punched cards only some 50 years ago and has transitioned through paper tape, magnetic tape, to magnetic disk, optical disk and portable memory such a flash memory to the present day. It is now extremely difficult to find card or tape readers if old archives of the originals come to light.

18.4.5 Data Is Bad at Self-Preservation

Unlike many analogue originals such as paper or paintings, data is very bad at self-preservation. Active measures must be taken at its birth to ensure that it survives longer into the future: this is known as the "retention intention" and is essential to data preservation. Data preservation cannot and must not be left to chance. At particular risk is the category of data which is "born digital' – that is, which has no analogue originals. A great deal of data is being produced in this category, much of which it is necessary to preserve: government documents, e-mails, electronic journals, dictionaries and encyclopedias, computer games, and, probably the most ephemeral category, web sites. While it is of course necessary to propose strategies for dealing with all categories of digital data, it is not feasible to propose that all digital data should be preserved for the long term.

18.5 Selection of Data for Preservation

In any format, analogue or digital, data is selected for long-term preservation because it is felt to have some long-term value. But whose values are taken into account, and how can they be known? Historians of the future will rely on what is preserved from today, but their needs will be different from those of present historians, and their research paths will be partly chosen by the data which is available. Given that it is not possible to preserve everything, it is a complex matter to decide what should be preserved. Even the world's major copyright libraries which are offered copies of every published product of their nation do not accept everything, though most of what is offered is stored somewhere. It is a vital strategic decision to have selection and retention policies for digital data, just as it is for analogue, and the decisions should be made on the value of the content, not the ease of preservation. It will take complex teams of data origina-tors, librarians, archivists, historians, and others concerned with the documen-tary heritage to decide upon robust selection and retention policies, and these are strategic issues of national and international importance.

The Digital Preservation Coalition has produced an interactive decision tree on the selection of digital resources for long-term retention (see http://www.dpconline.org/graphics/handbook/dec-tree.html). The first question posed in "Does the content of this resource fall within the institutional remit/

collection development policy?" Several surveys have found that while many institutions feel that they *should* have such a policy, very few have produced and implemented one. See for instance, Mind the Gap: Assessing digital preservation needs in the UK, a report prepared for the DPC (Waller and Sharpe, 2006) or the AHDS "Digital Images Archiving Study" and "Moving Pictures and Sound Archiving Study" (http://ahds.ac.uk/about/projects/archiving-studies/index.htm).

18.6 Methods of Preservation of Digital Materials

As is clear from the discussions above, the paradox of digital materials is that they are fundamentally simple, being made up of only two electrical states, but those states can be configured into patterns so complex using programming techniques that a limitless number of different documents and other artefacts can be represented. Digital data derived from different sources differs greatly in the amount of storage needed. Electronic text, even with complex encoding, is compact; still images can be very space hungry, with digital cameras now available which can capture files of 400 Mb or more from visually rich objects; sound and video, especially if captured at high quality, take orders of magnitude more storage than images or text; satellite images or complex maps created with GIS systems can be even larger. While file sizes can be reduced to some degree by compression of the data, the compression techniques which offer the greatest economies have the disadvantage that this comes at the price of loss of information.

There is also a great variety of media on which digital materials can be stored, from punch cards and tapes which represent the patterns as a series of holes, to the wide range of electronic recording materials: floppy disks, hard drives, tapes, CD-ROMs, DVDs, etc. The methods of digital preservation or digital archiving we propose to introduce here and are discussed in more depth in this book are:

- Technology preservation
- Refreshing
- Migration and reformatting
- Emulation
- Data archaeology
- Output to analogue media.

18.6.1 Technology Preservation

Technology preservation is the maintenance of the hardware and software platforms which support a digital resource, and if adopted as a preservation strategy this would need to be accompanied by a regular cycle of media refreshing. It is relatively impractical and financially unfeasible, given the large number of computers and programmes which would need to be managed over a long period of time: "any collection manager in charge of a large collection of digital resources who relied solely on this strategy would very soon end up with a museum of ageing and incompatible computer hardware" (Feeney, 1999, 42). One can imagine a library reading room littered with PCs with every version of Windows and Macintoshes running ten generations of operating system; that is to name just two current platforms. For certain rare and important resources, perhaps the technology could be preserved for a time, until a better long-term solution could be found, but this is an approach clearly fraught with difficulty.

18.6.2 Refreshing

Digital storage media have short lives, the length of which can be estimated but which is ultimately unknown. Data therefore has to be moved periodically to new media to ensure its survival. Sometimes this involves a change of media: CD-ROMs will be copied onto hard disks in a digital data store, floppy disks may be copied onto CD-ROMs, at other times refreshing may take place because a particular substrate has become unstable, and the files may be copied to a newer, more stable version of the same medium. Refreshing copies the bit stream exactly as it is, it makes no changes to the underlying data. It is a process that needs to be carried out whatever other preservation strategies are adopted. It is technically relatively straightforward, with low risk of loss if performed and documented properly.

18.6.3 Migration and Reformatting

Migration involves change in the configuration of the underlying data, without change in its intellectual content. This is necessary when hardware and software changes mean that the data can no longer be accessed unless it is migrated to the newer machines and programmes. Migration will generally involve some reformatting, which begs the question of whether the data still conveys the same content information as it did before it was migrated. The simpler the data structures, the more likely it is that the content will be preserved. With complexly linked artefacts such as web sites, it is difficult to see how they can be preserved without loss unless complex (and costly) documentation is produced which annotates the structures. If libraries and archives have to cope with a plethora of digital formats, one approach to their sustainability over the long term is to convert the digital objects into standard formats when they are first accessioned. This involves assessment of the object and extracting its data formats and inner structure, and conversion of the structures into the institution's own models. This is expensive initially, but could prove cost-effective over the long term, making migration easier and faster. The costs here are front loaded; with other preservation strategies they come later in the life-cycle.

18.6.4 Strategic Issues in Refreshing and Reformatting Data

Migration, reformatting, and refreshing of data are processes that may need to be carried out many times over the lifetime of digital objects identified as sufficiently significant for long-term preservation. Instability or obsolescence of media means that data will need to be moved regularly and changes in software and hardware platforms will dictate constant reformatting. Refreshing and migration cycles will not necessarily coincide, which means that documentation and management of the digital archives will be complex.

The main disadvantage of a reformatting approach to digital preservation is that *all* data must be converted in each reformatting cycle, whether there is any indication that particular resources will be accessed in the future or not. Missing a cycle could mean that the data is unreadable in subsequent cycles. Reformatting is costly and labour-intensive and is likely to stretch the resources of all libraries, large and small, which could compromise decisions about effort to be apportioned for other activities, digital and non-digital.

During refreshing and migration, too, time and care needs to be spent in validating data to ensure that there has been no corruption. The (relatively straightforward) process of copying the bit stream from one medium to another can sometimes be problematic, and even slight corruption can be cumulative, resulting soon in unrecoverable data. Reformatting *ipso facto* involves the loss of the original digital object, given that the premise upon which it is based is that the original is not preservable. Lorie says of migration:

> It is the most obvious, business-as-usual, method. When a new system is installed, it coexists with the old one for some time, and all files are copied from one system to the other. If some file formats are not supported by the new system, the files are converted to new formats and applications are changed accordingly. However, for long-term preservation of rarely accessed documents, conversion becomes an unnecessary burden. Another drawback of conversion is that the file is actually changed repeatedly – and the cumulative effect that such successive conversions may have on the document is hard to predict. (Lorie, 2001)

Migration is also time-critical and needs to be carried out as soon as new formats are defined and before the current format is obsolete. If a generation is missed, the data may already be difficult to recover; if more generations are missed, it could be completely lost. Migration cycles need to be relatively frequent – few digital originals will survive more than five to seven years without some attention.

18.6.5 Emulation

The more complex a digital object is, the more loss there will be in its migration to new formats and generations of hardware and software. This has led some researchers to suggest that for such resources emulation might be a better technique. "Without emulation it is unclear how interactive digital objects could be preserved in a useful way" (Holdsworth and Wheatley, 2000; see also 2001). Emulation is the process of recreation of the hardware and software environment required to access a resource. It would be theoretically possible to emulate either the hardware or the software: software could be re-engineered in the future if sufficient metadata about it could be stored, or the software and operating systems which created the digital object could be stored with it, and the hardware platform to run them could be emulated in the future. Russell is of the opinion that "although emulation as an approach for preservation has been viewed with some scepticism, it is gaining support because it offers potentially a solution for the very long term" (1999, 8). She argues that this is a long-term solution because the technical environment is only emulated when it is needed, rather than being preserved along with the data. This means that costs occur at a later stage than if data is constantly reformatted.

18.6.6 Data Archaeology

Sometimes it may be necessary to rescue a digital resource which has not been migrated and which contains vital information, or to which some unforeseen disaster which has occurred. Occasionally data is discovered on old disks or tapes that have been accidentally preserved and data archaeology has success-fully rescued it. A wide range of techniques can be employed for this, with varying degrees of success. Data archaeology has also been proposed as a pres-ervation strategy. In this model, data would be refreshed regularly, but no migration would be performed, and no programs would be preserved to be emulated at a later stage. Instead, data archaeologists of the future would be left to puzzle out the data structures and connections in order to reaccess the infor-mation. This is an extreme form of just-in-time rescue which has the virtue of being low-cost, but which is highly risky. One argument for it is that better tech-niques are likely to be available in the future to recover data, and if the resources are felt to be of sufficient value, methods would be developed. This is analogous to present recovery and interpretation methods of historians and archaeolo-gists, and has the virtue that it would be for them to decide what has value to their society, rather than current content creators and managers making deci-sions about the future which could easily be misguided. See the excellent report by Ross and Gow (1999) for some approaches to data archaeology.

18.6.7 Output to Analogue Media

For many years an integral part of the conservation of fragile materials was the creation of a high quality surrogate during repair, restoration, or rebinding. This might be produced using photography, but more likely microfilming or even high quality photocopying would have been employed to provide a surro-gate that would satisfy the access needs for the majority of users and would thus help to preserve the original. Now that valued originals are being captured in digital form, does there still also need to be an analogue surrogate of the item? Is the production of an analogue version of the data file an appropriate preser-vation strategy?

In any digitization project, consideration must be given to the question of whether to microfilm before the digital imaging is done. This provides a preser-vation copy in an analogue format and circumvents some of the concerns over the longevity of the digital files. However, there are often features in an original that microfilm cannot capture but digitization can, and so the digital file is a valuable primary surrogate in its own right. For access purposes high quality prints and also large sized screens for viewing might satisfy most users needs. The printing company Oce Limited even has technology that can print out full colour images straight on to vellum, thus recreating the experience of a manuscript as accurately as is feasible. However, these address only the preservation of the original analogue or the provision of analogue surrogates for access. To consider using analogue output as a preservation mechanism for digital files the options are fairly limited to "Computer Output to Microfilm" or "COM".

The COM process involves printing the digital data file directly onto microfilm – so that each page of data becomes a separate frame in the film. The COM approach is thus most successful for large volumes of straightforward alphanumeric text or for bitonal images, as the Cornell project found:

> The Cornell project showed that computer output microfilm created from 600 dpi
> 1-bit images scanned from brittle books can meet or exceed national microfilm
> standards for image quality and permanence. (Chapman, Conway, and Kenney,
> 1999)

It is not really suitable for greyscale or colour images, as too much information is lost in the process to consider it for preservation purposes.

The COM process is also limited in useful application to linear text-based resources such as books, journals, catalogues, or collections of individual images, such as engineering drawings. Other digital products are likely to be rendered almost meaningless in analogue form, unless what is stored is the underlying code, plus supporting documentation, from which they can be recreated. This is probably an unrealistic expectation.

18.7 Rights Management

Issues of intellectual property rights and copyright need to be considered when preserving digital materials for long-term access, and it may be necessary to obtain permission from the rights holders for any reformatting. Given that laws, customs, and practices differ from country to country, we offer no particular examples, here, but merely warn that this will be an issue that librarians must consider when preserving, reformatting, or even emulating data. As Day points out:

> Solving rights management issues will be vital in any digital preservation
> programme. Typically, custodial organizations do not have physical custody of
> digital objects created or made available by other stakeholders (e.g. authors or
> publishers). Instead they will negotiate rights to this information for a specific
> period of time. Permissions to preserve digital information objects will also need
> to be negotiated with rights holders and any such agreement may, or may not,
> permit end user access. A digital archive will have to collect and store any relevant
> rights management information which could be stored as part of the descriptive
> metadata. (Day, 1999)

The rights are similar in both the analogue and digital environments, with the obvious exception that in the digital environment almost every action taken on a digital object may be classed as making a copy, broadcasting, or performance.

18.7.1 Copyright

Copyright applies to work that is recorded in some way. Rights exist for musical and dramatic work as well as films, sound recordings, and literary, artistic, or typographic arrangements. It gives the author/creator specific rights in relation to the work, prohibits unauthorized actions (mainly copying or broadcasting), and allows the author to take legal action against such infringements.

In the UK and much of the western world, a person's work is automatically copyrighted. As a result there is rarely such a thing as copyright-free material, so even where no action has been taken to register or claim copyright, there is a copyright issue to be addressed. However, some material may have had its rights waived (such as certain kinds of public documents) or the rights may have expired.

The issues for copyright in digital preservation are:

- Under what circumstances does the preserving organization have the right or permission to ingest the content into the preservation system or storage environment? This activity may be deemed illegal copying under copyright laws unless the permissions to store and make available have been clearly agreed, with associated written evidence.
- Especially for moving image and sound recordings, there may be many creators and copyright holders. For instance, the background music for a documentary may have different restrictions on use from the visual content, and each of these will have to be addressed.
- There may be restrictions on the separation of elements of a work or their independent use. For example, removing a sound track from the visual track or GIS data from satellite imagery.
- Under what circumstances may the content being preserved be made accessible as this may be defined as publication, performance, or broadcasting? The digital domain creates this new problem because of the naturally one-to-many relationship of digital content and networked access. Dark archives may be able to address this issue of acceptable archiving but may then conflict with the initial purpose of preservation – to provide future access.
- Metadata to record and track copyright will be required to enable digital preservation and eventual use. Sufficient metadata fields and associated records must be available to record all the rights holders and their relationships with each other and the wider collection. Management of this data can be time-consuming and costly to achieve. Without it , however, the digital preservation strategy would remain open to litigation risk and continuing uncertainty in the long term.

Within the current UK law, the rules for making archival copies allow certain exclusions under which copyright may not apply to that activity. These circumstances include:

- for archival replacement
- unpublished documents

- material of historical and cultural importance
- out of print items
- abstracts (of scientific and technical papers).

However, such rules are not easily adapted to the digital preservation framework and the very properties of digital moving images and sound make them difficult both to preserve useful metadata and to deal with IPR issues arising.

18.7.2 Moral and Ethical Rights

Whatever the copyright circumstances, creators have moral rights under IPR that relates to paternity and integrity. The moral right of paternity is the right to be identified as the author of the work. Unlike copyright which will eventually expire, this moral right will persist for as long as the digital item persists or the estate of the creator is prepared to pursue the issue.

Ayre and Muir identify the moral right of integrity as being problematic as publishers and creators "interpret the right of integrity to mean that their digital publications should not be changed in any way as a result of preservation activities". However, a legal expert cited in their report states that the integrity right is to object to derogatory treatment of the work. From a digital preservation perspective the consideration will need to be whether reformatting, migration, or even different compression algorithms could be deemed as potentially derogatory. Whilst unlikely to lead to litigation, preservation organizations take moral rights seriously, and this issue remains a somewhat vague but present concern, without yet any definitive answer for moving images and sound content.

A person's image is also their property. If a person is to be filmed, then a release form should be signed allowing that filming. Click and Go have produced a release form template (see http://clickandgovideo.ac.uk/releaseform. htm). This may cause unexpected issues at the point of digitization and digital preservation. For example, a choreographer who, over many years, films rehearsals and performances of their work would not necessarily have written permission to film those performing. So, whilst they own copyright in their own filming, they may be restricted from what they can do with that film due to the lack of permissions to film the individuals involved.

18.8 Valuing Digital Preservation

It can be argued that concerns about the immediate value of digital preservation have created one of the most significant barriers to organizations developing their own digital preservation programmes. In the context of a rapidly changing and volatile environment, and the constant backdrop of the need for accountability and restraint in spending, it is understandable that managers have been likely to exercise caution before embarking on such a programme. Aschenbrenner and Kaiser suggest that "costs of a digital repository are hard to calculate due to the lack of hands-on data from other initiatives... the lack of experience with digital preservation costs obstructs a complete picture". (Aschenbrenner and Kaiser, 2005).

Whilst there is a strong growth in the general application of digital preservation technologies and techniques, we have yet to see a maturing of the economic basis for this activity. Mainly this is due to the costing assumptions used by institutions differing significantly from each other. Differences include the means of estimating the cost of labour and infrastructure, the cost of investment and expected returns, and how costs are allocated between distinct activities that share resources.

Most of the published material relates to cost models, rather than fully fledged business models. A cost model provides a framework in which all costs can be recorded and allocated or apportioned to specific activities. A business model shows how the service functions and outlines the method by which it can sustain itself. This involves both strategy and implementation.

However a number of factors have begun to emerge which point to a gradual shift away from an apparently stark choice of yes/no in the decision to develop a digital preservation programme. These factors can be broadly summarized into:

• Growing awareness of loss/risk of loss of digital materials
• Growing awareness of the brief timeframe during which action can be taken
• Increasing dependence on digital materials
• Increasing understanding of cost elements
• Increasing number of case studies with practical models for identifying costs
• Increased awareness and understanding of lifecycle management and a cyclical/iterative approach
• Increased influence of the OAIS model.

18.8.1 Risk of Loss

As the volume of digital information being created continues to grow exponentially, personal experiences of losing digital materials also grow to the point where everyone will have had some experience of losing their own material and/or access to something they had cited or bookmarked. Depending on what the material was and how great the consequence of loss is, this experience can range from a minor irritation, all the way through to a major catastrophe. No-one can give blanket advice on what could/should be kept but every individual organization will have some digital materials which are of such key strategic, business or legal importance to them, they cannot afford to risk losing it.

18.8.2 Brief Timeframe

We also know that the life of digital material can be alarmingly short. The UK Web Archiving Consortium refers to the average lifespan of a website being around the same as a housefly (44 days). In such an environment, the option available in the non-digital environment of leaving preservation until later, or to someone else, is not viable. Moreover, there are an increasing number of case studies which illustrate the cost-effectiveness of taking action sooner rather than later. This is not something which need only affect organizations with national responsibilities for permanent preservation, it will affect everyone at some stage.

18.8.3 Increasing Dependence

The degree to which we have all become dependent on digital resources to satisfy a whole range of information requirements has been accelerated by the increased ubiquity of quality digital resources and also by government initiatives, such as the UK's Modernising Government agenda. The move to open access is also fuelled by the obvious capacity of digital technology to provide rapid access to scholarly material to the benefit of those working in the same or related field of activity.

There is great potential to exploit the capability of digital technology to provide efficient, seamless access to a whole range of resources. The inevitable consequence of this is that *all* organizations, whatever their mission, whatever their size, will have made some investment in digital technology to assist them in meeting their mission. To make such an investment without giving thought to identifying which digital resources created by the organization need to be retained, whether for a defined period of time, or forever, is not economically sustainable. There will therefore be increasing economic and strategic imperatives to undertake digital preservation activity. The extent and nature of that activity, and the priorities for allocating resources for digital preservation, must be determined by the organization's mission.

18.8.4 Cost Elements and Practical Models

When organizations such as libraries and archives began to embark on digital preservation programmes ten or so years ago, it was really both a leap in the dark and a leap of faith. Early pioneers of digital preservation programmes had no basis on which to estimate their costs so it was a question of "learning by doing" and making the decision to allocate resources to this activity and then to develop from there. These were sometimes very difficult decisions as they often required reallocating resources from elsewhere, always a painful process.

It was therefore no surprise that those organizations making this commitment tended to be those who already had either a strong mandate to preserve national heritage and records (such as national libraries and archives) or were already in the business of preserving digital resources (such as digital archives). The situation is different now. Because cost has been such a frequently asked question, there have been a number of articles and studies which have defined cost elements to be considered, which provide some guidance.

Even more helpful are case studies which provide much more detail about the actual costs incurred in a practical context. While no-one would suggest slavishly following these or that there can be a kind of magic formula which can always be applied to work out costs – there are too many variables for that – it is now possible to determine cost with much more confidence and precision, the costs relating to the specific requirements of an organization. This can be assessed at least for a 3–5 year period (a significant time period in the digital environment).

18.8.5 Lifecycle Collection Management

The concept of lifecycle management has been used in libraries and archives for many years, to help them allocate costs associated with processing non digital materials. It also has the potential to be used as a tool for allocating costs of managing digital resources, particularly as the cost-effectiveness of managing digital resources rests heavily on decisions made early in the lifecycle of the resource.

Figure 18.1 shows the British Library's Collection Management model and illustrates all the activities which may be needed during the lifecycle of a non-digital resource, and their cyclical nature. It also reminds us that this to work within a wider context of national/international agreements and collaborations. The British Library has done useful work on using lifecycle costing for both digital and non digital materials, and this is now being explored further in the JISC-funded LIFE project (see http://www.ucl.ac.uk/ls/lifeproject/).

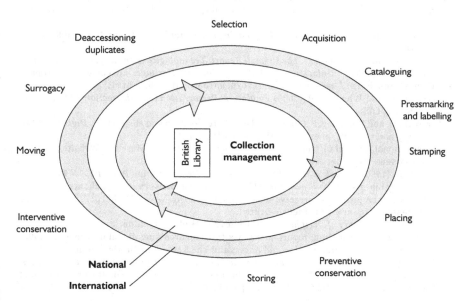

Figure 18.1 Lifecycle collection management (with thanks to the British Library).

18.9 Conclusion

The preservation of the written heritage in whatever format it is being produced is of crucial significance to civilized society. Given that it is so important, and that there are many strategic factors and costs which need to be established and predicted for the long term, it is an area where there are many uncertainties. Issues are hotly debated (sometimes in a wide public arena, as described about in the context of the disposal of newspapers) and different strategies have passionate adherents or opponents.

References

Aschenbrenner, A. and Kaiser, M. (2005) *White Paper on Digital Repositories*, March 2005, http://www2.uibk.ac.at/reuse/docs/reuse-d11_whitepaper_10.pdf.

Ayre, C. and Muir, A. (2004) *Right to Preserve? The Copyright and Licensing for Digital Preservation Project final report*, Leicestershire, Department of Information Science, Loughborough University, http://www.lboro.ac.uk/departments/ls/disresearch/CLDP/Project_reports.htm.

Chapman, S., Conway, P. and Kenney, A. R. (1999) Digital Imaging and Preservation Microfilm: the future of the hybrid approach for the preservation of brittle books. *RLG DigiNews*, 3(1), http://www.thames.rlg.org/preserv/diginews/diginews3-1.html.

Coleman, M. S. (2006) *Google, the Khmer Rouge and the public good.* Address to the Professional/Scholarly Publishing Division of the Association of American Publishers by the University of Michigan President, 6 February 2006, available at: http://www.umich.edu/pres/speeches/060206google.html.

Craig-McFeely, J. and Deegan, M. (2005) Bringing the digital revolution to medieval musicology: the digital image archive of medieval music (DIAMM). *RLG Diginews*, 9(3) http://www.rlg.org/en/page.php?Page_ID=20666#article1.

Day, M. (1999) Issues and approaches to preservation metadata. In *Joint RLG and NPO Preservation Conference: guidelines for digital imaging*, http://www.rlg.org/preserv/joint/day.html.

Feeney, M. (ed.) (1999) *Digital Culture: Maximizing the Nation's Investment*. National Preservation Office.

Geser, G. and Mulrenin, A. (2002), *The Digicult Report: Technological Landscapes for Tomorrow's Cultural Economy – Unlocking the Value of Cultural Heritage*. Luxembourg, European Commission, http://www.digicult.info/downloads/html/6/6.html.

Holdsworth, D. and Wheatley, P. (2000) *Emulation, Preservation and Abstraction*, http://129.11.152.25/CAMiLEON/.

Holdsworth, D. and Wheatley, P. (2001) Emulation, preservation and abstraction. *DigiNews*, 5(4), http://www.rlg.org/preserv/diginews/diginews5-4.html.

The International Council of Museums (ICOM), Disaster Relief for Museums Website. http://icom.museum/disaster_relief/.

Kenney, A. R. (1996) *Digital to Microfilm Conversion: a Demonstration Project 1994-96.* Cornell University Library, http://www.cornell.library.edu/preservation/pub.htm.

Lorie, R. A. (2001) A project on preservation of digital data. *DigiNews*, 5(3), http://www.rlg.ac.uk/preserv/diginews/diginews5-3.html.

Pope, M. (1975) *The Story of Decipherment*. Thames and Hudson, London.

Preserving Digital Information: report of the task force on archiving digital information (1996) The Commission on Preservation and Access and The Research Libraries Group.

Ross, S. and Gow, A. (1999) *Digital Archaeology: Rescuing Neglected and Damaged Data Resources.* A JISC/NPO Study within the Electronic Libraries (eLib) Programme on the Preservation of Electronic Materials, http://eprints.erpanet.org/47/

Russell, K. (1999) *Digital Preservation: Ensuring Access to Digital Materials Into the Future.* Leeds: CEDARS Project, http://www.leeds.ac.uk/cedars/Chapter.htm.

Singh, S. (1999) *The Code Book: the Science of Secrecy From Ancient Egypt to Quantum Cryptography.* Fourth Estate.

Tanner, S. (2004) *Reproduction Charging Models and Rights Policy for Digital Images in American Art Museums* (a Mellon Foundation study). http://kdcs.kcl.ac.uk/USart/.

Waller, M. and Sharpe, R. (2006) *Mind the Gap: Assessing Digital Preservation Needs in the UK.* A report prepared for the DPC, http://www.dpconline.org/docs/reports/uknamind-thegap.pdf

PART 7

From Information to Knowledge – the Human–Computer Interface

From the Information Age to the Intelligence Age: Exploiting IT and Convergence

Rae Earnshaw and John Vince

"Our ability to generate information and transport it about the planet on super highways of optical fibre is changing the way in which we communicate, work and live. There is not a single aspect of our lives that has gone untouched by the communication and computing revolution that is now upon us. As the pace of change gathers it will become clear that it will overshadow the impact of the printed word, industrial revolution, and physical transport. The next major wave of IT development must focus on the delivery of information and experience on demand, in the right form, at the right time, at the right price to fixed or mobile terminals anywhere. Ultimately, bandwidth, distance and time will no longer be significant cost elements as service and access become the dominant features of the changing demands of an information and experience focused society."

Professor Peter Cochrane OBE, former Chief Technologist at BT (http://www.cochrane.org.uk/)

19.1 Introduction

Digital convergence is bringing about a revolution in the way data are collected, stored, annotated, presented and accessed. Once stored they become information, which eventually enriches the intelligence base of the user population. There are four principal reasons why this is happening: reducing cost, increasing quality, flexibility of access and increasing system bandwidth. Moore's Law [1] results in ever-decreasing costs of processing and storage, whilst digital encoding ensures that all forms of media (text, image, sound and music) are held in a flexible, accurate, enduring format that previous technologies could not support. The ability to encode all types of media within a common format has made possible completely new ways of integrating and accessing information, such as web pages supported by sound, music and animation. Increased system bandwidth has resulted in mobile telephones capable of receiving text, voice, images, videos and web pages. Broadband internet services have transformed the quality and content of information services at a global level. Devices such as mobile phones, PDAs, PSPs and computers are increasingly more "intelligent", can be networked and are increasingly connectable through "Bluetooth" interfaces. User interfaces are becoming more adaptable and flexible, and can be tailored to particular application domains. Digital information is becoming seamless and invisible, enabling more attention to be paid to the content and the user's interaction with it. This revolution is having effects on the development and organization of information and artefact repositories such as libraries, museums, and exhibitions and the way in which physical and digital aspects are mediated to users. The changes that digital convergence are bringing about are substantial, ubiquitous and will be enduring.

Media is increasingly linked to technology because the capture, editing and dissemination of information is increasingly digital. It is cheaper, more accurate, and easier to transfer information from one medium to another. Thus students who study media in the 21st century benefit from an understanding of the framework brought about by digital convergence. In addition, today's entertainment companies are exploiting the distribution of their digital assets across all types of digital media platforms to maximize their investment in a particular production. This involves transformations applied to the original information in order to produce media outputs (e.g. film, DVD, website, game etc.). Television, the internet, mobile phones, and PDAs are all becoming part of a single distribution platform for information and entertainment.

A conference on *"Envisioning future challenges in networked information"* (6–7 July 2006) organized by JISC/CNI highlighted a number of aspects and issues related to networking. There were sessions on the following topics: Learning Spaces, E-Metrics, Interoperability across Scholarly Repositories, Digital Libraries in the Classroom, Access and Preservation, E-Theses, Open Access, How Users are Changing, Preservation and Curation, Massive Digitization Projects, Resource Discovery, and Future Challenges.

Here is a summary of the main outputs in terms of ongoing issues that institutions need to take account of in their forward planning for Libraries and ICT Services:

● **Massive Digitization Projects Worldwide**

University of Oxford, University of Michigan, University of California. The latter has digitized 34 million volumes from 10 University libraries.

The Oxford-Google mass digitization programme.[2,3,4]

● **The Net Generation**

The Net Generation (born between 1982–91) are now our students – they have a different set of priorities and ways of working – are we catering for their needs? Have we studied the way they learn, study, and work? *"The Net Generation has grown up with information technology. The aptitudes, attitudes, expectations, and learning styles of Net Gen students reflect the environment in which they were raised – one that is decidedly different from that which existed when faculty and administrators were growing up.*"[5,6,7,8]

- **Learning Spaces**

How do we define the characteristics of current and future learning spaces that are attractive to occupy and use? How do we extend learning spaces from the traditional environments of lecture room, classroom, and laboratories, into common spaces, social spaces, and virtual spaces?

University of Warwick Learning Grid – combines physical/group/virtual/VLE. [9, 10]

- **How Users are Changing**

Online search is increasingly replacing physical search. Changing practices of Learning, Teaching and Scholarship – for example in the way information is used and deployed. There are new genres of scholarly work. For example, the Perseus Project has been developing a digital library in the humanities. Initial work concentrated exclusively on ancient Greek culture, using this domain as a case study for a compact, densely hypertextual library on a single, but interdisciplinary subject. Since it has achieved its initial goals with the Greek materials, however, Perseus is using the existing library to study the new possibilities (and limitations) of the electronic medium and to serve as the foundation for work in new cultural domains: Perseus has begun coverage of Roman and now Renaissance materials, with plans for expansion into other areas of the humanities as well. The goal is not only to help traditional scholars conduct their research more effectively but, more importantly, to help humanists use the technology to redefine the relationship between their work and the broader intellectual community. "Perseus is an evolving digital library, engineering interactions through time, space, and language."[11] A further example is the work of Dr Peter Murray Rust at the University of Cambridge in the area of automated analysis of data in scientific publications, and the development of a Chemical Markup Language.[12] If these areas continue to expand, we need to consider how they are supported via new kinds of infrastructure.

- **NSF Cyberinfrastructure Directorate**

The new (March 2006) NSF Cyberinfrastructure Directorate has been set in place to address these challenges in the USA. Its objective is to "define and build cyberinfrastructure that facilitates the development of new applications, allows applications to interoperate across institutions and disciplines, insures that data and software acquired at great expense are preserved and easily available and empowers enhanced collaboration over distance, time and disciplines."[13,14]

- **Building Citations Databases from Blogs**

Technorati: "50 million blogs, some of them have to be good."[15]

- **Higher Level Structures are Needed in Universities**

IT strategy needs to be steered to meet new needs and requirements.

- **Institutional Repositories**

Microsoft, the Andrew W. Mellon Foundation, the Coalition for Networked Information, the Digital Library Federation, and JISC are working together to accomplish interworking between repositories.

- **Shared Services are Expected to Increase**

Shared services are expected to reduce duplication, increase efficiency, improve standardization, provide improved services to users, and facilitate sharing of best practice and latest products – thus collaborations between institutions will become increasingly important.

- **Library of the Future**

One example is at the Bodley Library, Oxford.[16]

- **Data Curators**

What have they learned from operating data services?

- **Interoperability of Services and Facilities, and Location-independent Working**
- **E-theses are expected to be a growing area**

There is a British Library Project in this area which is expected to be operational mid-2007. Dspace lacks some of the functionality that is needed for the future.

- **Strategies are needed for E-collections**

Contribution, archiving, retrieval.

19.2 Current Evolution

19.2.1 Technology

Blogs, wikis, tagging, MP3 players, online music, podcasts, AJAX, and Skype, to name but a few, have evolved considerably in the past year, and are moving mainstream. Companies have incorporated Blog-watching into their PR and marketing operations. Universities are also providing open content. Programmers are producing open-source software (some of this may be short-lived, some of it may be here to stay – often it is difficult to know at any point in time which is which). Further information on these areas is provided in the References section at the end of this paper.

ACM has an online Technology News web site with regular updates[17] and also online information on the latest computing trends.[18] Discussions with technology experts are available for download to your computer or MP3 player[19] and distance learning.[20]

The Foresight Programme of the Office of Science and Technology (OST) brings together key people, knowledge, and ideas to look beyond the present. Some technology trends are summarized on the Foresight website.[21] The OST has recently (26 January 2006) launched an initiative in the area of Intelligent Infrastructure Systems.[22] A central aspect of this initiative is the transformation of the *"information age"* into the *"intelligence age"*. This is a key theme for the future and it has therefore been made the title of this chapter.[23] Furthermore, there is information on the area of users and services in intelligent networks[24] and complexity and emergent behaviour in ICT systems.[25]

19.3 Utilizing Current Technology

Several questions arise concerning the utilization of today's technology. For example, how do we, or will we employ technology and address change? And perhaps, most importantly, how will students benefit from all of this? Here are some aspects to consider:

- Online, hybrid, or blended learning
- Distance learning and mobile learning
- Student induction and preparation – for a diverse range of students
- Factors that lead to student success
- Implementing technology in learning-centred environments
- E-portfolios and other online assessment tools
- Emerging technologies for teaching and learning (blogs, wikis, podcasts, etc.)
- Assessing information value and quality
- Open content and open source
- Multimedia resources and delivery
- Building and sustaining learning communities
- Using technology to enhance communication between staff and students
- Online student services (tutoring, advising, payments, hybrid – i.e. online plus human – etc.)
- Integrating online working with counter services, when required
- Facilitating institutional change with technology
- Professional development for faculty and staff
- Global learning or international education
- Gender equity, the Digital Divide, and access for everyone
- Educational technology use in Asia & the Pacific, Europe, South America, and Africa.

19.4 New and Emerging ICT Application Areas

19.4.1 Learning and Teaching

Over the next decade, three complementary interfaces will shape how people learn:

- The familiar webpages and windows "desktop"
- Multi-user virtual environments (including sensory immersion via virtual reality)
- Augmented realities based on mobile wireless devices and infused in real world settings.

The "millennial" learning styles ascribed to the Net Generation stem primarily from the desktop interface. However, the growing use of virtual environments and augmented realities is fostering new forms of mediated learning in users of all ages. The crucial factor leading to this "neomillennial" learning is that the desktop interface is not psychologically immersive, while in contrast virtual environments and augmented realities induce a strong sense of "presence." Psychological immersion enables a powerful pedagogy, situated learning, which is based on authentic contexts, activities, and assessment coupled with guidance from expert mentoring as well as tacit learning through collaborative activities. Through situated learning enabled by psychological presence, virtual environments and augmented realities are shaping participants' learning styles beyond what using sophisticated computers and telecommunications has fostered thus far, with multiple implications for education and training. (C. Dede, Harvard University, 2006)[26]

- **Areas for technology support:**

Blogging, video streaming, simulations, field reflections, scenario learning, concept mapping tools, and online journals.

- **Current best practices in:**

Online learning pedagogy including motivational techniques, learning style ideas, and blended learning strategies.

- **Learning Styles:**

Auditory, reflective, visual, and hands-on, or kinesthetic learners. Considerable research has already been undertaken in this area: *Implications of Emerging Learning Styles",* C. Dede[27] *"Planning for Neomillennial Learning Styles: Implications for Investments in Technology and Faculty"*[28] *"Planning for NeoMillennial Learning Styles"*[29] *"Millennial Learning: On Demand Strategies for Generation X and Beyond"*[30] *"The Millennial Learner – Challenges and Opportunitiest"*[31] *"Blogs, Blends, Boards, or Back to the Future: Building the Ultimate Online Learning Environment"*[32] and *"Blended EDU: Social Media Resources for Learning in the Digital Age"*[33]

19.4.2 Managing Knowledge, Information and Data

Profound and qualitative changes have been happening in the use of computers to manage information. Consider text (e.g. documents, books, journals, etc.). Some 20 years ago, storing text electronically was a very unusual practice! Documents and books lived in filing cabinets and libraries. In so far as computers were involved in their management, it was largely limited to library catalogue databases.

Today, billions of documents are online through the World Wide Web. They are being joined there by other containers of information and meaning such as images, sound recordings, movies and simulations. Computers have graduated from "data management" to "information management". They could even be said to have become tools for "knowledge management" in so far as they manage the digital resources that embody human knowledge.

One technique for gaining greater leverage over knowledge and information resources is the application of "metadata". In a sense, adding metadata is not very different from cataloguing a library or art collection. It's a question of classification and labelling. Its value is being recognized in various subject domains such as government, health, librarianship and archiving. However, in the context of a global Web, problems of classification and labelling get a whole lot more problematic: especially if you want the computer system to be more than just a passive container for knowledge and information resources, but an active ally in discovering and retrieving what is relevant to different users. Considerable research has already been undertaken in developing automatic tools to encode text, audio and image-based databases so that users can search and retrieve "intelligent" responses to their requests.

Enter a whole arcane vocabulary of problems and solutions: interoperability, category lists, Dublin Core, topic maps, thesauri, ontologies...

(With acknowledgements to the BCS Electronic Publishing Group)

19.4.3 The Semantic Web

"The Web was designed as an information space, with the goal that it should be useful not only for human-human communication, but also so that machines would be able to participate and help. One of the major obstacles to this has been the fact that most information on the Web is designed for human consumption, and even if it was derived from a database with well defined meanings (in at least some terms) for its columns, the structure of the data is not evident to a robot browsing the web. Leaving aside the artificial intelligence problem of training machines to behave like people, the Semantic Web approach develops languages for expressing information in a machine processable form. The Semantic Web is thus a mesh of information linked up in such a way as to be easily processable by machines, on a global scale. It is an efficient way of representing data on the World Wide Web, or as a globally linked database. It converts the World Wide Web from documents to accessible and usable knowledge. Your computer could, for example, automatically find the nearest dentist to where you live and book an appointment for you that fits in with your schedule".[34, 35, 36]

19.4.4 From ICT to e-Culture

An Advisory Report on the digitalization of culture and the implications for cultural policy was published by the Netherlands Council for Culture. [37] The objective of this study is to redefine and reassess the future shape and direction of cultural policy in the light of the changing media landscape in the digital age, especially in relation to the creative arts, cultural heritage, as well as information and media policies. "E-culture is not just something to do with computers – the cultural implications are far greater than the mere instrumental exploitation of technical opportunities. It is more than a medium – it is opening the door to new forms of expression, changing the roles played by cultural institutions, and placing the audience and the user centre stage."[38, 39]

- **Oxford Internet Institute**

The Oxford Internet Institute[40, 41] is a multi-disciplinary research organization devoted to the study of the societal implications of the Internet. It was launched in 2001 by an initial endowment of £10 million from the Steve Shirley Foundation plus £5 million of public funding from the Higher Education Funding Council for England.[42]

19.4.5 Computers in Entertainment

This includes the use of computers in animation, digital asset management, digital cinema, digital rights management, games, interactive television, the Internet, movies, music, performing arts, robotics, toys, and virtual reality. For further information refer to online publication "Computers in Entertainment"[43, 44] Interviews are also available with Nicholas Negroponte[45] and Dana Plautz.[46]

Full interviews and papers on the $100 laptop, digital cinema, games, MIT Media Lab, video services, *et al.* in *A Word from the Editor* and *Digital Library*.

19.4.6 Library of the future

The DaVinci Institute[47] sees the future of libraries pursuing the following trends:

- Communication systems are continually changing the way people access information
- All technology ends. All technologies commonly used today will be replaced by something new
- We haven't yet reached the ultimate small particle for storage
- But soon, search technology will become increasingly more complicated
- Time compression is changing the lifestyle of library patrons
- Over time we will be transitioning to a verbal society
- The demand for global information is growing exponentially
- The stage is being set for a new era of Global Systems
- We are transitioning from a product-based economy to an experience-based economy
- Libraries will transition from a center of information to a center of culture.

Recommendations for libraries

I. Evaluate the library experience

II.   Embrace new information technologies
   - Create a technology advisory board and stay in close communication with them
   - Recruit technologically-aware members of the community to hold regular discussion panels where the community at large is invited to join in the discussions
   - Develop a guest lecture series on the new technologies

III. Preserve the memories of your own communities.
   - Experiment with creative spaces so the future role of the library can define itself:
   - Band practice rooms
   - Podcasting stations
   - Blogger stations
   - Art studios
   - Recording studios
   - Video studios
   - Imagination rooms
   - Theatre-drama practice rooms.

19.5 Conclusion

The printing press was a technological breakthrough in the dissemination of the written word, but we must not fail to recognize the significance digital technology is having upon the storage, compositing and dissemination of every form of media we currently manipulate. Never before has a technology been discovered that offers the wealth of advantages offered by digital encoding. The challenges to harness the hidden potential of this technology are overwhelming and we should not be surprised that it will take considerable time to design and implement useful and enduring systems. No doubt many mistakes will be made, but progress will be speedier if individual sectors work with and influence the technologists behind the emerging systems.

As with previous industrial revolutions, today's digital revolution will bring dramatic changes in procedures, systems, jobs, careers, mobility and social behaviours. Some jobs and procedures will disappear completely, but they will be replaced by others, which will entail redundancies and retraining programmes. For example, today, the hot-metal production or type for newspapers has virtually disappeared. The changeover to computer-based technology was painful but inevitable, and now the technology is ubiquitous, no one would ever contemplate turning back the clock.

Today libraries are facing the challenges posed by digital technology. No one is suggesting that libraries will disappear, but they will change. Whether the number of libraries increases or decreases is anyone's guess, but the role of the library will change. What is certain, is that they will not just be custodians of books, they will be disseminators of information and knowledge no matter what its medium.

References

The Top Ten IT Issues: http://www.educause.edu/ir/library/pdf/ERM0530.pdf.
Educause Center for Applied Research (ECAR) *Students and Information Technology 2005: Convenience, Connection, Control, and Learning.* http://www.educause.edu/ir/library/pdf/ERS0506/ekf0506.pdf.
Educating the Net Generation. http://www.educause.edu/ir/library/pdf/pub7101g.pdf.
IT Networking in Higher Education: Campus Commodity and Competitive Differentiator. http://www.educause.edu/ir/library/pdf/ecar_so/ers/ERS0502/ekf0502.pdf.
Blogs. http://en.wikipedia.org/wiki/Blog and http://www.marketingterms.com/dictionary/blog/.
Wikis. http://en.wikipedia.org/wiki/Wiki.
Tagging of Metadata. http://www.flickr.com/
Podcasts. http://en.wikipedia.org/wiki/Podcasting.
AJAX. http://en.wikipedia.org/wiki/AJAX.
Skype. http://en.wikipedia.org/wiki/Skype.
Mobile Blogging, Skyping, and Podcasting – Targetting Undergraduates' Communication skills in Transnational Learning Contexts. http://www.microlearning.org/micropapers/MLproc_2005_oliver.pdf.
Libraries and E-Learning. http://elag2005.web.cern.ch/elag2005/media/workshop5.pdf.
Using a Course Management System to meet the Challenges of Large Lecture Classes. http://scooby.webct.com/webct_userconf_2005/papers/Bongey.pdf.
The Future of Networking in Higher Education (From Tin Cans to the Holodeck). http://www.educause.edu/ir/library/pdf/ERM0547.pdf
Education Guardian, 10 January 2006 – Special Issue of Educ@Guardian on IT in Schools. "With hi-tech learning aids such as stop-frame animation and video-editing now commonplace in many schools, Bett 2006 promises to be a mouthwatering prospect for the digital maverick." http://education.guardian.co.uk/elearning/story/0,10577,1682472,00.html.
How blogs can make the link. http://education.guardian.co.uk/appleeducation/story/0,16926,1682538,00.html.
Look to the new academics for a glimpse of the future. http://education.guardian.co.uk/higher/comment/story/0,9828,1682606,00.html.
http://www.demos.co.uk/.
Prof. Stephen Hepple, Learn3K Global Research Centre. http://education.guardian.co.uk/elearning/comment/0,10577,1682536,00.html.
http://www.learn3k.org/learn3k_launch/.
http://www.ncirl.ie/inside.asp?pageId=442&sectionId=6&level=1.
http://www.jonathansblog.net/stephen_heppell_learn3k_launch.
http://www.siliconrepublic.com/news/news.nv?storyid=single4830.
http://www.ultralab.anglia.ac.uk/pages/ultralab/team/stephen/contents.html.
Interactive Whiteboard. http://education.guardian.co.uk/getonboard/0,16957,1679885,00.html.
Game Theory Makes its Mark. http://education.guardian.co.uk/elearning/story/0,10577,1682478,00.html.
Nesta FutureLab's Games and Learning Handbook. http://www.nestafuturelab.org/research/handbooks.htm.
Teaching with Games. http://www.nestafuturelab.org/research/teachingwithgames.htm.
Digging for Data that can Change our World. http://education.guardian.co.uk/elearning/story/0,10577,1682496,00.h.tml
http://www.nactem.ac.uk/
Extreme Data – Rethinking the "I" in IT. http://www.cochrane.org.uk/downloads/csc_lef_extremedata.pdf.

1. http://en.wikipedia.org/wiki/Moore's_law.
2. http://www.bodley.ox.ac.uk/librarian/CNIGoogle/CNIGoogle.htm.
3. http://www.infotoday.com/newsbreaks/nb041220-2.shtml.
4. http://searchenginewatch.com/showPage.html?page=3447411.
5. http://www.educause.edu/content.asp?PAGE_ID=5989&bhcp=1.
6. http://www.educause.edu/ir/library/pdf/pub7101.
   pdf#search=%22net%20generation%22.
7. http://www.growingupdigital.com/.
8. http://www.riverdeep.net/current/2000/10/100400_netgen.jhtml.
9. http://www2.warwick.ac.uk/study/grid/.
10. http://www.denison.edu/learningspaces/.
11. http://www.perseus.tufts.edu/; http://xml.coverpages.org/perseus.html.
12. http://en.wikipedia.org/wiki/Peter_Murray-Rust.
13. http://www.adec.edu/nsf/nsfcyberinfrastructure.html
14. http://www.nsf.gov/dir/index.jsp?org=OCI.
15. http://www.technorati.com/.
16. http://www.bodley.ox.ac.uk/librarian/lotf/lotf_files/frame.htm.
17. http://technews.acm.org/current.cfm.
18. http://www.acmqueue.org/.
19. http://www.acmqueue.org/modules.php?name=Queuecasts.
20. http://www.elearnmag.org/
21. http://www.foresight.gov.uk/Previous_Rounds/Foresight_1999__2002/Informa-
    tion_Communications_and_Media/Reports/ITEC%20Technologies/Cover.htm.
22. http://www.foresight.gov.uk/.
23. http://www.foresight.gov.uk/esight/2006January/Index.htm.
24. http://www.foresight.gov.uk/Intelligent%20Infrastructure%20Systems/
    Reports%20and%20Publications/Intelligent_Infrastructure_Futures/Users_and_
    services.pdf.
25. http://www.foresight.gov.uk/Intelligent%20Infrastructure%20Systems/
    Reports%20and%20Publications/Intelligent_Infrastructure_Futures/
    Complexity%20and%20Emergent%20Behaviour/review_Summary.pdf.
26. http://www.gse.harvard.edu/%7Ededech/.
27. http://admin.acadiau.ca/paoffice/newsite/planning/Acadia.ppt.
28. http://www.gse.harvard.edu/~dedech/DedeNeoMillennial.pdf.
29. http://www.educause.edu/ir/library/pdf/eqm0511.pdf.
30. http://www.ltimagazine.com/ltimagazine/article/articleDetail.jsp?id=262368.
31. https://cbase.som.sunysb.edu/som/fac_retreat_uploads/85.pdf.
32. http://www.aace.org/conf/site/tutorials/index.cfm/fuseaction/ViewTutorial/
    eventID/1584.
33. http://blendededu.com/2005/10/technology-encourages-active-learning.html.
34. http://www.w3.org/DesignIssues/Semantic.html.
35. http://infomesh.net/2001/swintro/.
36. http://en.wikipedia.org/wiki/Semantic_web.
37. http://www.cultuur.nl/files/pdf/adviezen/E-cultuur_engels.pdf.
38. http://portal.unesco.org/culture/en/ev.php-URL_ID=27196&URL_DO=DO_TOPIC&URL_
    SECTION=201.html.
39. http://www.i4donline.net/nov04/ict_edu.asp.
40. http://www.oii.ox.ac.uk/.
41. http://en.wikipedia.org/wiki/Oxford_Internet_Institute.
42. Higher Education Funding Council for England.
43. http://www.acm.org/pubs/cie.html.
44. http://www.acm.org/pubs/cie/jan2006/docs/wordeditor.pdf.
45. Nicholas Negroponte.
46. Dana Plautz.
47. http://www.davinciinstitute.com/page.php?ID=120.

20

Cognitive Implications of Information Spaces: Human Issues in the Design and Use of Electronic Library Interfaces

Sherry Chen, Jane Coughlan, Steve Love, Robert D. Macredie and Frankie Wilson

20.1 Introduction

This chapter reviews some of the most important human dimensions applicable to the design and use of information spaces, with a focus on library applications. The chapter begins with an introduction to the area of information spaces, presenting an established view of human information processing that can be used to understand the way in which users make sense of information that is presented to them through information spaces. Designing effective systems that allow access to information spaces is a complex problem and there has been substantial research into the area. This chapter will turn to describing a set of well-established principles, drawn from the work of Norman (1988), that views consistent and well-grounded design as a key issue in alleviating problems of use by considering design in relation to users. To this end, a design case is presented to explore user task scenarios with respect to a particular library application, thus illustrating the emerging usability issues as they relate to interface design features. Notwithstanding the importance of the high-level design principles, the diverse background of the individual users accessing information spaces are not necessarily acknowledged or addressed. The chapter will therefore go on to present an analysis of what are argued to be the most important individual differences that can influence the way that users interact with systems and make sense of the information that they encounter. Finally, the chapter will consider the design of information spaces to allow for their context of use in terms of issues related to devices and mobility that are likely to become increasingly important in the coming few years for the provision of information spaces and the electronic library interface.

20.2 Information Spaces

Information spaces have been defined as "objects (real or virtual) to which the individual turns to acquire information" (McKnight, 2000: 730). It could be argued that this is the definition of both libraries and the Internet. As has been extensively argued within the library profession, the key to the success of libraries in the electronic age is the value of the interface that they provide between users and information spaces. Therefore, consideration of what users can or cannot do with the information available is key to the design of a successful library interface, whether traditional or electronic (Coleman and Oxnam, 2002). Dillon (2002) has detailed the advantages for users of an electronic information space. He explains that the electronic delivery of library services means that the user can access information rapidly, at a reduced cost, and that the information obtained can be easily manipulated, moved and shared across geographical boundaries and collaborative environments. While such advantages are clear, user interactions with electronic information spaces are cognitive in nature, involving perception, memory, attention, categorization, representation, problem-solving, decision-making, navigation and language processing. All of these are issues that are of concern in user-interface design, most notably in the field of human-computer interaction (Dillon, 2003).

Research from cognitive psychology forms the cornerstone in understanding the mental processes of users when interacting with electronic information spaces. As such, researchers have highlighted the critical research issues in designing effective user interfaces to such spaces. For example, Rapp, Taylor and Crane (2003) provided a review of findings of cognitive research and their application to the design of electronic libraries. They cited eight components of human information processing: integration (e.g., encoding and retrieval of information in memory); acquisition (e.g., knowledge representation); representation (e.g., format and content of representations in memory); comprehension (e.g., knowledge transfer); organization (organization of information in memory); retrieval (e.g., accessibility of representations); engagement (e.g., individual motivation) and individual differences relevant to the design of what they termed the "digital library". These components of information processing, and the issues that they raise for the way that users make sense of information presented to them, is important and underpins the detailed analysis of the way that users interact with electronic information spaces. However, there is a growing awareness of the limitations of information processing informed work (see for example Nardi, 1996; Hutchins, 1995; Suchman, 1987; Winograd and Flores, 1986). A key limitation is that this body of research has neglected the importance of how people work when using a computer interface in the real world (Landauer, 1987), suggesting that consideration of human-computer interaction requires a holistic approach. For many, such broadening of the focus of design issues beyond information processing adds unwelcome (though extremely important) complexity. An alternative approach is to start with high-level design principles. This will ensure that designers of electronic information space interfaces appreciate some central design concerns and common problem areas.

20.3 High-Level Design Principles

A famous set of principles comes from Norman (1988), whose intention was to set out the central issues that impact on the design and cognitive efficiency of interfaces. He drew on examples from the (mis) design of everday things before seeking to consider their application in computer systems. Norman's (1988) seven key principles for user-centred interface design integrate cognitive psychology issues with usability features of interfaces and can be thought of as a philosophy for design that remains as pertinent today as when Norman first proposed it. Each of the seven principles will now be introduced and explained.

20.3.1 Constraints

Constraints refer to making use of properties of objects to tell the users what they can and cannot do. Physical constraints are often used in the design of artefacts within the real world to limit the way in which a user can interact with the artefact. For example, a radio button, often used in the design of computer interfaces, can be "pushed" in and out, taking two states (usually used to denote "on" and "off"). There are, however, other types of constraints. Semantic constraints are those where the meaning of the situation in which the object of interest is used scopes the set of possible actions that might be taken. Such semantic constraints rely on the knowledge that we have of the world and the situation of the object's use. For example, it is only meaningful to sit facing one way on a motorbike. Cultural constraints are ones which rely on conventions, which form an accepted part of the culture in which the object resides and in which the user is operating. In Europe, for example, we accept that the colour red means "stop" in travel situations. Logical constraints are those that dictate what should be done through logic. For example, if a dialogue box appears which contains a message like "404 error" and an "OK" button; clicking anywhere outside of the box produces no action. It may be logically concluded that we are constrained to press the "OK" button if we want to proceed, despite the fact that we may not think that it is "OK" that the error has occurred. There is clearly a great interplay between the different types of constraints and the categories are not as clearly demarcated as the preceding discussion implies.

20.3.2 Mappings

Mappings entail making links clear and obvious. They are closely related to constraints and are often argued to reduce the reliance on other information held in memory. Mappings are concerned with the relationship between different things. For example, when using word processors the scroll wheel on a mouse can be used to scroll up and down a document, as can the scroll bar down the right-hand side of the document window. In both cases moving the interface object one way produces a corresponding movement type in the document. So, pushing the wheel up (i.e., away from the user) moves you up in the document (i. e., towards the beginning/top). This represents a natural mapping between the action of the user and the outcome in the application.

20.3.3 Visibility

Visibility refers to making clear what is happening to the user and is about providing the user with obvious, usually visual, information about the system, its use and the mappings between action and outcome. For example, it should be clear to the user what actions are open to him/her at any time. Feedback is an associated, often overlooked issue – when a user does something, there should be some form of feedback to indicate that the action has had an effect, and so to avoid multiple actions from the user before an effect is registered.

20.3.4 Consistency

Consistency refers to making things work and respond in the same way at different times. It is important that, when a user acts in a particular way in different contexts and at different times, the object or system responds consistently. For example, in all circumstances the scroll wheel should act in the same way – it should never scroll down in the document when it is moved upwards. There are many examples of inconsistency in interface design (and in the "real world") and they can cause both "errors" in use and great frustration for users.

20.3.5 Experience

Experience captures the importance of making use of what users already know. This is an obvious issue but can cause difficulties in that it tends to lead designers to make assumptions about users, which may be problematic. For example, the exploitation of experience may be problematic where systems are used across cultural boundaries and/or have a diverse user base. An example of where experience is drawn on heavily in interface design is in the use of standard interface objects (e.g., dialogue boxes) across multiple applications and platforms. The argument is that once you have the experience of them, you will be able to deal with them in varying contexts. There is clearly an association with the issue of consistency – if you are drawing on the experience of users by, for example, using standard interface objects, you must ensure that the objects act in the same way in different contexts, otherwise users will encounter difficulties and become frustrated.

20.3.6 Affordance

Affordance refers to making use of the properties of items to suggest the way that they should be used. In many ways it is a common sense concept, but one that is actually very complex when considered in detail. For example, the shape of a chair affords sitting on; its form and being does not suggest that you should, for example, use it to cut something. There are great debates in psychology about affordance and its relation to "knowledge in the world" versus "knowledge in the head". For our purposes, it is enough to think of affordance in a simple way: buttons afford pressing; sliders afford sliding, etc. There are links between the principal of affordance and those of visibility, constraints and mapping.

20.3.7 Simplicity

Simplicity refers to perhaps the most obvious and seemingly fundamental issue in the design of interfaces ¾ making the completion of tasks as simple as possible. However, electronic information spaces often require vast functionality, and this sometimes leads to complex interfaces and interaction design. Keeping simplicity at the heart of the approach to design is a good starting point but is often easier said than done. Simplicity is an overarching concept, which we can think of the other issues covered above as contributing to. If we can design in a way that is sensitive to the issues raised in Norman's (1988) principles it is more likely that the design will be seen as uncluttered and clean, with few distractions (e.g., an excessive number of options or choices); in other words, it will be a simple as possible.

These high-level design principles provide grounding for any approach to design. The next section details a real-life example of a library interface to vivify the application of the principles for design.

20.4 Design Case

In order to illustrate the facets of interface design that have been presented so far, this section will focus on a design case for a library application. The chosen example is the Brunel University Library E-journals gateway (provided by TDNet), which is a searchable catalogue of all full-text electronic journals subscribed to by Brunel University Library. The analysis of the attendant design problems in the design case is limited to a critique framed in terms of the high-level design principles presented previously.

20.4.1 Brunel University Library: E-journals Gateway

An electronic information space that is currently a feature of most libraries is a suite of electronic journals. The driver for this move from a traditional to an electronic format for this information space is the accessibility provided by desktop and remote delivery options. At Brunel University, there has been a number of methods of accessing this information space, from indexing on the catalogue (OPAC), to a home-grown A-Z list, through a commercially provided search algorithm for the home-grown list, finally arriving at the present, commercially produced searchable database. Presentation of the design case is firstly headed by a standard (and seemingly innocuous) request by a typical student (whom we will call Julie). The case has been divided into two scenarios (A and B) and is organized by the intended task to illustrate the nature of the user interaction with an electronic information space, along with a proposed context for the execution of the task. The task interface design problems as encountered by the user are then related and finally the usability issues emerging from such a design are highlighted.

Scenario A

Task: Finding a specific journal in electronic format from off campus.

Context: Julie has to give an assessed presentation in two days time for one of her first year modules. The assignment brief instructs her to use three specific references relating to the cognitive implications of information spaces. She has already borrowed the two recommended books from the library, and now needs to get the recommended article. She is a part-time student and prefers to work at home because of childcare responsibilities.

Task interface problems

There are four important elements for Julie to successfully find the journal article she requires: 1) secure remote login (Athens); 2) accessing the required journal; 3) ascertaining that she has access to the required year; and 4) navigating to the correct volume, issue and page numbers. However, this process is hindered by the fact that Julie must know that journals can be available electronically, and such journals are listed on the e-journals gateway.

1. Julie is forced to login using her Athens ID before she can view the search screen. However, the interface provides no information about which of the four University usernames and passwords is her Athens ID, and presumes that the user will know which to use. Fortunately, Julie had attended the Library induction at the start of the academic year, and has noted her Athens ID.
2. Julie types the journal title from her reference into the search box and activates the search.
3. The years available are displayed in the second column of the results screen. However, Julie does not notice this, and clicks directly on the title of the correct journal.
4. Brunel University Library purchases journals from a wide variety of publishers, each with their own unique interface for accessing content. When Julie is taken through to the publisher's page, she is initially disoriented as she has not used a journal from this publisher before. However, she quickly navigates to the correct volume, issue and page number, and downloads the PDF of the journal article.

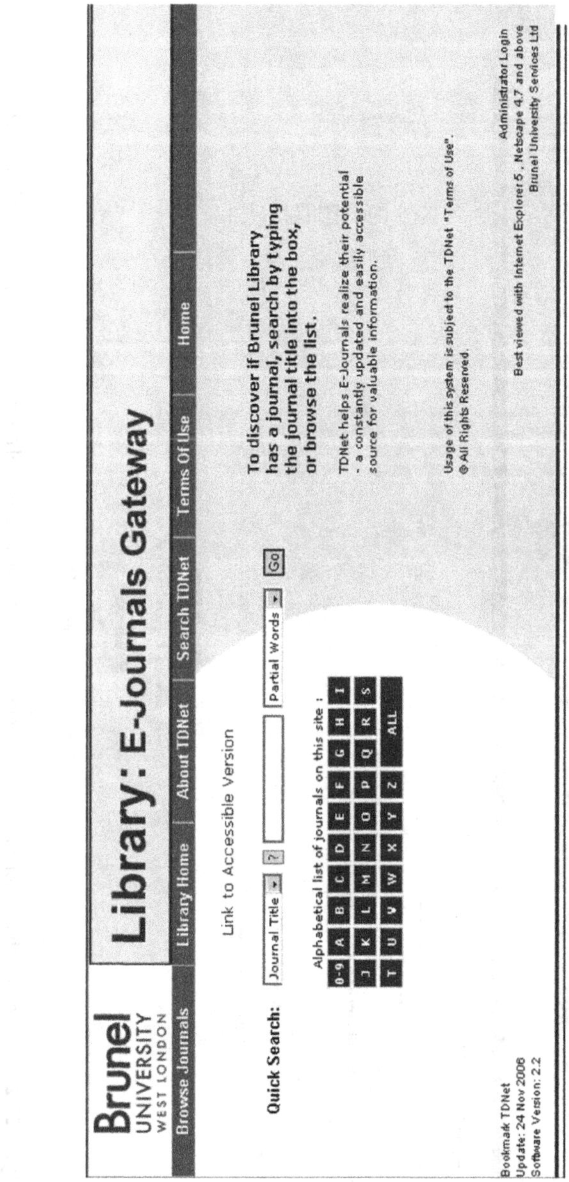

Figure 20.1   Search screen of Brunel University Library E-Journals Gateway (provided by TDNet).

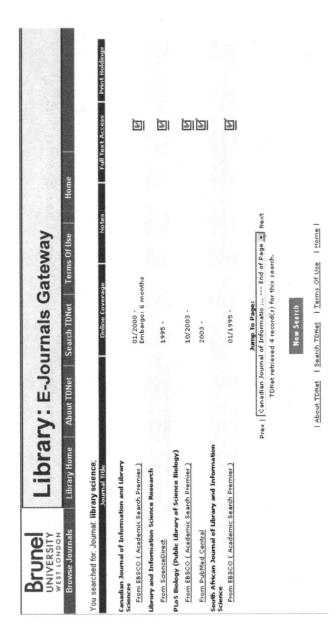

Figure 20.2 Result of search for "library science". User request: "I need to find journal articles on the cognitive implications of information spaces".

Associated task interface problems

1. Checking to see if the journal article is available in paper in the library requires checking the separate catalogue (OPAC).

Scenario B

Task: Finding journal articles on a specific topic.

Context: Julie's friend, Stuart, has read the three recommended sources, and wants to find additional journal articles on the topic to make his presentation stand out.

Task interface problems

Stuart is familiar with using the e-journals gateway and the catalogue (OPAC) to locate recommended journals. However, neither of these resources index journal articles and so searching for a topic is very unlikely to be successful.

1. Searching for the topic "cognitive implications of information spaces" produces no results. There is no information or suggestions about why the search has failed.

2. Stuart remembers the title of the journal that was on his recommended list. His search for "library science" produces a number of journals. Stuart clicks through to the access point for them, and uses the "search within" function (with which he is familiar from his use of "Google") to locate articles on the topic.

High-level design principles revisited

The usability of the Brunel University Library e-journals gateway interface is analysed according to the seven principles of design. The results of this analysis are displayed in Table 20.1.

As Table 20.1 illustrates, the information spaces to which libraries provide interfaces are complex, but the basic design philosophy that Norman's (1988) work represents provides a useful starting point for the design of new interfaces (or indeed the evaluation of existing interfaces). The principles provide a way of thinking about, and organizing, the design of the information space. They are general principles that do not consider individual users, but instead concentrate on the high-level issues that should be used to frame the core design approach. The interactions between the principles are clear and they should be seen as operating together as an underpinning approach to design. There are, though, differences in the way in which users approach and make sense of information that it might help to consider alongside these core design principles. These differences manifest at the individual level and there is significant, though often conflicting, evidence about their impact. The following section will introduce some of the key individual differences alongside a review of relevant research to help us to understand how we might seek to develop information spaces, and mechanisms to access them, which seek to cater for different users in terms of their individual differences.

Table 20.1 Correspondence of the e-journals gateway interface features to design principles.

Design principles	Interface features
Constraints	The library interface presents options to the user (see Affordance), which restrict the searches for journal articles to attributes of the journal itself (i.e. journal title, publisher, ISBN etc.). It is not possible to search journals using keywords on either the topic area of interest for journal articles or any indication of how this type of search may be achieved.
Mappings	There is a clear association between activating the search on search title and the presentation of the next screen detailing the results of the search.
Visibility	General navigation around the interface is fairly straightforward (see Mappings) but there is a number of redundant buttons on the screen, relating to the supplier of the system (TDNet) on the horizontal menu bar. Similarly, on the results of the search screen, there is a column for Print holdings although this is not populated with any useful information.
Consistency	The interface does appear to act consistently within the limits of the journal searches it offers.
Experience	The interface does appear to fit in with the general user's level of experience with activating search queries (see Affordance), though this may not be the case for all users; however, where the interface fails is in not offering journal searches that are consistent with the way that users might seek information on topic areas of interest (see Constraints).
Affordance	The interface is based on drop-down menu and input box styles of communication for activating searches, which is clear and obvious to the user without having to read the (unnecessary) instructions on the right (see Figure 20.1) and may be consistent with styles of interaction that the users have encountered before (see Experience). The results of the search (see Figure 20.2) are displayed in a way that affords access to the journal sought by the inclusion of a ticked checkbox, which the user can easily see at-a-glance the holdings and electronic availability of the library (see Visibility).

20.5 Designing for Different Users: Individual Differences

Users of electronic information spaces have a diverse background, in terms of knowledge, skills, and preferences and, according to Egan (1988), there are at least two reasons why interface designers should pay attention to such differences among users:

> "First, individual differences usually play a major role in determining whether humans can use a computer to perform a task effectively. Second, our understanding and technology have reached the point where it is possible to accommodate more user differences." (Egan, 1988, p. 544)

For these reasons, research into individual differences has grown significantly in the past decade. The individual differences examined include prior knowledge, cognitive style, and gender differences. The influences of these three individual differences elements are discussed below.

20.5.1 Prior Knowledge

Users' prior knowledge includes levels of computing skills appropriate to the system, (i.e., system experience) and existing understanding of the content area (i.e., domain expertise). The former refers to the users' knowledge of the system being used, including the general computing experience and experience of using library systems and the web; the latter refers to users' understanding of the content of the material presented in the system (Lazonder, 2000). Previous studies have indicated that both have an impact on users' information seeking, which will be discussed in the following sections.

System Experience

In the past few years, system experience has been investigated in several studies. Users' performance and behaviour are the main issues discussed in such studies. Fields *et al.* (2004) conducted a study to find to find out what makes experts better at finding information in the library. Two librarians and three users were involved in their study, the results of which (unsurprisingly) showed that librarians are able to be more successful than users at finding information. In addition to the possession of a better and more detailed knowledge of its user interface and internal structure, librarians are able to draw upon an extensive repertoire of strategies for finding information in the electronic library. The authors suggest that user interfaces should be constructed that will aid non-librarians to engage in some of the strategies that allow librarians to be successful.

In addition to library information spaces, the Internet also offers structured information repositories, such as directories, for users to locate information (Chen, Magoulas, and Macredie, 2004). In other words, the Internet can be considered as another type of electronic information space. Lazonder (2000) investigated the differences between novices and experts in searching for information on the Internet. Twenty-five students were divided into novice and expert classes on the basis of self-reported Internet experience and a proficiency test. They found that experts performed significantly faster and better on searches for sites using a search engine than did novices. Other studies also found similar results, including Fidel *et al.* (1999) and Hill and Hannafin (1997). In general, these studies suggest that users with more system experience have more efficient navigation strategies than users with less experience.

With regard to user behaviour, numerous studies have shown that users with differing degrees of system experience tend to adopt different strategies to find information. Farrell and Moore (2001) investigated whether the use of different navigation tools (linear, main menu and search engine) influenced users' achievements and attitudes. The results indicated a significant difference for experts using the search engine. Other studies have also shown that experts are more likely to make use of advanced search options, such as Boolean operators (Holscher and Strube, 2000) and "jump" tools (e.g., Go, History and Bookmark)

(Kim, 2001). Novices, on the other hand, tend to be less flexible in their information-seeking strategies (Vassileva, 1996), and often return to previous stages of their search rather than attempt to use different strategies (Holscher and Strube, 2000).

Domain Expertise

As with system experience, domain expertise has also been recognized as a critical factor, both in terms of the differences exhibited in navigation behaviour and in disorientation problems. In terms of navigation behaviour, individuals with a lower level of domain knowledge have been shown to use longer queries (the number of words used to search) than those with higher domain knowledge (Holscher and Strube, 2000). In addition, whilst both users with high and low levels of knowledge benefit from navigational aids, users with a lower level of domain knowledge tend to rely on navigational aids more than those with a higher level of domain knowledge (McDonald and Stevenson, 1998b).

In respect of disorientation problems, previous studies have found that users' domain knowledge influences the degree of disorientation in electronic information spaces. Another study by McDonald and Stevenson (1998a) examined the effects of domain knowledge and showed that subjects who lacked sufficient domain knowledge of the text topic demonstrated more disorientation problems than subjects with high domain knowledge. Non-knowledgeable users tended to open more additional notes, which suggested that they could not remember where they had been and had problems in finding the information that they required. Compared with non-knowledgeable users, knowledgeable users may experience fewer disorientation problems because their deep levels of understanding of the subject matter enable them to impose structure on the system. Mohageg (1992) asserted that knowledgeable users might avoid disorientation because they already possess a mental representation of the concepts in the domain that they are searching. Therefore, there is a need to provide non-knowledgeable users with appropriate navigational support that reduces disorientation problems.

20.5.2 Cognitive Style

Cognitive style can be defined as an individual's preferred and habitual approach to organizing and representing information (Riding and Rainer 1998). There is a variety of dimensions of cognitive style, such as Visualized vs. Verbalized, Right-Brained vs. Left-Brained, Global-Holistic vs. Focused-Detailed, or Field-Dependent vs. Field-Independent. Among these dimensions, Field Dependence versus Field Independence has a significant impact on users' information processing, because it reflects how well an individual is able to restructure information based on the use of salient cues and field arrangement (Weller *et al.* 1994). Field Dependence or Field Independence describes the degree to which a user's perception or comprehension of information is affected by the surrounding perceptual or contextual field (Jonassen and Grabowski, 1993). Their characteristics are:

I. Field Dependence: the individuals are considered to have a more social orientation than field independent persons since they are more likely to make use of externally developed social frameworks. They tend to seek out external referents for processing and structuring their information, are more readily influenced by the opinions of others, and are affected by the approval or disapproval of authority figures.

II. Field Independence: the individuals are more capable of developing their own internal referents, are more capable of restructuring their knowledge, and they do not require an imposed external structure to process their experiences. They also tend to exhibit more individualistic behaviours since they are not in need of external referents to aid in the processing of information. In addition, they are not easily influenced by others, and they are not overly affected by the approval or disapproval of superiors (Witkin *et al.*, 1977).

Recent studies have found that users' cognitive styles significantly influence their information seeking on the Internet. Wang *et al.* (2000) studied users' interactions with Internet resources, using 24 graduate student participants. The Group Embedded Figures Test (GEFT, Witkin *et al.*, 1977) was used to identify the participants' cognitive styles. The participants were asked to find answers from the Internet to two search questions, in one of which statistical significance of correlation was found between GEFT scores and the time spent for searching and the URLs visited. The participants with the higher GEFT scores conducted the longer search sessions and visited more URLs. The participants with the lower GEFT scores had the shorter sessions. Additionally, Palmquist and Kim (2000) investigated the effects of cognitive style and online database search experience on Internet search performance. The GEFT was administered to identify the cognitive styles of the 48 undergraduate students who formed the sample. Their results showed that Field Dependent novices frequently made greater use of embedded links than other users. Furthermore, a more recent study by Ford *et al.* (2005) sought to discover the effects of human individual differences on Internet search strategy. Their sample consisted of 250 Masters students and Cognitive Style Analysis (CSA) was used to measure their cognitive styles. The results indicate that there is a link between low levels of Boolean searching (where individual search terms are combined using operators such as AND and OR) and Field Independence and a link between high levels of Boolean searching and Field Dependence. The differences in approach and performance suggests that there is a need to accommodate both Field Dependent and Field Independent cognitive styles in the design of interfaces.

20.5.3 Gender Differences

Gender has long been recognized as impacting human-computer interaction and also as a broad issue affecting computer skills and computer design issues.

Previous research has shown that males have higher abilities and interest in computers than females. Males not only have lower computer anxiety, but also higher computer confidence and greater liking of computers than females do (Busch, 1995). As the Internet has become a popular tool for information dissemination, a growing body of research has been conducted to examine gender differences in users' information seeking on the Internet.

For example, Ford and Miller (1996) studied 75 postgraduate students (40 males and 35 females), and significant differences were found according to gender. Compared with the male students, the female students seemed relatively disoriented and disenchanted while seeking information on the Internet, and they generally felt themselves unable to find their way around effectively. In a more recent study, Ford et al. (2001) investigated individual differences in Internet searching using a sample of 64 Masters students with 20 male and 44 female participants. In line with previous findings, they found that female students had difficulties in finding their way effectively around the Internet, and were more likely to get lost and feel not in control. These studies suggest that females tend to experience more difficulties in finding information on the web and require support in terms of different user interfaces and navigation facilities.

Further to disorientation problems, gender differences also influence navigation styles. Roy and Chi (2003) examined gender differences in searching the Internet for information by analysing students' navigation styles. Fourteen students, with equal numbers of males and females, participated in the study. Searching behaviour was measured by using field notes along with computer logs of all the web pages accessed by students during their search. All search moves were categorized into one of the following four categories of search behaviour: 1) submitting a search query in the Google search window; 2) scanning the list of returned document excerpts which contain links to documents; 3) selecting, opening, and browsing a particular document; and 4) book marking a document location or taking notes. The findings showed that boys and girls had different navigation style. Boys tended to filter information at an earlier stage in the search cycle than girls, whereas girls were much more linear and thorough navigators than boys. In addition, boys navigated the information space in a horizontal way whereas girls navigated in a vertical way.

The findings of Roy and Chi (2003) are in agreement with the results of Large et al. (2002), who investigated gender differences in collaborative Internet searching. Their findings indicate that boys and girls make use of different navigation styles while searching information on the Internet. Boys tended to navigate in a broader way than girls. The results also revealed that the group of boys used fewer words to formulate queries submitted to search engines, and often expected to find relevant information from just entering a single word. The group of girls, however, tended to use natural language queries and open and closed quotations more often than boys. It is therefore necessary for interface designers to consider appropriate navigational support to address the preferred styles of both male and female users.

20.6 Accommodating Individual Differences

As argued in the previous three sections regarding users' prior knowledge, cognitive style and gender, individual differences significantly influence users' information seeking. Thus, how to accommodate individual differences has become an essential issue in interface design and has led to the introduction of a new generation of information systems, called adaptive hypermedia systems (Brusilovsky, 1996). Adaptive hypermedia systems seek to build a model of the goals, preferences and knowledge of the individual user and use this throughout the interaction to adapt the content, navigation support and layout to user needs (De Bra *et al.*, 1999).

In a broad sense, adaptive hypermedia systems provide two forms of adaptation: personalization and customization. Personalization uses *adaptivity* to tailor content, structure and/or presentation to each individual based on his/her user model (Treiblmaier *et al.*, 2004). Customization provides users with *adaptability* to modify the content presentation, format layouts and navigation facilities by themselves. Adaptivity is the capacity of a system for automatic adaptation to users' needs based on users' preferences, behaviour and trails. Adaptability allows users to modify the content presentation and navigation tools by themselves (Stephanidis *et al.*, 1995). These two approaches differ regarding who takes the initiative: the user or the system (Kay, 2001). The former is a system-driven process while the latter is user-driven. They have pros and cons with respect to the controllability offered to users (Jameson and Schwarzkopf, 2002). Giving control to the user can reduce the likelihood of incorrect adaptation. However, the cost of increased controllability is the additional effort required from users, as they may need to learn the adaptation component before being able to manipulate it (Tsandilas and Schraefel, 2004). Although this reflects an on-going debate in academic communities, especially in the field of human-computer interaction, there is a lack of empirical studies that compare user reactions to adaptability and adaptivity. In other words, it is a direction for future research to investigate how users react to adaptivity and adaptability and to examine how individual differences influence users' responses to these two types of approach.

As can be seen from the preceding and extensive discussion, it is essential that designers of electronic information spaces understand how to cater for the individual differences of users. The ultimate goal must be an information space where non-librarians are as successful in retrieving their desired information as librarians. Moreover, designers and providers of electronic information spaces must not only consider the user interface, but also the context in which the information space will be accessed. That is, a successful design will provide the user with their desired interrogation of the information space, irrespective of their context. Preece *et al.* (2002, p.207) define context of use as "the circumstances in which the interactive product is expected to operate" and include the social, technological, organizational and physical environment as elements of context. A crucial aspect for the design of current and future electronic information spaces is the increasing mobility of the devices used to access the space. The impact of this context of use is considered in the following section.

20.7 Mobile Technology Use in Public Places

Electronic information spaces may be accessed from computers in a wide variety of contexts: a desktop computer in the library, a computer room, an office or home; a laptop computer in any of these locations, with either a hard-wired or wireless connection; or a laptop computer with a wireless connection in a café, on a train, or any other "wi-fi" location. In this last case, people will be interacting with the electronic information spaces in very dynamic environments, and so could have distractions. For example, auditory distractions, or the presence of someone standing or sitting close to the user may actually put them off (or feel that they cannot or should not) using their device because of the social situation they are currently located in. In addition, users may experience network connection problems as they move from location to location that will affect their ability to use information spaces.

As well as wireless connectivity and accessibility issues, there are also security issues to be taken into consideration for all contexts that are not use within the library. For example, does the library want users to have to login before they can use all resources, or can they access some library systems and services without any formal signing in procedure? In addition, the library must ensure that it has a firewall in place to prevent hacking and the spreading of viruses. Users of wireless devices may also want to have a secure form of login, to ensure that their personal details are not captured and used by someone else to access their account or see their search history.

20.7.1 Mobile Technology Devices

In addition to the mobility of "traditional" computer devices, a recent development has been the advent of mobile devices such as PDAs and mobile phones that can also provide access to electronic information spaces. For example, in the USA, medical schools are leading the way in using handheld devices and wireless technology to their benefit. The advantages are seen as being an improvement in student-teacher communication, and the fact that students can have access to the latest up to date information as they move between classrooms, hospital wards as part of their training. According to Fallon (2002) about 20% of the country's medical schools require their third and fourth year medical students to carry handheld computers. The use of such devices creates specific challenges for designers of electronic information space interfaces.

Most of these mobile devices have a limited screen size, and the complexity of the information spaces likely to be accessed via a library interface mean that it is difficult to format the space for display without losing the quality of the content of the information. For example, a study conducted at Cornell University (Cook et al., 2003) found that one of the major drawbacks of trying to use a PDA to access external resources was that many third-party resources were inaccessible due to the web browser that was being used. However, there have been some successful developments in terms of making content such as library hours, contact information and upcoming library events accessible via such mobile devices (e. g., the Lincoln Trail Library System, Champaign, IL). It is likely that the accessibility and technical limitations of such devices will limit the nature of the information spaces they can be used to access, probably to interactions with traditional library management systems.

20.8 Future Directions

What might an electronic information space of the future look like following these design ideals? Firstly, it would be a federated search engine and provide a single interface to all resources available to the user (whether provided by the library or not). This would resolve the current issues of lack of consistency of resource search interfaces. However, there would be a choice of search interface to allow for the different needs of novice and expert users. One interface will be as simple as possible, and use natural language queries. The expert interface will use keyword Boolean searching, and allow the selection of a subset from the list of resources to be searched. From both search interfaces, there is the option to map search terms onto subject headings in a category tree. This will aid those who do not have extensive domain expertise both in their search, and also to gain an understanding of the domain. In addition, "similar" searches will be suggested, to aid those with limited domain and system experience both in their search and to learn. There will be a variety of tools for a user to track their navigation through the information space – including breadcrumbs and search history lists. This will help those who have difficulties with disorientation. The results will be presented in a consistent way, with the same format always used for references. It will be clear to users how they can access the full text of the items they have found, and the method will be simple. Options may include one-click access to an electronic library resource; one click access to Internet resources; electronic document supply to the user's desktop; or details of print holdings, both at local and federated libraries. These features will allow for different levels of experience, and confidence, as well as applying the principles of consistency, affordance, and simplicity. The interface will have secure single sign on authentication, and will be optimized for every operating system, internet provider and web browser. The key is to provide a multiplicity of methods of accessing the same information, to ensure that whichever path the user chooses, they will get to where they want to be.

References

Brusilovsky, P. (1996) Methods and techniques of adaptive hypermedia. *User Modeling and User-Adapted Interaction*, 6(2/3), 87–129.
Busch, T. (1995) Gender differences in self-efficacy and attitudes toward computers. *Journal of Educational Computing Research*, 12(2), 147–58.

Chen, S. Y., Magoulas, G. D. and Macredie, R. D. (2004) Cognitive styles and users' responses to structured information representation. *International Journal on Digital Libraries*, 4(2), 93–107.

Coleman, A. and Oxnam, M. (2002). Interactional digital libraries: Introduction to a special issue on interactivity in digital libraries. *Journal of Digital Information*, 2(4).

Cook, M., Morris-Knower, J., Mistlebauer, H., Hyland, N. and Wells, T. *Wireless PDA Accessibility and Application in Academic Libraries.* http://mobile.mannlib.cornell.edu/ [Accessed 5 December 2006].

De Bra, P., Brusilovsky, P. and Houben, G.-J. (1999). Adaptive hypermedia: from systems to framework. *ACM Computing Surveys*, 31(4es).

Dillon, A. (2002) HCI and the technologies of information. In *HCI and the Millennium* (ed. J. Carroll), pp. 457–74. ACM Press/Addison Wesley, New York.

Dillon, A. (2003) User interface design. *Macmillan Encyclopaedia of Cognitive Science*, Vol. 4, pp. 453–8. MacMillan, London.

Egan, D. (1988) Individual differences in human–computer interaction. In *Handbook of Human–Computer Interaction* (ed. M. Helander), pp. 543–68. Elsevier, Amsterdam.

Fallon, M. (2002) *Handheld Devices: Towards a More Mobile Campus.* http://www.campus-technology.com/print.asp?ID=6896. [Accessed 5 December 2006].

Farrell, I. H. and Moore, D. M. (2001) The effect of navigation tools on learners' achievement and attitude in a hypermedia environment. *Journal of Educational Technology Systems*, 29, 169–81.

Fidel, R., Davies, R. K., Douglass, M. H., Holder, J. K., Hopkins, C. J., Kushner, E. J., Miyagishima, B. K. and Toney, C. D. (1999) A visit to the information mall: Web searching behavior of high school students. *Journal of the American Society for Information Science*, 50(1), 24–37.

Fields, B., Keith, S. and Blandford, A. (2004) Designing for expert information finding strategies. In *People and Computers XVIII - Design For Life* (eds. S. Fincher and P. Markopoulos), pp. 89–102. Springer, London.

Ford, N. and Miller, D. (1996) Gender differences in Internet perceptions and use. *Aslib Proceedings*, 48, 183–92.

Ford, N., Miller, D. and Moss, N. (2001) The role of individual differences in Internet searching: an empirical study. *Journal of the American Society for Information Science and Technology*, 52(12), 1049–66.

Ford, N., Miller, D. and Moss, N. (2005) Web search strategies and human individual differences: cognitive and demographic factors, Internet attitudes, and approaches. *Journal of the American Society for Information Science and Technology*, 56(5), 741–56.

Hill, J. R. and Hannafin, M. J. (1997). Cognitive strategies and learning from the World Wide Web. *Educational Technology Research and Development*, 45, 37–64.

Holscher, C., and Strube, G. (2000) Web search behavior of Internet experts and newbies. *Computer Networks*, 33, 337–46.

Hutchins, E. (1995) *Cognition in the Wild.* Bradford, MIT Press.

Jameson, A. and Schwarzkopf, E. (2002) Pros and cons of controllability: an empirical study. *Proceedings of Adaptive Hypermedia*, pp. 193–202.

Jonassen, D. H. and Grabowski, B. (1993) *Individual Differences and Instruction.* Allen & Bacon, New York.

Kay, J. (2001) Learner control. *User Modeling and User-Adapted Interaction*, 11(1/2), 111–27.

Kim, K. (2001) Implications of user characteristics in information seeking on the World Wide Web. *International Journal of Human–Computer Interaction*, 13, 323–40.

Landauer, T. K. (1987) Relations between cognitive psychology and computer systems design. In *Interfacing Thought: Cognitive Aspects of Human–Computer Interaction* (ed. J. M. Carroll). MIT Press, Cambridge, MA.

Large, A., Beheshti, J. and Rahman, T. (2002) Design criteria for children's Web portals: the users speak out. *Journal of the American Society for Information Science and Technology*, 53(2), 79–94.

Lazonder, A. W. (2000) Exploring novice users' training needs in searching information on the WWW. *Journal of Computer Assisted Learning*, 16, 326–35.

Lincoln Trail Library System, Champaign, IL (http://ltnet.ltls.org/pda.html). [Accessed 5 December 2006].

McDonald, S. and Stevenson, R. J. (1998a) The effects of text structure and prior knowledge of the learner on navigation in hypertext. *Human Factors*, 40, 18–27.

McDonald, S. and Stevenson, R. J. (1998b) Navigation in hyperspace: an evaluation of the effects of navigational tools and subject matter expertise on browsing and information retrieval in hypertext. *Interacting with Computers*, 10, 129–42.

McKnight, C. (2000) The personal construction of information space. *Journal of the American Society for Information Science*, 51(8), 730–3.

Mohageg, M. F. (1992) The influence of hypermedia linking structures on the efficiency of information retrieval. *Human Factors*, 34, 351–67.

Nardi, B. A. (ed.) (1996) *Context and Consciousness: Activity Theory and Human–Computer Interaction*. MIT Press, London.

Norman, D. (1988) *The Psychology of Everyday Things*. Basic Books, New York.

Palmquist, R. A. and Kim, K.-S. (2000) Cognitive style and on-line database search experience as predictors of web search performance. *Journal of the American Society for Information Science*, 51(6), 558–66.

Preece, J., Rogers, Y. R. and Sharp, H. (2002) *Interaction Design: Beyond Human–Computer Interaction*. John Wiley & Sons, Chichester.

Rapp, D. N., Taylor, H. A. and Crane, G. R. (2003) The impact of digital libraries on cognitive processes: psychological issues of hypermedia. *Computers in Human Behavior*, 19, 609–28.

Riding, R. and Rayner, S. G. (1998) *Cognitive Styles and Learning Strategies*. David Fulton Publisher, London.

Roy, M. and Chi, M. T. H. (2003) Gender differences in patterns of searching the web. *Journal of Educational Computing Research*, 29(3), 335–48.

Stephanidis, C., Savidis, A. and Akoumianakis, D. (1995) Towards user interfaces for all. *Proceedings of 2nd TIDE Congress*, pp. 167–70.

Suchman, L. (1987) *Plans and Situated Actions*. Cambridge University Press, Cambridge.

Treiblmaier, H., Madlberger, M., Knotzer, N. and Pollach, I. (2004) Evaluating personalization and customization from an ethical point of view: an empirical study. *Proceedings of the 37th Hawaii International Conference on System Sciences*.

Tsandilas, T. and Schraefel, M. C. (2004) Usable adaptive hypermedia systems. *New Review of Hypermedia and Multimedia*, 10(1), 5–29.

Vassileva, J. (1996) A task-centered approach for user modelling in a hypermedia office documentation system. *User Modeling And User-Adapted Interaction*, 6, 185–224.

Wang, P., Hawk, W. B. and Tenopir, C. (2000) Users' interaction with World Wide Web resources: an exploratory study using a holistic approach. *Information Processing and Management*, 36(2), 229–51.

Weller, H. G., Repman, J. and Rooze, G. E. (1994) The relationship of learning, behaviour, and cognitive styles in hypermedia-based instruction: implications for design of HBI. *Computers in the Schools*, 10(3–4), 401–20.

Winograd, T. and Flores, F. (1986) *Understanding Computers and Cognition: A New Foundation for Design*. Ablex, Norwood.

Witkin, H. A., Moore, C. A., Goodenough, D. R. and Cox, P. W. (1977) Field-dependent and field independent cognitive styles and their educational implications. *Review of Educational Research*, 47(1), 1–64.

21

Mobile Media – From Content to User

Antonietta Iacono and Gareth Frith

21.1 Mobile Devices and Operating Systems

21.1.1 Types of Handheld Device

A handheld can be described as a small, pocket sized computing device that is used whilst being held in one's hand. Examples of handheld devices:

- PDA
- Smartphone
- Mobile Phone
- Handheld Games Console
- Ultra-Mobile PC
- Converged Devices
- Portable Multimedia Devices.

PDA

Handheld devices with large screens and typically a touch-screen interface with stylus are often referred to as PDAs (Personal Digital Assistants). These have evolved from personal organizers, and only a few of these devices are capable of telephony, although many new models are now reaching the market. Newer, more powerful devices are generally capable of some type of wireless connectivity (e.g. Wifi or Bluetooth). Few of the devices include cameras, which are the norm with smartphones. Devices which provide "SD I/O" slots can expand their capabilities.

Smartphones

A smartphone can be defined as a phone that uses an open[1] operating system that allows for the installation of natively-coded software. Such operating systems include Series 60 and UIQ; these provide a standardized interface and platform for application developers.

Feature Phones

Most other phones can be defined as "feature phones", having less power than their smartphone counterparts. The vast majority of feature phones do however support the mobile java environment and several have numerous advanced features although some capabilities will be limited. These account for a large percentage of the market share, due to their lower cost and increased multi-media functionality. These devices only support Java mobile applications, but are able to take and send pictures, play music and record/watch video clips like other smartphone devices.

Converged Devices

Devices that have both the features of a mobile phone and what is traditionally known as a PDA are sometimes referred to as "converged devices". These sometimes are also used to describe smartphones.

Ultra-Mobile PC (UMPC)

A specification for small form factor tablet PCs, known as the Ultra Mobile PC, is a joint initiative between Microsoft, Intel and Samsung. These devices run Microsoft Windows XP Tablet PC Edition 2005, but are limited in processing capabilities, typically with a 1 GHz processor. They can, in theory, run any standard PC application supported by Windows XP; however, some minor interface modifications may be needed.

Portable Multimedia Players

These devices are media centric and do not generally provide any telephony capabilities. Some are single function i.e. audio playback. More sophisticated devices (such as the video iPods) have more advanced functions such as the ability to view video and image files and/or record audio. The Apple iPod, for

---

1   This is not to be confused with "open source" software, but it does allow manufacturers and others to modify and develop it.

example, has had remarkable success despite its limited functionality when compared to today's multi-functional mobile phones and PDAs. These devices do not generally have wireless capabilities, and are connected to a PC using via cables such as USB.

21.2 Mobile Operating Systems

Symbian OS

Symbian is an operating system designed specifically for mobile devices. It is a descendant of Psion's EPOC system, and runs exclusively on ARM processors, which in 2002, accounted for almost 75% of embedded devices[2].

The popularity of the Symbian OS can be directly related to its "open" system, allowing lots of flexibility for manufacturers, who can customize the OS to their own needs. Being an "open" system, many manufacturers use their own implementation of the Symbian OS; even the "low-end" feature phones implement limited versions of Symbian, even though this is not always directly evident. It is currently in its 9th version, which has brought several new features to the already mature mobile operating system – notably, greater customization, improved security and a generally improved OS that takes advantage of the improved specifications of contemporary mobile phones.

Windows Mobile OS

This OS is designed to be somewhat similar to desktop versions of Windows, but with vastly cut down functionality. Common features of this OS include:

- Today Screen showing date, owner, emails, tasks etc.
- Taskbar
- Outlook
- PC Synchronization capabilities
- Windows Media Player
- MS Office application readers (although with limited functionality)
- Connection to Microsoft Mobile SQL 2005.

The new Windows Mobile 5 solves some known issues (such as accidental loss of data) with previous versions, as well as adding greater functionality and application integration. Some of the new features include:

---

2   Industry Analyst Andrew Allison, January 2002, http://www.arm.com/products/ CPUs/

- New PIM and Telephony classes allow developers to access messaging and telephony services as well as tasks, calendars and contacts.
- Direct push email technology to compete with Blackberry (with Exchange Server 2003)
- Soft-keys
- Closer adherence between PocketPC and Smartphones version UI
- Hotmail and MSN capabilities
- Video Calling
- Wifi support for Smartphones.

Even though the PPC and Smartphone versions of this OS have converged somewhat, development for both platforms is not as unified as it may seem. There are still separate Pocket PC, Pocket PC Phone and Smartphone editions. Due to the nature of these devices and the inherent functionality they provide, development for each of these is still somewhat separate, although nearly 90% of the API is consistent between editions.

Linux Mobile

Linux has been of increasing interest to manufacturers, in particular, with low-mid end phones. In comparison to Symbian and Windows Mobile, Linux is a completely open source solution allowing a completely free and flexible OS for manufacturers. It has been used in phones on a limited basis since 2004. The majority of Linux handhelds have been shipped to Asia, in particular, China and Japan. Linux based mobile handsets have been released primarily by companies without a share in Symbian such as NEC, Panasonic and Motorola.

Blackberry

Developed by Research in Motion (RIM), the Blackberry communication device has been very successful, mostly due to its email "push" capabilities and ease of use. Some devices by other manufacturers such as Nokia, incorporate Black-Berry email push technology into their devices.

Recently, more multimedia friendly business phones have been released by RIM with advanced functions. These feature cameras, video record and playback, and MP3s like other smartphones, as well as usual BlackBerry functions such as "push" delivery of email.

Java

Although not specifically a "mobile operating system", the mobile version of java (J2ME) is an OS independent development platform supported by the vast majority of contemporary mobile phones. J2ME stands for the Java 2 Micro Edition, a specially designed cut down version of java for limited devices, such as mobile phones and PDAs. This is the Java version that handheld devices support in the current mobile market. J2ME comprises of a variety of different packages each offering a different set of functionality. Most handheld devices used the Connected Limited Device Configuration (CLDC). Upon this lies MIDP, the Mobile Information Device Profile, this allows mobile java application or "MIDlet" to be deployed.

21.3 Development Technologies

The choice of mobile operating system will dictate the choice of technologies needed to develop software solutions for the client and the server.

Symbian C++

Symbian is considered to be a very stable, mature mobile OS. It uses the C++ syntax, and is renowned for having very strict object models and programming paradigms, thus creating a steep learning curve for programmers and longer development time. On the other hand, it is very robust and provides greater opportunities when accessing phone functions such as calendar, phone book and camera functions. Symbian applications can also be run as background processes.

NET Compact Framework

Microsoft compact version of the .net framework is a development environment designed specifically for limited devices such as mobile phones and PDAs. It is hardware independent, and each edition of the Windows Mobile OS will be consistent on each device, in comparison to Symbian that exists in different versions to make full use of device capabilities.

Java

J2ME applications can be easily designed using Sun's Wireless Toolkit, also known as WTK. The Sun WTK allows development of MIDlets (java applications) and is the basis for all mobile java development. Several development environments connect to or include the WTK, some of which are open source and free to download (NetBeans and Eclipse).

Flash

FlashLite is a cut-down version of the Flash player specifically for limited devices, such as mobile phones. It is native to only some mobile devices, others can download the flash player.

FlashLite 1 was extremely limited, based on version 4 of the desktop edition. FlashLite 2 supports Actionscript 2, the most current revision of the Flash scripting language. Although there are still some limitations (i.e. memory), this allows for much richer, interactivity. It uses a cut down version of the PC based API, but it is still quite substantial in terms of functionality. A flash-based application is very quick to build in comparison to Java and C++, and can also be used to quickly develop prototype user interfaces, even if not considered robust enough for full scale applications.

Server Side Technologies

In addition to client-side development technologies, which allow the presentation of content and applications on mobile devices, there will also be technologies which exist on the server-side. These may not be connected to continually, but will be required for the transfer of data at some point either to or from the client devices.

Application Signing

For security and protection (and to prevent malicious code) an unsigned mobile application will warn the user before accessing certain features on the phone. It is important to note that although application signing brings several benefits, it can be a costly procedure depending on the chosen platform.

Rapid Development Tools

These allow for reduced development time, a small application needs to be installed on the client device. This is a good method for trialling software design ideas with users without investing large amounts of development time.

Python
Python is a prototype and rapid development high-level programming language.

mForms
Integral Mobile Data mForms offers a suite of products for rapidly developing and deploying mobile data applications, with a particular emphasis on forms.

Appforge

Another rapid application development tool, called Crossfire. This supports a wide variety of OS and versions, including Symbian (S60+ and UIQ), Windows Mobile and Blackberry. This technology has to be licensed before use.

21.4 Device Specifications

There are hundreds of different mobile devices available today, all with a variety of different technical specifications. Rich media content such as images and video require higher specifications in terms of display and storage. Devices also require a certain amount of bandwidth for the application to be delivered appropriately. The sophistication of the device is directly related to the content that needs to be supplied.

Camera

To be able to take pictures and video, a device must already incorporate that functionality. A small percentage of PDAs feature a built in camera, although many others allow the extension of a camera. Most new mobile phones and converged devices feature some kind of camera, but the difference in quality can be varied. Some devices that are specifically aimed at the enterprise (such as the BlackBerry) intentionally do not include cameras due to corporate security issues.

Camera phones support a variety of different resolutions which varies according to manufacturer and target audience. The standard VGA resolution, 640 × 480, is of very low quality. Although these can seem to be of decent quality when viewed on the device itself, once transferred to a larger screen or print, the poor quality of some mobile cameras becomes directly evident. Some cameras may also not work well in varying light and other conditions. MMS (Multimedia Messaging) only supports limited image resolution.

Video

Even devices that do not have a camera may support video playback. The standard mobile format is 3gp which has been defined specifically for mobile phones. 3gp is a cut down version of MPG-4 and comes in 2 different versions:

- 3gp for GSM mobiles and
- 3g2 for CDMA mobiles (3G).

The 3gp format does not have native support on desktop PCs and therefore needs to be converted or have a special codec installed. Newer versions of Apple Quicktime support 3gp video as standard.

Video resolution and frame per second rate varies depending on mobile device capabilities and user settings. Resolution is usually much lower than camera resolution, this is typically 176 × 144 pixels as this fits within the constraints of a generic smartphone screen, taking into account headers and other information (battery/networks) that is displayed on screen.

Most devices will have an option to view videos full screen (landscape), making use of the full screen.

Audio

Most contemporary phones include some method of recording audio although with various limitations. Low-end devices may only record a few seconds, high-end devices can impose little or no restrictions. Regardless of software limitations, disk space needs to be sufficient to store the data needed.

Mobile phones do not support mp3 and wav by standard although many do. The standard mobile sampled audio formats are are .amr, a lossy compression format. The .amr (Adaptive Multi-Rate) format is optimized for speech coding and is the standard for Multimedia Messaging Service. It therefore has the widest support amongst mobile phones in comparison to other formats. It is also the standard speech codec supported by 3gp. The .amr format does not have native support on desktop PCs and therefore needs to be converted or have a special codec installed. It should be possible to convert this automatically on a server without further user interaction.

Screen Size/Display Resolution

Small screens can be hard to read and only a certain amount of text can be displayed clearly. Mobile screens can vary from 96x96 pixels up to 800x600 (full desktop size). Inevitably a large screen device is usually bigger in size. In terms of text display, a small mobile screen may only be able to show 3–4 lines of text at any given time.

Persistent Storage

Available storage space in each mobile device can vary greatly according to capabilities and purpose. Some low-end devices can have as little as a few hundred Kilobytes and have no slots available to add additional memory. Mid to high-range devices can have larger amounts of internal memory and/or support flash memory cards as external storage, theoretically extending the available space to up to 4 GB[3]. Newer devices now feature "hot swappable" cards so that they can be taken out and inserted while the device is still running.

---

3   Devices do not always support large volume flash memory. Depends on what was available at release.

Input

There are a few methods of input available for mobile devices.

Touch Screen
Usually used in conjunction with a stylus (although fingers can be used with less control). Handwriting recognition software present with the device can convert written text to type, however, users must learn relevant shorthand and calibrate the system properly before use.

Keypad (One-Hand)
The traditional mobile phone input is a standard keypad featuring numbered keys that each represent sets of letters for textual input. Other OS-dependant shortcut keys are also available for opening menus, changing settings and the like. Usability of these can often depend on a variety of factors.

Built-In Keyboard
Some mobile devices feature small "qwerty" keyboards arranged in different styles. These do not appeal to all users and provide an often cumbersome method of input.

External Keyboard
With other devices, external keyboards can be connected via either a proprietary serial connection or via Bluetooth. These often have full-size keys arranged in a compact form, similar to laptop keyboard. Often these keyboards also hold the device (like a small monitor) while it is being used, and usually fold down into a smaller, portable size when not being used. These are usually only supported by smartphones and PDAs (not feature phones).

Voice

Speech recognition technology has advanced substantially in recent years. Contemporary desktop speech-to-text conversion software is now considered very accurate. Packages, such as the Dragon "Naturally Speaking" adapt to the user voice and require little or no training for the user. "Naturally Speaking" is also available in Medical and Legal versions, that support specialized vocabularies.

Speech recognition software can only really understand a single user as it is not yet possible to accurately convert speech from multiple voices in commercial applications. It is also important to note that speech-to-text conversion accuracy is directly dependant on the quality of the original source. Poor quality recordings, distortion, microphone quality, background noise are all factors that can affect the speech-to-text recognition process.

Mobile devices also support some methods of voice recognition, but these are somewhat limited in comparison. These include the ability to add voice tags to mobile functions, such as calling a contact or opening a menu. Additional software can be installed to add further voice controlled functionality.

Due to their limited processing and memory capabilities, mobiles can not yet exploit the full potential of today's speech recognition technology. It is, however, possible to dictate and record into an audio file. This can then be transmitted to a desktop PC or server that will convert the audio to a text-based file.

Browser

Most mobile devices feature some type of browser. Windows-based mobiles feature a Pocket version of Internet Explorer. Others use different browser implementations; one of the main ones in use is Opera.

Most mobile browsers will reformat the page for the device before display. The Opera browser is particularly efficient at this. What can be accessed is determined by networks, most standard websites will not actually work on a mobile device. Other websites will display, but the content has not been appropriately for the small screen. Certain technologies and settings interfere with mobile browsers, in particular: JavaScript, frames, DHTML, Flash, unsupported fonts and oversized images. Many websites don't work as they have not been considered for mobile web. However, it is relatively easy to re-skin content for display on the mobile platform.

OS Integration

Many of the newer technologies allow access to system tools and functions such as access to personal folders, contact list, connections, etc. Unsigned applications will warn the user about such events and actions.

Office Document Support

Many mobile devices feature some kind of Office document support, although supported features may be limited.

Windows Mobile OS

Windows Mobile devices are more likely to support proprietary MS Office files (such as .doc and .xls) using their mobile office suite. Windows mobile 5 supports more desktop-like formatting and functions as well as adding support for Powerpoint files. It is important to note that the MS package does not come pre-installed on some devices such as smartphones. The office suite also lacks support for some smartphone mobiles. It comes pre-installed on Pocket PC versions.

Non-Windows Mobile OS
With OS such as Symbian, MS document support is licensed. Some pre-installed applications will only view MS office file types (.doc, .xls).

Battery Life

High-powered devices naturally have shorter battery life. This has become much more evident as we meet the limitations of current battery technology. Larger screens and faster processors all consume more power. PDAs generally have higher power consumptions than mobile phones and smartphones. Device specifications and documentation usually provide information on how long the battery is expected to last under different use. Network connections such as Wi-Fi and Bluetooth drastically affect battery life when in use.

External Device Support

Digital Pens
These pen-shaped devices, when used in conjunction with special paper or clipboards, remember exactly what has been written in digital form. They can digitally capture handwritten notes drawings and ideas. Some software can convert handwritten information into text.

Anoto
Most of the digital pens available are based on Anoto's proprietary technology and require special, compatible paper that uses the Anoto pattern. This patented pattern, appears as a shade of gray to the naked eye, but is actually a grid of very small dots, 0.1mm in size .

Digital Clipboard
The alternative to the digital pen is a clipboard device that uses standard paper such as the ACECAD Digi-Memo. These often have much thinner pens that make writing feel more natural. More advanced models feature a small screen that displays the digital equivalent of the text that has been written.

Unlike the Anoto based systems, this form of digital pen technology requires no special paper. On the other hand, small movements of the paper can interfere with the accuracy of the system.

External Cameras (SDIO/Bluetooth)

Some Bluetooth-enabled, standalone cameras have been released, although they are somewhat limited.

21.5 Usability

Usability is vital in any mobile device or application. It is possibly the most important factor in the success of a service. On the whole, users prefer a device that works easily rather than a sophisticated device with a steeper learning curve. Good usability is down to both hardware and software design.

21.5.1 Considerations

Difficulties tend to cluster around two main areas: input and display. Input is difficult because mobiles and handhelds are usually small, and entering large amounts of text is difficult, as is sophisticated navigation. Display is generally an issue, again because of the size of the device and hence the screen. More innovative forms of input and display need to be explored.

All devices have some learning curve with new users. In fact, the majority of the more sophisticated mobile applications and functions (such as Mobile Internet and Multimedia Messaging) are not often used by the bulk of phone owners whose devices have the capability. There are many reasons for this a major one being difficulty in set-up and usage not to mention an initial lack of services.

In terms of software design, the developer is always limited by the actual device. There have been many failings in application and device usability in the mobile arena in Europe as well as some notable successes. Voice calls and text messaging remain by far the most popular activities for users but other data services such as the Mobile Internet failed to gain expected uptake upon initial launch, although usage is growing. This was in part because of difficulties of usability and poor content availability.

21.5.2 Content Design Guidelines

In terms of content, usability is key to a successful user experience. Content usability guidelines are issued from various sources, usually labelled as "user experience guidelines" or "visual Guides". These are generally published by Operators and Manufacturers as a guide to developers of specific technologies (Java, Symbian etc.) Some of these guidelines have been inherited from the PC, though there is special consideration made to small screens and user input. W3C Mobile Web Best Practices Working Group has produced a useful document containing recommendations for Mobile Web design[4].

Usability guidelines can be summarized into the following categories:

- **Consistency:** Respecting conventions of a chosen system. If a given phone has a particular navigation system, the content should attempt to emulate it so that rather than having to learn the device and the application, the user only needs to learn one methodology. Following some regular Web and

---

4   http://www.w3.org/TR/mobile-bp/

Computer conventions can sometimes be appropriate depending on the user and the application (far more people own a mobile than own a computer).

- **Input:** Consideration of different input methods. In particular, bulky text input is not advised without an additional keyboard and complex navigation sometimes needs to be achieved with one hand. Voice activation is also a possible input method. Speech recognition services are available as are fold out keyboards and the like. Predictive text can also be helpful. Where input is required, selection from drop-down lists or checkboxes is often the easiest.
- **Navigation:** Must be logical and simple for the user. Searching numerous options and menus can be cumbersome. A large screen is not available to lay out numerous options, so navigation has to be "linear" rather than spatial. Ideally, the main options of any application should be available from just one or two button presses.
- **Text:** Appropriate, readable font sizes. There is something of a compromise to be made between being able to fit content on a screen and being able to read it easily. The choice of words in the actual text can be very important. Sentences should be efficient rather than excessively wordy. Bullet points and space improve readability but there is not a lot of free space for the designer to play with. W3C suggest "Writing content in the traditional journalistic 'front loaded' style can assist users determining whether information is of interest to them and allow them to skip it more easily if it is not."
- **Colour:** Higher contrast provides better usability (e.g. between text and background colour). Generally the same issues apply as to regular Web design. Background images to text are to be avoided.
- **Audio:** Should be used sparingly and control given for the user. It can be useful to signal if the user has completed an action or something similar.
- **Control:** Ability to enter/exit application easily. The user must be able to locate the limits of the application and not have it "take over" their device.
- **Filesize:** Suggested sizes for delivery to mobile phones will vary depending on the application requirements and infrastructure availability. The general rule of thumb is the smaller the better.
- **Efficiency of content:** Any unnecessary material delivered to a mobile device will only reduce the quality of user experience in addition to leading to greater cost and likelihood of transmission failure. In particular, delivered content should be limited to what the user has requested. There should be no links to material that cannot be viewed effectively on the device in question. Images that are considerably larger than the screen size can be irritating, requiring significant scrolling to view them.

21.5.3 Accessibility Issues

Special, purpose-built accessible mobile devices are available from certain suppliers, who also provide tools to support disabled mobile device users. These are somewhat similar to those available on standard PC systems, though specifically adapted for mobile phones and functions.

Tools include:

- text-to-speech conversion (SMS, Contacts, battery levels, alarms + other mobile functions)
- speech-to-text conversion for sending messages
- screen magnifier, some with the ability to change colours.

21.6 Networks and Connections

As a mobile device moves around the environment, the available networks the device can connect to may change. Wireless support in today's mobile devices can vary, with higher-end devices supporting a wider range of networks. A wireless application must be prepared for breaks in the connection. This could be permanent or temporary, but the application needs to be able to function whilst it regains connection or finds alternative solutions (such as other networks or local storage).

Many devices offer more than one method of connection, this is much more apparent in new devices where various connections are offered as standard. For e.g. 3G phones all support GPRS for when the 3G connection is not available. Many new phone models support Wi-Fi. The application needs to take into account differences in

- Quality of Service, data rate, latency etc.
- Cost structure (free, based on connection time or data transferred)
- Battery usage considerations (repeated connection attempts can vastly drain battery types).

Current Technologies

SMS
Short Message Service (SMS) is the text messaging service supported by the large majority of digital mobile phones. It can be used to exchange small amounts of information as it is limited to 160 characters per message. Can be used to exchange basic information between devices and applications that support it, it can also be used to initiate an application using push technology.

MMS
The Multimedia Message Service (MMS) has evolved from SMS technology, but allows graphic, video and audio attachments. Media is usually compressed by the device before sending. Not all content is compatible between mobile devices.

Wi-Fi – 802.11a/g
Wi-Fi is cheap to implement and offers high bandwidth data rates. Many mobiles now support it, but it can drastically affect battery life when switched

on. 802.11a offers 11Mbps, 802.11 54Mbps and security is dependant on network settings.

GPRS (2.5G)
GPRS (General Packet Radio Service) is a mobile data service available to GSM mobile users that modestly improves available bandwidth. Several classes exist increasing the available downlink and uplink to up to 80kbps and 40kbps respectively.

EDGE (2.75G)
Standing for Enhanced Data rates for GSM Evolution, the EDGE technology is an addition to the GSM/GPRS networks. It can allow download speeds of up 236Kbps. Although several EDGE networks exist, availability in the UK is somewhat limited, as the networks have concentrated on implementing 3G technology instead. EDGE is not really needed in areas where 3G is available.

3G
3G – standing for 3rd Generation, is a term usually used in the context of mobile communications. It is not a technology in its own right, but more a collection of systems and services brought together in a family of standards, known as the International Mobile Telecommunications Programme "IMT-2000".

Podcasting
The term "podcasting" combines the words "iPod" and "broadcasting" to define a method of distributing multimedia files (usually audio and video), over the internet to mobile devices such as an iPod, mp3 player or mobile phone. Podcasts are typically separated into "shows" or "episodes" and these are generally transmitted on a regular basis. The media is delivered to the mobile device by "push" technology using existing web feeds such as RSS and Atom. Once a user has subscribed to a service, Podcasts can be automatically downloaded to the device as they become available. Podcast feeds can also be possible over mobile networks.

Bluetooth
Bluetooth, also known as IEEE 802.15.1, is a Personal Area Network (PAN) technology that provides a short-range, low-powered method of connection between mobile devices such as cameras, PDAs, phones, printers. The development of the Bluetooth technology is driven by the Bluetooth Special Interest Group (SIG). It uses the same radio frequencies as Wifi (2.4 GHz), but with lower power consumption, thus providing a much lower bandwidth of 721kbps.

There are different classes of Bluetooth available each with different power consumptions. Bluetooth uses a "pairing" system which can provide extra complications when connecting to a device. Novice users can experience difficulties with this process if they do not understand the fundamentals of the technology.

Ultra-Wideband (UWB) – 802.15.3

A new system potentially giving 100 Mbps with very low power consumption, UWB can also pinpoint the precise location of the source. The signals are spread over a very wide bandwidth (many GHz) and hence just appear to be negligible weak interference to other systems. The committee was not able to agree on the standard specification, and two rival systems are now competing in the development marketplace.

ZigBee – 802.15.4

An extremely low-powered system intended for use with home control and automation, and is specifically designed for devices that require low data rates and power consumption. Data rates vary between 20 Kbps and 250 Kbps depend on carrier frequency (2.4GHz/915MHz/868MHz).

Future Technologies

WiMAX

WiMAX (Standing for Worldwide Interoperability for Microwave Access) has been defined and developed by the WiMAX forum, to promote the IEEE 802.16 standard as the future of broadband internet. WiMAX is not a technology as such, but a certification/ stamp of approval given by the WiMAX forum to a device that conforms to the IEEE 802.16 standard. It is similar to Wi-Fi in terms of its interoperability with supported networks, but is very different in the way it works. It is expected that WiMAX will provide mobile wireless broadband connectivity without the need of direct line of sight with a base station with a typical cell radius of 3–10km. Systems can be expected to support up to 40 Mbps per channel, with enough bandwidth to support hundreds of simultaneous connections. The WiMAX forum expects the technology to be incorporated in mobile devices starting 2007. The WiMAX technology could be particularly disruptive to the world's cellular network providers as it could offer users a realistic alternative that is based on the traditional "internet" charging structure.

Wi-Fi – 802.11n

802.11n uses multiple spatially-separated channels to increase data capacity: this is the MIMO method (Multiple input, multiple output). There are at least three ways of achieving this, but all require very challenging engineering; however, the problems are being overcome, and MIMO could enhance the power of other communications systems as well.

3.5G HSDPA

HSDPA (standing for High Speed Download Packet Access) is a technology for improving existing 3G WCDMA networks download performance. It offers much greater potential download speeds (800kbps -14.4 Mbps).

3.75G HSUPA
Standing for High Speed Upload Packet Access builds on HSDPA to increase the upload speeds of the W-CDMA networks to up to 5.76Mbps.

3.9 G
A term given to technologies based on existing 3G networks that exhibit characteristics closer to 4G expectations.

4G
Short for 4th generation, a successor to 3G wireless communications technology. The IEEE's official name for 4G is "3G and Beyond (B3G)", this is planned for implementation in 2010–2015. The Japanese company NTT DoCoMo and Samsung are testing 4G at bandwidths of up to 100 Mbps for a moving device and 1Gbps whilst stationary. The service should also provide uplink speeds of approximately 20Mbps. The increase in bandwidth available with 4G communications should allow seamless, near instantaneous download of full-quality video/audio and much richer multimedia in general.

Synchronization

Some method of synchronization is available with most mobile devices. This is usually completed when connecting to a PC. It is also to automatically synchronize devices without user interaction (i.e. when the device is in range).

Exchange Server 2003
Microsoft's Exchange Server includes built-in support for wireless synchronization of email and calendar information with devices that support Exchange ActiveSync. Windows mobile devices support this by default, although the software may need to be upgraded to take advantages of newly added features[5]. Other, non-windows mobiles can connect to the Exchange Active sync using 3rd party tools. One such program is RoadSync™, developed by DataViz Inc. This, along with similar programs, has to be installed on the individual clients, requiring no changes to existing servers.

BlackBerry
Required for BlackBerry direct push email functionality and is supported by BlackBerry as well as other devices[6] that incorporate the BlackBerry technology.

---

5   Full list: http://www.microsoft.com/windowsmobile/business/5/default.mspx
6   Supported by devices aimed at corporate users, such as Nokia 6810, 9300, 9500, Sony Ericsson P910, Qtek 9000.

21.7 Security

Server

Microsoft Exchange Server 2003 features new security features that include central password administration and "remote wipe", the ability to remotely reset a mobile device should it have been lost or stolen. It also supports certificate-based authentication to gain access to corporate networks.

Exchange Server 2003

Service Pack 2 improves functionality by adding several new and improved features. These include secure, direct push technology and central password administration.

Client Blacklisting

UK networks have recently joined forces and signed up to a common charter to disable the majority of lost and stolen handsets within 48 hours of them being reported. The networks will now work from a shared blacklist database to enable them to block stolen phones, permanently. This is after increasing pressure from the government after a large increase in mobile related thefts. Each individual phone has a unique IMEI number, a 15 digit code that identifies each mobile handset. By blacklisting this code, a phone is unable to make/receive any calls, but all other device functions, such as listening to an MP3, are still intact.

Antivirus

Mobile viruses have been of particular interest recently, and have been targeting Windows Mobile and Symbian devices. Some of the PC antivirus developers, such as Trend Micro, have begun to release special mobile versions of their antivirus software. These are compatible with Windows Mobile, Symbian S60 and UIQ.

Security Codes

All mobiles that use the cellular networks contain SIM cards that authenticate the user on the network. Devices usually also have security pins that can be activated on the clients, users have to enter these at start-up and / or after a given amount of time.

Biometric

Some high-end mobile devices feature biometric fingerprint readers to authenticate users. Access to these functions is usually built in to the device and relevant development environment.

Digital Certificates

Such certificates can be stored on the device and used by applications. These can be provided by companies such as VeriSign and can be used to authenticate users before allowing the connection to the server.

Digital Signatures

Signatures play a big part of our every-day life, they are unique and can be differentiated from one another. They can be easily recorded using touchscreen capable devices. The information can be translated to a vector object and transferred/stored for future use.

Signature recognition is the process of authenticating and verifying a user's identity by checking the signature written by the writer and comparing this against the samples that are stored within a database. The authentication process can be based on pattern matching, whereby the signature is split into coordinates, these are compared to existing data in the database.

PART 8

Historic Collections and Case Studies

Special Collections Librarianship

Richard Ovenden

22.1 Introduction

The last three decades have witnessed considerable changes in the nature of librarianship, and Special Collections librarianship has changed as much, if not more, than other branches of the profession.

When I first entered the profession of librarianship in the UK at the University of Durham just over twenty years ago, special collections was regarded as the dry and dusty backwater of a profession that had in other respects had entered the world of information technology with all the zeal of a recent convert. At least this is what the librarians at Durham in departments other than special collections (or Rare Books as it was known there and then) were keen to tell me. The impression they presented was that I was wasting my time entering a sector of librarianship that had nothing to do with the future, and that was only interested in the past. Part of this feeling was no doubt engendered by the recent move to create a new University Library building on the Stockton Road campus, leaving Special Collections behind in the medieval buildings of Palace Green (where they nestled peacefully with the undergraduate collections of Music and Law, and the library's store of "secondary sequence" books). Automation had hit the Durham catalogue in every respect except for special collections. Philip Larkin is known to have regarded the GEAC mainframe at Hull as "the beast in the basement", but in Durham it was a machine that would drive librarianship into a modern, professional and "relevant" future. I knew instinctively, but did not have the experience at the time to realize empirically, that these well-meaning souls had missed the point. From my stints, both official and voluntary in special collections I gradually became aware that the part of the library with the closest ties to the research community was Special Collections: there were numerous examples. Dr Anthony Ian Doyle had retired as Keeper of Rare Books by the time I arrived as a trainee but was still very much in evidence in the library not least in his capacity as Honorary Reader in Bibliography. Ian Doyle

was both research active at a very high-level (his facsimile and introduction to
The Vernon Manuscript (Bodleian Library MS Eng.poet.A.1) was published by
D. S. Brewer during my time as a trainee), and an amazingly generous teacher,
both formally to MA and PhD students doing either English degrees or his own
course in Historical Bibliography, or informally to a group of individuals like
myself who were involved some way in the world of books, manuscripts and
libraries and to whom he was willing to become involved as a beneficent bookman. Ian was happy to involve me in research projects by utilizing the skills I
already had and supplementing them with codicological, bibliographical, historical and palaeographical skills I didn't. I was encouraged and financed to set
up a dark room in the Library, to take both traditional photographs, and to
deliver a programme of beta-radiographs of 15th century English printed
books in Durham collections for Lotte Hellinga's BMC volume XI (amazingly
published during December 2006 at the time this essay was finished). This generosity of spirit provided an amazing opportunity for me to develop my experience and skills in special collections librarianship, but also encouraged me to
work harder for the library, because I could see the value of the enterprise in
research terms. The other staff in special collections at the time were similarly
imbued with this generous spirit. Two individuals in particular played key roles
in encouraging an eager young librarian: Beth Rainey (Ian Doyle's successor as
Keeper of Rare Books) was ever-vigilant to provide interesting opportunities
and to introduce me to interesting visiting scholars and librarians. David
Pearson, then a project-funded cataloguer of rare books, now Director of
Research Library Services at the University of London, became a collaborator in
various bibliographical projects, and was equally willing to share his experience and "take" on things. Beth as line manager was able to take a rounded view
and provide me with a thorough training in both the mundane but essential
routine tasks, as well as opportunities to work on exhibitions, special catalogues
and publications.

Looking back to that time I also perceived Durham's special collections as making a major contribution to the research culture of the University. Ian Doyle's
knowledge of the manuscripts, and his expertise as a serious scholar of Middle
English brought researchers from across the world to Durham generating what
in RAE terms would be called "evidence of esteem" and bringing, more particularly, graduate students to the University.

22.2 Library School at UCL

My Durham experience was then followed by a period at the Library School at
University College London where again Special Collections was very much
resigned to ghetto-like courses in Historical Bibliography and Palaeography.
The Palaeography course was considered hopelessly rarified by many of my
contemporaries, and only a handful of us were, accordingly, treated to the scholarly erudition, generosity and kindness of Professor A. G. Watson. Andrew
regularly produced important publications in his Professorial capacity, but
continued the role of Ian Doyle in providing guidance and encouragement to

younger scholars and budding special collections librarians. Apart from the two specific courses, other aspects of the profession were however, given short shrift. In Historical Bibliography we were taught about collations and other aspects of descriptive bibliography, but we were not taught how to catalogue a rare book in the cataloguing courses. Preservation and conservation were skimmed over, and the management courses did not really cover standards properly (I don't recall ever coming across BS 5454 at the time, but I suspect the Archives students being aught in the same building were exposed to realities of temperature and humidity control, and the practicalities of running a repository to accepted standards).

22.3 The British Library

International collaboration only reared its head during my useful and enjoyable placement: a month in the ESTC office in the British Library where I encountered technology again. Not only online cataloguing using MARC fields and authority files, but NETWORKING, and live cataloguing on the RLIN file: serious work that involved collaboration with the ESTC team at the University of California, Riverside and the people in the Research Libraries Group. Amazingly this aspect of librarianship (that is to say collaboration) had not been mentioned at all at Library school and it encouraged me to view the profession completely differently. Under the guidance of Mike Crump I saw for a few weeks that librarianship was a collaborative activity that at the Special Collections end of things was just as implicated in the technological future as any other part of the profession, and in many ways was more technologically-focussed. My experience at ESTC also showed how special projects could not only infuse an institution with new ideas and energy, but could also act as a focus for research activity.

22.4 The National Library of Scotland

By the time I arrived at the National Library of Scotland to serve my apprenticeship as a Special Collections curator, the funding-drift away from libraries in general and Special Collections in particular was in full flow. I was interviewed at NLS by Robert Donaldson, Keeper in the British Antiquarian Division in the August of 1989. By the time I arrived in Edinburgh to begin work in October 1989 plans were already being laid for his retirement party and for the integration of British Antiquarian in to the Department of Printed Books. By the time I left in 1999 British Antiquarian had morphed into Rare Books, which had merged into a new Department of Special Collections with Maps, Music, and Manuscripts (following on from developments in the Bodleian that I shall come onto later). Rare Books had been left with one senior staff member where a decade earlier there had been four. The gradual decline of special collections at the NLS was to continue after my departure for Edinburgh University Library in 1999, and now no such department exists, although the four constituent parts remain as curatorial units in an administrative unit called Collections. Similar nuclear solutions were put in place in the National Library of Wales and the British Library.

This decline may in part have been due to the parallel activities that were taking place in the higher education sector. The advent of serious project funding following the Follett Report of 1993 and the Anderson Report of 1996 delivered two successive programmes: NFF and RSLP brought project management, collaboration, automation, digitization, and new staff to libraries in HE and to special collections in particular. Throughout the 1990s special collections ceased to be perceived as lame ducks by chief librarians and other library staff, and became sources of new technology, new staff, and external income. NFF and especially RSLP began to match library collections with research activity, and in the era of the RAE, encouraged a more entrepreneurial approach among special collections staff at the very least it honed the skills of grant-writing and developed a bidding-culture. This was the world I entered in 1999, recruited by the charismatic and energetic Ian Mowat who had played a key role in NFF, and I was thrust into the bidding stages of RSLP at the institution that hosted Ronald Milne and his team at RSLP. Edinburgh University Library had done well under NFF and was to do even better under RSLP at one stage EUL was involved in 16 projects, the majority of them being in Special Collections, including leadership of three projects and being the major contributing partner in several other projects, especially the CURL 19th century Pamphlets project (only Oxford under Reg Carr's leadership was involved in more). What I noticed was that other parts of the library service were now seen as being rather dull and dreary, and staff began to be jealous of special collections, and resentful of the energy and excitement (this was a view shared by some of the older and wearier staff in special collections itself). I began to be aware of other funding sources, especially JISC, AHRC and HLF and soon developed an appetite and enthusiasm for grant-writing and seeking collaboration, often in partnership (or indeed healthy and friendly competition) with colleagues in the digital library side of EUL. Two factors had helped to bring this situation about. First was the growing focus on research within UK HE, and the consequent shift in resources and university planning to support activities that fostered research and could demonstrate success. Secondly was the burgeoning interest in collaboration: and here CURL was highly important.

22.5 CURL

CURL had begun in 1992 as a group of institutions with major research collections, especially special collections. In the vanguard of the organization were Oxford, Cambridge, Edinburgh, Glasgow, and Manchester. These were not just the institutions with the big holdings of printed books and the big staff numbers and annual budgets but were the institutions with manuscripts, archives, rare books, and other special collections. CURL provided a framework for benchmarking for the big-hitters within which special collections became one of the key membership factors. In other words to library directors, special collections were a key to achieving membership of the club of big-players.

The same soon became true of RLG where membership by UK libraries and archives began to grow in the late 1980s an 1990s. RLG developed new services like ESTC and the Hand Press Books database, but with its increasingly digital focus encouraged further inroads to be made by the special collections community into new areas of technological development and service delivery made remotely through networks. RLG was of course another arena for library directors to benchmark and network, and through its collaborative ethos, UK libraries were exposed to important developments such as Encoded Archival Description (EAD) and digitization, and a new era of professionalization began in special collections librarianship, where the skills of a digital age began to be added routinely to those of the material culture of the book and the research domains which relied on physical textual artefacts. The leading role played by Reg Carr as Chair of RLG was transformational not only in that organization, but in bringing the best of American energies, interests, and enthusiasm into the UK HE scene. My own engagement with this phenomenon began in EUL where Ian Mowat encouraged me to take the lead in Edinburgh's engagement with RLG, especially over the Cultural Materials Initiative (Ian of course was famously locked into the OCLC community at a high level – especially when he became a board member). My first encounter with Reg Carr was at an RLG meeting in Ottawa in 2001 where he displayed similar qualities of encouragement and involvement to a young and rather green Deputy.

Although RLG has fallen into abeyance as an independent force, and OCLC has wound up as the dominant library collective, it nonetheless played an important role for several of the larger UK institutions in exposing them to a higher level of professional activity, much of it surrounding the world of special collections.

22.6 CILIP

What of the British players in the field of professional organization and guidance? I joined the Library Association as a Library school student in 1986 and never renewed my membership after the first year. It seemed to me to be an organization obsessed with the world of public libraries and political correctness. Little has changed in the intervening years except that I have rejoined the organization (now known as CILIP) and have become the Chair of its Rare Books and Special Collections Group (my first act as Chair being to rename it. Although the Group itself remains lively, strong, and closely attuned to the work and interests of its members, sadly the parent body has spent the last few years lurching from one crisis to another. Of the professional bodies in the Special Collections field the Society of Archivists is one that has undergone something of a renaissance. The Archives community in general has embraced the digital information very successfully and the professional organizations in the UK and USA (the Society of American Archivists) have provided a great deal of leadership in the information profession more generally. It has been particularly impressive to see how the Archives community has engaged in meaningful ways with the digital library community – helping to bring a truly archival sense of information management to the world of digital libraries (look at the ways in which EAD has become utilized for describing other forms of collections: in the California Digital Library for example). It's hard to imagine Cliff Lynch giving the closing address to CILIP, but in 2000 he spoke at the Society of American Archivists in Birmingham, Alabama, about the challenges facing archives of the cultural implications of digital information.

Looking at the applicants for professional posts (academically-related) at Oxford and Edinburgh University Library, the products of the UK library schools have tended to perform less well at interview than their equivalents from the Archives courses. I do not have hard data to base this statement on, but rather the anecdotal evidence based on interviewing hundreds of candidates for dozens of jobs over the past decade or so. This is not to say that applicants for rare books jobs have not been excellent they have, but on the whole they tend to be candidates with an existing research background in the field of book history, an aptitude for digital technologies, and (probably) no formal training in librarianship. Many of these individuals then play catch-up by acquiring the professional qualifications through the Aberystwyth long-distance course, but many will admit that this is purely for the qualification rather than for what they might learn on the course. The Archivists, by comparison, tend to have learned much more about the application of digital technologies to their branch f the professional, in addition to, rather than at the expense of, skills like palaeography. They have also been introduced to the legislative background of Copyright and IPR, Data Protection and Freedom of Information, knowledge that is just as applicable in the traditional as the digital aspects of special collections librarianship. As an employer, then, I think that the British Library schools (of which I am proud to be a product) need to have a serious look at how they are skilling their graduates. Can we actually afford to run the education of librarians and archivists in almost total isolation from one another?

22.7 Fundraising

Finally, the aspect of special collections librarianship that has changed most dramatically in the past thirty years or so is the emphasis on fundraising. This is an aspect of the profession that Reg Carr has made just as dramatic a contribution as in the field of digital information. When I joined the profession at Durham, the profession relied very heavily on the core funding that the University received from the old University Grants Committee, a sum of money that seemed to me, from my very lowly perspective in among the grass-roots, to be subject to wild fluctuations, and which subjected services like special collections to a constant round of self-justification, as it continually lost the numbers game against services which operated principally on the "pile-'em-high, flog-'em cheap" principles of undergraduate provision. As I have already indicated this position changed somewhat with the advent of the research focus in higher education during the 1990s, and the impetus provided by the NFF and RSLP programmes in support of the new research agenda. These two programmes, along with JISC and Elib helped to create a "bidding culture" within libraries in the higher education sector (although still absent from the national libraries: I was to witness the different cultures very markedly when I moved from the National Library of Scotland to Edinburgh University Library in 1999). These skills have become an integral part of the special collections librarians work toolkit, just as applicable to the other funding sources, for acquisitions as well as projects. Under Reg Carr's leadership at Oxford Special Collections benefited from funding brought in from the Heritage Lottery Fund, National Heritage Memorial Fund, V & A Purchase Grant Fund, JISC, HEFCE (NFF and RSLP), National Art Collections Fund, Friends of the National Libraries, the Andrew Mellon Foundation, the Samuel H Kress Foundation, the Getty Grant Program, the Delmas Foundation, the Paul Mellon Center for Studies in British Art, the Frits Thyssen Stiftung, and the Kultur Stiftung der Lander (among others). But it has been the shift toward funding from private individuals (often through charitable trusts) that has been such a marked feature of Reg Carr's contribution to special collections at Oxford. His tireless work, and inspired leadership, have show how the principles under which the Bodleian was founded in the early seventeenth century are just as applicable today as they were four hundred years ago. In many ways our counterparts in the big research libraries in the US had come to this conclusion a generation ago: that the best way to ensure sustained funding to ensure the continuity of the great research collections can only be achieved through endowment of staffing posts. Only by going down this route can the vagaries of funding driven by political imperatives be avoided. At an extreme level the Beinecke Library at Yale must serve as the paradigm case, where three members of the same family all Yale graduates who had accumulated considerable wealth through the business interests (in the Beinecke case Green Shield stamps) combined together to build a striking new facility on the Yale campus, to populate it with their outstanding family collections, and give it an enviable endowment to ensure that staffing and acquisitions funds would not be a problem. Like Bodley four hundred years earlier the Beinecke example "stirred up other men's benevolence", and other gifts and bequests, both financial and bibliographical, soon followed. This had very much been the pattern in the Bodleian's early history, but the endowment was squandered by the University over the next few hundred years, partly through a "forced loan" to Charles I during the Civil War of half of the endowment, a debt that was returned as such in our annual accounts for over 150 years and eventually given up.

22.8 Conclusion

Special Collections librarianship stands at an interesting moment in time. It faces many challenges: many of us work in institutions with a legacy of hundreds of years of collecting, and in which these collections have survived in what Cliff Lynch has described as "regimes of benign neglect". The financial and organizational burdens inherent with these legacy collections are made doubly difficult in a climate of competing for increasingly scarce resources, and where special collections are often seen as either "soft" targets or the financial responsibility of already hard-pressed humanities divisions. We must re-assert our traditional roles as stimulators and incubators of research and researchers, and as the part of our research libraries and professional organizations that take the long-view and regard preservation as an inherent component of access. We must continue to lead the vanguard in entrepreneurial activity and continue to embrace new technologies to make us work "faster, better, and cheaper". In some ways we must learn form our Archivist colleagues and find ways of working with them. Finally we must not neglect our traditional strengths: as knowledge of how to manage information becomes more pervasive throughout society, experience and expertise in books as physical objects will become increasingly valuable skills.

Defending Research and Scholarship – United Kingdom Libraries and the Terrorism Bill 2005

Clive D. Field

23.1 Introduction

During the winter of 2005–6 the library community of the UK unexpectedly found itself catapulted on to the national political stage, and at loggerheads with Her Majesty's Government over some aspects of the Terrorism Bill 2005. While not being opposed to the general purposes of the Bill, which sought to tighten counter-terrorism measures (not least in the wake of the 7/7 London bombings), the community did have serious concerns about the potential implications, arising from infelicitous wording, of the proposed new offence of disseminating terrorist publications. It was fearful of the prospect of the criminalization of libraries and librarians for carrying out their legitimate (and sometimes statutory) public duties to collect and make available information to support research, learning and enquiry across the full field of human knowledge.

In particular, in relation to the dissemination clause, the library community had apprehensions about:

- the lack of requirement for the investigative and prosecuting authorities to prove actual intention on the part of the defendant, thus reversing the customary burden of proof, of innocent until proved guilty
- the wide and indeterminate nature, and the subjective and inconsistent definition, of a terrorist publication, which appeared to depend upon time and context, and upon the behaviour it induced in the user

303

- the limited nature, and the specificity, of the available defences, making them seemingly difficult or impossible to invoke
- the possibility of conflict, for libraries covered by these Acts, with the provisions of The British Library Act 1972 and the Legal Deposit Libraries Act 2003
- the likelihood that, in order to minimize the reputational and financial risks of prosecution, libraries would exercise a degree of self-censorship over their collecting and circulation processes, thereby introducing a "chilling effect"
- the danger of thoughtless and spontaneous enforcement of the dissemination clause by the authorities, especially in the highly-charged atmosphere which would follow a major terrorist atrocity.

The reality of these concerns was confirmed by two separate pieces of independent legal advice commissioned by The British Library (BL) and the National Library of Scotland (NLS).

This essay first describes, in a chronological narrative, the events of that winter and then analyses some of the main conclusions which can be drawn, and the lessons which can perhaps be learned for future political mobilization of librarians, from the library community's involvement with the Bill. It does not seek to address some of the broader ethical and professional issues affecting libraries and counter-terrorism, such as surveillance by the authorities of library users and access to their library records, which have been reviewed by Sack (2006) and are also implicitly raised in recent draft Government guidelines to higher education institutions (Dodd, 2006).

23.2 Chronology

The Government had announced its plans to bring forward new counter-terrorism measures during the passage of the Prevention of Terrorism Act 2005. Preparations were already well under way in advance of 7/7, but the London bombings had given added urgency and suggested further areas for legislation. One of these was the creation of a new offence of dissemination of terrorist publications, to plug a perceived gap in Section 58 of the Terrorism Act 2000, which had already made it illegal to compile or hold information that might be of assistance to the commission or preparation of an act of terrorism but had not explicitly banned its dissemination. This offence was accordingly included, as Clause 3, in the draft Terrorism Bill 2005 which was published on 15 September, Government's intention being to allow a limited degree of political consultation before the measure was formally introduced into Parliament.

The draft does not appear to have been noticed by libraries at that time, but it was fairly rapidly seized upon by the leading civil liberty and legal groups such as Liberty, the Law Society and JUSTICE. They picked up on the limitations and dangers of Clause 3, being especially critical of its breadth, the lack of requirement to prove intent, and the weakness of the defences. They had numerous other concerns about the draft Bill, also, and were invited to give oral evidence before the House of Commons Home Affairs Committee on 11 October, but they were not specifically questioned about Clause 3. Charles Clarke, the then Home Secretary and architect of the Bill, was, however, by Ann Cryer, and he used the words "nonsense", "laughable" and "ridiculous" in answer to charges that, under certain circumstances, a London A–Z, an Underground map or *Who's Who* could be considered as terrorist publications. He also disagreed with Cryer in her comment about the lack of intent in the clause and the possible difficulty for the prosecution to "prove the thoughts and beliefs of absent terrorists". These exchanges were eventually published on 25 October (House of Commons Home Affairs Committee, 2005, QQ. 37, 39).

The Bill was introduced into the House of Commons on 12 October and given a First Reading (*Hansard: Commons*, 437, col. 295). By then the dissemination provisions had become Clause 2. The explanatory notes issued alongside the Bill made it clear that it did apply to libraries. On the same day, the Government also published the advice (dated 5 October) of Lord Carlile, its independent reviewer of anti-terrorist legislation, in which he expressed residual concerns about the Bill's potential for criminalizing academic and Parliamentary research, but he did not flag up an analogous threat to libraries (Carlile, 2005, para 28). Although the Bill attracted much media attention, Clause 2 was not especially in the spotlight. It is thanks to the vigilance of Terry Hanstock, a librarian at Nottingham Trent University, that the potential impact of Clause 2 on libraries was identified and relayed. He posted an alert on the lis-link and lis-law listservs on 13 October and on lis-cilip on 14 October. This was immediately picked up by the present author at the BL, who soon spotted the Bill's significance for libraries, and who in turn escalated the matter on 13 October both with his own senior collection colleagues and with the officers of the Consortium of Research Libraries in the British Isles (CURL) and the Society of College, National and University Libraries (SCONUL). They reacted with their initial concerns on 14 October. Quite independently, at that stage, public librarians were also becoming apprehensive about the Bill which was a topic of conversation at the Public Library Authorities Conference on 19–21 October, at which the Museums, Libraries and Archives Council (MLA) first seems to have been warned about Clause 2.

For a few days, the BL took the lead in unpicking the ramifications of Clause 2 and making informal enquiries of DCMS, the Government department with policy responsibility for libraries. On 21 October the BL registered a formal concern with the Bill with DCMS, on its own behalf and for other libraries, copying in MLA, and it also commissioned external legal advice on the Bill's implications (subsequently extending its instructions to its solicitors on 26 October). CURL sent a general alert to its members the same day. By 25 October DCMS officials, having contacted the Home Office, reported that the latter's view was that the Bill would affect libraries no differently than the Obscene Publications Act, with which, in the eyes of the Home Office, they appeared to have lived without difficulty. This was not entirely reassuring, given the attempted prosecution of one university in 1997–8 under that Act (University of Central England, 1998). DCMS advised the library community through the BL that it should take matters up direct with the Home Office. Unbeknownst (at that time) to the libraries, 25 October was also the day on which Bob Marshall-Andrews, a leading QC and MP, prepared an analysis of the Bill, subsequently circulated to the Labour Representation Committee, in which he highlighted the lack of intent in Clause 2 as a clear contravention of Article 10 of the European Convention on Human Rights.

It was against this background that representatives of nine library organizations met at SCONUL's offices in London on the morning of 26 October to consider next steps. The bodies represented were the BL, the British and Irish Association of Law Librarians (BIALL), the Chartered Institute of Library and Information Professionals (CILIP), CURL, MLA, NLS, the Scottish Confederation of University and Research Libraries (SCURL), the Scottish Library and Information Council (SLIC) and SCONUL. At the meeting they reviewed a draft letter to Charles Clarke which had been prepared by the BL and agreed on various changes. The letter ran to two pages and sought amendments to the Bill to address the concerns of libraries. Given the urgency, the Bill coming before the House of Commons for its Second Reading later the same day, the letter was faxed there and then to the Home Secretary, with copies going to the Secretaries of State for Culture, Media and Sport and Education and Skills, to the Minister for Culture, to DCMS officials, and to the members of the All Party Parliamentary Group on Libraries and Information Management (APPGLIM). Over the next few days the letter was also sent by the library consortium, with a covering note, to a targeted selection of MPs, with yet more copies going out to further MPs identified by individual libraries and librarians.

The Second Reading debate in the House of Commons on 26 October (*Hansard: Commons*, 438, cols. 322–423) was a disappointment to libraries. The Government secured a substantial majority on the division on the whole Bill, 472 votes to 94, and no explicit references were made to libraries during the debate. In introducing Clause 2 Charles Clarke confidently stated: "The Bill extends the provisions to those who disseminate terrorist material, including on the internet, but makes clear that those who simply transmit material that does not reflect their views will not be caught." However, Dominic Grieve, the Shadow Attorney General, was not so persuaded and alluded to the "sloppily drafted" nature of large parts of the Bill, including the wide drafting of Clause 2. The BL followed this up with Grieve on 31 October. The fears of the libraries were heightened still further on 26 October when the BL received the initial legal advice from its solicitors, the final advice arriving on 2 November. The solicitors confirmed that the Bill as currently drafted raised "significant difficulties for the British Library and other legal deposit libraries", with the BL in "a particularly awkward position".

The library consortium met for a second time, at the BL, on 31 October to take stock. At the meeting a second and elaborated letter to the Home Secretary was agreed, running to three pages and with three additional signatories, the National Library of Wales (NLW), the Research Information Network (RIN) and the Society of Chief Librarians (SCL), making twelve members of the consortium in all. The first edition of a set of scenarios, designed to translate the potential impacts of the Bill on libraries into some real-life situations, was drawn up. There were eight scenarios, with a further two being added for the second edition on 2

November (reproduced in Appendix 1). The letter and the scenarios were immediately sent to Charles Clarke, with a similar distribution list for copies as the first letter. The consortium also signed off an outline strategy for handling the remainder of the House of Commons stages for the Bill. A stock letter to MPs was produced, for the organizations in the consortium and their memberships to use in lobbying local MPs. Armed with this documentation, electronically distributed via organizational email lists, during week-commencing 31 October libraries contacted MPs on a large scale, by letter, telephone and through personal briefings, to explain the difficulties which the library community had with the Bill. Some efforts were particularly co-ordinated; for instance, the South-West Museums, Libraries and Archives Council mass-mailed all the MPs in its region. A refreshed stock letter to MPs was produced on 8 November.

This lobbying had begun to have some impact on MPs by the time of the two (guillotined) sessions for the Committee Stage on the Bill, which took place on the floor of the House of Commons on 2 and 3 November (*Hansard: Commons*, 438, cols. 832–938, 985–1073). Although there was insufficient time for a substantive discussion of Clause 2, which continued to stand after Committee, consideration of a number of amendments affecting Clause 1 put forward by various MPs did stray into the area of the lack of intent in Clause 2. Also, Bob Marshall-Andrews made explicit reference to the concerns of the BL expressed in a letter and telephone call to him, while Alan Simpson noted that "the British Library cautioned the Government about the draconian consequences that would follow" for libraries, in the event the Bill was not amended. Elfyn Llwyd made similar points on behalf of NLW.

The consortium's strategy for Report Stage, on 9 November (*Hansard: Commons*, 439, cols. 310–438), was to have a probing amendment from the consortium tabled, to get the concerns of libraries on to the Parliamentary record in a substantive way. This amendment was finalized on 4 November and involved the porting of the take-down notice from Clause 3 (relating to Internet publication) to Clause 2. Lyn Brown, chair of APPGLIM, and Rob Marris were signed up to move this amendment but, unfortunately, were not called since the debate centred on other issues (not least in respect of Clause 23, dealing with the period of detention without charge, on which the Government was defeated on its proposal for 90 days), and it was, in any case, guillotined. Of particular interest to libraries was the acceptance, on division, of a Government amendment to Clause 1 (relating to the encouragement of terrorism) to introduce the requirement for intent and recklessness. This was an important concession and precedent on which the consortium was later to draw in its arguments for a similar approach in Clause 2.

The final stage in the House of Commons took place on 10 November when the Bill was given an unopposed Third Reading after four hours of discussion (*Hansard: Commons*, 439, cols. 492–553). The debate's main significance for libraries was the marker put down for the House of Lords by Dominic Grieve. In expressing the overall support for the Bill of the Official Opposition, he noted that there had been insufficient time to discuss certain aspects of the measure, including Clause 2:

We have ... failed to resolve whether there should be a defence for the dissemination of terrorist publications. That has been of great concern to academics and librarians because, as the Bill stands, if one hands out an al-Qaeda manuscript to students so that they can write an essay on it at a university, one commits a serious offence. Only the discretion of the Director of Public Prosecutions will prevent prosecution. That is unsatisfactory. It is not sufficiently unsatisfactory to make us abstain or vote against the Bill, but it must be tidied up in another place.

The Bill thus immediately passed to the House of Lords, where it had a First Reading on 10 November (*Hansard: Lords*, 675, col. 820). It had become increasingly clear to the library community that, with the preoccupation of the House of Commons with "bigger" issues such as 90 days and glorification of terrorism, it was going to be in the House of Lords that the library voice stood the best chance of being heard. The consortium's preparations for the Lords' stages had begun on 3 November, when initial contact was made by the BL with two prominent members of the Upper Chamber, Shirley Williams (who had directly relevant experience with the effect on American libraries of the US Patriot Act 2001) and Helena Kennedy. This was followed up by a BL briefing of Lord Tope, vice-chair of APPGLIM, on 9 November. The consortium met for a third time at the BL on 11 November to review tactics, by which time it had acquired a thirteenth member, the Library and Information Services Council (Northern Ireland), a province which naturally had its own knowledge of the interest of the authorities in so-called terrorist publications during the time of "the Troubles". A stock letter to selected peers was agreed on 15 November, and despatched by the consortium on 17 and 18 November, with individual libraries contacting further peers with whom they had links. A follow-up meeting with Baroness Williams and her Liberal Democrat colleague Lord Goodhart took place on 16 November, which marked the start of an effective working partnership between the consortium and the Liberal Democrats in the Lords.

Meanwhile, in parallel with the Parliamentary effort, contact was being maintained with Government, through the intermediation of the BL with officials in DCMS, in the hope of securing a breakthrough with the Home Office. The action was stepped up on 17 November when Lord Eatwell, chair of the BL's Board, telephoned Charles Clarke's office to express concerns about Clause 2. The Home Secretary promptly followed up the conversation with a three-page letter to Eatwell on 18 November, substantially drawing upon Government's standard replies to MPs who had written in on behalf of libraries. Taking issue with the legal advice obtained by the BL, the letter stated that it was not the intention of Government to restrict the vast majority of librarians and that it did not think the Bill would have that effect. Clarke argued that a very high test for prosecution of librarians had been set and that there were adequate safeguards in the statutory defences in Clause 2, the requirement on libraries being not dissimilar to that under the Obscene Publications Act. Identical arguments were put forward in the 30-minute face-to-face meeting between Clarke and Eatwell at the Home Office three days later, also attended by four Home Office officials and advisers and the present author. The Home Secretary was not especially conciliatory and was adamant that he would not move to insert intent into Clause 2, but he did provide some general assurances to libraries and agreed to look again at the wording of the sub-clauses dealing with the defences. In preparation for the meeting with Clarke, the consortium had produced a fresh three-page briefing for him, seeking five amendments to the Bill, and attaching the second version of the scenarios.

The meeting between Clarke and Eatwell took place on 21 November literally while the Second Reading debate was in progress in the House of Lords, and references to the meeting were made in the latter part of the debate (*Hansard: Lords*, 675, cols. 1384–1492). Leading for the Government, Baroness Scotland explained Clause 2 in terms which mirrored the Home Secretary's when he introduced the measure into the House of Commons: "The Bill extends the provisions to those who disseminate terrorist material, including on the Internet, but makes it clear that those who simply transmit material which does not reflect their views will not be caught." Although the outcome of the very lengthy debate was an unopposed Second Reading, peers from all sides of the Chamber raised concerns about Clause 2, especially its lack of intent, on behalf of libraries and academics, including Baronesses Carnegy, Sharp, Warwick and Williams and Lords Carlile, Clement-Jones, Eatwell, Goodhart, Griffiths, Henley, Kingsland and Parekh. The Liberal Democrats were especially eloquent. Williams proclaimed "the drafting of this legislation is terrifyingly weak and terrifyingly far-reaching", noting that even the US Patriot Act did not undermine the First Amendment in this respect. Clement-Jones criticized the failures of DCMS in addressing the concerns of libraries, and Goodhart observed that "The Government's test for guilt is not what was in the mind of the defendant, but what might be in the mind of some unidentified persons who are, in all probability, unknown to the defendant". Also of great significance, given his role as independent reviewer of anti-terrorist legislation, was Lord Carlile's recognition that there was a case to be made for librarians and academics. In summing up for the Government, Scotland restated that there was nothing in the Bill which would threaten innocent librarians, but she did undertake to see whether any changes might be necessary to the defences in Clause 2.

In the wake of the House of Lords Second Reading, the library consortium met for a fourth time on 23 November and fine-tuned its Parliamentary tactics. Separate meetings followed with the Conservative and Liberal Democrat leads on the Bill in the Lords on 29 November and with the convener of the cross-benchers on 1 December. Lord Eatwell wrote to Baroness Scotland on 29 November, summarizing the questions he had posed to her at Second Reading and particularly pressing the need to amend Clause 2 to incorporate intent. Government, however, was apparently still not for moving, since, on the very same day, Hazel Blears, a Home Office Minister, sent a three-page reply to all the signatories to the consortium's original 26 October letter to the Home Secretary, restating the Government's position as outlined by Charles Clarke to Eatwell. The consortium agreed a succinct two-page rejoinder to Blears on 2 December arguing that, notwithstanding Government assurances, libraries continued to harbour grave concerns about the Bill, pointing out that the drafting did not seem to reflect Government's articulated purposes, seeking a full reply to the scenarios, and highlighting the illogicality of the Home Office's position on intent, which it was prepared to see in Clause 1 but not in Clause 2.

The fifth meeting of the library consortium was on 30 November. It was significant because representatives of the two university groupings which had been
lobbying against the Bill, Universities UK and (as it then was) the Association of
University Teachers (AUT), were in attendance. Henceforth, the concerns of
librarians and academics were fully aligned, and campaign resources were
pooled. The same afternoon, on behalf of both communities, Baroness Warwick
(Chief Executive of Universities UK) hosted an open meeting for peers in a Parliamentary committee room, to brief them on the Bill. Eight peers attended, two
from the Labour benches, three Liberal Democrats and two cross-benchers. In
preparation for Committee Stage in the Lords, the enlarged library and academic consortium drafted a new stock letter to peers, which was mailed on 2
December, the same day that the legal advice to NLS came through, reaffirming
that libraries had every reason to be concerned about the Bill unless amended.

Committee Stage began on 5 December and was overshadowed by the publication that day of a report from the Joint (Parliamentary) Committee on Human
Rights (2005) which, in its analysis of Clause 2, identified the potential for
incompatibility with the European Convention on Human Rights. It recommended a new public interest defence to protect freedom of expression and also
the incorporation of a requirement to demonstrate intent or recklessness. This
cut no immediate ice with Government. In opening Committee Stage (*Hansard:
Lords*, 676, cols. 421–69, 485–504), and in answering early interventions from
Baroness Williams and Lord Eatwell, Baroness Scotland was at pains to provide
assurances that the Bill was not designed to, and would not in practice,
criminalize the activities of librarians and academics, but also announced that
Government would bring forward at Report Stage amendments to strengthen
the defences in Clause 2. However, she was resolute about continuing to exclude
intent.

Scotland maintained the same stance on the second day of Committee, 7
December (*Hansard: Lords*, 676, cols. 619–80, 700–36), when Government was
faced by a whole series of amendments to protect academics and librarians, elo-
quently advocated by Baronesses Carnegy, Warwick and Williams, and Lords
Eatwell, Goodhart, Kingsland, Lloyd, Lyell and Thomas. Scotland was conciliatory in her approach and was clear that "We do not wish librarians and academics in any way to be disadvantaged or to discharge their duties in a significantly
different way from what they do now. They do so honourably and to the credit of
our country." She envisaged few prosecutions under Clause 2 and all tightly controlled by the Director of Public Prosecutions. She said that she was in listening
mode to ensure that the revisions already promised would meet all remaining
concerns, but she and, in her later absence, Lord Bassam held out firmly against
any concession on intent. The contrary case, for the incorporation of intent, was
strongly put by peers on all benches who condemned the Government's position as illogical, legally flawed and a threat to freedom of expression. In the
event, these and other amendments aimed at protecting libraries (by Baroness
Williams to exclude from Clause 2 libraries covered by The British Library Act
1972 and the Legal Deposit Libraries Act 2003, by Baroness Williams to reduce
the maximum penalties under Clause 2, and by Lord Goodhart to introduce an
evidential, or lower, burden of proof) were withdrawn and not pushed to

division, leaving Clause 2 unamended. The universities, however, were placated by an amendment to Clause 6, on the training of terrorists, which addressed their concerns on that score, leaving them to focus on Clause 2 issues for the future. The third and fourth days of Committee, on 13 and 20 December, did not especially affect libraries (*Hansard: Lords*, 676, cols. 1118–98, 1213–46, 1631–70).

The Christmas Parliamentary recess then intervened, with a month before the next key legislative stage in the House of Lords, but the library and university consortium was far from inactive during this period. Two formal gatherings of the consortium, the sixth and seventh, were held on 19 December and 6 January, and membership was further extended into the archive domain: the National Council on Archives, the Society of Archivists, the Association of Chief Archivists in Local Government and the British Records Association all joined the campaign in early January. There were further meetings with the Liberal Democrat leads in the Upper Chamber, on 15 and 19 December and 12 and 16 January (that on 12 January also involving Lord Williamson for the cross-benchers). There was significant contact with the Conservatives, a meeting with Lord Kingsland on 20 December, letters to David Cameron (the new Tory leader) on 4 January and to other members of his front-bench team in the House of Commons on 9 January, and a meeting with Dominic Grieve on 11 January. In addition, on 11 January the consortium mailed, jointly with the universities, all peers other than those on the Government benches, with further personal letters going to around 30 Lords over the following day or so.

The early New Year also saw two self-inflicted setbacks for the Government. On 5 January Hazel Blears wrote from the Home Office to Derek Wyatt MP in reply to his letter of 6 December on behalf of the BL. She reaffirmed Government's commitment to strengthen the defences in Clause 2 and went on to set out why further changes were unnecessary. Towards the end she added, ominously: "As with obscene publications, libraries must act with due care in handling such publications and restricting access to them as they deem proper, in order that proper academic research is possible whilst not allowing impressionable people to see such publications." This statement, and notably the reference to "impressionable people", seemed to confirm all the libraries' worst fears about the Bill, and it came back to haunt Government at subsequent stages in the House of Lords. The letter was widely circulated during early January.

The next blow to Government came on 9 January, with the delayed publication of a letter sent on 28 November by Louise Arbour, the UN High Commissioner for Human Rights, to Nicholas Thorne, British Ambassador at the UN, together with the Home Secretary's reply, in the form of a written ministerial response. In her letter the High Commissioner recommended further work on the Bill to ensure that it aligned with the UK's obligations under international and regional legal instruments. In respect of Clause 2 she highlighted its broad and sweeping nature, the omission of intent, and the lack of proportionality. In his response, Charles Clarke pointed to improvements to the Bill which had already been made or were planned and rejected the High Commissioner's criticisms (*Hansard: Commons*, 441, cols. 1WS–2WS). Government's apparent withholding from the House of Lords (at Committee Stage) of the High Commissioner's critique led to an acrimonious debate in the Upper House on 11 January (*Hansard: Lords*, 677, cols. 163–7).

Whether triggered by these immediate events, or by a broader assessment by the whips of its chances of getting Clause 2 through the division lobbies in the Lords, on 12 January Government announced an apparent change of heart. In a letter to Lord Kingsland, copied to Lord Goodhart, Baroness Scotland explained that, having considered the arguments advanced by Lord Eatwell, Baroness Warwick (both Labour peers) and others, Government would be tabling an amendment to Clause 2 to incorporate intent with subjective recklessness, as well as amendments to strengthen the defences, as previously promised. Eatwell was sent a similar letter on 16 January. This news naturally led to cautious jubilation on the part of the libraries and universities and left them with no choice but to cancel their media release planned for 16 January, embargoed for 17 January. Unfortunately, when the Government's amendments on intent were published on 13 January they were found not to be a mirror of the equivalent section in Clause 1 and altogether lacking the clarity and simplicity of the various Opposition amendments to Clause 2. They also seemed to imply the screening of library users. A hastily-convened eighth meeting of the leaders of the consortium on 16 January, while expressing disappointment with the Government's amendments, resolved initially not to oppose them but to see where the debate in the House of Lords at Report Stage went. Later that day, however, there were some second thoughts about this.

Report Stage commenced on 17 January, the first day going fairly badly for the Government (*Hansard: Lords*, 677, cols. 549–613, 630–54). For a start it lost a critical division on glorification, which was excised from the Bill. Then it ran into difficulties with the libraries and universities, whose cause was pressed by Baronesses Warwick and Williams and Lords Butler, Dearing, Eatwell, Goodhart, Kingsland and Lloyd. This was despite Baroness Scotland making it clear that the Government's concern was with "radical texts and extremist pamphlets" which had played a major role in "radicalising vulnerable and susceptible young people, particularly changing Muslims from law-abiding members of the community to potential terrorists". She was early put on the spot by Williams and Eatwell about the Blears letter of 5 January, of which Scotland had to concede she had absolutely no knowledge. While Government's amendments to strengthen and generalize the statutory defences in Clause 2 were accepted without division, and new defences for the BL and other legal deposit libraries were not pursued, their Lordships voted by 234 to 134 to accept the Opposition parties' crystal-clear amendment on intent with subjective recklessness in preference to the Government's more opaque proposals. The second day of Report on 25 January (*Hansard: Lords*, 677, cols. 1186–1254) held no significant library interest, although there was one disquieting reference to the possibility of seizure of publications from a library during the debate on an amendment to Schedule 2 moved by Lord Bassam for the Government.

Immediately after the first day of Report, on 18 January, Baroness Scotland informed Baroness Warwick that the Government would be bringing forward compromise amendments on intent in Clause 2 at Third Reading which would fit better with the Bill as a whole. She handed out copies of these amendments at a meeting with Baroness Warwick and Lords Eatwell, Goodhart, Kingsland and Lloyd on 25 January, the day after the consortium's ninth meeting. The new amendments were considered by the consortium's leaders on 26 January, in the light of advice received from Opposition parties in the Lords, and were deemed satisfactory to the libraries and universities. On 27 January the BL also agreed with Government not to press for an amendment to deal with the potential for conflict with its own statutory responsibilities under the 1972 and 2003 legislation but to accept assurances on the Parliamentary record. It provided a form of words for this purpose which Government subsequently adopted verbatim.

A final consortium meeting with the Liberal Democrat leads in the Lords on 31 January preceded Third Reading in the Upper Chamber on 1 February (*Hansard: Lords*, 678, cols. 197–242). Lord Bassam moved the Government's compromise amendments on Clause 2 on intent, which also stood in the names of Lords Goodhart, Kingsland and Lloyd, to emphasize the cross-party support for them. Baronesses Carnegy, Warwick and Williams and Lords Eatwell, Goodhart and Stoddart spoke in favour of them, and the amendments were approved without division. Eatwell sought assurances for the BL on possible conflict with its duties under the 1972 and 2003 Acts, not least against the background of the unsettling Blears letter, and received them from Lord Bassam. Baroness Williams tackled Bassam about his reference at Report Stage to the seizure of publications and received an assurance from him that it was not the intention to seize material from deposit or other legitimate libraries. Through DCMS, Government checked with the consortium via the BL on 15 February whether the libraries were now broadly content and was given an affirmative reply.

The journey was still not quite at an end, however. The 49 amendments made to the Bill as a whole during its passage through the Lords, a few of them very controversial, now had to be validated by the House of Commons. They came before the Lower Chamber on 15 February, where all were agreed to without debate or division, apart from those affecting glorification, which was reinstated (*Hansard: Commons*, 442, cols. 1427–98). Since the consortium had not made glorification a principal concern, it was therefore possible to send a "home and dry' message out to the membership, on the basis that all the amendments otherwise affecting libraries and universities had been upheld by the Commons. The glorification clauses returned to the House of Lords on 28 February, where they were again rejected (*Hansard: Lords*, 679, cols. 136–77). They were reinstated by the Commons on 16 March (*Hansard: Commons*, 443, cols. 1664–87), and sent back to the Lords on 22 March, where they were finally accepted (*Hansard: Lords*, 680, cols. 241–60). The Bill received Royal Assent on 30 March, with most of the provisions of what was now the Terrorism Act 2006 coming into force on 13 April, the date of the last electronic Bill update sent to the consortium. Between late March and early May a large number of thank-you letters were sent out by the BL to Parliamentarians on behalf of the consortium.

23.3 Analysis

The UK's library community had cause to be pleased with the outcomes of its uncharacteristic and unexpected excursion into Parliamentary politics, to see off the threat which the Terrorism Bill had been thought to pose. In particular, through collective action on a scale and with a determination never before seen, librarians and their allies from other sectors had secured two major amendments on the face of the Bill, in respect of Clause 2 on the dissemination of terrorist publications: the incorporation of intent with subjective recklessness, and a strengthening and generalizing of the statutory defences. They had also obtained from Government increasingly explicit assurances, on the Parliamentary record, which put beyond any shadow of doubt that the everyday activities of legitimate libraries and librarians in collecting and disseminating publications on behalf of their users were not the anticipated targets of the Clause, assurances which the investigative and prosecuting authorities would need to bear in mind in contemplating any action under the Clause. In short, the libraries had mounted a victorious campaign, but what were the critical success factors, and what lessons can be learned for future political activity by the library community?

Starting with Government, it is clear that Home Office ministers and officials entirely failed to anticipate the concerns which libraries would have with the Bill, and, once voiced, struggled to appreciate their seriousness. They genuinely saw resonances with the provisions of the Obscene Publications Act and thought the wording of the Bill fully reflected their stated purposes, that those who simply transmitted material which did not reflect their views would not be caught and thus that legitimate librarians could never be criminalized by the Bill. Therefore, for a long while, the Home Office in general, and the then Home Secretary in particular, could not comprehend what all the fuss was about. They had accordingly seen no need for prior consultation with the community, nor even (it would seem) with DCMS, the Government department with responsibility for libraries, which was taken as much off-guard by the introduction of the measure as were the libraries themselves. The Home Office probably had little practical experience of the working of libraries, and they declined, despite repeated offers by the consortium, to enter into a serious direct dialogue with its representatives, in strong contrast to the discussions which officials evidently held with Internet Service Providers over Clause 3 of the Bill. Communication with Government during the crisis was thus largely conducted in circuitous fashion through the BL into DCMS civil servants. The latter did their best under difficult circumstances, but they did not appear to exercise any significant influence over the Bill Team in the Home Office for whom the anxieties of libraries were a fairly low priority. Only when Parliamentary defeat over Clause 2 started to stare Government in the face in the New Year did the Home Office come forward with amendments and assurances which defused the situation.

Although Parliament ultimately provided the mechanism through which the library community was able to register its concerns and ensure they were addressed, the early legislative stages were not especially auspicious. For the House of Commons the big issues of principle in the Bill were around the period of detention of suspects without charge and the concept of glorification of terrorism; relative to these, the preoccupation of librarians was not a key story for debate. Matters were exacerbated by the very tight controls which Government imposed on the duration of each stage in the Commons, which effectively squeezed out "lesser" topics. The community was quick to recognize this challenge, and to accept that the only realistic objective for the Commons phases was to place a marker on the Parliamentary record that there were deficiencies in the Bill from a library perspective which had to be rectified in the House of Lords. In this they were successful, especially through the intervention of the Shadow Attorney-General.

The trust which libraries placed in the role of the House of Lords as a revising chamber was fully vindicated, and they were assisted by differences in Parliamentary procedure applicable to the Lords. In the Upper Chamber the convention is that all tabled amendments have to be debated, and that Ministers have to respond to all of them, so there could be no question of library issues being timed out or buried. There was a real prospect that Government could be worn down through persistence, and this is what eventually happened. The effectiveness of the libraries and their allies in the House of Lords owed much to the fact that, through their vigorous lobbying, they were able to draw upon cross-party support, from the Conservatives, Liberal Democrats, cross-benchers and some peers under the Labour whip (most notably, and bravely, Lord Eatwell and Baroness Warwick, both of whom went out on a limb with Government on behalf of libraries and universities). Liberal Democrat peers in general, and Lord Goodhart and Baroness Williams in particular, were especially powerful advocates for libraries and universities and were able to lift the concerns beyond the narrowly technical and theoretical to the plane of freedom of thought and expression, which commanded a broader appeal. They were also a source of tactical advice and of expertise in the law. Sadly, while a few individual members of APPGLIM were helpful to the library cause in both Houses of Parliament, the Group as a whole was not a critical success factor in the campaign.

The House of Lords' engagement with the library agenda owed remarkably little to any spotlight which the print and broadcast media were casting on it. In fact, media publicity played a very small role in the successful outcome for libraries. The initial strategy of the library consortium had been to give Government the opportunity to respond to its concerns, before seeking to fan any flames of public opinion, and so it consciously targeted politicians rather than journalists with its arguments and adopted a reactive stance to media enquiries. The universities, through Universities UK and AUT, by contrast, took a more media-assertive line, and this led to some incidental surfacing in the media of the Bill's implications for libraries. For instance, there was a short burst of coverage during the second week of November, in Edward Stourton's interview with Professor Drummond Bone of Universities UK on Radio 4's "Today" programme on 8 November, a piece by Curtis and Taylor (2005) on "law-breakers" in higher education libraries, and a similar story by Fazackerley (2005). Some of the professional library and information journals also covered the library issue, notably

Mark Chillingworth of *Information World Review* (Chillingworth, 2005, 2006), but, being monthly or less frequent, they were obviously challenged to keep up in a fast-moving Parliamentary environment. The CILIP website, however, did carry some basic information about the Bill and the library campaign throughout.

The consortium modified its media stance to become more proactive during the House of Lords stages of the Bill, thereby aligning with colleagues from the universities. A major tactic to coincide with the start of Committee Stage was an opinion piece to which Baroness Williams had lent her name, and whose line was around the need to protect freedom of thought and expression and the pursuit of knowledge. It was anticipated that the *Sunday Times* would publish the article on 4 December, but their last-minute editorial decision was against publication, so it is appearing in print here as Appendix 2 for the first time. Similarly, the consortium had planned to precede Report Stage with a joint press release with the universities on the theme of "Terrorism Bill could criminalise librarians and academics", for issue on 16 January (Appendix 3). This launch had to be cancelled on 13 January when Government introduced its own amendments on intent in Clause 2, thereby defusing some of the tension and, for many journalists, seemingly reducing the chances of its defeat on the issue. Newspapers such as *The Times*, which had seemed poised to run the story on 16 January, became much less interested when a lost division was no longer on the cards. In the event, of course, Government did lose a vote on Clause 2 in the Upper Chamber on 17 January, when its own amendment on intent was rejected in favour of an Opposition one. This gained some coverage in the media on 18 January, albeit as a footnote to the Government's defeat on glorification in the same debate.

If media positioning was not a critical success factor, then to what besides the House of Lords can a good outcome be ascribed? Two other overarching explanations might be advanced. First, having been caught off-guard at the outset, when they lost a whole month before realizing the Bill posed a potential threat, a simultaneous failure in Government consultation and communications and of the library sector's Parliamentary intelligence, the libraries recovered to build an effective working consortium and disciplined campaign organization drawn from all parts of the UK and representing all types of library. This was led by the BL, underpinned by BL administrative support and public affairs expertise, guided by the early legal advice taken by the BL (both on the Terrorism Bill and the Racial and Religious Hatred Bill, which was also before Parliament), and informed by the BL's recent practical Parliamentary experience in connection with the Legal Deposit Libraries Act. However, it was also a consortium that was co-operatively and transparently managed, according to a rolling action plan which always worked several stages ahead, rather than simply responding to current developments, and with constant communications and opportunities for direct involvement. Regular meetings of the consortium were held, frequent (often daily) updates posted by the BL and others to a closed email list to synthesize the political news, all key documents were put out for comment in draft, and invitations were extended to members to join in meetings with politicians. After a slightly hesitant beginning, the constituent bodies in the consortium empowered their representatives to commit on their behalf, trusting the consortium's collective judgement and thereby speeding up the decision-making process.

Second, an effective organization was paralleled by a simple and focused message, delivered with a minimum of emotion and rhetoric. It was made abundantly clear that the philosophical objection was not to the general purposes of the Bill, which libraries supported, but to the unintended consequences which would be potentially brought about for libraries and their users by the infelicitous drafting of certain clauses. The tactical objective was not particularly to get librarians on the march but to persuade Parliament of the need to amend the Bill through reasoned and evidentially-based argument. The legal advice taken by the consortium was influential, adding weight to the various other legal objections which were being raised with Parliament. The scenarios had an instant impact, graphically illustrating for those with limited knowledge of libraries how an unamended Bill would jeopardize their normal operations and undermine the public interest. The scenarios powerfully demonstrated that the campaign was not driven by a selfish desire to keep librarians out of jail but to protect the values of a free and open society. Neither was the message diluted. The consortium could easily have jumped on to more general bandwagons around the Bill, not least to make common cause with those who were lobbying to excise glorification, but it concentrated on a limited agenda around Clause 2, and increasingly on the single issue of the inclusion of intent therein. The libraries accordingly chose their allies carefully, benefiting significantly from their growing collaboration with the universities and, at the very end, archives. Some contact was maintained with the Internet Service Providers, but the publishing and bookselling trade bodies did not significantly engage, in public at least, and Research Councils UK perceived no great danger in the Bill, leaving it to the universities and peers to fight the research corner alongside the libraries.

23.4 Conclusions

Was the campaign worthwhile? Did it warrant the enormous commitment of time and energy of the leadership of so many library organizations? Were librarians, many of them paid out of public funds, justified in setting themselves up in apparent opposition to Government? Certainly, none of those involved in the consortium felt entirely comfortable with wearing the political mantle. But they never doubted the necessity of their cause. Looking across the world to Australia, we can now glimpse what might have been in the UK had libraries and universities not pointed out the flaws in the Terrorism Bill 2005 and succeeded in getting them rectified. As Maslen (2006a, 2006b) has shown, the new Australian anti-terrorism laws are already being used to curtail academic research into Islamic fundamentalism and to prevent libraries from stocking the relevant texts. Nearer to home, one journalist, Gadher (2006), tried to make capital out of the fact that "The only man convicted in connection with the 9/11 terrorist attacks began plotting the downfall of western society from the austere surroundings of the British Library", a reference to a reader's pass which Zacarias

Moussaoui had obtained in 1994 while he was a postgraduate student at South Bank University. On the contrary, as the consortium expressed it in its never-published press release:

> Libraries and universities underpin this country's revered tradition of freedom of thought and expression, and the pursuit of knowledge. These freedoms are the envy of the world and attract thousands of overseas scholars and students to study here. This inadequately drafted legislation risks undermining the very liberties that the terrorists seek to destroy, and would inhibit the very research and educational activities which can play a key part in preventing terrorism.

In this way, through their successful and wholly unprecedented collective action during the winter of 2005–6, the library community of the UK made an important contribution to preserving the country's democratic ideals and traditions and to passing them on for future generations to enjoy.

References

Lord Carlile (2005) *Proposals by Her Majesty's Government for Changes to the Laws against Terrorism*. HMSO, London.

Chillingworth, M. (2005) Terrorism Bill poses threat. *Information World Review*, **219** (December), 8.

Chillingworth, M. (2006) Lords defend libraries in debate over Terrorism Bill. *Information World Review*, **220** (January), 2.

Curtis, P. and Taylor, M. (2005) Law-breakers in the library. *The Guardian*, 8 November, Education, 1–2.

Dodd, V. (2006) Universities urged to spy on Muslims. *The Guardian*, 16 October, 1–2.

Fazackerley, A. (2005) Libraries urge clarity on terrorism criteria. *The Times Higher*, 11 November, 7.

Field, C. D. (2006) A very British campaign: challenging the Terrorism Bill. *Library & Information Update*, 5(7–8), 22–3.

Gadher, D. (2006) British Library quest of 9/11 plotter. *Sunday Times*, 6 August, 1.7.

House of Commons Home Affairs Committee, Draft Terrorism Bill 2005: oral evidence, Tuesday, 11 October 2005, HC 515-I.

Joint Committee on Human Rights (2005) *Counter-Terrorism Policy and Human Rights*, HL Paper 75-I and HC 561-I.

Maslen, G. (2006a) Study into suicide bombing curtailed. *The Times Higher*, 29 September, 11.

Maslen, G. (2006b) Anger at ban on books on terror. *The Times Higher*, (6 October, 10.

Sack, T. (2006) Anti-terrorism measures and the impact on public libraries in the UK: surveillance versus user privacy and confidentiality, and the attitudes, views and reactions of the library profession towards it. *MSc Dissertation*, City University.

University of Central England (1998) *After a Year out on Loan Mapplethorpe Book is set to return to Library Shelves*. http://www.uce.ac.uk/mapplethorpe/.

Appendix 1

Second edition of scenarios, 2 November 2005

Scenario 1 – Two different individuals can access the same information for quite legitimate or terrorist purposes.

For example, a reader accessing human traffic information on the London Underground during rush-hour, in addition to train and station design reference material and various London maps, street atlases and mainline station information could quite as easily be a postgraduate or journalist researching anti-terrorist intelligence operations as a terrorist seeking information on where explosives might best be placed. The definition in Clause 2 relies on the use made of publications and the reader's intentions as opposed to the content of the work itself. This may also apply to historical texts, where an individual studying Nelson Mandela's memoirs is in one context looking at an account endorsing a form of state terrorism and in another, the actions of a courageous freedom fighter.

Scenario 1a – International "terrorism" information at specialist institutions

A library specializing in the study of the Commonwealth and its member nations, has collections including a wide range of material, particularly material published in these countries, relating to their history and social sciences, including political movements. Some of these political movements are of course oppositional in nature; some have been labelled, or are currently labelled "terrorist" organizations. The material includes pamphlets and political ephemera from bodies such as the African National Congress, SWAPO (Namibia) and Zimbabwe African Nationalist Union (ZANU). It is important that this material is available for the study of political movements, political change, etc.

Scenario 2 – The Bill could put all libraries at risk of prosecution.

A researcher in the House of Commons Library accesses submitted enquiry responses looking at security at major sporting events. The researcher obtains copies of several submissions raising concerns over lack of strategic security at the Olympics, including structural faults in the stadium and communications problems with police antennae. The researcher, although security checked at the time, may use this information several years on for terrorist training purposes. The House of Commons Library is liable to prosecution (it provided access to the information) until it proves it did not endorse the material.

Scenario 3 – Libraries could be committing an offence by negligence in lending to other institutions.

The British Library lends material to other libraries, either in the UK or abroad and provides copies of documents to Higher Education through the remote document supply service. For example, the material, a research paper on terrorist training techniques is studied in a lecture theatre, interpreted outside of the controls of the library by individuals unknown to the library, who are not reader pass holders. These third parties then commit a terrorist act or pass on publications that lead to a terrorist act. The British Library may have committed an offence "by negligence" in carrying out the normal duties prescribed by the British Library Act 1972.

Scenario 4 – Terrorist material could be kept legitimately as part of an academic library.

A university library collects material to support courses and research in international relations and religious studies. These courses and research could contribute to a better understanding of terrorism, and help to develop ways of preventing it. It is possible that some of these materials could meet the definition of "terrorist publications". Most academic libraries have publicly available catalogues of their material, and, in addition to their own staff and students, many allow access to the library for research purposes to individuals outside the academic community.

Scenario 4a –Defending alleged terrorists in the courts.

A solicitor undertaking criminal work and defending individuals accused of terrorist offences would need to research relevant materials. The firm's librarian is asked to obtain these materials and lend them to the solicitor who might pass them on to the defending barrister. Is the librarian and the law firm partnership committing an offence in obtaining and subsequently keeping them in the firm's library for possible use in future work, where it could be seen and influence one of the firm's employees?

Scenario 5 – It is impossible to second guess and keep track of all uses of library reference material.

A "terrorist publication" has been identified as being made available by the library and has led to a terrorist attack in a public space either directly or indirectly. The Library, according to the Bill is responsible for having "provided a service" under Clause 2 and could be deemed responsible and its Directors liable to corporate manslaughter charges.

Scenario 6 – "Take down" notices applying to the internet will not cover archived material.

An individual member of the public submits material to a website message board, such as the BBC online "Have your Say" section. This website is routinely archived as part of undertaking the web archiving programme, in line with regulations under the Legal Deposit Libraries Act 2003. Later, it is deemed that the comment should be removed and the web service provider is asked to do this or be at risk of "endorsing" the material. Yet it will exist on a permanent record of the website and searchable as part of the British Library's web-archiving site. Clause 3 of the Bill treats the web as non-permanent yet it remains a static record for research purposes by law.

Scenario 7 – Fictional works by their very nature are open to interpretation.

A work of fiction is read at a public book reading event. The reader endorses the book as a fine piece of fiction and a fantastic critique on terrorist activities but a member of the audience uses the ideas and themes discussed in a future terrorist act. The reader and/or author will not endorse the acts that may be depicted in the work itself but the Bill leaves the reader and author open to prosecution.

Scenario 8 – Forfeiture of a "terrorist publication" is problematic.

A publication is deemed to be "terrorist" in nature and ordered to be recalled and pulped. It is unclear how this will work in practice if the publication in question has had a print run of thousands, with copies available in a large number of libraries, bookshops, publisher and distributor warehouses, and so forth – around the world as well as in the United Kingdom.

Appendix 2

Article offered for publication in the *Sunday Times*, 4 December 2005

Much has been made of the Government's recent defeat in Parliament over its proposal to introduce a 90-day detention period for terrorist suspects. While there is no doubt that this was a rare event, focus upon it has directed attention away from the many other deficiencies that blight the Terrorism Bill currently before Parliament. The Government has now signalled its intention not to debate the detention issue in the House of Lords, so an opportunity has arisen for the grave concerns of a wide cross-section of society to be examined.

Of particular moment are the fears being articulated by the UK library community, a community never before so united behind one issue. In short, the implications of the Bill are that any librarian, and any university lecturer or professor, might be criminalized should they disseminate what is considered to be terrorist material. These are not just the idle thoughts of a "spineless Liberal", to quote the Home Secretary; they are based on senior legal opinion. The library community has every reason to fear that they will be profoundly restricted in their first and inescapable obligation – to promote knowledge and access to it – by this badly drafted yet far-reaching legislation.

Libraries are particularly worried about the wide and obscure definitions of what constitutes a "terrorist publication", and their potential for retrospective application. For example, a publication on passenger flows in London underground stations could conceivably be of use to both a transport engineer as he seeks to redesign Victoria underground station, and a terrorist looking to maximize the impact of his intended attack. The Bill depends upon the reader's intentions to decide if an item is a "terrorist publication", but how can the intentions of hundreds of readers be ascertained by librarians as they carry out their work? This could also apply to historical texts, where an individual studying Nelson Mandela's memoirs is in one context looking at an account endorsing a form of terrorism against the state and, in another, at the actions of a courageous freedom fighter. These definitions must be made much more explicit.

An even more alarming feature of the legislation is the complete reversal of one of the most fundamental principles upon which this country's judicial system is based: the right of someone to be considered innocent until proven guilty. This Bill would assume guilt until the defendant can demonstrate his or her innocence. As the Bill is currently drafted, it will be virtually impossible for a librarian, or lecturer at a university, to prove that he or she did not distribute an item with the knowledge that it would be used to encourage or facilitate a terrorist act. The Bill must be amended to incorporate at a minimum a requirement to prove intent to commit an offence.

None of us can for one moment support the capricious and cruel activities of terrorists that have destroyed the lives of a great many people, and may well destroy the lives of others. The library community strongly supports effective action to combat terrorism and isolate terrorists. But any law in this delicate and difficult area must be absolutely clear, consistent and workable. It must also protect the fundamental liberties that define a free and open society. In its present form, the Bill fails all these tests in its treatment of terrorist publications.

One of the greatest tools at our disposal in the war against terrorism is the freedom to acquire and disseminate the widest possible range of printed and digital information, absolutely essential for full and free-ranging debate and a deeper understanding of what it is that leads people to commit terrorist acts. How far are we to go in destroying the liberties we have enjoyed for centuries in an effort to prevent terrorism and, in doing that, how far would we be going in giving the terrorists exactly what they want? Libraries and universities underpin freedom of thought and expression in our country, and the pursuit of knowledge. These freedoms attract thousands of scholars and students from outside Britain to study here. This inadequately considered legislation, whatever the Government's intentions, threaten them all.

Appendix 3

Press release intended to have been issued on 16 January 2006

Terrorism Bill could criminalise librarians and academics

The library and university communities of the UK have grave fears that freedom of expression will be undermined by the Terrorism Bill, about to enter Report Stage in the House of Lords on 17 January. As drafted, it could potentially criminalise the legitimate and vital activities that librarians and academics carry out.

Specific concerns regard the Bill's efforts to restrict the dissemination of terrorist publications. The UK library and university communities fully support Government's efforts to combat the terrorist threat, but want to ensure that sound legislation is produced. The two main issues are:

- The uncertain definitions as to what constitutes a terrorist publication
- The alarming shift in the burden of proof from the prosecution to the defence in respect of the dissemination of terrorist publications.

An article on crowd flows in stations could legitimately be used by an engineer working on the redesign of a London Underground station, or by a terrorist looking to maximize the horror of a planned attack. Should such an attack take place, and the terrorist be found to have obtained the article from a library in order to facilitate his planning, the librarian who distributed the item could be liable to prosecution. A librarian cannot be expected to accurately judge the intentions of a reader when carrying out his or her legitimate duty to provide access to information.

The Bill also shifts the burden of proof to the defence. Rather than being considered innocent until proved guilty, a librarian or lecturer would have to demonstrate their innocence of the charge of knowingly distributing material that would either incite or aid an individual in carrying out a terrorist act. This is an unprecedented reversal of one of the historic cornerstones of the British judicial system.

Speaking on behalf of the library and university communities, Dr Clive Field, Director of Scholarship and Collections at the British Library, argues that: "Libraries and universities will suffer damage to their reputations and expense in answering unnecessary cases made against them, when all they have done is to facilitate access to published information. This will lead to self-censorship, and undermine the important role that they play in combating terrorism through fostering a better understanding of it."

Professor Paul Wilkinson of the Centre for the Study of Terrorism and Political Violence, University of St Andrews, adds: "Libraries and universities underpin this country's revered tradition of freedom of thought and expression, and the pursuit of knowledge. These freedoms are the envy of the world and attract thousands of overseas scholars and students to study here. This inadequately drafted legislation risks undermining the very liberties that the terrorists seek to destroy, and would inhibit the very research and educational activities which can play a key part in preventing terrorism."

Appendix 4

Terrorism Act 2006, Section 2: Dissemination of terrorist publications

1 A person commits an offence if he engages in conduct falling within subsection (2) and, at the time he does so-

    a. he intends an effect of his conduct to be a direct or indirect encouragement or other inducement to the commission, preparation or instigation of acts of terrorism;

    b. he intends an effect of his conduct to be the provision of assistance in the commission or preparation of such acts; or

    c. he is reckless as to whether his conduct has an effect mentioned in paragraph (a) or (b).

2 For the purposes of this section a person engages in conduct falling within this subsection if he-

    a. distributes or circulates a terrorist publication;

    b. gives, sells or lends such a publication;

    c. offers such a publication for sale or loan;

    d. provides a service to others that enables them to obtain, read, listen to or look at such a publication, or to acquire it by means of a gift, sale or loan;

    e. transmits the contents of such a publication electronically; or

    f. has such a publication in his possession with a view to its becoming the subject of conduct falling within any of paragraphs (a) to (e).

3 For the purposes of this section a publication is a terrorist publication, in relation to conduct falling within subsection (2), if matter contained in it is likely-

    a. to be understood, by some or all of the persons to whom it is or may become available as a consequence of that conduct, as a direct or indirect encouragement or other inducement to them to the commission, preparation or instigation of acts of terrorism; or

    b. to be useful in the commission or preparation of such acts and to be understood, by some or all of those persons, as contained in the publication, or made available to them, wholly or mainly for the purpose of being so useful to them.

4 For the purposes of this section matter that is likely to be understood by a person as indirectly encouraging the commission or preparation of acts of terrorism includes any matter which-

   a. glorifies the commission or preparation (whether in the past, in the future or generally) of such acts; and

   b. is matter from which that person could reasonably be expected to infer that what is being glorified is being glorified as conduct that should be emulated by him in existing circumstances.

5 For the purposes of this section the question whether a publication is a terrorist publication in relation to particular conduct must be determined-

   a. as at the time of that conduct; and

   b. having regard both to the contents of the publication as a whole and to the circumstances in which that conduct occurs.

6 In subsection (1) references to the effect of a person's conduct in relation to a terrorist publication include references to an effect of the publication on one or more persons to whom it is or may become available as a consequence of that conduct.

7 It is irrelevant for the purposes of this section whether anything mentioned in subsections (1) to (4) is in relation to the commission, preparation or instigation of one or more particular acts of terrorism, of acts of terrorism of a particular description or of acts of terrorism generally.

8 For the purposes of this section it is also irrelevant, in relation to matter contained in any article whether any person-

   a. is in fact encouraged or induced by that matter to commit, prepare or instigate acts of terrorism; or

   b. in fact makes use of it in the commission or preparation of such acts.

9 In proceedings for an offence under this section against a person in respect of conduct to which subsection (10) applies, it is a defence for him to show-

   a. that the matter by reference to which the publication in question was a terrorist publication neither expressed his views nor had his endorsement (whether by virtue of section 3 or otherwise); and

   b. that it was clear, in all the circumstances of the conduct, that that matter did not express his views and (apart from the possibility of his having been given and failed to comply with a notice under subsection (3) of that section) did not have his endorsement.

10 This subsection applies to the conduct of a person to the extent that-

   a. the publication to which his conduct related contained matter by reference to which it was a terrorist publication by virtue of subsection (3)(a); and

   b. that person is not proved to have engaged in that conduct with the intention specified in subsection (1)(a).

11 A person guilty of an offence under this section shall be liable-

    a. on conviction on indictment, to imprisonment for a term not exceeding 7 years or to a fine, or to both;

    b. on summary conviction in England and Wales, to imprisonment for a term not exceeding 12 months or to a fine not exceeding the statutory maximum, or to both;

    c. on summary conviction in Scotland or Northern Ireland, to imprisonment for a term not exceeding 6 months or to a fine not exceeding the statutory maximum, or to both.

12 In relation to an offence committed before the commencement of section 154(1) of the Criminal Justice Act 2003 (c. 44), the reference in subsection (11)(b) to 12 months is to be read as a reference to 6 months.

13 In this section-
"lend" includes let on hire, and "loan" is to be construed accordingly;

"publication" means an article or record of any description that contains any of the following, or any combination of them-

    a. matter to be read;

    b. matter to be listened to;

    c. matter to be looked at or watched.

Politics, Profits and Idealism: John Norton, the Stationers' Company and Sir Thomas Bodley

John Barnard

24.1 Introduction

The only formal contact between Sir Thomas Bodley and the Stationers' Company is the latter's order of 1610 which first established copyright deposit in England, an often told story.[1] This important event looks significantly different when set in a wider context than that of Sir Thomas and the Stationers alone. That additional context is provided by the Company's own ambitions, by the accession of James I, and by the career of Bodley's bookseller, John Norton.

John Norton (1556/7–1612)[2] was a bookseller, publisher, and finance capitalist, an extremely successful entrepreneur active on several fronts, including the continental trade. Further, Norton's business pre-eminence was intertwined with his role as a cultural broker and facilitator. Supplying books for Sir Thomas Bodley's new library was only one of his concerns, and Norton's business shows how far early seventeenth century capitalism depended upon the effective utilization of the openings provided by kinship, clientage, patronage and government favour. His example also suggests that historians should consider more regularly the evidence provided by book history and bibliography. "The cultural impact of printing and the book trade was out of all proportion to its economic significance."[3]

I will start with Bodley's library, and then locate Sir Thomas's dealings with his bookseller within an account of Norton's career, his relevant publications and his connections with James I, before returning to the beginnings of copyright deposit in England – a narrative from which John Norton is usually absent.

24.2 Bodley's Library

Sir Thomas Bodley's broader intentions need to be highlighted. He saw his new library as a "publike benefit" and expected it to be "a most admirable ornament aswell of the state, as of the Vniversitie".[4] (Bodley's success in attracting gifts and donations from the aristocracy, clergy and more widely, shows how swiftly it became a co-operative national enterprise, not just one man's obsession.[5])

The kind of public benefit to the state which Bodley, a staunch Protestant,[6] had in mind for his library is clear from a comparison with that established slightly later by Archbishop Tobie Matthew at York.[7] Matthew's remarkable library, housed in his palace at Bishopsthorpe, "was the largest private library in England at the time". He made it available to writers and preachers, regarding it as a "theological arsenal, for attacking his Counter-Reformation enemies". Like Bodley's library, that of Matthew needed continental Catholic texts (even those proscribed) as well as Protestant ones.[8] Norton's expertise in the continental book trade was essential for the creation of Bodley's knowledge base for the furthering of Protestant learning and the defence of the Anglican church.

The relation between Sir Thomas and the University in the library's foundation is simple and well documented – one of institutional gratitude to a generous and visionary benefactor. There is also a wealth of evidence in Sir Thomas's letters to his librarian, Thomas James, about his dealings with Norton and John Bill (successively Norton's apprentice, agent and successor) from 1601 onwards.[9]

Much more complicated was the relationship between the University and the London Stationers' Company, which controlled the book trade. The success of Bodley's negotiations with the Company is surprising because its interests and those of the two Universities were opposed: throughout the seventeenth-century the Stationers were frequently at loggerheads (and law) with one or other of the universities. The cause was the longstanding rights awarded by the Crown for both universities to print limited classes of books. This represented a direct threat to the Stationers' otherwise total monopoly over book production in England, Wales, and Ireland. The agreement to deposit copies of all newly published works in the Bodleian Library was, on the face of it, an unlikely one. What other publishers' association, particularly one defending an altogether more aggressive monopoly than the Net Book Agreement, would instruct its members to give away their product for nothing? The arrangement came about only through a complicated inter-reaction between the institutions and individuals involved – one group made up of Sir Thomas Bodley, Thomas James, his librarian, and the University authorities, and the other of the Stationers' Company as a corporate body, its officers, and the members of the London book trade. In addition, after his accession in 1603, James I had direct or indirect influence on all the parties. These overlapping spheres of influence are all involved in the beginnings of copyright deposit in England. (Unlike France, it was not established by a royal *diktat*: there, in 1537, Francis I's Montpellier Ordinance had required every publisher throughout France to give a copy of every new book to the Royal Library at Blois.[10] Things were done differently, and much later, in England.)

24.3 John Norton's Career

A good sense of John Norton's standing and business is given by his activities in 1601, the first year he is recorded as buying books for the library. That year Sir Thomas's bookseller, then aged forty four, presented the new library with a copy of Gerard's Herball, which he had published with his cousin, Bonham, in 1597 or 1598. Norton specially employed an artist to hand-colour the engraved portrait of Gerard and the highly elaborate engraved title-page, of which there are colour reproductions in Treasures from the Bodleian (1979).[11] In addition, the ornamental capitals are carefully coloured throughout the book, and so too, most importantly, are the numerous woodcuts of plants (which include the first printed illustration of a potato plant). These appear on almost every page of this very large folio – and all of them are represented in realistic colours. The four representations of maize or "Turkie Wheate" (or, as it used to called, "Indian corn") on page 76 of the Herball demonstrates the implicit colonial dimensions of the work.

When I saw the book, I was amazed to find that the final pages were extremely badly worn. This was not due, as I first thought, to a lack of care for Norton's expensive gift. As Clive Hurst showed me, the wear was entirely due to its intensive use by early readers. The serious damage is restricted to the book's index section – once that's realized, it is evident that although the images of plants still have a pristine brightness, the outer margins of every page are grey with generations of handling. Norton's gift was as useful as it was beautiful.

John Norton was one of only two book tradesmen to make gifts in kind to the new Library.[12] No doubt his present reflected the element of client-patron relationship between the bookseller and his customer, but Norton's care in having this reference work expensively illustrated, especially when put together with his later role in trying to enforce copyright deposit, suggests that here was a man acting out of an idealistic belief in learning.

I'll come back to the question of John Norton's idealism, or otherwise, later. The publication history of this botanical atlas, the second largest book Norton ever published,[13] tells a good deal about the kind of commercial advantage he had over his rivals. Firstly, he shared the costs with his cousin, Bonham Norton (spreading the risk of expensive publications was essential to his business success). Secondly, not only was Gerard's folio in part a translation of an earlier continental work by Rembert Dodoens, first published in 1573, but Norton had borrowed (or, more likely, rented) all but a few of the nearly 1,800 woodcuts required from the Frankfurt printer, Nicolaus Basseus (the blocks were originally cut for an earlier German work of 1590).[14] Thirdly, he employed an English engraver, William Rogers, to cut the splendid title-page and portrait. This very large investment, made only three years after Norton had set up business in London, demonstrates his willingness to risk large scale investment. It also shows him making the latest botanical knowledge available to the wealthy English reader, and using continental texts and continental craftsmen to do so. At the same time the publication offered some employment for the nascent English engraving trade. One or more of these features occurs in Norton's other illustrated publications, but the single most important factor is his working relationship with the Continental trade.

Three of Norton's other activities in 1601 enforce the importance of these links and their importance to his career. In March that year, Sir Henry Savile, the friend of Bodley, Warden of Merton and later Provost of Eton, was consulting the bookseller about how and where to publish his proposed edition of the fourth century Church father, St. John Chrysostom – should it be London, Paris or Frankfurt? This monumental eight volume scholarly work, intended for a European readership, entirely set in Greek characters and on a scale new to England, was to be delayed for another decade, when Norton was once again to be involved.[15]

Norton's connections with the continent, and also with Scotland, appear in an altogether less idealistic light later the same year. In June 1601 Robert Barker, the Queen's Printer, brought a petition against "John Norton, an Englishman and stationer of London" and Andro Hart of Edinburgh. Barker accused them, in partnership with John Norton's cousin, Bonham, of infringing his rights by importing cheap Bibles which they'd had printed in Dordrecht. These undercut Barker's Bible monopoly and threatened, he claimed, the livelihoods of thirty people dependent upon his business.[16] This was very clever sharp practice on the partners' side: by financing the printing abroad themselves, the partners not only undercut Barker's expensive London-produced Bibles, but also saved the additional expense of employing a continental middleman. The partners in London and Edinburgh thereby profited twice over.

Towards the end of the year Norton was in trouble again, this time with the Stationers' Company, for falsely registering a book by Piscator as his copy (again continental connections were involved[17]), which he was forbidden to print.[18] Despite this, the Company appointed him an Assistant in January 1602.[19]

By 1601 therefore Norton had developed good connections with men like Bodley and Savile, had a first hand knowledge of the London trade, was on his way up the hierarchy of the Stationers' Company, knew the continental trade, and had contacts in two of its most important centres, Paris,[20] and Frankfurt, as well as in Dordrecht. It is also evident he was willing to break his Company's rules for his own benefit.

There is one further startling fact about John Norton's activities in 1601, one which has gone unnoticed. Early that year, John Norton carried a letter to James VI of Scotland, as part of the Earl of Essex's conspiracy against Queen Elizabeth. Henry Cuffe, one of the conspirators, confessed on 2 March 1601, only eleven days before he was executed –

> ... Norton the bookseller carried the Earle of Essex letter to the Scottish Kinge, which Norton received at Barwike [i.e., Berwick on Tweed], and that one parte of the letter was to persuade the coming uppe of the Earle of Marr to London by the first of Februarie ... the King of Scottes shuld retourne his aunswere in disguised woordes of thre bookes, which the King did accordinglie.[21]

Cuffe recognized the dangerous position in which this involvement placed the man he called his "honest friend": in his will Cuffe left Norton £40, partly for unpaid bills, but "allsoe to give him some recompence for the trouble which this great tempest (I feare) is like to bring vppon him."[22] No action was taken against Norton, which may mean he was ignorant of the letter's contents: but he must have shared the conspirators' belief in the need to secure the Protestant succession by ensuring that James became the next King of England.

The connection with James I and VI will come up again in Norton's career. But the immediate question is, how had John Norton, the son of a Shropshire yeoman,[23] come to occupy the position he did in 1601?

Two factors, apart from innate ability, are accountable – the strong kinship networks in the English book trade, and Norton's involvement in the lucrative import trade in continental books, which until the very end of the sixteenth century was the monopoly of immigrant booksellers.

This is evident from the outline of John Norton's early years in the trade. He was apprenticed in 1578 at the unusually late age of twenty one, by which time his father was dead.[24] His master was his Shropshire born uncle. William Norton was one of the original members of the Stationers' Company, and founded a wealthy merchant dynasty. A summary account of the family's success is given by the monument which Jane Norton, the wife of Bonham, erected in St Faith's under Paul's, the parish church of the booksellers in St Paul's Churchyard.

It gives a somewhat sanitized version of reality. Bonham Norton, who is described as "Esquier, Stationer and sometimes Alderman of this City", had in fact died in prison, a result of his long standing and unscrupulous attempts, which included physical violence, to gain the office of King's Printer held by Robert Barker, which included the Bible monopoly (the very one he had earlier attempted to undermine with John Norton and Andro Hart). None of the five other stationers with memorials in St Faiths are described as "Esquiers", but status was evidently important to both Bonham and Jane Norton. There is a complaint as early as 1597 that he, a mere "Bookseller", had improperly purchased himself armorial bearings:[25] he also married well into a local Shropshire family. Jane Owen was the daughter of an Elizabethan judge who had built the magnificent Condover Hall for his son and her half-brother, Sir Roger Owen. Condover church, immediately adjacent to the Hall, still has the impressive family monument erected by Jane Norton: it has four kneeling figures – her father, half brother, husband and herself.[26]

William, John and Bonham Norton did very well. All three became Master of the Stationers' Company, all three amassed considerable wealth, and all three bought property in or around their birthplaces – in particular, Bonham Norton built up a substantial number of properties in Church Stretton and is credited with rebuilding the town after the disastrous fire of 1593.[27]

John Norton's future trade required him to know Latin: he became a student at Queen's College, Cambridge in 1570, but left without taking a degree.[28] He was probably already under the care of his uncle, who later sent his son, Bonham, to Cambridge in 1580–1. [29] It seems likely that his uncle saw the possibility of displacing the immigrant London families (the Birckmanns and de Renialmes) who monopolized the import trade in books. Certainly that was what happened. From the beginning of the seventeenth century the Latin trade was to be taken over first by John Norton, then by John Bill his former apprentice, and later by Henry Fetherstone, Bonham Norton's apprentice from 1598.

This would explain why, when John Norton completed his apprenticeship in 1586 aged thirty, he set up business, not in London, but in Scotland.[30] By 1587, he and the young Edinburgh bookseller, Andro Hart, claimed to have been importing books from Germany,[31] a claim supported by Christophe Plantin's ledgers – from as early as 1588 John Norton was buying and selling through the Antwerp merchant (though on a much smaller scale than Ascanius de Renialme).[32] Norton, that is, learnt the Latin trade in Edinburgh, outside the jurisdiction of the London stationers. The business was successful enough for Norton to employ an agent, Edmond Wattes, with whom he'd earlier been a fellow apprentice.[33] They ran into problems with Andro Hart and other Edinburgh booksellers in February 1593 when they tried, against city regulations, to expand their wholesale business into the retail market,[34] but Hart and Norton were to continue to work together, as the 1601 Dordrecht Bible shows.

In 1594 John Norton moved to London, but maintained his Edinburgh business. [35] His shop was in St. Paul's Church Yard. There is a description of it in 1649: "... a Celler (all vnder the said House) In the ffirst Story, a Shopp, an Inner Roome and a Closett, In the Second and Third Storys, Two Roomes and a Closett in each of them, and Two Garretts over the same. And all those Two Vaults lyeing under the Quire of Paules Church, on the North side thereof."[36] The shop was on the East side next to St. Paul's School. This was opposite his old master's shop, now in the hands of his cousin.[37] His business prospered: by 1607 he needed more space and had to rent an additional room in Stationer's Hall.[38]

Following the early death of his agent Wattes in 1596, Norton sold his Edinburgh stock and debts to Andro Hart and Edward Cathkin for the considerable sum of £400[39] (equivalent to over £57,000 in today's money). It is probable that this sale was prompted more by the need to finance his publishing ventures than the difficulty of replacing Wattes – between 1597 and 1598 he jointly published three books, including Gerard's *Herball*, with his younger cousin, Bonham, who had inherited his father's estate in 1593: John Norton presumably supplied the business expertise and his cousin the extra capital required. Of significance here is Norton's publication in 1600 of a catalogue of manuscripts in Oxford and Cambridge[40] by Thomas James, Bodley's librarian. This must have established at least indirect contact with Sir Thomas himself, and this book additionally marks the start of a long publishing partnership with George Bishop, an older man and a senior figure in the trade. James's catalogue was among three London published books advertised in the Frankfurt Book Fair catalogue for autumn 1600.[41] This was probably Norton's doing: from 1604 to 1612 Norton was to advertise regularly, if in a small way, in the Frankfurt catalogues, the first English bookseller to do so.[42]

24.4 John Norton and James I

It was these Frankfurt advertisements which first alerted me to the political dimensions of a group of John Norton's publications aimed at continental readers. These are all connected with James I, who succeeded to the throne in 1603, and had a significant impact on John Norton's future, without which he might never have become Master of the Stationers' Company.

So you need to remember, as I pursue John Norton and James I, that throughout the years from 1601 to 1612 John Norton, with the help of his newly freed apprentice, John Bill (also from Shropshire), was in continuous contact with Sir Thomas, advising and consulting, providing bibliographical information and giving him access to catalogues both printed and in manuscript. Above all, they regularly brought back books from the twice yearly Frankfurt book fairs, while from the age of twenty five John Bill searched the whole of Europe for books – France, Italy, and Spain, as well as the Low Countries and Germany. Sir Thomas either went to Norton's London shop or had Norton bring the books to his home where he could examine them at leisure in his gallery.[43]

James VI of Scotland succeeded to the English throne on 24 March 1603: he thenceforth ruled both countries as well as Wales and Ireland, and so became the first King of the new "Great Britain". James I did not reach London until May, three months later. On 28 March, only four days after James I had been declared King, John Norton and five other men registered their copyright in James's book, *Basilikon Doron*. This manual, written for his son on the duties of a monarch, was originally meant for strictly private circulation – the King had just seven copies printed in 1599. A revised Edinburgh version appeared in 1603. In England the demand was such that Norton and his partners hastily printed at least three London editions, dividing the work among different printing shops for speedy production – a copy is recorded as being available a mere two days after registration.[44] Norton, with his Scottish connections, must have been the prime mover of these London editions.

On 17 May 1603, shortly after reaching London, James I granted Norton the office of King's Printer of Latin, Greek and Hebrew, which included the money-spinning grammar monopoly.[45] This can only have been the King's reward for the delivery of Essex's letter in 1601 and Norton's publication of the *Basilikon Doron*, particularly since James's grant was extremely doubtful legally – the office already belonged to another man, John Battersby. (Norton's new privilege was, indeed, promptly challenged by its owner, though the two men eventually reached a settlement, and Norton was able to rent out the grammar publishing to partners.[46])

But grammars were not the only business of the King's Printer of Latin. He also supplied the King's Latin books,[47] which Norton did and for which he was paid. [48] As T.A. Birrell has demonstrated, James I's library was

on the one hand a clear reflection of his personal taste, and on the other hand an organ of state – but even as an organ of state it reflects the distinctive personal policy interests of the monarch.... [It was] a combination of a Home Office library and a Foreign Office library.... James I was the first English monarch systematically to keep dossiers on subjects that interested him.[49]

He was particularly concerned by the continental books in Latin, often virulent in tone and content, like those by the Catholic polemicists Caspar Scioppius and Jacob Gretser, written in reply to his own publications. He used John Norton (and subsequently John Bill and Bonham Norton, who took over as King's Printer of Latin) to collect them as "library agents in the modern sense".[50] As King's Printer, then, John Norton's continental purchases for James I ran alongside, and, to an important degree, overlapped with, his purchases for Bodley's new library.

The King's collection of books was a working library for his international propaganda war with the Papacy. As W.B. Patterson's recent revisionist account shows (but again with no reference to Norton),[51] James I's defence of Divine Right provoked a European-wide debate, and was a serious attempt to forge an alliance of Protestant princes, denying the Pope's claims to superior authority over them and their subjects. It also involved arguing for the historical legitimacy of the Anglican church and state. The furious debate centred on James I's own substantial 112 page pamphlet defending the Oath of Allegiance, *Triplici nodo, triplex cuneus. Or An Apologie* [i.e., defence] *for the Oath of Allegiance* (1607) (written with the help of James Montagu, Master of Sidney Sussex and Master of the Chapel to James).[52] The Oath of Allegiance had been imposed on James I's Catholic subjects in the after-shock of the Gunpowder Plot, and was intended to distinguish between those Catholics who accepted the temporal authority of the British monarch, and those who believed in the papacy's superior authority. It had been precisely the Pope's power to release subjects from their allegiance to heretic princes, and to displace or even assassinate them, which had led to the Gunpowder Plot.

John Norton's appointment involved him directly in this campaign since he was the official publisher of the Latin translations of James I's own works, and was better placed than any other London bookseller to ensure their European circulation. Between 1604 and 1612 Norton not only published Latin books and pamphlets by James and his clerical supporters, but advertised them in the Frankfurt Book Fair catalogues.[53]

There is a very immediate account of how this propaganda war and the Frankfurt catalogues impacted on the King's immediate circle. On 6 April 1611 Patrick Young, his Librarian, reported that John Bill had returned the previous day from Frankfurt, bringing the latest catalogue. Young immediately looked up the replies to James I's latest publication. Their titles alone were enough to excite his outrage. (I paraphrase his Latin.) "There you can see the monsters brought forth every year, like that foulest shit-demon, Eudaemonis, and other publications by Lessius and Scioppius [all three virulent attackers of James I's ideas]: like a swarm of locusts they roar violently at James's Preface,[54] which is said to be one from Antichrist and his forebears."[55] This network (Frankfurt Book Fair, John Bill, the King's Librarian, and the King himself both buying these works and contributing to the debate himself) shows how close the work of Bill and

Norton brought them to the political and religious centre of the English establishment.

Norton was also indirectly involved in the publication closest to James I's heart, the 1611 Authorized Version. The right to Bible publishing, the one infringed by the Nortons and Andro Hart in 1601, involved a heavy initial capital outlay, even if, properly managed, it could bring considerable rewards: Robert Barker's income from the monopoly was thought to be £3,000[56] (about £370,000 in today's money) and in the time of James and Charles I the post itself was worth the equivalent of nearly £4,000,000.[57] If the Bible patent was normally capital intensive, the massive cost of publishing the Authorized Version made it even more so. Barker is reputed to have paid no less than £3,500[58] for the manuscript and copyright of the new translation. The stakes were high: the Court of Chancery believed in 1619 that Bonham Norton's "moiety" in the office of King's Printer was worth £11,000 (more than a million pounds).[59] It now appears that between 1610 and 1612 Barker was forced to sell a very large proportion of his stock, possibly worth as much as £6,900, to a consortium of seven booksellers headed by John Norton in order to raise sufficient capital to print the necessary editions of the new translation. Neither Barker nor members of the consortium seem to have realized that John Norton had been in a lucrative three way partnership with his cousin, Bonham, and John Bill since 1605, importing books from the continent. Barker's forced sale of his stock seems to have played into the hands of the Norton cousins and John Bill, who saw the opportunity of taking over the Bible trade for themselves.[60] Following John Norton's death, Bonham Norton and John Bill eventually succeeded in wresting control of the Bible trade from Barker, a struggle detailed in the prolonged acrimonious litigation between Bonham Norton and Barker.[61]

James I appears in these years as the dedicatee of three other important books financed by John Norton, once more with partners, each representing a "first" in English publishing. In 1607 Norton, together with George Bishop, published the first folio edition of Camden's *Britannia*, originally published as an octavo in 1586 (with the encouragement of his friend, Ortelius, the continental cartographer[62]). This much enlarged edition of Camden's historical and geographical account of the nation, is the first to have county maps, and Norton advertised it in the Frankfurt catalogues.[63] It has an elaborate engraved title-page and there are no fewer than 55 double leaf and two single leaf maps, 21 of which are signed by William Hole (who also engraved the title-page) and 34 by William Kip, both English engravers.[64] In 1610 Norton, in partnership with five other tradesmen, again including George Bishop, published the first English translation of Camden's work, once more in folio and again with the maps and title-page, at last making it available for the wider general public in England.[65]

The third publication is the most outstanding, and complex, of all John Norton's publications, this time financed jointly by himself and John Bill. Following his publication in 1602 of the first pocket sized world atlas in English, an epitome of Ortelius's *Theatrum Orbis Terrarum*,[66] Norton went on to publish the whole work. This imposing English version of Ortelius's atlas is dated 1606 but was probably not published until 1608. The English *Theatrum* had 166 plates and was, according to R.A. Skelton, the "tallest volume printed in England up to that date ..[and] also the largest collection of intaglio prints in a single book yet published in England".[67] Norton arranged with the plates' owner, Baptist Vrients, to have the maps printed in Antwerp, and then shipped over to London where the English text was printed.[68] It is striking that the English edition actually has more plates than any of the continental editions – and includes a new map of England and Ireland with a tree of English monarchs culminating in James I, to whom it is dedicated by Vrients.[69] All the maps were hand coloured, and the edition seems to have been no larger than three hundred.[70] Skelton notes that the atlas "could have exercised a formative influence on the ideas of Englishmen whose minds were turning towards world geography, oceanic commerce and overseas colonization". He also calls it "decidedly a book fit for a king".[71] That's evidently what Norton intended. He had the arms of James printed on the back of the title-page, to which he was misguided enough to add two couplets of his own in the panel at its foot:

> The sway by Sea & Land, great Iames doth beare,
> His Birth, His Bloud, These Kingdomes figure here,
> But were his seuerall virtues to be crown'd
> A World, past thine, Ortelius, must be found.

Facing this is the bookseller's own dedication of his work to the King, taking the form of a memorial inscription: it reads:

> TO THE
> MOST HIGH,
> MOST MIGHTY,
> AND MOST HAPPY
> PRINCE, IAMES BY THE
> GRACE OF GOD, KING
> OF GREAT BRITAINE,
> FRANCE AND IRE-
> LAND, DEFEN-
> DER OF THE
> FAITH, &c.
> Iohn Norton
> HIS MA-
> IESTIES MOST
> HVMBLE AND
> FAITHFVLL SER-
> VANT CONSECRATETH
> THESE IMMORTALL LA-
> BOVRS OF ABRAHAM
> ORTELIUS, TRANS-
> LATED INTO
> ENGLISH.

It was an extremely unusual gesture for a bookseller to dedicate his own work to a monarch. Norton believed in the importance of his status as King's Printer.

Yet this was the man routinely referred to in Sir Thomas Bodley's correspondence as a mere functionary – as my "bookseller" or my "stationer".

24.5 Copyright Deposit

Not surprisingly, given his standing, prosperity, and family connections, John Norton was elected Master of the Company in 1607–8 and again in 1611–12, when his position in the Company was to prove important for the Bodleian Library. The imaginative idea of persuading London's stationers to donate copies of their new books had been that of the librarian, Thomas James, as Bodley himself admitted – "For the stationers gifte, I am of your opinion, that it is to be accounted, a gifte of good moment: & I thinke I had hardly thought vpon it, if yow had not moved the mater at first", adding, "for the effecting whereof, I have found notwithstanding many rubbes and delaies."[72] Sir Thomas's first point of contact in this affair must have been John Norton.

The Stationers' grant, made during the Mastership of Thomas Man (among the more important of Norton's partners), is dated 12 December 1610 and was sealed at the University's congregation on 17 February 1611.[73] Five months later Bodley was complaining of the slow delivery of the Company's books,[74] a complaint which echoed down the years. Matters had not improved by 1 January 1612 when he wrote, "Mr Norton ... hath promised faithfully to [see that the books are delivered] with speede."[75]

Norton kept his promise. He had become Master of the Company a second time in July 1611: on 28 January 1612,[76] three weeks after Bodley's letter, the Company passed an ordinance which added teeth to its earlier decision. From now on, failure to comply was to be punished by a fine of three times the book's value.[77] Appended to this enforcing order of the earlier agreement was a commendation from the High Commission, the ecclesiastical equivalent of Star Chamber. This commendation was made at the requested of the Stationers, led by Norton, and resolved to "maintain the perpetual execution" of the ordinance: the nineteen signatories are headed by the Archbishop of Canterbury.[78] John Norton had done all he could to enforce copyright deposit: fortunately both he and Sir Thomas died before they could realize the new order was to be no more effectual than the first.

It is quite clear from Bodley's complaints, and later those of the University, about the difficulty of getting the books from the Company, that the trade's everyday membership resented the ordinance handed down by its oligarchy requiring them to give away their goods for nothing. Why, then, did the governing body of the Stationers' Company decide to support Bodley's new library at this time? There is no reason to disbelieve that, as their original grant said, they were responding, in part at least, out of their desire "to further a work of so much pietie and benefit to the generall state of the Realme".[79]

The King's endorsement of Bodley's venture, signalled by his visit to the University in 1605, had underlined its national role (even if his promise of a gift of

Royal manuscripts came to nothing). The Stationers' Company itself must have felt particularly confident of its future in the years 1610–12. During James's reign, they had consolidated their monopoly over the majority of the regularly profitable publications like almanacs, educational and law books (this joint stock venture, called the English Stock paid its investors 10% and 12½% a year for the remainder of the century[80]). The Company's Hall had been used for the final checking of the Authorized Version in 1611, and by 1612 they were able to purchase the site for a new Hall[81] (which had to be rebuilt after the Great Fire[82]).

The years 1610–12 also at last saw the publication of Sir Henry Savile's splendidly printed eight volume edition of Chrysostom's works dedicated to James I. Although this was financed by at great expense by Savile himself (he reportedly spent £8,000 of which £2,000 was for the paper alone[83]), the Company had given crucial support in kind,[84] and the edition's publication was organized by their Master, John Norton.[85] (When Norton advertised the edition in the Frankfurt catalogues he was proud enough of his connection with Savile's project to use his official title – 'Typographus Regius' – for the first and only time.[86]) The Stationers' leading members had every reason to believe in the security of their standing in the country's polity in the years between 1610 and 1612. As a corporate body, one in which John Norton played a leading role, their support for Sir Thomas's library reflected their national standing.

24.6 Conclusions

What are we to think of John Norton?

He was clearly an astute, imaginative and energetic businessman who amassed considerable wealth and was investing in Shropshire property. He was also capable of sharp practice, as Robert Barker and John Battersby knew only too well. But Norton was motivated, at least in part, by idealism. One sign of that is his commitment to the Stationers' Company. John Norton died on 19 December 1612.[87] His will left the Company the very considerable sum of £1,000 to fund interest-free start-up loans for poorer members of the trade. This provision exactly imitates a clause in his uncle's will of 1593, but far more generously (£50 p.a. as opposed to only £6).[88] There is also an observable ideological and religious consistency in his career. His activities as Latin publisher and propagandist for the king on behalf of the Protestant cause are functions of his official position, but all the signs are that they reflect the bookseller's own beliefs. The publication of the world atlas in English, in a pocket version as well as the grand folio, and of the two versions of Camden's *Britannia* were undoubtedly business ventures but they played a part in the country's developing colonial project and in James I's ambitions to redefine the nation as "Great Britain".

This can be put another way. There is a remarkable convergence between the cultural and political objectives of the King (and of Sir Thomas Bodley) and John Norton's business ambitions, entrepreneurial skills, continental network and senior position in the Company. For Norton, the political, religious and cultural aspirations of James I's "Great Britain", into which Bodley's new library fitted with remarkable neatness, provided a highly profitable context in which to do business while acting as a cultural broker.

Finally, there is an unanswered question. On 6 May 1603 Bodley wrote to his librarian, Thomas James –

Sir, I pray yow speake to Mr Vicechancellours Deputie in my behalf, and intreat him to suffer yow, to send me hither Mr Nortons Herball for which he has present, and very special vse. Howbeit I shall be assured of another as good, or rather better. I pray yow faile not send it by the first.[89]

What pressing "very special vse" can Norton possibly have had which persuaded Bodley to contemplate breaking his own library's rules against lending books? Norton's promise to give the library "another as good, or rather better" can have only one implication: Norton wanted it as a presentation copy. Bodley's letter was written on 6 May, James I had left Edinburgh on 5 April, was received at Charterhouse on 7 May, and on 17 May granted Norton the office of King's Printer of Latin, Greek, and Hebrew. Did Norton want the Bodleian's "painted" copy of Gerard's *Herball* as a gift for the King? It's hard to think of anything else which could have persuaded Sir Thomas to act as he did. If his urgent request was obeyed, then what the Bodleian Library now has is a *second* "painted" copy. Neither the extant documents or the book itself offer any further evidence, nor have I found a copy of Gerard's *Herball* owned by James I.[90] I'd like to believe, therefore, that John Norton's outrageous request was refused pointblank by Bodley's librarian.

References

1. See W. D. Macray, *Annals of the Bodleian Library, Oxford, A.D. 1598–A.D. 1867* (London, Oxford, and Cambridge, 1868), pp. 30–31, 44–6, and R. C. B. Partridge, *The Legal Deposit of Books throughout the British Empire* (London, 1938), pp. 2, 17–21, 288–92. The most recent account is by Ian Philip, *The Bodleian Library in the Seventeenth and Eighteenth Centuries: The Lyell Lectures, Oxford 1980–81* (Oxford, 1983), pp. 27–30. Of these only Philip, who recognizes his importance, mentions John Norton (if necessarily briefly and not in this context).
2. See *The New Dictionary of National Biography* entry by Ian Gadd. Norton died on 19 December 1612 (John Barnard, 'The Financing of the Authorized Version 1610–1612: Robert Barker and "Combining" and "Sleeping" Stationers', *Publishing History*, 57 (2005), 5–52 (at p. 9). The earlier date is that from the International Genealogical Index, where his birthplace is given as Billingsley, Shropshire, which matches the entry of his apprenticeship in 1578 (see Edward Arber, *A Transcript of the Records of the Company of Stationers of London*, 5 vols. (London and Birmingham, 1875–94), ii.82.
3. Introduction, *The History of the Book in Britain, Volume 4: 1557–1695*, ed. John Barnard and D.F. McKenzie, assisted by Maureen Bell (Cambridge, 2002), p. 1. Ian Gadd notes that in 1557 the Stationers' Company was ranked 56th out of 63 guilds and that it was still among the poorer companies in 1692 (Ian Gadd, "'Being like a Field': Corporate Identity in the Stationers' Company, 1557–1684" (D. Phil. thesis, University of Oxford University, 1999), pp. 125–6.
4. Ed. G. W. Wheeler, *Letters of Sir Thomas Bodley to Thomas James, first Keeper of the Bodleian Library* [1599–1613] (Oxford, 1926), No. 83, p. 88 (7 June 1603).
5. The evidence for this is brought together very compactly by R. A. Beddard, "The Official Inauguration of the Bodleian Library on 8 November 1602", *Library*, 7th series (2002), 255–83, at pp. 257, 259–62.

6. D. J. B. Trim's important article, "Sir Thomas Bodley and the International Protestant Cause", *Bodleian Library Record*, 16 (1997-99), 314-40, establishes the intellectual, religious and European dimensions of Bodley's career. R. A. Beddard's account of Bodley's collection supports this paragraph ("The Official Inauguration of the Bodleian Library", pp. 274-6).

7. Matthew became Archbishop of York in 1606.

8. J. B. Gavin, "Elizabethan Bishop of Durham: Tobias Matthew, 1595-1606" (Ph. D. thesis, McGill University, 1972), p. i. See also John Barnard and Maureen Bell, *The Early Seventeenth-Century Book Trade and John Foster's Inventory of 1616*, Proceedings of the Leeds Philosophical and Literary Society, xxiv (1994), pp. 29-30. Foster's inventory includes entries for "One Cattalogg of the Mart" worth 4d. and 24 "Cattaloges of the Martes" valued at a shilling altogether (p. 70). These were most probably for the Frankfurt Fair and seem to have been among the books for sale. Matthew had an incomplete run of the catalogues for the years under consideration here: this is now in York Minster Library (xv. L. 76-77).

9. Wheeler, *Letters of Sir Thomas Bodley*.

10. Partridge, *The Legal Deposit of Books throughout the British Empire*, p. 2.

11. The two leaves in the *Herball* containing the portrait and title page were cut out and stolen in the 1980s: these high quality photographs are now the only record of the two painted leaves.

12. Robert Barker was a donor in 1604 (Macray, *Annals of the Bodleian Library*, p. 25). It is noteworthy that, in view of John Norton's connection with them, that Sir Henry Savile and William Camden were also donors of the library in 1601 (p. 19).

13. The largest was Bishop Jewel's *Works* (1609, 1611), which contained 399 sheets: Gerard's *Herball* was made up of 371 sheets (i.e., 185.5 sheets per partner). Thereafter, with the exception of Jewel's *Works* and Calvin's *Institutes* (1611), John Norton's share in large books was 116 sheets or less.

14. The woodcuts were originally used in Tabernaemontanus' *Eicones plantarum* (Frankfurt, 1590). See Blanche Henrey, *British Botanical and Horticultural Books before 1800*, 3 vols. (Oxford, 1975), i.36-54, 247, for the fullest account of the complexities of Gerard's authorship and the illustrations. See also Wilfrid Blunt and Sandra Raphael, *The Illustrated Herbal* (London, 1979), p. 165.

15. HMC, *Buccleuch and Queensberry*, i. 33-4.

16. HMC, *Salisbury*, xiv.179-80. For the edition involved see STC 2184.5. For the Order in Council supporting Barker's case, see ed. John Roche Dasent, *Acts of the Privy Council 1601-4* (London, 1907), pp. 14-15.

17. Eds. W. W. Greg and E. Boswell, *Records of the Stationers' Company 1576 to 1602 - Register B* (London, 1930), p.82.

18. Greg and Boswell, *Records of the Stationers' Company*, p. 82 (5 October).

19. Greg and Boswell, *Records of the Stationers' Company*, p. 84.

20. In 1601 John Chamberlain began using Norton's shop as a *poste restante* address for his correspondence with Dudley Carleton in Paris (ed. Sarah Williams, *Letters written by John Chamberlain during the Reign of Queen Elizabeth*, Camden Society, 1st series, lxxix: London, 1861, p. 147).

21. Ed. John Bruce, *Correspondence of James VI. of Scotland with Robert Cecil and others in England....*, Camden Society, 1st ser., 78: London, 1861, p. 90.

22. Bruce, *Correspondence of James VI. of Scotland*, p. 92

23. See note 2 above.

24. He was apprenticed on 8 January (Arber, *A Transcript of the Records of the Company of Stationers of London*, ii.82).

25. "A briefe discours of the right use of givinge armes with the late abuses aboute that mattere and the best means by which they maie be reformed orderly"; the author claims Norton had purchased "the cote both of Talbott and Mortimer" (Bodleian Library, Rawlinson Ms. B.56, fol. 23r). This document was "Written upon the appointment of the earl of Essex as marshal (fols. 36, 35b, 44) in 1597 by a grandson of Thomas Howard, fourth Duke of Norfolk, who was restored to the office of earl marshal by Q. Mary in 1553 (fol. 16b), and apparently addressed to the former nobleman" (*Catalogi Codicum Manuscriptorum Bibliothecae Bodleianae Partii Quintae ... Ricardi Rawlinson, J. C. D. ...* , ed. W. D. Macray, 1 vol. in 5 parts (Oxford, 1862-1900), i. col. 465). Other examples of this abuse cited include "Lacye the Mercer", the Queen's embroiderer and a fishmonger.

26. The monument, which on the wall of the North side chapel is about 7 feet by 20 feet tall. Its inscription reflects Jane Norton's considerable self-regard (but also gives a full list of their children): "Here lieth the Body of Mrs Iane Norton the Eldest Davghter of | Thomas Owen Esq one of the Iustices of the Common Pleas to | Qveene Elizabeth; she was the wife of Bonham Norton Esq. 45 | Yeeres and had issve by him 7 sonnes Bonham William Thomas | Arthur Iohn Roger George AID [sic] | 4 Daughters Sarah Vrsvla Mary | and Margaret she lived a widow 6 yeres and died Jvne 3 1640 | being aged 70 yeres. This monument is erected by her appoint | ment in memorial of her father her eldest brother Sr Roger | Owen her husband and her selfe This structure was finished .... . 651 [?]". It is significant that Bonham Norton's profession is omitted in favour of his social standing. He was made Sheriff to the county in 1611.

27. Ed. C. R. J. Currie, *Victoria County History, Shropshire*, x (Oxford, 1998). 79, 92–4.

28. J. and J. A. Venn, *Alumni Cantabrigienses....Part I from the earliest times to 1751*, 3 vols. (Cambridge, 1922–27): there John Norton is identified as "Doubtless" the stationer. However, Venn also says, "Perhaps adm. as Fell.-Com., 'of Kent'", but all of John Norton's connections are with Shropshire, though his uncle had property in Kent (Henry R. Plomer, *Abstracts from the Wills of English Printers and Stationers from 1492–1630* (London, 1903), p. 32. The fact that Bonham also matriculated at Cambridge adds force to the identification.

29. Venn, *Alumni Cantabrigienses*. Bonham matriculated at Trinity College in Lent 1580–1.

30. For the best account of Norton's activities in Edinburgh, see Alastair J. Mann, *The Scottish Book Trade 1500–1720: Print Commerce and Print Control in Early Modern Scotland. An Historiographical Survey of the Early Modern Book in Scotland* (Linton, 2000), pp. 14, 91, 136–7.

31. J. Lee, *Memorial for the Bible Society* (Edinburgh, 1824), p. 50.

32. R. Lauweart, 'De handelsbedrijvigheid van Officina Plantiniana op de Büchermesse te Frankfurt am Main in de XVIe eeuw', *De Gulden Passer*, l (1972), 124–80 (at pp. 169–70), reports London importers in Plantin's records as follows: Ascanius de Renialme (S 1586-Q 1600) as buying 585/2/6 guilders worth of books and selling 58/19/0. John Norton (Q 1588-S 1600) bought 72/2/0 guilders worth and sold 6/4/0; James Rimé (S 100) sold 14/0/0 guilders worth; and Hans Wantemeel (Q 1592-Q 1597) bought 12/0/0 guilders worth: Joseph Barnes of Oxford also bought 12/0/0 guilders worth in S 1600. It is unusual for an Englishman to deal direct with Plantin at all as early as 1588.

33. Wattes was freed in 1589: he had been apprenticed to William Norton on 5 August 1583 (Arber, *A Transcript of the Records of the Company of Stationers of London*, ii.118), so the two men were together in their master's shop for three years.

34. Mann, *The Scottish Book* Trade, p. 14.

35. Norton had a business presence in London prior to 1594. In 1591 he sent his uncle parcels of books published in Scotland (which were impounded, but most of these are innocent except for two works by John Penry, the Marprelate author, exiled in Scotland: also include were James VI's poems (Arber, *A Transcript of the Records of the Company of Stationers of London*, ii.38), on 9 August 1592 he apprenticed John Bill for eight years, and he entered and published STC 14938 in 1593, a book by George Ker, previously published in Edinburgh by Robert Waldegrave.

36. Peter W. M. Blayney, *The Bookshops in Paul's Cross Churchyard*, Occasional Papers of the Bibliographical Society, No. 5 (1990), p. 53, cited from Guildhall Library, MS. 11,816A, fol. 73a.

37. Blayney, *The Bookshops in Paul's Cross Churchyard*, pp. 53–54, figs. 8 and 11. The shop's frontage was 42 feet: it was 28 feet deep. Bonham Norton inherited his father's shop, the Queen's Arms, first leased to William Norton in 1573: by 1599 Bonham Norton had an interest in additional shops (pp. 35–37).

38. William A. Jackson, *Records of the Court of the Company of Stationers 1602 to 1640* (London, 1957), p. 25. The annual rent was £1/6/8d.

39. David Calderwood, *The History of the Kirk of Scotland*, ed. Thomas Thomson (Edinburgh, 1844), v.511.

40. *Ecloga Oxonio-Cantabrigiensis*.

41. *Catalogus universalis pro nundinis Francofurtensibus* (Frankfurt, Autumn 1600), sig. C4v (Bodleian, Antiq. e. G. 1): on a few occasions my information is based on the Leipzig version of the catalogues, *Frankfurt and Leipzig Fair Catalogues: Michaelmesse 1594-Michaelmesse 1860*, ed. Bernhard Fabian (Hildesheim, 1977–83).

42. Further see, John Barnard, "Financing the Authorized Version 1610-1612", Appendix 2.
43. See *Letters of Sir Thomas Bodley*.
44. See Stanley Rypins, "The Printing of *Basilikòn Dôron*, 1603", *Papers of the Bibliographical Society of America*, 64 (1970), 393-417. John Manningham reports the work's publication in his diary entry for 30 March 1603 (p. 393n). Norton and his partners were immediately threatened by Edward Allde's pirated edition of 1,500 copies. Although the Stationers' Company fined Allde, the partners were also fined on 13 April for selling the book at an excessive price (Jackson, *Records*, pp. 2-3).
45. *Calendat of State Papers Domestic 1601-1610*, 17 May 1603: see Nancy A. Mace, "The History of the Grammar Patent, 1547-1620", *Papers of the Bibliographical Society of America*, 87 (1993), 419-36. Arnold Hunt gives a succinct account of this patent and of patents more generally in "Book Trade Patents, 1603-1640", *The Book Trade & its Customers: Essays for Robin Myers*, ed. Arnold Hunt, Giles Mandelbrote and Alison Shell (Winchester and New Castle, Del., 1997), pp. 27-54. As King's Printer, Thomas Berthelet was paid by Henry VIII for printing proclamations but he also acted as the King's bookseller, supplying Latin books among others (see the account worth £117/0/6½d for the years 1541-43, Arber, *A Transcript of the Records of the Company of Stationers of London*, ii.50-60.
46. Mace, "The History of the Grammar Patent", p. 430.
47. Just as Robert Barker, the King's Printer of English books, supplied James I with books in the vernacular (Paul Morgan, "A King's Printer at Work: Two Documents of Robert Barker", *Bodleian Library Record*, 13.5 (1990), pp. 370-74).
48. These are as follows: 100 marks on 23 January 1608 "for certain books for the Prince"; £173/16/4 on 13 November 1609 "for binding sundry books, covered with velvet, &c. for the King's service"; £60/2/8 on 12 March 1610 for books for the Duke of York, testified for by his tutor, Thomas Murray (*Calendar of State Papers Domestic 1601-1610*); £50 on 5 April 1611 "for books for the King's use" (*Calendar of State Papers Domestic 1611-18*).
49. T. A. Birrell, *English Monarchs and their Books: from Henry VIII to Charles II: The Panizzi Lectures 1986* (London, 1987), p. 26.
50. Birrell, *English Monarchs and their Books*, pp. 26-7.
51. *King James VI and I and the Reunion of Christendom* (Cambridge, 1997, 2000).
52. STC 14400. This first English version was printed by Robert Barker in 1607 (as King's Printer in English), as was, more surprisingly, the first Latin edition in the same year (STC 14403). Norton published the Latin translation again in 1608 (STC 14404) and advertised it in the Frankfurt catalogues (*Catalogus universalis* (Spring 1608), sig. B1r (York Minster, xv. L. 76 (5))). On the work's composition, see David Harris Wilson, "James I and his Literary Assistants", *Huntington Library Quarterly*, 8 (1944-45), 35-57, at pp. 40-42.
53. Eds. Julian Roberts and A. G., *John Dee's Library Catalogue* (London, 1990), p. 13.
54. That is, STC 14405 (1609), the Latin translation of *Triplici nodo triplex cuneus* which has a general title-page, *Apologia pro juramenti fidelitatis* with the addition of a "Premonitory" preface (see D. H. Wilson (above, n. 52), pp. 40, 44-5), was advertised in the Frankfurt catalogue for autumn 1609. James sent a copy of his 'Premonition', on a subject which touches all Christian princes, 7 June 1607, to Archduke Albert of Austria, with a covering letter saying that a copy has been received by the King of France, and copies were sent to the King of Spain and the Emperor (HMC, *Salisbury*, 21, p. 64). D. H. Wilson (pp. 48-9), notes that these copies were elaborately 'bound in velvet and stamped and cornered in gold'.
55. Johannes Kemke, *Patricius Junius (Patrick Young) Bibliothekar de Könige Jakob I. und Karl I. von England*, Sammlung Bibliothekwissenschaftlicher Arbeiten, vol. xii (Leipzig, 1898), p. 9.
56. Henry R. Plomer, "The King's Printing House under the Stuarts", *Library*, n.s. 2 (1901), 353-75, at 354.
57. Morgan, "A King's Printer at Work", p. 370.
58. *DNB*, citing William Ball, *Treatise concerning the Regulating of Printing* (1651), p. 27.
59. The figure had been reduced to £8,000 by 1629.
60. John Barnard, "The Financing of the Authorized Version 1610-1612", pp. 5-52. This modifies Plomer's account of the way in which the Authorized Version was financed.
61. Plomer, "The King's Printing House under the Stuarts", pp. 353-75, provides the standard account of the struggles in the courts between Bonham Norton and Robert Barker. These courtroom battles are re-examined by Maria Wakely in a forthcoming article in the *Library*.

Graham Rees has a forthcoming article on the King's Printers in this period in the *Huntington Library Quarterly*.

62. The two men met when Ortelius visited England in 1577 (*DNB*).

63. *Catalogus universalis* (Autumn 1607), sig. C1v (York Minster xv. L. 76 (4)).

64. R. A. Skelton, *County Atlases of the British Isles 1579-1850: A Bibliography* (London, 1970), No. 5.

65. Skelton, *County Atlases*, No. 6.

66. Abraham Ortelius, *An Epitome of Ortelius* ... (STC 18857). dated "[1601?]" by STC, which also notes that it was printed for John Norton in Antwerp by H. Swingenij. However, see C. Koeman, *Atlantes Neerlandici: Bibiography of Terrestrial, Maritime and Celestial Atlases and Pilot Books Published in the Netherlands up to 1800*, 5 vols. (Amsterdam, 1967-71), Ort 65, where it is dated "1602": Norton came to an arrangement with Baptist Vrient to use the plates from his Latin 1601 Antwerp edition of the work for his own London edition (Ort 58) (as he did for his edition of the full work in 1606-8 - for which see next note and text above). I have accepted Koeman's date here on the grounds that Vrient would not have wanted an English edition competing with his own in the same year. STC dates the other contemporary London edition of the *Epitome*, printed abroad for J. Shawe, London (STC 18856), as 1603, based on the imprint. Koeman reports that this (Ort 65) is the English version of a 1601 Antwerp Latin edition with the Galle maps (Ort 63), which was itself competing with Vrient's Antwerp edition. It may be, however, that both English editions came out in 1603 and so were in competition simultaneously as the Latin ones had originally been on the Continent. (There is a problem about the format of Norton's *Epitome*: STC records as obl. 8°, whereas Koeman says it is obl. 32°, giving the source as *List of Atlases in the Library of Congress*, 418.) John Bill was paid 20s. for a copy of "Ortelius Epitome" among the books sold to the Duke of Northumberland, 1610-2 February 1611: it was among the more expensive books - a large English Bible cost 50s. (HMC, 6th Report, pp. 229b-230a).

67. Koeman, *Atlantes Neerlandici*, Ort 37, citing ed. R. A. Skelton, *Theatrum Orbis Terrarum: A Series of Atlases in Facsimile*, 1st ser., No. 3 (Amsterdam, 1968). Remarkably, John Norton had seven copies of Ortelius' *Theatrum* as early in his career as October 1596. See the letter of Jacobus Colius Ortelius (1563-1628), a wealthy silk merchant, to Abraham Ortelius (1527-98): "I sent to Norton for sale six copies of the map of Germany and six of that of Utopia; the former he has sold, the latter not yet. 4. He tells me that he has had seven copies of your 'Theatrum', whereas you wrote to me of four only" (ed. J.H. Hessels, *Ecclesiae Londino-Batavae Archivum, Tomus Primus. Abrahami Orteli ... et ad Jacobum Colium Orteliarum ... Epistolae ....* (Cambridge, 1887), Letter 294, p. 696. (The Latin says only "Nortono": Lawrence Worms believes, I think correctly, that John not Bonham Norton was the bookseller involved.)

68. This sequence is the reverse of normal practice: the plate mark left by the maps made it more sensible to print the letterpress first (Koeman, *Atlantes Neerlandici*, Ort 37).

69. Koeman, *Atlantes Neerlandici*. Ort 37, map (12) [148].

70. P. R. van den Broecke Marcel, *Ortelius Atlas Maps: an Illustrated Guide* (t'Goy, Netherlands, 1996), p. 19.

71. Ed. Skelton, *Theatrum Orbis Terrarum*, pp. xvii, viii.

72. *Letters of Sir Thomas Bodley*, No. 201, p. 206, dated 26 February [1611].

73. Philip, *The Bodleian Library in the Seventeenth and Eighteenth Centuries*, p. 27. The document (Oxford University Archives, 1606-11) is transcribed by Partridge, *The Legal Deposit of Books*, pp. 288-90.

74. *Letters of Sir Thomas Bodley*, No. 216, pp. 216-17, dated 23 July [1611] .

75. *Letters of Sir Thomas Bodley*, No. 220, p. 219.

76. This date is usually given as 18 January, but the transcript gives the decade as "vicesimo" (Partridge, *The Legal Deposit of Books*, p. 290).

77. Oxford University Archives, A.27; printed in Macray, *Annals of the Bodleian Library*, pp. 34-36, Partridge *The Legal Deposit of Books*, pp. 290-91.

78. Macray, *Annals of the Bodleian Library*, p. 36, and Partridge *The Legal Deposit of Books*, pp. 291-2.

79. Partridge, *The Legal Deposit of Books*, p. 289.

80. Cyprian Blagden, *The Stationers' Company: A History, 1403-1959* (London, 1960), p. 96.

81. They had also, like the other London trade Companies, been obliged to invest in the Ulster Plantation in 1610 (Jackson, *Records*, pp. 45ff.), which was to bring in useful rents.
82. Gadd, "'Being like a Field': Corporate Identity in the Stationers' Company", p. 24 and note, corrects, with advice from Peter Blayney, the history of the Company's permanent and temporary premises.
83. *DNB*. The edition was not a financial success: the original asking price for the 1,500 copies was £9 but was later sold for £3.
84. On 10 June 1610 the Company gave special allowance to the printer Melchisidec Bradwood to take on six extra apprentices for the work and to set up a press at Eton (printing was jealously restricted to London normally), where Savile could oversee the work (Jackson, pp. 42–3). A handful of other works were published from Eton by the team of Savile, Bradwood and Norton: see STC 12346, 14622 (1610); 2353.5 (1611).
85. In the event, Savile himself also used his own circles in an attempt to sell the edition. On 17 September 1610 David Hoeschelius wrote to Jacobus Colius Ortelius from Augsburg asking for a note to be delivered to Savile, and saying that the editon of Chrysostom is looked forward to eagerly (ed. Hessels, *Ecclesiae Londino-Batavae Archivum*, Letter 354, pp. 835–6. For his part, Norton advertised the book on the continent: see *Catalogus univeralis* (Frankfurt, autumn 1612 and autumn 1613), sigs. A4v and sig. B1r (York Minster Library, xv. L. 76 (9), xv. L. 77 (2)).
86. See previous note: Norton's title is given in the autumn 1612 advertisement but not in the shortened one in the following year.
87. See note 2 above. Patrick Young told Bishop Richard Montagu that Norton was seriously ill on 17 November 1612 (Kemke, *Patricius Junius (Patrick Young)*, pp. 15–16. On 2 December, Bonham Norton was acting as Master in his place.
88. Plomer, *Abstracts from the Wills of English Printers and Stationers*, p. 46.
89. *Letters of Sir Thomas Bodley*, No. 80, p. 84.
90. Hand-coloured copies of Gerard's *Herball* (1597) are rare. There is a copy, bound in two volumes, in the King's Library in the British Library (35.g.13), which has some of the images coloured in, like the Bodleian copy, but the task was never completed – the portrait, title-page and decorative initials are uncoloured. The two volumes give no sign of having been owned by James I.

Acknowledgements

My thanks are due to the Friends of the Bodleian for inviting me to work on what has proved a fascinating topic. I must also thank Jon Stallworthy, Michael Turner, T. A. Birrell, Julian Roberts, Giles Mandelbrote, Paul Hoftijzer, Dirk Imhof, Martin Butler, Clive Hurst, Geoffrey Groom and, in particular, Ian Gadd for their generous help and advice in preparing this lecture. And, like anyone who has worked on the Stationers' Company, I have to express my gratitude for the indefatigable labours of the Company's Archivist, Robin Myers.

25

William Drummond of Hawthornden: Book Collector and Benefactor of Edinburgh University Library

John Hall

25.1 Introduction

Great libraries owe much to the generosity of benefactors and, in common with many other libraries of historic foundation, the early years of Edinburgh University Library attest to the enlightened philanthropy of donors. The new University of Edinburgh, founded in 1583, was fortunate in having immediate access to a collection of theological books bequeathed in 1580 to the town and kirk of Edinburgh by Clement Little, one of the town commissaries. This small nucleus of 276 volumes, containing 325 works (Finlayson, 1980), was quickly transferred by the town councillors to the fledgling university which they had established. Subsequent development of the library is characterized by a pattern of benefaction. The first books acquired by the library were presented by students when they graduated and these early donations from students such as John Ruthven, third Earl of Gowrie, and his brother Alexander Ruthven, William Little (nephew of Clement Little), or James Reid and Robert Foster still survive in the library (Finlayson, 1963, 3–5). In due course the practice of graduation gifts was sensibly replaced by the payment of graduation fees made over to the library for book purchases so that duplicates could be avoided. In the early years after its foundation, the library also received bequests of money which proved to be a valuable source of income, since the financial base of the library had not been properly established at the outset. And so a pattern of acquisition and library development was established which led up to the donations of the first major benefactor of Edinburgh University Library, William Drummond of Hawthornden, in the 1620s and 1630s.

Figure 25.1 William Drummond.

25.2 Early Developments

William Drummond of Hawthornden was born in 1585, the eldest child of Sir John Drummond, gentleman usher to King James VI, and his wife Susannah, sister of the poet William Fowler, secretary to Queen Anne, consort of King James (Spiller, 2004–6). Drummond was educated at the high school of Edinburgh, and subsequently attended Edinburgh University, where he graduated M.A. in 1605, presenting as his graduation gift a copy of Ramus' Arithmeticae libri duo (Frankfurt, 1599) (EUL (Edinburgh University Library) De.4.41). In 1606 he visited London on his way to France, and the following two years he visited Paris and Bourges, studying law at the latter. When he returned to Scotland in late 1608, he brought back with him a substantial quantity of books to be added to his private library. He revisited London in 1610, but on his father's death that year he became laird of Hawthornden and, abandoning the notion of practising law, retired to his estate and his books, undertaking a reconstruction of Hawthornden Castle as a place for honest ease, as recorded on a contemporary panel in the castle. Up to the early 1630s Drummond's interests were literary, and it is in this period that he wrote his poetry, inspired by Petrarch and his followers, particularly the French Pléiade group of poets led by Pierre de Ronsard. He devoted the later part of his life to politics and history, and his History of Scotland from the Year 1423 until the Year 1542, though completed in his lifetime, was only published posthumously by his kinsman Lord Scotstarvet in 1655. Drummond died in December 1649.

Drummond's donations to Edinburgh University Library in the 1620s and 1630s were remarkable at the time and surviving books and documents provide evidence as to how Drummond assembled his library and how books circulated in his day, evidence that was not used fully in the extensive account of Drummond's library published by R.H.MacDonald in 1971. For example, Mac-Donald (1971, 46) suggests that Drummond began his book buying after his graduation. Drummond's graduation gift to Edinburgh University Library in 1605, noted above, may well be the first book which he can be shown to have owned. The evidence of the presentation inscription on the title page of this volume predates other documentary sources, yet it is unlikely that Drummond only started collecting books after this date. Drummond was born into an educated and literate family and there is every reason to suppose that he came into contact with books from an early age. Furthermore, his university education at Edinburgh must have demanded some contact with books, since the university library was not for the use of undergraduates, and Drummond himself was not admitted as a member until November 1637 (EUL MS Da.2.1). Suitable texts for all the subjects which Drummond would have studied (Shepherd, 1983, 2–3) can be identified in Drummond's library and demonstrate that the poet possessed the type of course book which university students of the day would have recourse to. The graduation gift itself, reflecting the popularity of Ramist views in the Scottish universities, also finds numerous echoes in Drummond's library. Though it is not possible to prove that Drummond began to collect books before his graduation, it does seem unlikely that the year 1605 should be so crucial (Bevan, 1983, 19–20). If one considers the habits of book collectors generally, it is far more likely that he began to collect at an early age and was able to indulge his love of books to a greater extent after 1605.

25.3 Book Collector

In support of the view that Drummond began to collect books before 1605 is the fact that he must have handled books at his home. He listed the few volumes which he inherited from his father Sir John Drummond after the latter's death in 1610 (National Library of Scotland (NLS) MS 2059, fol.10, identified by MacDonald as List F), fortunately so, as none of the books has survived. Apart from one or two literary works, such as Sidney's Arcadia and a translation into English of Ovid's Metamorphoses, the books were of a more practical nature, and included works on popular medicine, husbandry and French grammar. Drummond also obtained books from other members of his family, for example his cousin Alexander Drummond of Midhope who had owned the copy of the works of Saint John of Damascus (EUL De.1.1), and his maternal uncle William Fowler, who died in 1612. Six books in Drummond's collection bear Fowler's characteristic autograph: a French translation of Thucydides (EUL De.1.8), a tract by the French humanist lawyer Guillaume Budé (EUL De.4.1), and works by the Italian authors Giovanni Maria Bonardo and Filippo Gesualdo (EUL De. 1/1.30, De.2.4, De.4.3), as well as a translation into Italian of Du Bartas' epic La Semaine (EUL De.2.16). These Italian imprints could well have been part of the bale of books which Fowler is known to have purchased from a Venetian book-seller in 1593 (Fowler, 1940, xxvi). Drummond inherited William Fowler's literary papers in addition to his books. Various drafts of Fowler's poems, miscellaneous treatises and correspondence are to be found in the Hawthornden manuscripts in the National Library of Scotland (MSS 2063–7). Drummond did not retain the whole collection for his own use and presented some of his uncle's manuscripts to the University Library, notably the manuscript of Fowler's sonnet sequence modelled on Petrarch entitled The Tarantula of Love (EUL De.3.68), and his translation into English of Petrarch's Triumphs (EUL De1.10). A further work by Fowler given to the Library in manuscript, the Verses dedicated to the Ladie Thirlstane (MacDonald, 1971, 225 no.1360), has since been lost. The manuscript of Sir Philip Sidney's sonnet sequence Astrophel and Stella (EUL De.5.96) may also have come into Drummond's possession through his uncle William Fowler, as the manuscript was written for Sir Edward Dymoke, patron of poets and scholars, who met and exchanged verses with William Fowler at Padua in 1591 or 1592 (Fowler, 1940, xxiv–xxvi; Sidney, 1962, 540).

The books from members of Drummond's family came to the poet some time after he had begun to buy books in earnest himself, a period that can indeed be situated after his graduation at Edinburgh. Drummond's travels to London and cities in France between 1606 and 1610 gave opportunities for book buying, as indicated by the inscription written by Drummond on the title pages of his books. Most of these inscriptions relate to Drummond's stay in France: 36 books in the Edinburgh collection were bought at Paris in 1607, and one at Bourges in the same year; and in 1608 Drummond purchased a further 19 items at Paris and 9 at Bourges. He also bought one book at Rouen in 1608. Inscriptions relating to purchases on this side of the Channel are far less numerous: only two books at London in 1606, two more at Edinburgh in 1609 and one at London in 1610. Paris was noted as a cosmopolitan centre in the book trade and this is certainly borne out by Drummond's purchases. Over a quarter of the books were printed outside France, in Italy, Germany, Switzerland and the Low Countries, and similar, foreign books were bought at Bourges. For the most part Drummond bought secondhand books but he did pick up certain items just off the presses, such as a collection of *Sententiae* of German Reformers published in 1607 and bought in Bourges in 1608 (EUL De.2.7), or Anthoine Du Breuil's *Petit dictionnaire de l'ortographe françoise* published by the author in 1608 and purchased in Paris in the same year (EUL De.1/2.62). While Drummond was in France, he was probably still perfecting himself in various foreign languages, and so added various grammars to his collection. He also studied law at Bourges and there is a fair representation of the subject in his purchases. However, apart from a few classical texts, such as Virgil and Ovid, and Neo-Latin writers such as Salmon Macrin, most of the books reflect Drummond's vernacular literary interests, and his interest in French literature of the sixteenth century in particular. Thus Marguerite de Navarre's *Les Marguerites* (EUL De.1/2.2) and Guevara's *Le mespris de la court* (EUL De.1/2.10) are counterbalanced by the works of the Pléiade poets Du Bellay (EUL De.4.74) and Baïf (EUL De.2.70), as well as more recent publications.

In 1611 Drummond took stock of his books and compiled a catalogue of all those in his possession at that time (NLS MS 2059 fols.370r-397r; MacDonald 1971, 46-7, 147-8). He listed them in various categories, beginning with the Italian, Spanish, French, English, Greek and Hebrew books, and then proceeded to list the Latin books, first according to subject – theology, philosophy and law – and then according to form, whether poetry or prose. The 1611 catalogue lists 546 titles, of which only 130 or so match titles surviving in Edinburgh and elsewhere. The figure is slowly increasing, however, as items from Drummond's library are rediscovered and can be identified against the 1611 catalogue. Item 24 in the Philosophy list, for example, an edition of Dionysius Periegetes' *De situ orbis* (MacDonald, 1971, 155 no.119, now EUL JA3819) which was formerly in the library of Thomas Dampier, Bishop of Ely and the Chatsworth collection, was acquired by Edinburgh University Library in 1982. The 1611 catalogue provides not only vital information as to the contents of Drummond's library which is not available elsewhere but also further evidence of the growth of Drummond's collection. The recording of prices paid for 401 of these books, and the currency gives additional information on Drummond's book buying habits (MacDonald, 1971, 37). The prices in fact are a confirmation of the pattern shown by the inscriptions where the place of purchase is recorded. Of these 401 books, 323 were bought in France, 76 in England and only 2 in Scotland. The cheaper prices in France than in England explain why Drummond was keen to build up his library during his travels abroad.

Further light on Drummond's collecting habits can be shed by the various reading lists he compiled between 1606 and 1614 (MacDonald, 1971, 228-231). Not all the books in these lists have been identified with surviving copies known to have been in Drummond's library, and MaccDonald only includes a proportion of them in his catalogue of the library. If titles which Drummond claimed to have read do not appear in the 1611 catalogue, this may not necessarily indicate that he did not own the volumes in question. As a serious book collector Drummond would surely have preferred to possess his own copies rather than borrow from friends and he could have passed on his copies to others before 1611. There is evidence at a later date that items left Drummond's library before his major gifts to Edinburgh University Library. Drummond himself gave away in 1620 an edition of Aristophanes to Sir John Scot of Scotstarvet for his newly founded class library in St Andrews (MacDonald, 1971, 227 no.1395) and two of his volumes were given as graduation gifts by university students in 1622 (EUL JA962, *W.21.8) and a further volume in 1623 (EUL T*.25.15).

The titles which Drummond claimed to have read in these years correspond well with his known preferences, with a large proportion of French and English literary texts, yet there is scarcely any overlap between the reading lists and the books with a known purchase date. Drummond's copy of Giovanni Battista Gelli's *La Circe* (EUL De.2.68) which he bought in Paris in 1607, and his edition in French of Petrarch (EUL De.5.14) bought in the same city in 1608 appear in the reading lists for 1607 and 1610 respectively but that is the only correspondence between the two sources. Although every book collector has on his shelves books acquired and not yet read, it is unlikely that Drummond bought dozens of books which he read but never owned. The survival of items recorded in the reading lists, together with the evidence of the 1611 catalogue of his library and the published catalogue of his donation to Edinburgh University, *Auctarium Bibliothecae Edinburgenae* (1627), reinforce the view that the books enumerated in Drummond's reading lists were in his possession at some point.

If the reading lists are a somewhat ambivalent source of evidence about the growth of Drummond's library, they can at least give other indications. They can show that Drummond studied certain books soon after their acquisition: for example his copy of Sir George Buck's *Daphnis Polustephanos* (EUL De.2.76), published in 1605, was read in 1606, and Spenser's *Faerie Queene* (EUL JY1069), Drummond's copy of which was published in 1609, appears in the list for 1610. Similarly his copy of Folengo (EUL De.5.12) was bought at London in 1610 and perused the following year in 1611. On the other hand certain items were put on one side for some time: Thomas Lodge's *Phillis* (EUL De.3.106) and the anonymous *Zepheria* (EUL De.2.77) were both bought at London in 1606 but not read until 1611. In all this Drummond seems no different from any other book collector, who buys when the opportunity presents itself and who reads at a later date when there is time for leisure.

The date of publication of the books in Drummond's collection gives another perspective to his book collecting habits. Approximately half the books now in Edinburgh University Library were published in Drummond's lifetime, and a third of the total are from the seventeenth century, the period which we can reasonably assume to represent Drummond's book collecting career. Practically all Drummond's books published after 1600 bear no marks of previous ownership, and were probably acquired as new books, but of course not necessarily in the year of publication. Occasionally, however, Drummond received presentation copies from authors, for example his copies of various Neo-Latin poems by John Leech, published between 1617 and 1626, which were brought together in volumes with suitable presentation inscriptions (EUL De.5.63, De.5.119). Even after Drummond had begun to donate books to Edinburgh University Library, he was still collecting and there are a handful of imprints between 1626 and 1636, which in some cases must represent his most recent acquisitions. The latest publication date is 1633 on a copy of James Hume's *Pantaleonis vaticinia*, published at Rouen (EUL De.1/2.61), and presented by Drummond to the Library in 1636.

Some of the items in Drummond's library were acquired as a result of personal contacts and family connections. During the course of his visit to the home of Sir William Alexander at Menstrie, Drummond was shown Alexander's books and papers (Masson, 1873, 40–44). These doubtless included the manuscript of Alexander's poem *Doomesday* which came into Drummond's possession at this time, featuring in the reading list of 1613 and subsequently being given to Edinburgh University Library in 1624 (EUL De.4.72). Alexander was later to give Drummond a copy of Henry Briggs' *Arithmetica logarithmica* to be added to the collection in Edinburgh University (EUL De.1.5, inscribed by the donor). The Drummond manuscript of Samuel Daniel's play *Hymen's Triumph* (EUL De.3.69), which was written for the marriage of Jean Drummond, daughter of Patrick, third Lord Drummond, to Robert Ker of Cessford, first Lord Roxborough, was presented by the author to the bride and at some stage passed to her distant kinsman William Drummond (Daniel, 1994, xvii). By 1621 Drummond owned the Roxborough manuscript, since he wrote in this year to Sir Robert Kerr of Ancram to ask for a more perfect copy of the manuscript to send to the press:

> Though I haue no sute at Court to trouble you with, yet so long as Daniell lastes (who, dying as I heare, bequeathed to you his scrolls) or Done, who in his trauells lefte you his, I will euer find a way of trafficking with yow by letters. Not long since there came to my hands a Pastorelle tragecomedye of Samuell Daniell's, which for her sake at whose mariage it was acted, and to whom it is giuen, I intended to send to the presse. But it both wanting the title and hauing no Chorus, I thought I would first intreate you if there were a more perfect coppye among the Author's papers. (Daniel, 1994, xviii)

Drummond's correspondent Sir Robert Kerr also acquired a collection of manuscripts from John Donne just before the poet left England in 1619 as chaplain to the embassy of Viscount Doncaster (Donne, 1978, xlix), and Drummond's copies of Donne manuscripts, no longer surviving (MacDonald, 1971, 225 nos.1346–7), may have come to him from this source. Similarly Drummond's copy of Alexander Montgomery's *Poems* (EUL De.3.70), the so called Margaret Ker manuscript, is likely to have been acquired through the connection between Drummond and his neighbour John Lord Herries of Newbattle Abbey, father of Margaret Ker.

If Drummond's seventeenth century books were generally new when he acquired them, his pre-1600 imprints were secondhand, for the most part. This is borne out in particular by marks of previous ownership and textual annotation of varying degrees, which can provide further clues to Drummond's book collecting. Several of the books which Drummond is known to have acquired in France were from other collections. The copy of Joannes Raymundus' *Epistolarum legalium* (EUL De.5.42) bought at Bourges in 1608, was formerly in the possession of Jean Mercier, a pupil of Cujas and dean of the faculty of law at Bourges after the death of Cujas in 1590. Apart from the ownership inscription, Drummond was careful to note himself the provenance of the book – "Avariti Biturgia ex libris J.Mercier 1608" – as he did with another book acquired at Bourges (EUL De.5.82), which previously belonged to François Ragueau, another pupil of Cujas and professor of civil law at Bourges. Another interesting book, bought this time at Paris in 1608 (EUL DE.4.16), came from the collection of François Ier Dinteville, Bishop of Auxerre; besides his ownership inscription, there is the note of the subsequent owner, his nephew François II Dinteville, also Bishop of Auxerre, recording the fact that he had received the volume from his uncle. In these instances there is no need to rely on the marks of ownership to indicate where the volume was acquired, but with other volumes which bear no indication as to where they were purchased, it is possible to infer that they were acquired in France on account of ownership inscriptions. The association in this way of names such as Estienne Chauvyn, Vincent Cossard, Blaise Grenieres, J.Boucher, P.Jacquart, E.Jassard, F.Jarry or J.Moulin with books published in France is an indication that these were probably obtained in the country of publication when Drummond visited Paris and Bourges. As is so often the case with provenance research, it is not always possible to identify previous owners conclusively and many identifications must remain conjectural. Was the Fransoys Dolu who signed the title page of Aulus Persius Flaccus' *Satires* (EUL De.4.97), for example, none other than the Président of the Chambre des comptes at Paris of this name in the late sixteenth century? Other books deriving from continental collectors include a blindstamped pigskin binding dated 1579 on E.Cordus' *Opera poetica* (EUL De.2.82/1), with a presentation inscription from Ericus Lange to Vilhelm Fuler of 1599, and a volume formerly in the ownership of Andreas Mitz (EUL De.3.116). Again these and other continental owners can suggest, for want of any other evidence, where Drummond acquired certain books in his collection.

25.4 Continental Books

That Drummond acquired large numbers of books on the continent should not be taken to imply that continental books were not circulating in Scotland during his lifetime. However, the evidence of the Drummond collection clearly shows that books with a Scottish provenance, and especially a pre-Reformation provenance, do not have other than Scottish marks of ownership and it is safe to conclude that these books were circulating in Scotland and acquired by Drummond in Scotland. The contents of these early Scottish libraries have been listed, as far as surviving books permit, in J.Durkan and A. Ross' Early Scottish Libraries (1961) and many are represented in

Drummond's books. Drummond owned only one book from the largest single recorded collection belonging to a Scottish owner of pre-Reformation times, that is Henry Sinclair, Bishop of Ross (Cherry, 1963), an edition of Homer's Odyssey printed in Paris by Wechel in 1528 (EUL De.2.81). The volume in question also bears the inscriptions of Sir William Sinclair of Roslin and his son of the same name, who held the Sinclair estates until 1612 (Lawlor, 1897-8, 90-120). There are a number of books in Drummond's collection associated with other notable early Scottish collectors: for example, the copy of B.Ochino, Il Catechismo (EUL De.5.39) from the library of Adam Bothwell, Bishop of Orkney (Cameron, 1932, 409), the edition of English Statutes (EUL De.4.49) from the library of John Leslie, Bishop of Ross, Sebastian Münster's edition of Sphaera Mundi (EUL De.3.10) from the library of John Duncanson, canon regular of St Andrews and Principal of St Leonard's College, A.Tiraqueau, Commentarii (EUL De.2.80) from the library of John Marjoribanks, lawyer, two works on cosmography (EUL De.3.75/1-2) from the library of William Hay, Principal of King's College, Aberdeen, and a breviary printed in Paris (EUL De.2.23) owned by William Forsyth, monk of Kinloss.

Other volumes demonstrate the transmission of books from one Scottish collector to another. Thus, Drummond's edition of William Cranston's *Dialectica compendium* (EUL De.3.46) passed from the ownership of James Foulis, secretary to James V to Hugh Chapman, a student in St Leonard's College who gave it to his fellow student George Sinclair; the copy of Ovid's *Epistolae* (EUL De.4.60) was owned variously by David Guthrie, doctor of laws, John Monypeny and Adam Johnson; a volume from the library of John Sinclair, Bishop of Brechin when Dean of Restalrig (EUL De.1/2.79) also bears the ownership inscription of Robert Anderson, Regent in St Salvator's College; two volumes have ownership inscriptions of Edward Henryson and his son Thomas Henryson (EUL De.4.59, De.4.65); the first in a collection of theological treatises (EUL De.4.50/1) owned by William Scheves, Archbishop of St Andrews was also in the possession of the Edinburgh Dominicans, Thomas Sinclair and William Sinclair of Roslin; and the Paris edition of Xenophon (EUL De.4.31/1-2) was owned by John Rutherford, Provost of St Salvator's College, George Buchanan and his nephew William Morison.

Later Scottish collectors are also well represented among Drummond's books, including items formerly owned by Isaac Brown, advocate and nephew of Clement Little (EUL De.2.114), John Jablonne of Edinburgh (EUL De.3.76), Robert Rollok, the first principal of Edinburgh University (EUL De.5.61), James Forrester of Corstorphine (EUL De.1/2.65, De.2.48), several books from the library of James Livingstone (eg. EUL De.1/2.72, De.2.26, De.4.32) and a few items from the collection of Andrew Melville, including one volume presented to him by Théodore de Bèze (EUL De.2.30). All these Scottish provenances indicate a lively booktrade which Drummond exploited to the full in order to add to his collection. In all this there does not appear to be any distinctive pattern in Drummond's buying, and it is more the case that he bought what interested him when it was available to him.

25.5 Edinburgh University Library

Having formed a substantial collection of books over a number of years, it is still something of a mystery why Drummond chose to give a large proportion of it away to Edinburgh University Library. Not that all the books came to the Library at once. Drummond's first donation, after his graduation gift, came in 1624, when he presented to the Library copies of his own poetical works – the second impression of the Poems of 1616 (EUL De.4.55) bound with his Forth feasting of 1617, the 1623 edition of Flowres of Sion (EUL De.4.53), as well as the manuscript of Sir William Alexander's poem Doomesday, already discussed. These few were not the first of Drummond's books to come to the Library, however, as strays from his collection were donated as graduation gifts by Adam Sinclair and Joseph Johnston in 1622 and by William Brown in 1623, as noted above. Nevertheless, the donation of 1624, with its emphasis on Drummond's own work came almost as a harbinger of the overwhelming generosity of 1626.

On 22 November 1626 the Principal of the University, John Adamson, made known to the Town Council of Edinburgh the extent of Drummond's gift, and it was agreed there and then that an inventory of the books should be printed (Wood, 1936, 15). Not surprisingly, two days later on 24 November, Drummond was admitted as a burgess and guildbrother by the Council (Wood, 1936, 16). The donation of 1626 numbers just over 550 items, about one third of Drummond's library, and the catalogue which had been agreed by the Town Council, the *Auctarium Bibliothecae Edinburgenae*, was published by the heirs of Andrew Hart the following year. As a catalogue of the books, it is not a very distinguished production: there are numerous errors in the dates of the books catalogued, places of publication become titles, and in one case a manuscript by Sir William Cockburne which was known to have been given to the Library by the author was nevertheless included in the catalogue.

Yet the purpose of the *Auctarium* was much wider than a mere catalogue of books. Principal Adamson, who seems to have been responsible for the production, and indeed may have induced his friend Drummond to part with books for the benefit of the University, included in the volume a Latin translation of Drummond's essay *Of libraries* preceded by a list of the main benefactors of the Library up to Drummond's time. The list is of course headed by Clement Little, whose bequest of theological books to the city and kirk of Edinburgh in 1580 laid the foundations of the University Library. Next comes William Rig, a Town Councillor who in addition to money left to support a professor of divinity gave 300 merks to the Library to be spent on books. After William Rig comes James Heriot, an Edinburgh Town Councillor, then Thomas Fisher, Sir Archibald Douglas, a senator of the college of justice, Thomas Hope of Craighall, David Williamson, and finally James Raith of Edmonstoune House, Dalkeith, a graduate of Edinburgh University and member of the Faculty of Advocates, whose wife Eliza Fowler was an aunt of William Drummond. Apart from William Rig's bequest, the importance of which was recognized by a commemorative broadside listing the 26 books purchased, these gifts were not very extensive, and so the publication of the catalogue of Drummond's extensive donation was intended to inspire by example and elicit further donations from benefactors.

Drummond was quick to follow up his first donation with further gifts and between 1628 and 1636 he presented a further 175 items to the Library. A number of books not listed in the *Auctarium* were given either with no presentation inscription at all or with an undated inscription, and though it is impossible to specify the year when these were presented, it is likely that they were given after 1627. Similarly it is not possible to determine any pattern in Drummond's various donations. There is some overlap between the reading lists already discussed and the *Auctarium* which implies that Drummond was disposing of books which he had read. However the overlap here is so small that it would be unsafe to apply this conclusion to the whole collection. Moreover there is no discernible pattern from a subject point of view, and similar books were given on different occasions over the whole period. On the other hand, the books made a significant impact on the Library's collections at the time, since they represented about one third of the total Library stock listed in the press catalogue begun in 1636. The accession of Drummond's books widened considerably the scope of the Library's collections. Apart from books given by benefactors, accessions to the Library were all graduation gifts of students and as such were largely a reflection of the university curriculum of the day. Drummond's books, on the contrary, were not closely related to the university curriculum, being an expression of his own personal interests, and in this way the Library came to own a varied selection of literary and historical texts in the vernacular. In terms of size and scope, the Drummond donation was the most significant in the early history of Edinburgh University Library.

25.6 Conclusions

If Drummond was persuaded to present a large portion of his private library to Edinburgh University by his friend Principal John Adamson, he was also driven by loftier ideals. Drummond's love of books and libraries is evident not only from his gifts to Edinburgh University but also in his writings. In his essay Of Libraries, Drummond explains how books are best able to preserve for posterity the deeds and reputation of good men.

> As we find Republicks to have flourished in Power and Glory, so do we find them to have been eminent and come to the Height in Knowledge and Letters; and as they builded Arsenals and Store-houses for Arms to serve in Time of War, so did they Libraries, furnished with Books for Peace and War. Wits, howsoever pregnant and great, without Books, are but as valiant Soldiers without Arms, and Artizans destitute of Tools. (Drummond, 1711, 223)

Drummond asserts that nations owe much to those who lead the way in various endeavours – "who like Torches waste themselves to shine and give Light to others" – and thus he recalls with pride previous founders of libraries in ancient and more recent times:

... how much is Florence adebted to the noble Laurentius of Medices, for his Library, and to Bessarion, once Bishop of Nice, who at his Death devouted to it a Library, valued at Thirty Thousand Crowns? And what oweth Oxford, nay this Isle, to the most worthy Bodley, whose Library, perhaps, containeth more excellent Books, than the Ancients by all their curious Search could find? (Drummond, 1711, 223)

Drummond took the view that all lovers of learning should contribute to the good work of a library which develops from small beginnings, and asserts that a library should contain all manner of books. He concludes with a clarion call to his fellow men to plant knowledge in libraries by giving books:

As good Husband-men plant Trees in their Times, of which the After-age may reap the Fruit, so should we, and what Antiquity hath done for us, do for Posterity, that Letters and Learning do not decay, but ever flourish to the Honour of God, the Publick Utility, and the Conservation of Humane Society. (Drummond, 1711, 223)

Drummond also writes about the power of libraries in another essay *Bibliotheca Edinburgena Lectori*, in which the library itself speaks out. He suggests that the good deeds of benefactors will be publicized by the contents of the library which they have helped to enlarge, but recognizes the duty which the library has of keeping the memory of such benefactors alive:

All that I would set down and say, is, That which is so oft reiterated in my Volumes, that Ingratitude is the Height of all Vice; and to be forgetful of those who have been beneficial to me, were the Height of all Ingratitude. (Drummond, 1711, 222)

From this it can be seen that Drummond's various benefactions to Edinburgh University were driven by thoughts of lasting fame for himself, yet his call to cherish the memory of library benefactors is as valid today as it was in the seventeenth century.

References

Bevan, J. (1983) Seventeenth-century Students and their Books. In *Four Centuries: Edinburgh University life, 1583–1983* (ed. G. Donaldson). University of Edinburgh.

Cameron, A. I. (ed.) (1932) *The Warrender Papers*, Vol. 2, 396–413, Scottish History Society.

Cherry, T. A. F. (1963) The Library of Henry Sinclair, Bishop of Ross, 1560–1565. *The Bibliotheck*, 4(1), 13–25.

Daniel, S. (1994) *Hymen's Triumph* (ed. J. Pitcher). The Malone Society Reprints.

Donne, J. (1978) *The Epithalamions, Anniversaries and Epidicedes* (ed. W. Milgate). Clarendon Press, Oxford.

Drummond, W. (1771) *The Works ... consisting of those which were formerly printed, and those which were design'd for the press, now published from the author's original copies.* James Watson, Edinburgh.

Durkan, J. and Ross, A. (1961) *Early Scottish Libraries*, John S. Burns & Sons, Glasgow.

Finlayson, C. P. (1963) *Benefactors of the Library in Five Centuries. An exhibition of books and manuscripts selected from donations to the Library from the 16th to the 20th century.* Edinburgh University Library.

Finlayson, C. P. (1980) *Clement Litill and his Library, the origins of Edinburgh University Library*, Edinburgh Bibliographical Society and the Friends of Edinburgh University Library.

Fowler, W. (1940) *The Works*, Vol. 3 (ed. H. W. Meikle, J. Craigie and J. Purves). Scottish Text Society, Third Series, 13.

Lawlor, H. J. (1897–8) Notes on the Library of the Sinclairs of Rosslyn. *Proceedings of the Society of Antiquaries of Scotland*, **32**, 90–120.

MacDonald, R. H. (1971) *The Llibrary of Drummond of Hawthornden*. Edinburgh University Press.

Masson, D. (1873) *Drummond of Hawthornden: the Story of His Life and Writings*. Macmillan.

Shepherd, C. (1983) University Life in the Seventeenth Century. In *Four Centuries: Edinburgh University life, 1583–1983* (ed. G. Donaldson). University of Edinburgh.

Sidney, Sir P. (1962) *The Poems* (ed. W. A. Ringler). Clarendon Press, Oxford.

Spiller, M. R. G. (2004–6) Drummond, William, of Hawthornden (1585–1649), poet and pamphleteer. In *Oxford Dictionary of National Biography*. Oxford University Press.

Wood, M. (1936) *Extracts from the Records of the Burgh of Edinburgh, 1626–1641* (ed. M. Wood). Scottish Burgh Records Society.

de Gaulle and the British

David Dilks

26.1 Introduction

Both admired and demonstrated courage, physical and moral; both revered the memory of Napoleon; each had a profound conviction of his own country's worth. Both wrote and spoke sublimely; each had a strong poetic vein. Both believed in the power of the great man and the individual will to shape events. Each understood that a political leader in the 20th century must know how to reach the people by the new means of communication. Each moved among words as a friend and appreciated the supreme importance of words to a politician. Both regarded politics as being in part a theatrical performance. Each was a serious student of history and built a history of the war around the experiences of himself.

de Gaulle confides at the opening of his memoirs that he formed in his imagination "une certaine idee de la France".[1] In his mind and emotions, austerity and passion blended. In Churchill, there burnt a fire of equal strength for England and her institutions, for "the grand old British race that had done so much for men, and had yet some more to give.'[2] de Gaulle tells us how his conception of France was imbibed from his father, "homme de pensée, de culture, de tradition, ... impregné du sentiment de la dignité de la France. Il m'en a découvert l'Histoire.'[3]

To Churchill, France meant the land of sunshine, of Pol Roger, of warm days and painting in the clear light of the south. He would reflect upon the moods and nature of France, in terms which leave no doubt of his love of the country or rather, of more than one France: for there was the France which rose against all tyrants, the tradition which Clemenceau had represented; and another France, that of Foch, ancient, aristocratic, graceful, chivalrous, the France of Versailles. Between those two conceptions flowed the blood-river of the Revolution and towered the barriers which Christianity raises against agnosticism. All the same, when Clemenceau and Foch contemplated the inscription on the golden statue of Joan of Arc, "la pitie qu'elle avait pour le royaume de France", their two hearts had beaten as one.[4]

My first thought was to address the roles which Britain and France played in the war and perhaps to dwell upon some of the misconceptions which have continued to shape our affairs. For example, few people in Britain have any idea of the scale of French sacrifices in the campaign of 1939–40; the loss of some 100,000 men amounted to about a fifth of that sustained by Britain and the Commonwealth in almost six years, and that is to make no mention of 1,800,000 French prisoners of war. But I will select a broader theme: and the fact that it is possible to consider "de Gaulle and the British" testifies to the position which the General won for himself during the war and again from 1958, and the degree to which in both phases he came to embody the spirit of France. So great were his qualities, so inflexible his will, that the France of the war reflected part of de Gaulle, and the France of 1958 to 1969 still more. Neither de Gaulle's springs of action nor Churchill's derived simply from profound reflection and study; each at critical periods expressed something which welled up from powerful emotion and united with the skills of the man of arms and the man of statecraft. No more than de Gaulle did Churchill have any time for a history which consists of vast impalpable forces, one in which individuals do no more than strut upon a stage and retire without effect. Much of the Prime Minister's admiration for France derived from the performance of the French armies during the First World War. Napoleon he placed upon a plane of genius equalled only by the likes of Caesar. We cannot know how often he measured de Gaulle or the France of the Second World War by the yardstick of earlier times. What is certain is that he will have indulged this process, for his habits of mind were such that he was capable of doing none other.

M. Reynaud remarked with justice that Churchill rendered France great service by saying to de Gaulle in London in that summer of 1940 "I regard you as the leader of the Free French", for that enabled de Gaulle to assemble those compatriots who wished to continue the struggle.[5] To the British, the de Gaulle of June 1940 represented two kinds of force: the political and the spiritual. In politics, he offered a rallying point, someone of energy and youth and will, around whom could gather the nucleus of a French government in exile. In its turn, that fact might provide the means of retaining for the Allies the human and material resources of the French empire overseas. But General de Gaulle stood for more than that; he represented what remained of Britain's hopes and convictions about the old France, the France which could surely not collaborate with the Nazis, still less let its army or fleet fight against the British.

On 18 June 1940, the anniversary of Waterloo, General de Gaulle issued a statement of magisterial defiance in language worthy of comparison with that which Churchill himself uttered in those ever-memorable weeks, de Gaulle rightly discerned even then that what was opening was a world-wide war. He roundly condemned the panic and servitude to which France was being surrendered and, like the Prime Minister, said that he had only one purpose. Churchill's aim was victory at any cost, no matter how hard the road; de Gaulle's a victory at which France must be present. "Alors, elle retrouvera sa liberte et sa grandeur."

26.2 de Gaulle comes to London

Reliant upon the British for almost everything, including cash and uniforms, de Gaulle and his few comrades of the Free French took up their headquarters in Carlton Gardens, home of that doughty defender of British interests Lord Palmerston and next door to the mansion of Lord Curzon. In these first months, the nobility of his words and conduct stood in startling contrast with a good deal which was to be seen in metropolitan France. His comradeship with the British was strong enough to survive the assault upon the French fleet, an event which brought profound pain to officers of the Royal Navy and to the Prime Minister himself, who said that it had been "a terrible decision, like taking the life of one's own child to save the State."[6] Indeed, Churchill had insisted that because he must bear the responsibility before history, he should himself sign the message to the commander of the British fleet off Oran.[7] General de Gaulle was mistaken to suggest in his own memoir of the war that the Parliament and press of Britain gloried in the action taken at Mers-el-Kebir.[8]

This little-known French soldier had undertaken an act of the highest courage. He had conquered those inhibitions, and the by no means empty formalities of the oath of loyalty, which paralysed many officers equally valiant. As Churchill would have expressed it, he had risen to the level of events. It went without saying that if he should fail, he would die the death of a dishonoured traitor. Though chafing at dependence upon the British, he could be generous in his appreciation. If he seemed impossibly haughty one day, he would behave modestly the next. If he argued for small points, then his British companions tried to remind themselves that in the nature of his mission General de Gaulle had to make a resolute stand for the interests of a France distinctively different from that of Vichy. For his part, de Gaulle admired the close-knit character of the British official machine, and its capacity to be by turns distant or friendly, pressing or detached.[9] The British machine, it has to be confessed, found collaboration with the Free French a prickly business. The rivalries in Carlton Gardens and elsewhere burned intensely. Petty squabbles occupied too much time. The General dealt with them in his lofty manner. "Ce n'est rien, tout cela" he said after one of these episodes. "Ce ne sont que les troubles de l'emigration."[10]

26.3 de Gaulle and Churchill

We must record with sadness that the relations between Churchill and de Gaulle, which had been warm, indeed intimate, in the summer and autumn of 1940, grew steadily worse. It would have helped no end if de Gaulle could occasionally have shown a greater measure of gratitude. Churchill did his best for a long time. On one occasion he said to the General "I know that there can be, and indeed are, Frenchmen who do not like the British. They have a perfect right to their opinion; mais ce ne sont pas les Français que je recherche."[11] By the autumn of 1941, the Prime Minister was saying with sorrow to General de Gaulle that he now felt he was no longer dealing with a friend. He had been pained by the trail of Anglophobia left behind during a visit to the Middle East and the Levant by the French leader, whose behaviour towards the representative of the War Cabinet in Cairo had been so hostile, even insulting, that some of the bystanders wondered whether de Gaulle was wholly in his senses. Perhaps we see a part of the reason in de Gaulle's response to Churchill in this conversation of September 1941. Denying that anyone could believe him an enemy of Great Britain, he drew pointed attention to the treatment which he and the representatives of the Free French in Syria had received. In normal times, such difficulties would be smoothed out by ambassadors. But when France was "broken and humiliated", his own efforts to vindicate her must fail if he met with such behaviour. Mr Churchill explained that while the British had no imperial ambitions in Syria, the populations of Syria and the Lebanon saw no sense in driving out the Vichy French only to see them replaced by the Free French. They had been promised their independence and must have it. By comparison with other European powers, France would remain pre-eminent in the Levant after the war. Of this neither Churchill nor Eden, Macmillan nor Duff Cooper, could ever convince de Gaulle, or rid his mind of the suspicion that the British were determined to oust France from the Levant to their own imperial advantage. No issue did more harm to the relations of our two countries during the war and indeed after it.

Churchill begged de Gaulle to give no grounds for any suspicion that he entertained hostile thoughts towards Britain or had even moved towards certain authoritarian or fascist views. With dignity, de Gaulle asked Churchill to understand that the leaders and members of the Free French were "necessarily somewhat difficult people". Otherwise, they would not be where they were. If that difficult character sometimes coloured their attitude towards their great ally in daily actions or utterances, Mr Churchill must be assured nevertheless that the loyalty of the Free French to Great Britain remained unimpaired.[12]

At least these antagonisms in the Middle East raised difficulties chiefly between Britain and the Free French. For the British, however, there was an element in their relations with de Gaulle which loomed even larger; the effect upon the government of the United States, and especially on the State Department and the President himself. The seizure of Saint-Pierre et Miquelon exemplifies antagonisms which go beyond the printed record or rational explanation. The Canadian government naturally protested; Roosevelt was furious, and Secretary of State Hull so angry that he could barely speak. Mr Churchill, at this moment when at long last America was entering the war and everything turned upon good relations with Washington, hated the embarrassment which such episodes brought, the more so when it turned out that despite categorical assurances which de Gaulle had previously given, he had also issued secret instructions to Admiral Muselier to take the two islands. Some of the Prime Minister's entourage disliked de Gaulle heartily. General Spears in the Levant, once a warm admirer of de Gaulle, came to detest him. Those in the Foreign Office, notably Mr Eden and Sir Alexander Cadogan, who well understood the importance of de Gaulle in the war and of a strong France after it, were undermined by each instance of de Gaulle's impetuosity and hauteur. For his part, de Gaulle was acutely aware of America's hostility and loathed the attitude of the US

Government towards Vichy. "Don't ask me to quarrel with the President over de Gaulle" Churchill said repeatedly during the next four years. As Sir Alexander Cadogan, the Permanent Under-Secretary of the Foreign Office, remarked on one of these occasions, "No one asks him to but we do wish he would reason with the President.'[13]

26.4 de Gaulle and Anthony Eden

The Foreign Secretary, Eden, had a lifelong passion for France, where he had spent part of his youth; he spoke excellent colloquial French, and was widely read in the classics of French literature; he had inherited from his father a taste for Monet and the Impressionists. He has not yet had anything like his due from history and there are few aspects of his tenure of office in the war which reflect greater credit upon him than his policy towards France. Even he was driven to explain to de Gaulle in the summer of 1942 that attitudes of suspicion to the British in everything made good relations impossible, de Gaulle replied that he had very little suspicion of the British, but a deep suspicion of the Americans. Eden tried to make him understand that this method of treating the American government was miscalculated, de Gaulle retorted "After all, I represent that part of France which wishes to fight. I have therefore much responsibility but my resources are very small and that makes it necessary for me to be watchful.'[14] On another occasion, in the autumn of that year, when Churchill sent a friendly message to say that he did not forget the part which General de Gaulle had played in 1940 and after, de Gaulle rejoined that he knew himself for a man of quick spirit and temper; had he not been so, he would not have become leader of the Free French movement. He firmly believed that he himself represented France, and that to do so it was essential for him to make himself difficult. His British interlocutor, Major Morton of the Prime Minister's private office, was probably less than reassured by the General's observation that "he had given his policy further deep thought and had always returned to the same conclusion."[15]

Although the Poles, the Greeks and the Yugoslavs all had more men under arms than had the Free French and French circles in London were notorious for leakage and indiscretion, the fact that the British would not share military information, even where the operations involved Free French forces or French territory, hurt de Gaulle profoundly as a man of honour and a professional soldier. Eden pleaded with the Prime Minister:

> I hope that you will help me and that some attempt will be made to consult him [de Gaulle] a little in regard lo events present and future. There is no need to tell him military secrets in order to do this ... he responds every time that he is approached in these matters.[16]

An official paper midway through the war remarked in a purely factual style that General de Gaulle "gives us more trouble than all the Allied Governments in London put together.'[17] Eden made much the same point to the General, only to receive the reply "I have always maintained that France is a very great country.'[18] After a new spate of difficulties in respect of the Levant, Churchill and de Gaulle held another fretful conversation. The Prime Minister told him in terms that he, de Gaulle, was making a continuous attempt to assert his local position in the Middle East in a way which had no connection with the common cause, de Gaulle blamed the local British representatives and by plain implication Spears. He even said to Churchill's face that he could not make out whether the British preferred to make arrangements with Vichy or with the fighting French. The issues in the Levant called in question the collaboration between France and England:

> "Not France and England" said the Prime Minister; "between General de Gaulle and England."
> "Why are you discussing matters with me" asked de Gaulle "if I am not France?"
> "It is all written down" Churchill replied. "You are not France, but fighting France."

And so the wrangle went on. de Gaulle explained that he was fighting with, but not for, England. He spoke for France, to which he was responsible. When Churchill observed that the hope that the two countries would conduct their campaigns together had been frustrated because General de Gaulle was so combatant that, not content with fighting Germany, Italy and Japan, he wished also to fight England and America, de Gaulle rejoined that "he took this as a joke, but did not regard it as a very good joke." When Churchill said that he could not understand why the General did not try to make things go well, and Eden interjected that other allies did not find the British so difficult to deal with, they received the reply that General de Gaulle could not accept any diminution of the position of France anywhere. He must be intransigent, or he would count for nothing in France. That is not only my duty, but a political necessity.'[19]

No doubt it would be a great mistake to take Churchill's stern expressions in conversation – a little later in the year, for example, he said "Well, Darlan is not as bad as de Gaulle anyway'[20] or on paper –'There is nothing hostile to England this man may not do when he gets off the chain'[21] – as embodying settled convictions. If de Gaulle was often impossible, he was also a genius, and Churchill would feel that from time to time, de Gaulle's demeanour at the time of the landings in North Africa in November 1942, when he at once said that the Free French must not split and that he would be willing if necessary to serve under Giraud,[22] his grim humour when informed of the death of Darlan – "What a pity! He was making numberless converts for me'[23] -, the growing evidence of strong support for the Free French within France itself, strengthened the realization that if the British broke with de Gaulle, they would merely hand a triumph to Vichy; so much so, indeed, that when he addressed one of his splendid orations to the Members of Parliament they spontaneously burst into the Marseillaise, an event previously thought impossible. Shortly before de Gaulle's departure from British shores, the Prime Minister under pressure from Roosevelt and Hull tried hard to persuade the War Cabinet to abandon him. But that row like many others had simmered down, de Gaulle came to bid an official farewell to the Foreign Secretary. "Le peuple anglais a été merveilleux" he remarked graciously.[24] Mr Eden understood that this genial memory would not embrace the British government.

26.5 de Gaulle in North Africa

Once in North Africa, de Gaulle steadily gathered power to himself by strength of character, personality and sheer superiority of mind. There he struck up close relations with Mr Harold Macmillan, who like many of de Gaulle's French collaborators suffered from the General's moods and habits. Reporting an observation of de Gaulle that the Anglo-Saxon domination of Europe was a mounting threat and that if it continued France after the war would have to lean towards Germany and Russia, M. Jean Monnet remarked that he found it difficult to make up his mind whether the General was a dangerous demagogue, or mad, or both.[25] Macmillan discovered with surprise that he and General de Gaulle held similar views about the changes which would be necessary in British and French society after the war, a mean to be found between capitalism and socialism, the widening of opportunities for the millions. Macmillan played a truly remarkable role in the Mediterranean during the war, displaying political talents of the highest order. He would often persuade his American colleagues to moderate the more violent strokes of policy against de Gaulle which President Roosevelt desired, and would exert himself to compose differences between the squabbling French factions. Even Macmillan had to say of the General "He is a difficult kind of horse. He either starts down the course before the gate has been raised, or he won't start at all until the other horses are half-way round."[26] Nonetheless, after listening to de Gaulle's exposition of the French crisis, which he said had begun in 1789 and had lasted until the outbreak of war, and the problem of so managing the affairs of France after the war that disorder on the one side and extreme policies on the other were avoided, Macmillan recorded in his diary that de Gaulle stood head and shoulders above his colleagues in the breadth of his conceptions for the long term.[27]

There is no need to dilate here upon repeated difficulties which arose between Britain, France and America in the second half of the war, or the offence which de Gaulle gave by his reluctance to appear at Casablanca in January 1943. A good deal was said and done which would have not been said and done in calmer times. The Prime Minister felt half-angry, half-admiring. At Casablanca, he gazed as the columnar figure of the General strode down a path.

"His country has given up fighting, he himself is a refugee, and if we turn him down he is finished. Well, just look at him! ... He might be Stalin, with 200 divisions behind his words. I was pretty rough with him. I made it quite plain that if he could not be more helpful we were done with him." "How did he like that?" someone asked. "Oh, he hardly seemed interested" the Prime Minister replied. "My advances and my threats met with no response." "France without an army is not France" mused Churchill later in the same conversation, "de Gaulle is the spirit of that army. Perhaps the last survivor of a warrior race."[28]

26.6 de Gaulle and the USA

The State Department in Washington, conscious of de Gaulle's dependence upon British money, seemed to believe that the British had connived at or even financed violent attacks upon the USA by the Free French.[29] In vain did the Prime Minister, Eden and others labour to disabuse Mr Hull of such notions. With some justice, Eden feared that the Americans might well commit a folly which would give de Gaulle a martyr's crown, or control of the French army, or both.[30] As for the Prime Minister, he said sorrowfully about de Gaulle "I brought him up from a pup, but never got him properly trained to the house."[31]

We need scarcely add that the American policy of collaboration with Vichy, whatever its practical merits, was openly harmful to the blockade which the British were trying to enforce. That many of the Americans should have regarded de Gaulle as a puppet of the British is not without its humour. Admiral Leahy, who had been the American Ambassador to Vichy, was still telling President Roosevelt in the spring of 1944 that Petain, not de Gaulle, was the man to rally France after the allied forces had landed.[32]

So accustomed have we become to the preponderance of the United States in the Western alliance that we remember with difficulty how, until this moment in June 1944, Britain and the Commonwealth countries had more divisions in contact with the enemy, the world over, than had the United States. In other words, the British and their immediate allies had borne the brunt of the fighting on land for nearly five years. The landings in Normandy would have been out of the question without the massive deployment of their sea power, the bulk of the United States Navy being engaged in the Pacific. Once the beachheads were established, the military balance tilted rapidly and the political balance within the coalition likewise. To General de Gaulle and his colleagues, the events of June 1944 brought a sense of frustration that France had been so largely excluded from the initial phases, an opportunity to show that they had been right in stating that the Free French embodied the soul of France and, to be more prosaic and immediate, the ability to take control of the government. The British Ambassador to the French National Committee, Mr Duff Cooper, was to demonstrate often his love for France. Even he, after reading the files in the Foreign Office, had become convinced that the General was a "potential source of mischief and a standing menace to Anglo-French, and what is even more important, to Anglo-American relations" and wondered whether the British government should not allow some of the information to transpire, so that more people would be aware of objectionable acts by de Gaulle.[33] This temptation, to their credit, the Prime Minister and Foreign Secretary resisted, with more difficulty on Churchill's part than Eden's. Indeed, though those two Ministers were closer to each other than any others in the government, the Prime Minister felt at one moment that they might come to a public breach over their differences in respect of France, and in one of his altercations with the Foreign Secretary threatened to denounce de Gaulle and carry the House of Commons.[34] But at that stage of the war and until the last months of it, both Churchill and Eden believed that the great problem of post-war Europe would lie not with Russia but in the possible resurgence and rearmament of Germany. On that reading, as Eden constantly pointed out, a strong France mattered more than ever.[35]

The wrangling between Britain and America about recognition of the new French Committee of National Liberation as the provisional government of

France and the failure to consult him about the landings in Normandy must have hurt de Gaulle to his core. Under protest, he went to see the Prime Minister on the latter's special train near the south coast of England on 4 June 1944. This was the train of which Eden remarked "It was hell. There was only one bath and one telephone. Winston was always in the bath and Ismay always on the 'phone." Churchill explained that the landings were imminent, de Gaulle protested against various features of the arrangements. Angry and resentful, his own nerves stretched taut, Churchill made a remark to the effect that Britain would always side with the USA against France. It comes as no surprise that someone with a sense of history so highly developed as de Gaulle never forgot this. Indeed he quoted it to, and against, Mr Macmillan in the negotiations of 1962. But he partly misunderstood the point. Churchill did not mean that Britain would consistently side with the United States, or seek opportunities to align herself against France. He meant that if in some dire crisis a choice between the two had to be made, the British would choose the United States; for which he can scarcely be blamed, least of all in the circumstances of 1944.

The tragi-comic episodes of 5 and 6 June 1944 are too well recorded to require elaboration tonight. It must be deemed a failure on the side of de Gaulle and the British alike that on the eve of so momentous an event, the parties should have been arguing in an almost hysterical way. Let it be recorded to General de Gaulle's credit that after an intervention by Duff Cooper, he mellowed a little. Perhaps he had responded to the Ambassador's fine fighting record, his trenchancy and independence, his passion for France. Against the Ambassador's note of a statement by de Gaulle that while he was always making concessions nobody ever made any to him, the Prime Minister wrote "Good Lord".[36]

We are told that possession is nine points of the law. Certainly it constitutes a goodly part of political power. While the allies still wrangled over the terms of recognition, de Gaulle in effect took control of one part of France after another. He managed this process with consummate skill. However vigorously everybody might deny it, almost all the people by whom the state had to be run, the civil servants, the local government officers, the judiciary, had been Petainists. Roosevelt welcomed the General to Washington in July; and then, as the Prime Minister himself showed some signs of melting and proposed to visit de Gaulle in Algiers, the General replied in effect that he did not wish to see Churchill. The eventual recognition of de Gaulle's government came in an undignified scramble. After all the Prime Minister's efforts to ensure that de Gaulle should not intrude between him and the Americans, the British learned with reactions varying from amusement to incredulity that the United States had decided to recognize de Gaulle's government as the provisional administration of France without even informing London.

According to de Gaulle, Churchill had once alleged that if the Free French took power alone when France was liberated, open revolution would stalk the streets; Roosevelt had said the same at the first Quebec conference in 1943. When Churchill and Eden came to Paris on Armistice Day 1944, an enormous good-natured throng cheered them and the British troops lustily, de Gaulle pointed to the enthusiasm and said to Eden "Regardez-moi ce peuple en revolution."[37] The two British ministers were accompanied that day by General Ismay, who met an old military friend with whom he had worked in the early part of the war. The French officer said to his British colleague *"Have you forgiven us for quitting the fight?"* Ismay replied that such thoughts should be dismissed. Who were the British to cast stones? After all, they had been so powerless to help and had owed their salvation to twenty miles of salt water. His French colleague replied There will be Frenchmen who will not forgive you for two generations. You made our shame so great by fighting on."[38]

Meanwhile, the Prime Minister had insisted upon renewing his homage to Napoleon, of whom he was fond of saying "Genius never gazed upon mankind from a nobler countenance." He went to inspect Napoleon's tomb, remarking pointedly to de Gaulle "In all the world there is nothing greater." Although the General's reception of this observation is not recorded, he did have the grace to salute Churchill as the author of victory. When they dined that night, he asked the Prime Minister what had struck him most about France? "Your unanimity" Churchill replied. "I felt as if I were watching a resurrection."[39]

It would be consoling but misleading to record that this cordial temper prevailed to the end of the war. Churchill and Eden fought hard for France at Yalta, exclusion from which conference de Gaulle and the Free French naturally resented. Thanks largely to British efforts, a zone of occupation in

Germany was secured for France. The Prime Minister was deeply puzzled to know what to make of Stalin's attitude to France. "Does he not know her history?" Churchill asked.[40] de Gaulle assured Duff Cooper that there was nothing he desired more than a pact between Britain and France; but it must be a genuine alliance with all outstanding questions settled. The Prime Minister was in no hurry for any such agreement, fearing snubs and blackmail from de Gaulle. In any event, there was the running sore of the Levant. It would seem incredible, were the facts not in evidence, that Britain and France should have spent the summer of 1945 at screaming pitch over the Lebanon and Syria at the very moment when allied arms were at last triumphant in western Europe. General de Gaulle was in a state of incandescence, and so doughty a hero of the Resistance as M. Bidault scarcely less so. We must take it as one more piece of evidence that the foreign policy of old-established states runs in deep grooves, from which it is not easily deflected, that de Gaulle should have told Duff Cooper in June 1945 with apparent regret that France was not in a position to declare war on Britain. *"But you have insulted France and betrayed the West. This cannot be forgotten."*[41]

26.7 Eden Resigns

In the autumn a tremulous settlement was patched up, and by then Churchill and Eden had left office. The latter was perhaps the only British minister of whom de Gaulle consistently spoke and thought well. When Eden was old and frail in retirement, de Gaulle treated him with exquisite courtesy. I take these sentences from a letter written in the General's own hand in 1965, after he had read Eden's account of the war years:

... Sans employer aucun artifice, vous y mettez en relief le contraste qui a confronté, d'une part le caractère - combien dramatique! - des évenements, d'autre part, associée a l'impetuosité de Churchill, votre action inlassablement raisonnée, equilibrée et efficace. En votre personne, c'est vraiment un grand homme d'Etat qui avait alors en charge la ministère britannique des Affaires Etrangères.

Comme j'ai pu vous voir l'oeuvre dans la térrible guerre ou Angleterre jouait son destin, comme ce destin entratnait celui de mon pays, comme vous avez toujours agi sans meconnaitre ni la France ni l'Europe - equité et perspicacité alors bien rares et méritoires! - je salue, une fois de plus, avec respect et avec amitie, l'oeuvre qui fut la votre ... [42]

26.8 End of the War

In that summer of 1945, a time of exhaustion, hope and fear, de Gaulle strove to assuage the quarrels and dress the wounds of a France desecrated and profaned by the Germans, but a part of which had in his and other eyes dishonoured its fair name by collaboration or feebleness. If Mr Churchill announced that he had not become his Majesty's first minister in order to preside over the liquidation of the British Empire, de Gaulle felt equally towards French possessions in the Levant and Africa. Roosevelt had stated, without sensing any contradiction with his previous policies, that he could accept no responsibility for post-war France, which he regarded as Britain's business. Indeed, he made it plain that the American forces would withdraw from Europe promptly. As for himself, de Gaulle found the conditions of French politics irksome. After his abrupt retirement from office in January 1946, viewed with mixed feelings in London, the General retreated to Colombey and as the years passed, devoted himself to laborious composition of his memoirs. He seemed to have put politics behind him. Whereas Churchill dictated all his speeches and books - as he used to say with a grin, "I live from mouth to hand" - de Gaulle wrote in manuscript, with concentrated thought and countless corrections. His three volumes are suffused by his abiding faith in France's culture and destiny. As the work progresses, the General himself becomes simply "de Gaulle" as if he already represented a figure from the realms of history. Written in a French at once majestic and allusive, the work stands on a par with Churchill's own chronicle of the war.

The spectacle of instability which the Fourth Republic presented, the manoeuvrings of the parties, confirmed de Gaulle's distaste for ordinary politics. He disliked the plans for a European army embodied in the E.D.C. He was hostile to any notion of federalism. Not until 1957 was there any serious talk of his return to power and even then the prospect looked distant. [42] By chance, the President of the United States was Eisenhower and the Prime Minister of Great Britain Harold Macmillan, both of whom had known de Gaulle closely in the war. The British hoped that it might be possible to make an accommodation between the Six who had signed the Treaty of Rome and the nascent European Free Trade Association. Dr Adenauer told the British Prime Minister of the profound harm done to the soul of Germany by Nazism. He even said that Germany had got rich again too quickly, and did not wish to see Germany get strong again too quickly. That was why he yearned for European unity and, in view of France's weakness, for British participation.[43]

The repeated changes of government had made post-war France a difficult ally from the point of view of the British and other governments. France after 1958 was to be equally difficult or more so, but for different reasons. The stability which de Gaulle brought, in place of fluidity and perpetual changes of allegiance, was welcome; but soon that stability began to resemble rigidity, or (in the eyes of the British) the rigidity to resemble hostility. Nevertheless, many of them, and not least the Prime Minister, felt admiration for de Gaulle because he restored dependable government to France, because of his undoubted political courage and his indifference to danger. Even before he returned to power, de Gaulle had said to the British ambassador Sir Gladwyn Jebb how deeply he admired England. He would never forget what had happened in 1940. Nor, he added, could he ever forget the way in which he had been treated in respect of Syria. During this interview, de Gaulle wept as he read to the Ambassador the passage from his book in which he reflected upon the comparisons between Churchill's career and his own, meditations stimulated by his memory of the news of Churchill's defeat in the election of 1945.[44] "Whatever else may be said about the General," Jebb reported to London, "it must be admitted that he is not like anybody else, either physically or psychologically."[45] We do not know how much illumination British ministers were able to derive from this assessment.

26.9 de Gaulle and Macmillan

When de Gaulle assumed office at that dire moment in the summer of 1958, the British imagined that they would face at least two major demands from him: first, the acknowledgment of France's right to her own nuclear force; secondly, the right to much closer consultation with the United States or, to put the point more provocatively, a refusal to accept dictation from the Anglo-Saxons. The British had a clear interest in making de Gaulle's tenure of office successful. France had to find a policy in Algeria; she had to resolve an economic crisis; and the Communists were counting on de Gaulle's failure. All three grounds provided the British with ample argument for supporting him. NATO and the alliance with the United States were quite another matter. Each subject was crucial, and on neither could de Gaulle and the British agree in 1958 or for that matter in the ensuing decade. The British understood well de Gaulle's instinctive resentment of the notion that French sovereignty should be impaired by membership of the Six, and understood it the better because de Gaulle's reservations on that subject were very similar to those which had been entertained in London from the beginning. Nevertheless, the British had no desire to undermine the Six, or to encourage France to be difficult in that connection;[46] on the contrary, they regarded the Six, together with NATO and the Western European Union, as the basis upon which German co-operation with the West was founded. The alliance needed the strength of Germany; and the wider community required regular reassurance that as the rearmament of Germany proceeded, a development which would have seemed inconceivable even a few years earlier, that country would find herself always in the company of strong partners.

General de Gaulle said grandly to Mr Macmillan at the Hotel Matignon on the evening of 29 June 1958 that while there was no doubt the Soviet Union represented a great danger to the free world, the old Russia persisted and in the course of time the Russians would bury Communism as they had buried the Czars. This distinction between Communism and Russia, he insisted, must never be lost to sight. Mr Macmillan agreed in part. The Russians, he commented, wanted the profit of war without war itself and he believed there was small danger of a major conflict so long as the West did not throw away its power.[47] But this of course represented the nub of the disagreement, as it developed over the years, between de Gaulle and the British in these military matters. The ties between Britain and the USA were close at every level; their nuclear collaboration, begun during the war, was just resuming, after years of extremely expensive duplication of effort. The British knew well that although it might have been possible to stave off defeat without America in the war, there could have been no question of victory either in the Far East or on the mainland of Europe. The Americans had immense military power, on which much of NATO depended, and great economic strength. In a word, the British could not afford to separate themselves from the USA in any matter of the first importance.

Walking with Macmillan in the garden of the Matignon after dinner that evening, General de Gaulle remarked spaciously that Morocco was a state, Tunisia was a state, but Algeria never had been. It was nothing but a heap of dust. He explained some of the ways in which that most pressing problem might be tackled, seemed conscious of the difficulties and, to Mr Macmillan's mind, displayed a modesty and simplicity of approach which was quite new to me. All the old conceits and prejudices seem to have gone … He spoke personally to me at the end of our conversation of his pleasure in seeing me again, and of his affection for Britain.

Here we may pause to add that Macmillan had cause to revise at least some of these judgments within a year or two. The Prime Minister recognized General de Gaulle's anxiety to perform his duty, whether he succeeded or failed, de Gaulle said in this same conversation that the reason why he had been so tiresome during the war was that he was representing a country that was ruined and dishonoured beyond anything he could have believed possible. That was the terrible grief that he had had to carry.[48]

During the next four years and more, Mr Macmillan and his colleagues tried to impress upon de Gaulle the importance of avoiding unnecessary disagreements in Europe; they refused to accept that the issue between the Six and EFTA was only or chiefly an economic one; they pointed to Britain's wide interests in the Commonwealth, which General de Gaulle repeatedly said he wished to sustain and strengthen. Like de Gaulle, they never felt wholly sure of German intentions. The General even became quite lyrical about the prospects of the Channel tunnel, the possibilities of driving backwards and forwards, selling goods more easily and the increase of Anglo-French friendship which would follow.[49] In principle, de Gaulle said, he favoured the extension of economic co-operation in Europe provided that means could be found which would damage neither the French economy nor the Treaty of Rome. These were large, and we must add somewhat elastic, conditions.

Within a few days of Macmillan's visit to de Gaulle in Paris in the summer of 1958, the crisis in the Middle East, with American and British military intervention in the Lebanon and Jordan, revived all the painful memories of the war and the Levant. The British learned confidentially that General de Gaulle believed he had been deceived not only by Mr Macmillan but by Mr Dulles; at least, this was reported by no less an authority than M. P.-H. Spaak, who had learned it from the French Foreign Minister. The Prime Minister wrote patiently and fully to General de Gaulle to explain what had happened; the reply was less than wholly forthcoming.[3]

For a time, Mr Macmillan made himself almost an apologist or interpreter of de Gaulle. When Dr Adenauer complained furiously of the latter's behaviour, Mr Macmillan replied that he had a longer experience of de Gaulle than almost anyone then in international politics. *"He is apt to treat his friends with this curious ineptness and rudeness. It is because of his mysticism and egoism ... a proof of clumsiness but also of innocence ..."* At least from this moment at the end of 1958, the British had clear warning that France might retreat from NATO. In Macmillan's diary for November of that year we also find *"The outlook for the European Free Trade Area seems bad. The French are determined to exclude the United Kingdom, de Gaulle is bidding high for the hegemony of Europe ..."*[51]

Only the close relations now established between France and Germany enabled de Gaulle to adopt such a policy. Repeatedly the Prime Minister asked how, if the other powers were to be progressively excluded from the markets of the Six, political antagonisms as well as economic rivalries could be prevented from springing up? To Macmillan, with his close interest in French affairs and not a censorious interest at that, de Gaulle appeared increasingly as the new Napoleon, owing his civilian power to military prowess and his record in war. In France the President enjoyed, especially in time of emergency, powers which no British prime minister possessed, whereas there are marked points of resemblance between the American constitution and that which the General established for the Fifth Republic.

de Gaulle tackled the Algerian issue boldly, and offered self-determination in 1959. Thus some of the positions of 1956 had almost been reversed. The British had by then gone far down the road towards independence in West Africa and elsewhere, whereas the French had appeared to be clinging to their colonial territories in North Africa. There was of course an important difference of scale between the two countries; while France was essentially a European, Mediterranean and North African power, the countries of the British Commonwealth were scattered all over the world – indeed, Europe was the only continent in which there was no Commonwealth country – and the Commonwealth was far more important in relation to Britain than were the colonies to France.

The European Free Trade Area came into existence not long after the Treaty of Rome entered into force; Macmillan did his utmost to persuade the German and French governments that the British had not gone soft about Berlin; repeatedly he assured de Gaulle that a strong France and a positive French leadership of the Six were strongly desired by Britain.[52] de Gaulle handled the Summit Conference in Paris in 1960 with an aplomb which Macmillan admired, refusing to be upset by Kruschev's blusterings about the invasion of Russian air space by the U2 aircraft. "Every few hours" said de Gaulle to Kruschev, spreading his hands towards the heavens, "this sputnik is invading the air space of France. Yet I do not propose to call off the Conference on that account."[53] It was perhaps this meeting in Paris, with the realization that with so much at stake for the world Britain had not the power or influence to press either the Russians or the Americans into more sensible courses, that did more than anything else to make up Macmillan's mind about joining the Six. Certainly he was influenced by far more than trading advantages.

To be sure, it was no easy business to collaborate with President de Gaulle. Even his ministers seemed to know little of his inner thoughts. The British Embassy in Paris had to glean what it could. The imperial tone of the regime did not diminish. When the General insisted upon flying to Britain in April 1960, and said he was quite confident there would be no fog, an official of the Foreign Office minuted on the file "I can only assume that among the special powers he has now assumed he includes control of the weather."[54]

de Gaulle's firmness and fierce pride; his unfeigned belief in the mission of France; his powers of decision – all this and much more the British could readily acknowledge, while being baffled by displays of unexpected and almost irrational hostility. How, they asked themselves, could de Gaulle make so little allowance for their own interests and outlook? How could he recognize Europe's dependence on the USA, and yet withdraw from NATO? Why did he harp so often upon old grievances? Did he not value the military and other contributions which the British were making in Europe? M. Monnet explained that General de Gaulle always tried to look at each problem from the point of the historian coming a generation later; thus he did many things which ran counter his nature and sometimes to his philosophy, and which he disliked intensely. Monnet cited de Gaulle's Algerian policy as an example; it had gone against the grain for de Gaulle to do what he had done, but equally he had felt quite certain that in twenty-five years' time the historian would have to say that it was necessary to do, and that the General had been right to do it.[55]

26.10 The European Community

The President had asked whether Britain was prepared to enter the European community. The British, after many agonized discussions, had in effect replied "Yes". Mr Macmillan told de Gaulle pointedly that the economics could be arranged if there were a will; political questions were more important. Did not Britain and France have a basic community of interest in holding Germany to the West? de Gaulle agreed, and said that he was averse to an integrated Europe, which was not practical, sensible or desirable, for the result would be a materialist, soul-less mass, with no idealism left. The national identity of the European nations should be preserved. With this the British could readily agree. What they could not do was to persuade de Gaulle that the United Kingdom could join the Common Market if such countries as Canada were excluded; but if they were included, he .argued, the United States would also have to be brought in, she would be too strong and Europe would not be re-formed. With the utmost earnestness, Macmillan said that President de Gaulle should understand that this was a turning point in history and for Europe. If no progress could be made in the negotiations, he would have to explain the reasons; and if he had to say that the failure had been caused by the impossibility of making arrangements about New Zealand, and of a kind which would not shatter her economy, or because agreement could not be reached about a few thousand tons of wheat, people would think that the real cause of failure was that the United Kingdom was not wanted in Europe.[56]

Perhaps that would not serve as a bad summary of what happened in the next few years. Plainly, the British could not walk away from their obligations to the Commonwealth and EFTA. By patient negotiation, most of the immediate difficulties were worn down. Macmillan's government invested an enormous amount of political capital in this process, of which de Gaulle was well aware. For his part, the President remarked that he had found that confederation, rather than integration, was possible in Europe; this had removed the political disadvantages, and he had simultaneously come to realize – as he delicately expressed the point – that the "Common Market had certain economic advantages for France."[57]

de Gaulle acknowledged that the British pursued seriously their application to join the Six. Mr Macmillan pressed again and again the importance of taking at the flood this tide in the affairs of the world.[58] Negotiations proved tedious. After hours of wrangling over a single word in a communique concerning NATO, the British Foreign Secretary once said to his French opposite number *"For God's sake, Couve, telephone to the General and tell him that the alternative word will do just as well."* M. Couve de Murville replied, *"One does not telephone to General de Gaulle"*. Lord Home could only apologize for his foolish suggestion.[59]

At the Chateau de Champs in the summer of 1962, Macmillan thought that he had made good progress and convinced the General of Britain's sincerity in desiring to accept the Treaty of Rome,[60] with conditions no more onerous than those which France herself had demanded at the time of her accession. Others believed that de Gaulle, who for all practical purposes constituted the government of France, remained implacably opposed to Britain's entry, de Gaulle's success in the elections of 1962 and President Kennedy's decisive handling of the Cuban crisis strengthened the French position, de Gaulle talked gloomily at Rambouillet in December 1962 of the impossibility of finding a basis for the political organization of Europe, and disputed Macmillan's suggestion that the Common Market was a political organization or at least tending in that direction. The Prime Minister argued that without the essential economic base, there was no chance of reviving the civilization, life and power of Europe.

It may be, as has often been alleged, that de Gaulle interpreted what Macmillan told him about the future of Britain's nuclear weapons as a clear sign that the British would always give prime place to their relations with the United States. Indeed, the President pointed out that Mr Churchill had said that in the war; to which Mr Macmillan made the sharp reply that when Britain had faced the choice, she had stood alone to defend the independence of Europe.

de Gaulle explained that in the Six, France had weight and could say "No" even against the Germans. She could stop policies with which she disagreed. Once the United Kingdom and the Scandinavians and others had entered, things would be different; and the rest of the world would no doubt demand special arrangements. Who by that point would be strong enough within the Common Market to resist such pressures? The result, he said, *"would be a sort of world free trade area which might be desirable in itself, but would not be European."* The Prime Minister, who had explained once more that the British and French were at one in desiring that governments should govern and that everything in Europe should not be run by civil servants, made the obvious retort that the opinion which the President had expressed constituted a fundamental objection of principle to the British application; and if that really were the French government's view, it should have been put forward at the start.[62]

France's rejection of Britain's application came less than a month later, in wounding terms. Though not unexpected,[63] it fell like a blow upon a bruise, de Gaulle's oldest political ally, M Reynaud, protested against this treatment of the British, only to receive in the General's hand a reply marked *"If absent, please forward to Agincourt (Somme) or Waterloo (Belgium)"*. Within a few days, France signed a treaty with Germany, and made approaches to the Soviet Union. Neither policy produced the results which de Gaulle might have liked. As he remarked *"Treaties are like young girls or roses. They last as long as they last."* No more than Britain did Germany wish to be forced to choose between the Americans and the French. As for the breakdown of negotiations about the Common Market, General de Gaulle expressed his desire for particularly good relations with Great Britain but remained convinced that negotiations could not have succeeded at that time. It was for the British to decide when the moment was ripe.[64] Neither Mr Macmillan nor Lord Home believed in the explanations given about French agriculture or the impossibility of reconciling the Commonwealth's economic interests with those of Europe. As Macmillan used to express it, There was a farmyard with a number of hens and one cock. The last thing de Gaulle wanted was two cocks."

The irony is apparent. The British, who in the earlier stages had judged for good reasons that they could not become part of a federal Europe, then found that the Europe des patries espoused by de Gaulle was one with which they could identify; but the principal proponent of that Europe was the one determined to keep them out. In due course, Mr Harold Wilson and Mr George Brown were to discover that they had no greater persuasive powers, and no greater commitment to Europe, than Mr Macmillan and Lord Home. The next British application was rejected as decisively as the earlier one. What de Gaulle had done would not have been possible without the close and unlikely alignment between France and Germany. Each needed the other, and for the moment France was the stronger of the two. Indeed, we must place this reconciliation with Germany high in the list of de Gaulle's achievements; which is to say much. If we apply M. Monnet's test of the historian's backward glance over the span of twenty-five years, we may add the resolution of the Algerian question, so intractable and perilous, with all that it entailed for the primacy of civilian rule in France; and the creation of the constitution which has given France stable government. On this commemorative occasion, let us salute above all the de Gaulle of 1940 and 1944, and not dwell unduly upon our differences. In the noble oration which the President delivered to the Houses of Parliament during his State Visit of 1960, he remarked that if in those days of June 1944 he had not always found himself entirely in agreement with Churchill,

> c'est peut-être parce que le succés, desormais certain, nous portait a quelque intransigeance. Quatre ans plus lot, nos discussions étaient moins obstinées! Mais voyez comme le temps se charge de mettre en relief ce qui compte et d'effacer ce qui importe peu![66]

Less than five years after that speech, Churchill died. He had taken pains about his own funeral. Vehement and even violent as his disagreements with de Gaulle had been, those who gathered in St Paul's Cathedral in January 1965 discovered that Sir Winston had arranged for the French to come first, the Russians second and the Americans third. President de Gaulle towered over the company in more senses than one. He was dressed as a poilu, with no medals or decorations. I owe that vignette, and a great deal else besides, to Sir William Deakin, formerly Warden of St. Antony's College.

26.11 Conclusion

Let us in a like spirit of respect and reconciliation remember, as part of our gratitude to those who made possible the liberation of Europe, how collaboration between Britain and France has worked to the benefit of ordered freedom, whereas estrangements between our two countries have been a tragedy for them and for a wider world. The relations between General de Gaulle and the British serve as an allegory or epitome of so much else in Anglo-French affairs of the last hundred years. I also express the conviction – which I realize is far from fashionable – that the issues in which France and Great Britain have a common interest, in Europe and beyond, far outweigh those about which we disagree.

References

1.　de Gaulle, C. *Memoires de Guerre: L'Appel 1940–1942* (Paris, 1954, paperback edition), p. 5.
2.　Churchill, W. S. *The Second World War,* Vol. I (London, 1948, Reprint Society edition), p. 217.
3.　de Gaulle, *loc. cit.*

4. Churchill, W.S. "Clemenceaif", in *Great Contemporaries* (Odhams Press edition, London, 1949), pp. 236-7.
5. Reynaud, P. in *Churchill by his Contemporaries* (ed. C. Eade) (Reprint Society edition, London, 1955), p. 221.
6. Lord Moran, *Winston Churchill, The Struggle for Survival 1940-1965* (London, 1966), p. 259
7. Deakin, F. W. *Churchill The Historian* (University of Basel, 1970), p. 17.
8. de Gaulle, *op. cit.*, p. 99; cf. *The Memoirs of Lord Ismay* (London, 1960), p. 149.
9. de Gaulle, *op. cit.*, p. 176.
10. I owe this information to the late Valentine Lawford, who was present as interpreter.
11. Raczynski, E. *In Allied London* (London, 1962), p. 176.
12. Record of a meeting between Churchill and de Gaulle at 10 Downing Street, 12 Sept. 1941, Public Record Office, London (PRO), Prem. 3/120/2.
13. Dilks, D. N. (ed.) *The Diaries of Sir Alexander Cadogan 1938-1945* (London, 1971), p. 629.
14. Eden to C. Peake, 13 June 1942, PRO Prem. 3/120/10A.
15. Major D. Morton to Churchill, 30 Oct. 1942, PRO Prem. 3/I20/10A.
16. Eden to Churchill, 4 June 1942, PRO Prem. 3/120/7.
17. Memorandum annexed to Eden to Churchill, 20 Sept. 1942, PRO Prem. 3/120/6.
18. P. Reynaud, *op. cit.*, p. 221.
19. Record of a conversation between Churchill, Eden and de Gaulle, 30 Sept. 1942, PRO Prem. 3/120/6.
20. Earl of Avon, *The Eden Memoirs: The Reckoning* (London, 1965), p. 351.
21. Minute by Churchill, 30 May 1942, on Eden to Churchill, 27 May, PRO Prem. 3/120/7.
22. Dilks, D. N. (ed.), *op. cit.*, p. 490.
23. *ibid.*, p. 500.
24. Harvey, J. (ed.) *The War Diaries of Oliver Harvey 1941-1945* (London, 1978), p. 262.
25. Macmillan, H. *War Diaries* (London, 1984), p. 97; for a similar observation by Macmillan himself, *ibid.*, p. 101.
26. *ibid.*, p. 79.
27. *ibid.*, pp. 289-90.
28. Moran, *op. cit.*, p. 81.
29. Eden, *op. cit.*, p. 402.
30. *ibid.*, p. 394.
31. Lord Halifax's diary, 22 May 1943, cited in Dilks, *op. cit.*, p. 529.
32. Eden, *op. cit.*, p. 447.
33. Charmley, J. *Duff Cooper* (London, 1986), pp. 168-70.
34. Eden, *op. cit.*, p. 455.
35. For an example see Eden, *op. cit.*, p. 398.
36. Charmley, *op. cit.*, p. 179.
37. Eden, *op. cit.*, p. 493.
38. Ismay, *op. cit.*, pp. 380-1.
39. de Gaulle, *War Memoirs*, Vol. III (English edition, London, 1960), p. 53.
40. Moran, *op. cit.*, p. 224.
41. de Gaulle, *War Memoirs*, Vol. III (English edition), p. 192.
42. de Gaulle to Eden, 24 March 1965, Avon papers, University of Birmingham, AP 23/24/22B. I am indebted to the Countess of Avon for permission to quote this letter.
43. Home, A. *Macmillan*, Vol. II (London, 1989), pp. 32-3.
44. de Gaulle, *op. cit.*, Vol. III (English edition), pp. 201-2.
45. Sir G. Jebb to Selwyn Lloyd, 24 March 1958, PRO Prem. 11/2338.
46. See, for example, Selwyn Lloyd to Sir G. Jebb, 24 June 1958, PRO Prem. 11/2326; and, for de Gaulle's apparent acceptance of the point, Jebb's reply of 25 June, same file.
47. Record of the conversation between de Gaulle and Macmillan, Paris, 29 June 1958, PRO Prem. 11/2326.
48. Note by Macmillan of his private conversation with de Gaulle, 29 June 1958, *ibid.*
49. Note by Macmillan of his private conversation with de Gaulle, 30 June 1958, *ibid.*
50. Sir F. Roberts to Selwyn Lloyd, 1 Aug. 1958, PRO Prem. 11/2335; Macmillan to de Gaulle, 5 Aug. 1958, and reply, 9 Aug., ibid.
51. Home, *op. cit.*, pp. 111-12.

52. For an example, see the record of Macmillan's private conversation with de Gaulle at the Palais d'Elysée, 21 Dec. 1959, PRO Prem. 11/3132.

53. I owe this reminiscence to Mr Macmillan; for a more elaborate version, see H. Macmillan, *Pointing The Way, 1959–1961* (London, 1972), p. 206.

54. Minute by J. E. Killick, 10 Feb. 1960, on WF 1051/40, PRO FO 371/153906.

55. Minute by E. Heath, 8 March 1961, PRO FO 371/161093.

56. Records of Macmillan's conversations with de Gaulle, 24 and 25 Nov. 1961, PRO FO 371/161246.

57. Record of a conversation between de Gaulle and Macmillan at Rambouillet, 28 Jan. 1961, PRO Prem. 11/3322.

58. For example, see the records of Macmillan's four conversations with de Gaulle at the Chateau de Champs, 2 and 3 June 1962, PRO FO 371/166978.

59. Earl of Home, *The Way The Wind Blows* (London, 1976), p. 151.

60. Macmillan to President Kennedy, 5 June 1962, PRO FO 371/166978.

61. Record of conversation between de Gaulle and Macmillan at Rambouillet, 15 Dec. 1962, PRO Prem. 11/4230.

62. Record of a conversation between de Gaulle, Macmillan and others at Rambouillet, 16 Dec. 1962, PRO Prem. 11/4230.

63. See, for example, Sir P. Dixon (Paris) to the Foreign Office, 1 Jan. 1963, PRO FO 371/169109, commenting on de Gaulle's broadcast of the previous evening.

64. Sir P. Dixon's record of his conversation with de Gaulle, 23 Nov. 1963, PRO FO 371/172078.

65. Mr Macmillan made this remark, with variations, on several occasions during the years when I worked as his research assistant.

PART 9

High Level Applications of Content and its Governance

27

Great Libraries in the Service of Science

Alan Eyre

27.1 Introduction

This chapter first describes briefly the three greatest libraries in the world's history, along with a glimpse of a few of their associated personalities, and an appraisal of their service to science. These are the "Pharmacy of the Mind" in Thebes, the Imperial Library of China, successively in Xian, Loyang, Nanking and Beijing, and, the greatest of all, the incomparable Alexandriana. This is followed by a brief tour of a few great contemporary science libraries in nine cities across the world: Canberra, Cape Town, Cluj-Napoca, Kraków, Leipzig, St. Andrews, Venice, Vienna, and Washington. These are a small but significant selection of many in which and for which it has been my privilege to work. This is a very private and personal journey, a re-living of a few golden, or bizarre, moments in a professional career dedicated to international science research evaluation and abstraction. Without librarians of these great collections, science and scientists would be unimaginably poorer.

27.2 The "Pharmacy of the Mind"

In Thebes in Upper Egypt (the modern Luxor) there can be seen today the remains of the Ramesseum. One of the ruined buildings in this monumental complex from the second millennium BCE is the "Pharmacy of the Mind", the psyches hiatreion as the Greeks translated the hieroglyphic inscription still visible on the doorpost. This was the great national library of Pharaonic Egypt, also known as the "Hall of Books". By the entrance was a sculpture of Saf, the goddess of writers, and within were statues of the baboon god, the guardian of libraries.

The 515-year period 2778–2263 BCE, usually called the Old Kingdom period of Egyptian history, was the world's first great age of science. The most important books in the "Pharmacy" were, according to René Taton, *"the brilliant creations of the first scientists"*[1] Taton emphasizes that Egyptian science was pragmatic and utilitarian, not philosophical. Whatever worked was painstakingly recorded; whatever didn't work was scrapped. The leading sciences in this remote but exciting period of human history were pharmacology, medicine and, of course, engineering and architecture. The "famous physicians of old", meaning those of the third millennium BCE were obligated to record their "findings" for posterity in written forms that were as nearly permanent as possible. Some papyri that have survived are absolutely breathtaking in their beauty and state of preservation. Unfortunately, Egyptian culture, including science, became fossilized, with scientific masterworks acting more as holy books rather than as stimulants to further research and experimentation.

27.3 The Imperial Library of China

The golden age of the great imperial libraries of the world was the first millennium BCE. In addition to huge libraries of papyrus books in Egypt, archaeologists have proven the existence of vast collections of clay tablets at Nineveh, Babylon, Nippur, Shushan, Ecbatana, Persepolis and other royal cities in west Asia. It is possible that the Chinese Imperial Library had its beginnings almost three thousand years ago. Certainly by the third century BCE, at the time the Alexandriana had reached full development and world status, the Chin Imperial Library in Xian was a large, well-funded and renowned institution in the service of science. Moreover, it is the longest continuously operating library in the world. Apart from three removals, from Xian to Loyang, then to Nanking, and from Nanking to Beijing, and some brief hiatuses due to wars, its doors have been open to scholars and readers for more than two thousand years. Because of this, access to its resources has enabled scholars to document in great detail the development of science in China during the whole of that period. The most useful survey in the English language is the enormous, erudite, multi-volume work by Joseph Needham of Gonville and Caius College, Cambridge, Science and Civilization in China. This monumental study extends to more than twenty-four thousand pages and nineteen million words. Today, as the Chinese at home and abroad begin to take a leading and a global place in science, it behoves English-speaking scientists to become acquainted with this immensely informative, though now somewhat dated, publication.[2]

The first collections of scientific observations in China included records of astronomical and meteorological ephemera such as eclipses, droughts, storms and floods. Some of these, from 1300 BCE, are on pieces of bone. Perhaps used for astrological purposes, they are known today as "oracle bones".

As early as the beginning of the second century BCE, the importance of libraries to the Chinese state was recognized. The scholar Lu Chia, known as "the bookworm", made this clear to the Han Emperor. When the Emperor asked, *"What is the use of a library?"*, Lu replied, *"You may have conquered the empire on horseback. But it is not on horseback that you will be able to govern it. War and peace are two aspects of an eternal art. Only by humanity and righteousness can you govern a kingdom. For that you need books"*. And so, soon afterwards, a government university was established in Xian with its own library.

In 4 CE the first scientific Congress known to history was convened in Xian, the capital of China. More than a thousand scientists "learned in the ancient records" assembled in the precincts of the Imperial Library. Although no conference proceedings have survived, we know that presentations were made in meteorology, astronomy, chronology, mathematics, acoustics and musicology, philology, historical geography, the medical sciences, horticulture, botany, and, to add a special flavour, filial piety (qualifying as a social science?). It is possible that the first public demonstration of a magnetic compass was made at this Conference. Just a century later, the bibliophile Hsu Shen published the world's first great dictionary.

Bibliographic evidence indicates that more than two thousand years ago, the science of endocrinology was well established in China. The method used by the Chinese twenty-one centuries ago was not "discovered" in Europe until 1909 by Adolf Windaus. Explicit recipes for the large-scale extraction of androgens, estrogens and gonadotrophins from human urine have survived the centuries, showing that it was a large-scale industry. The pills so manufactured had as a typical directive: *"take five to seven pills with warm wine or soup before breakfast"*.[3]

The Chin dynasty (265–420 CE) oversaw a period of great scientific and technological development in China. Canal building, improved irrigation techniques and better water management yielded increasing surpluses which enabled a science-based civilization to emerge. Emperor Huang Ti was the head of a united China. A group of scientists led by Lu Pu-Wei wrote treatises, copies of which were deposited in the Chin Imperial Library.

The books were of two types. The more valuable items were rolls of high quality bamboo paper, impregnated with insecticides, sized or varnished, and treated with a preservative. For exceptionally valuable books a special paper called *kung chih* was used. "Run of the mill" volumes and brief works were on *phien* or tablets. As might be expected, the Imperial Library was a legal deposit library; the requirement was fifty copies of every book produced in the country! It may have been this demanding national regulation that eventually spurred the invention of printing books by movable type.

The millennium between 450 and 1450 CE is considered the "Dark Ages" of world civilization. But this is a purely Eurocentric viewpoint. In stark contrast to the intellectual and scientific eclipse of the "West", China enjoyed a golden age, led by brilliant scholars orbiting the great library. Pao Phu Tzu in the fourth century CE must be counted among the world's great naturalists and Yang Chien among its most erudite economists. The massive gazetteers and systematic geography texts of the same era are unrivalled for any nation in history. The library even had a separate section for relief models of landscape. In 510 CE Li Tao-Yuan published a classic volume *Commentary on the Waterways*.

The Sui dynasty (581–618 CE) was the age when the infrastructure of China made its first "great leap forward", an age of monumental building projects. Under the Emperor Yang Ti a network of navigable waterways was constructed. The greatest of these was the Grand Canal, which employed five and half million workers. These massive undertakings *"benefited posterity to ten thousand generations"*.[4]

The evident economic success of this and other similar works led the Chinese to their deeply-held preference for mammoth projects and to their belief in the power of their indigenous science and technology. All projects were documented in great detail and the books and plans deposited in the great library. The sheer volume of material with which the librarians had to cope was such that a suite of new buildings on an appropriately imperial scale had to be built c. 610 CE. At this date the Sui Imperial Library was by far the largest operating library in the world. Ironically, at the very time that this vast new library in China was opened, its nearest rival in size, the great Theodosian Library in Constantinople, was deliberately destroyed by the Byzantine Emperor Leo III, and its 120,000 priceless volumes of classical literature and science incinerated.

The new Sui Library had fourteen reading rooms. When a librarian escorted a reader to a room, he stepped on a device and the doors of the bookcases automatically flew open. On leaving, they would close and curtains would drop down to protect them. Among the many scientific works deposited in these bookcases, a very large number were in the field of agronomy. This is understandable, given the need to develop scientifically the vast areas newly available to highly intensive agricultural production. Whereas from early Classical times the frontier of European science was theoretical and what has been termed "pure" science, the Chinese excelled in all the applied sciences. Indeed it was a combination of Chinese agronomy and transport technology which made possible the levels of population density and growth that led to the Chinese becoming a fifth of the human race.

In the eighth century CE the demand for academic textbooks was so great that it led to the invention of block printing and the special inks and papers needed to produce mass editions of major works. Textbooks were printed in runs of tens of thousands, and popular books in the hundreds of thousands. In 774 CE the Imperial Academy of Science (today the Academia Sinica) was founded, and we can assume that the Imperial Librarian was a prominent figure in its activities.

Under the Sung dynasty, established by Emperor Thai Tsu in 960 CE, China *"rose to a height of culture and science previously undreamed of"*.[5] The Imperial Library, relocated in Loyang, played a crucial role in the service of science. In 1086 CE, during the Liao dynasty, Shen Kua, chancellor of Han-Lin Academy (University), organized a great deal of the scientific material and engaged in field research himself. He was not a specialist but a deeply-learned compiler of facts from several of the sciences. These included astronomy, mathematics, palaeontology, cartography, metallurgy and descriptive biology. The following is a list of the fourteen sciences for which there were extensive holdings in the Imperial Library, in order of their importance as indicated by Shen Kua: biological sciences, medicine and pharmacology, astronomy and chronology, meteorology, engineering and metallurgy, geology and mineralogy, geography and cartography, mathematics, ying and yang and geomancy, agronomy, architecture, hydraulics, physics, and chemistry. The first "modern" geologist was not James Hutton (1726–1797) but Shen Kua. His geological works have been available for study for a thousand years. *"When I went to Hopei on official duties I saw that in the cliffs of T'ai-Hang Shan there were strata containing whelk-like animals, oyster shells and echinoids. So this place, though now a thousand li west of the sea, must once have been a shore. Thus what we call the continent must have been made of mud and sediment that was once below the water. By muddy, silt-bearing rivers the substance of the whole continent must have been laid down".*[6]

A story is told of Ch'ao Mei-Shu, Assistant Director of the Imperial Library, which reveals the prestige and influence of librarians in national affairs. Like the Alexandriana, the Imperial Library was also what would be called today a museum, and Ch'ao was curator of a wonderful collection of clocks designed by the great horologist Su Sung. Among these was one ten metres high which was both a clock and an astronomical observatory. It "struck" every quarter hour *"with a great sound of creaking and splashing, clanging and ringing".*[7] In 1094 CE, the government decided that it did not want to preserve these priceless artefacts. Horrified, a determined Ch'ao went persistently up the bureaucratic ladders in his efforts to save them, until he finally got the receptive ear of Chang Tun, the Prime Minister.

By the eleventh century CE movable typesetting was general. It is suggested that the most influential bibliophile and library scientist of all time was Pi Sheng, who between 1041 and 1048 perfected the art and technology of book printing. It was from his presses that these skills were carried centuries later to Europe. Rare visitors from outside China marvelled at the amazing speed at which thousands of books were produced, bound and distributed, and also at the ability and alacrity of library staff to retrieve items on request from their collections.

The twelfth to fifteenth centuries saw the publication of the Chinese encyclopaedias, compiled in the Imperial Library. Among these, two classics are noteworthy. These were the Imperial Medical Encyclopaedia of 1111 CE, edited by twelve of China's leading medical scientists, and the Great Science Encyclopaedia. Three thousand scholars combined their efforts to produce this gigantic work, consisting of 11,095 volumes bound in yellow brocade.[8] In 1421 the Imperial Library was relocated to its final home in Beijing. With its estimated eighteen million books, its librarians are facing the challenges of the twenty-first century with confidence and enthusiasm.

27.4 The Alexandriana

The Alexandriana Library was founded c. 300 BCE, with Demetrios of Phaleron as its first and greatest Director. Its patron and chief fund-raiser was Ptolemy Soter, Macedonian ruler of Egypt, who, *"encouraged by the celebrated Demetrios of Phaleron, put into execution a plan for the formal endowment of literature and science".*[9]

In Athens there is a Metro station with the name Neos Kosmos. Five kilometres south, along Andrea Syngrou Avenue, is the fashionable coastal suburb of Paleo Faliro or Old Phalaron. Somewhere beneath the cafes, boutiques and chic high-rise apartment blocks is the birth site of Demetrios (350–282 BCE). Born to his parents in conditions of servitude, his father's master evidently saw potential in this child and ensured that he was well educated. Demetrios went on to become a philosopher, orator, statesman, diplomat, scholar, man of letters, and above all, librarian. Without question the leading intellectual of his time, his fame rests solidly on his brilliance as the world's first director of a great public library open to all. All the great libraries before had been royal libraries mainly for matters and persons of state. The Alexandriana was the first great library in history to be devoted to the pursuit of universal knowledge, and above all in the service of science. To cite Weniger, *"the highly cultured Demetrios of Phaleron created the magnificent scientific institution"* of the Alexandriana.[10] Demetrios' towering achievement as "Keeper of Books" in the Alexandriana Library was to place on a firm foundation the four basic principles of librarianship: collection, classification, storage, and access. If there ever is to be a "Nobel" award for librarianship, it surely must be the Demetrios of Phaleron Prize.

Callimachos of Cyrene, chief librarian from 260 to 240 BCE, *"fixed the canons of cataloguing, which have been incorporated, more or less, in our Library of Congress, European, and other systems"*. The catalogue of the Alexandriana, known as the *Pinakes*, was essentially the work of Callimachos, and was *"the first great library catalogue of western civilization"*.[11] The books were catalogued by author and also by subject. Parsons gives one example of the latter: there was a division *Cook Books,* which had an alphabetical list of authors under each subdivision such as *Pastry Cooking,* and so on.

The holdings of the Science Library provided both bibliographic sources and records of experimental data. These made possible a quantum leap in applied science during the first three centuries of the Library's existence. In applied maths and computing, mechanical calculators were developed which contained elaborate arrangements of gear wheels for counting and then displaying the results. An example of one of these computers used for navigation was recovered from a wreck sunk around 5 BCE near Crete (the Antikythera computer).[12]

In the third century BCE medical science in particular was well served by the Alexandriana. It made available to scholars the experimental work of medical scientists going back two and three centuries before the Library's foundation. Outstanding was the work of Alcmaeon of Croton (c. 500 BCE), the "father" of scientific dissection, who had identified and described the nerves proceeding from the eyes to the brain, and correctly surmised that vision was interpreted in the brain, with the eyes themselves performing a strictly mechanical function. Erasistratos (c. 260 BCE) wrote and deposited a large number of works, notably on comparative anatomy, abdominal pathology, haemoptysis, nutrition, and hygiene. He carried out post-mortems and much experimental research on cadavers, examining the mammalian brain in great detail. From the brains of hare, stag, and man, he hypothesized that the number of convolutions varied with the degree of intellectual development. One of Erasistratos' most notable scientific discoveries was that the arteries carry both oxygen ("the breath of life") and nutrients to the tissues, while the nerves carry messages to and from the brain ("the psychic life"). He accurately described peristalsis of the bowel, and analysed the processes of digestion and excretion. He was the first medical scientist in history to identify the brain as the central seat of the intelligence and the emotions, with the heart serving only as a sophisticated mechanical pump. Erasistratos placed great emphasis on what is now, in the twenty-first century CE, termed "wellness". He opposed drastic "medical" interventions such as blood-letting and violent purging, encouraging instead the benefits of carefully regulated physical exercise and physiotherapy.

One section of the library was devoted to musicology. Pythagoras (of right angle triangle fame) left a corpus of studies to the library which showed the mathematical relationships between the notes of a musical scale and the lengths or sizes of vibrating strings, bells or columns of air among various musical instruments. These can be said to have prepared the way for the modern symphony orchestra. It is a significant testimony to the influence of the library that Alexandria became a renowned centre for the manufacture of musical instruments, including hydraulic organ building in which several firms were world famous.[13]

The acquisition of the Indian collection, its cataloguing, and the creation of a special reading room at the Alexandriana for the enormous number of documents in Sanscrit, formed one of the most extraordinary bibliographic achievements of antiquity. It was greatly aided by the fact that Chandragupta, ruler of the Indian Empire, worshipped Alexander the Great as a god. As a young man, Chandragupta witnessed the siege of Taxila and Alexander's conquest of western India. It was in this way that ancient Indian science cross-fertilized Greek, Babylonian and Egyptian science. It was this meld that later influenced Arabic science during the European Dark Ages.

What was the most important influence of the great Alexandriana upon science, then and since? Of this, there can be no doubt. One of the earliest professors at the university associated with the Library was Euclid (320–260 BCE). He founded the school of mathematics there. But he did much more. With his axioms, postulates, theorems, and hypotheses, he created the basic framework and methodology of science and rational inquiry. Indeed, the very concept of "proof" comes from Euclid through the Alexandriana. Doubt, about anything, could be resolved by reference to the great collection of data. The convention was established that sources must be compared, verified, and acknowledged, not only in the sciences, but in all areas of knowledge. The philosophical works of Philo the Jew, another professor at the university, reflect this rational outlook. Even in religion, this became the accepted approach. *"Prove all things"*, wrote the apostle Paul, *"hold fast to that which is good"*.[14] The use of supporting citations in speeches and writings is another feature of the Alexandrian legacy. This also is seen in the New Testament.[15]

The last librarian of the Alexandriana was John Philoponus, but he never took up his post. His application was referred to Caliph Omar by "Amr, the Muslim governor of Egypt. His response was that no other books were needed besides the Quran. The destruction of the Alexandriana in the seventh century CE was a tragedy not only for science as a human endeavour, but especially in the realm of human health. It has always been my view that the Dark Ages can be dated from the bonfire of books in 646 CE when the last surviving treasures of the Alexandriana were allegedly used to heat Omar's bathwater.

27.5 The Australian National University Mount Stromlo Library, Canberra

The Mount Stromlo library, as its name implies, was located on a mountaintop several kilometres from the Canberra campus. Although by 2003 the most sophisticated observations were carried out at Siding Spring and Parkes in New South Wales, some of the telescopes and other instruments at Mount Stromlo were still operational, and the library housed the greatest collection of astrophysical monographs in the southern hemisphere.

27.6 The National Library of South Africa, Cape Town

A favourite in my personal "collection" of great libraries is the National Library of South Africa. Tracing the previously forgotten African wanderings of the nineteenth-century black Jamaican scientist Isaac Edmestone Barnes, my abiding memory of "NLSA" is the graciousness and helpfulness of the staff.

Barnes was a mineralogist and civil engineer trained at the University of Leipzig. He was South Africa's first black executive manager of an international diamond mining syndicate. The Orangia Syndicate, a public stock company, was financed principally by the ninth Earl of Elgin and Nathan Rothschild, among many others, and had two (or more) diamond mines in the Kroonstad (OFS) area of South Africa. Barnes had many Afrikaner burghers as his close friends. Nevertheless, the racist hostility of a handful of British and Irish army officers prevailed, and he was hounded out of the country in 1909 after a six-year residence in Kroonstad and Cape Town.[16]

Oddly for a library on the southern tip of Africa in a city only four hundred years old, it is famed for its collection of medieval scientific manuscripts.[17] However, my own "lucky find" on this mission was in an adjunct library with a magnificent collection of Africana, the Mendelssohn Library. In my South African quest I must acknowledge the courteous help of a great, yet humble, librarian, Peter Coates, retiring editor of The Quarterly Bulletin of the National Library of South Africa.

It was fascinating that my visits to the ruins of the "Pharmacy of the Mind" in 1985 and to the National Library of South Africa twenty years later spanned Africa from north to south and also four thousand five hundred years of librarianship. What is this myth of the "dark continent"?

27.7 Babes-Bolyai University Library, Cluj-Napoca

University education in the ancient city of Cluj-Napoca in Romania, and the libraries underpinning it, have had a long and somewhat turbulent history. This has been due to the multi-ethnic character of Transylvania. For a thousand years four "nations", languages and cultures have competed for dominance in the region: the Magyars, Szeklers, Saxons and Vlachs (pre-Roman Dacians). In 1872 the library took its present form, its name honouring bacteriologist-haematologist (and politician) Vincent Babes (1854–1926) and Janos Bolyai (1802–1860), renowned author of The science absolute of space.18 The university has the unusual distinction of being the first in the world to establish a department of speleology.

A visit to Babes-Bolyai in Cluj-Napoca, Romania, was attractive in prospect and in theory. From the distance and insularity of the West Indies, the idea seemed innocent enough. The urging came from a Szekler (Magyar-speaking Romanian) professor living at the time in London.

In practice and experience this academic excursion turned out to be a scholastic version of negotiating a minefield. Beginning as a somewhat unconventional attempt to seek research data from a very prestigious institution within a reclusive totalitarian dictatorship.

I got lots of data from Babes-Bolyai, filtered through the chief librarian. Working in the library was a very strange experience. Unlike the British Library, for example, where coats *must* be removed before entry, all readers wore massive identical ankle-length black coats with deep pockets, along with identical grey fur hats which were never removed. There was another peculiarity that must have had some political significance. You could never make a left turn. To do so, you had to turn right and circle the building. In the street outside, pedestrians had to do the same.

The first library in Cluj was probably founded by the Romans who occupied the town of Napoca, with a view to bringing literacy and civilization to the "barbarian" Dacians. There were later halcyon days in the sixteenth century when Ferenc David was the illustrious head of the Academy and Library of the Unitarian Brethren and Prince Janos Sigismund Zapolya was its generous patron.20 David was the only prominent academic and religious leader in the world of his day to advocate through national legislation the concepts of liberty of conscience, academic freedom, freedom of the press, mutual tolerance, and the peaceful resolution of conflicts. Sadly, the success of his efforts was short-lived, as the fanatical seventeenth century wars of religion bear tragic testimony.

Babes-Bolyai was once a great and famous library, but neither Babes nor Bolyai would have been amused at its fate and disutility in 1982. No doubt as Romania joins the European Union, it will become great once again.

27.8 The Jagiellonian Library, Kraków

The historic city of Kraków was the royal capital of Poland, and is still its heart and pride. Two great ancient libraries, administratively independent but sharing many common concerns, are located in the city's centre: the Jagiellonian Library, established in 1364, and the Czartoryski Library, an originally private collection founded at a later date.

The sixteenth century was the golden age of the Jagiellonian Library. Of course, its shining star was the Pole Mikolaj Kopernik (1473–1543) widely known as Copernicus. Kopernik, a classics and mathematics graduate of the Jagiellonian in 1494, went up to the great Italian universities of Bologna and Padua where he studied astronomy, medicine, and (then almost a compulsory subject for any brilliant scholar) canon law. His developed cosmology went much further than merely proof that the earth and the planets circled the sun. He explained the seasons, the precession of the equinoxes, and, most astonishingly, grasped the concept of astronomical distances, demonstrating that the "fixed" stars were not really fixed at all, but moved quite independently of our solar system and at a vast distance from it. His scientific work was supposed to be a hobby while a canon at Frombork cathedral. But it became far more than a sideline, especially after his *magnum opus, De revolutionibus,* was completed in 1530. The library's first copy is dated 1543, the year of his death.

My quest in Kraków was for original documentation on the educational policies and curricula of the *Braci Polskich* (Polish Brethren in Christ) in the sixteenth and seventeenth centuries, especially in science. At most European universities at that time, the faculties of arts and natural philosophy (science) were subordinate to the faculty of theology. This reflected the view that Augustine the "father" of theology was greater than Aristotle the "father" of science. The principle of Thomas Aquinas was strictly applied: "whenever natural science and theology speak with different voices, the former has to be dismissed as false. It is wise, however, to find out where science has erred, for, whenever possible, actual knowledge is preferable to blind faith".[21] By contrast, the Brethren in Christ in Poland and elsewhere in Europe were not bound by Aquinas. They were the first religious body to encourage students to widen their minds through a unified process of discovery, scientific and religious. Beginning at the Altdorf Academy near Nuremberg, and later fully organized at their own Academies at Raków in central Poland and Kieselin in the western Ukraine, religion and science were seen as two facets of the "whole counsel of God". The many publications of the Polish Brethren in Latin and Polish strongly influenced philosophers and scientists across Europe, including John Locke and Sir Isaac Newton in Britain.

The two Kraków libraries, because they had been spared destruction in World War II, are rich in source material. But the decade of the 1970s was not an easy time for library research in Poland by an English-speaking Jamaican. Dr. Tadeusz Franczik, the Czartoryski librarian, would only speak Polish, Russian or French. He claimed that no one in either the Jagiellonian or the Czartoryski could speak a word of English. In some cases the catalogue listed a Latin copy of a document (which I could read) and a Polish copy (which at the time I could not), but for some obscure and inexplicable reason only the Polish copy could be located.

27.9 Universitätsbibliothek, Leipzig

This great and justly renowned library was founded in 1543. In that year university chancellor Caspar Borner salvaged the libraries of several abandoned pre-Reformation monasteries in the Leipzig area of Germany, and the Duke of Saxony donated the Pauliner monastery to house the precious collection. The size and topical breadth of the new library was impressive from the start, and its renown was such that in 1711 it was opened to the public for two hours a week! Today the "Bibliotheca Albertina" on Beethovenstrasse is the splendid hub for forty satellite libraries.

My purpose at the Universitätsbibliothek Leipzig was to obtain information on the Jamaican scientist Isaac Edmestone Barnes, born in 1857, referred to earlier. Barnes studied at the University of Leipzig at the end of the nineteenth century. At that time the university was at the peak of its fame. Its Institut für Mineralogie, Kristallographie und Materialwissenschaft was the world's most prestigious school of mineralogy, and it was here that Barnes acquired his legendary expertise in diamond prospecting and mining. It took many hours of searching, but eventually the library and registry staff came to the firm conclusion that Barnes had been the only black man of any national origin in more than five hundred years to graduate from the University of Leipzig. As well as his major in mineralogy, he also seriously studied land surveying, geology and civil engineering, and dabbled in philosophy and theology.[22] The university archives have photographs of classes he attended, but all those pictured are white and German. With some embarrassment, it was concluded that either he was deliberately omitted, or painted out.[23] Barnes is widely believed to have discovered the first diamonds in West Africa, in the same area where "blood diamonds" funded the career of Charles Taylor in the 1990s, although this cannot be established with certainty.

Nobel laureate Werner Karl Heisenberg (1901–1976) was Professor of Theoretical Physics at the University of Leipzig from 1927 to 1942. He was the "founder" of quantum mechanics. More importantly, as a scientist-philosopher he closed the era of certainty, determinism and "proof" initiated by scientist-philosopher Euclid at the Alexandriana two thousand two hundred years before. The present era of "uncertainty" and "chaos theory" in the sciences began. Working at the "Albertina", even for a brief period, made a significant impact on me personally. In particular, a video on the work and influence of Heisenberg on scientific thought has undoubtedly affected my own philosophical outlook.

27.10 St Andrews University Library, Scotland

Nearly six hundred years old, this great university and national library manages to reconcile age, size and intimacy. One of the great advantages of research at St. Andrews is the remarkable accessibility of reference material on the open shelves. On one occasion I had Wilhelm Korff's Lexikon der bioethic, John Button's A dictionary of green ideas, del Hoyo, Eliott and Sargatal's massive ten volume Handbook of the birds of the world, Levin's Encyclopedia of diversity, Knobil and Neill's four volume Encyclopedia of reproduction, Currie and Padian's Encyclopedia of dinosaurs, and Zeuner's History of domesticated animals all on my desk within less than fifteen minutes.

I have a special affinity with St. Andrews because the university and its library wrought two revolutions in my own view of science, nature and indeed of the very concept of "life" itself. The first was due to my study of the work of James Bell Pettigrew, who was Chandos professor at St. Andrews from 1882 to 1905. His classic multi-volume masterwork *Design in nature,* published a century ago, figuratively opened my eyes very wide indeed.[24] I became a passionate, lifelong investigator of design, form and function in the natural world from crown shyness and arboreal architecture in the tropical rainforests to the exquisitely precise formulation of weird and lethal toxins by the tiny spiders in my garden and of luciferin (cold light) in synchronously flashing fireflies.[25] I have been urging the re-publication of Pettigrew's best work in a centenary volume.

The disciplines of marine biology and microbiology are quite strong at St. Andrews, and I have been intrigued during my visits by the recent advances in these areas of science. Truly, an extraordinary revolution in our understanding of the biosphere is taking place. More than thirty years ago I toured the Negev with Israeli scientists who showed me "living rock" – strata in which microbiota were actually a part of the rock itself, extending over large areas of the desert. I was one of very few scientists who believed them then. Then I learned in South Africa that living organisms are found in gold-bearing quartz rock too hot to touch two kilometres deep below Johannesburg. My concept of "life" and "living" has been shocked once again by marine scientists at St. Andrews who now tell me that "tiny microbes may inhabit vast regions of the Earth's interior, way beyond the reach of any other life forms".[26] Living creatures have been collected from hundreds of metres beneath the seabed in sediments dated millions of years old. How do they survive, and reproduce? Are they immortal? It has been suggested that the total biomass *within* the earth may outweigh all the living organisms in the ocean, on the earth and in the atmosphere put together.

27.11 The Biblioteca Marciana, Venice

During the 1980s, I had a short period working at the famed Libreria Sansoviniana, otherwise known as the Marciana Library, in Venice. I was looking for some sixteenth and seventeenth century manuscripts in Italian. I found a lot more than I expected, so this historic library stands high in my esteem. Also, to my surprise, I found that I could read the old Italian handwriting far more easily than manuscripts of the same age in English.

Designed in a monumental style beside the Grand Canal by the architect Jacopo Sansovino in 1537, it was described by the great Palladio as "the finest building since antiquity". However, prior to its opening, the vaulting collapsed, and Sansovino was imprisoned while having to rebuild at his own expense. Ceiling paintings by Paolo Veronese celebrate Arithmetic, Geometry and Music.

The Marciana was once a great library in the service of science, the glory of the Serene Republic. But it was eventually eclipsed in that role by other Italian libraries in more dynamic cities. Today, it is a historic relic, of little significance in the modern world. Even when I was there twenty years ago, all the staff were living and working in a kind of time warp, immensely proud of a wonderfully photogenic library from a past age.

27.12 The Austrian National Library, Vienna

There is no doubt that this is a great library. The building is in the Grand Imperial Style. You are awed by the long echoing corridors. What I recall most about my research in this place is the extraordinary regimentation. Each day I was allowed to examine six items. Books, maps, reports, manuscripts anything: under no circumstances whatever could I see, examine or even request more than six items. I was a visiting scientist from Washington, from the Library of Congress in the United States of America? No, we are really sorry, but it is six items a day and no more. I had to assume that the idea was to ensure that I enjoyed the delights of Vienna for as long as possible. The card catalogue (this was before computers) was replete with many items that I would have loved to lay my greedy hands on and photocopy. No, we are sorry, but the rules of the library restrict this and forbid that. And pleading was useless.

It was freely admitted that some of the items I requested had not been past the issue desk for more than a century. But they cannot be retrieved today, or tomorrow. There is a two week waiting time for copying that item, but we can send it to you in a few weeks time by air mail, for a fee.

Surely in a great library, access is as important as conservation.

27.13 The Library of Congress, Washington DC

I had two periods on the staff of the Library of Congress. The first was for seven years, from 1966 to 1972. I was in my thirties, and they were the most interesting and intellectually stimulating of my long professional career as a scientist. Washington DC has always remained my favourite city. I was recruited in 1966 in a most extraordinary way.

If you want an indication of how fundamentally America and the world have changed since the mid-1960s, my appointment at the Library of Congress would suffice. Because of the peculiar nature of the institution, the letters of appointment and dismissal of senior staff bear the President's signature. So I rather treasure the signatures of Presidents Lyndon Johnson and Richard Nixon in my *curriculum vitae!* Notwithstanding, though a humble (or perhaps not so humble!) Jamaican national, I was taken on in a senior position on the strength of a telephone call and without a formal interview. Some years later, Marie Tremaine, my redoubtable section head, retired and I hazarded the comment that she had taken quite a risk in hiring me in this manner. *"Not at all"*, she replied promptly, *"I am a shrewd judge of human nature"*. The fact is that the Americans were in a fierce and furious space race, and were desperate to recruit young scientists from anywhere, especially those with some facility with foreign languages and willing to travel. I suppose I was also potentially attractive at that time in that I had qualifications in geology, geography and meteorology – in other words, under, on and above the earth. By the time I left DLC I had gone even higher, into space science and cosmology!

The Library of Congress houses well over twenty-five million printed items and fifty million manuscripts. The library's collections of Russian, Chinese and Japanese materials are far and away the largest in the world outside those countries. I never lost my sense of awe at this vast temple of human learning. I never did discover how many lifts (elevators) there were, but I did once find myself eleven storeys down from ground level.

It would be tedious to recount many of the fascinating forays in research abstraction that the Library of Congress enabled me to make. So as a sample I will mention five large and three extremely large research evaluation projects that came to fruition on my desk. In every case the Library of Congress proved to be the ideal base for the data collection and evaluation. Because of its incomparable collection at one site and the simplicity and efficiency of source identification and retrieval, each project could be both comprehensive and completed in a relatively short time. It is very doubtful if at that time this would have been possible anywhere else.

The Americans were suspicious that during the Stalin dictatorship in the USSR, there had been a very serious nuclear disaster in the vicinity of Sverdlovsk (now Yekaterinburg) in western Siberia, and subsequently kept secret. The seriousness and the effects of the disaster were matters concerning which the western powers were intensely curious. Using librarians, Congress was able to gain a very detailed insight into all aspects of this quite horrifying disaster. An interesting feature of this investigation was the route by which much of the sensitive data reached Washington. Jewish scientists in the Soviet Union reported in Hebrew to colleagues in Israel, and institutions such as the Harman Science Library at Givat Ram then passed the data on to the Library of Congress.[27]

Another event of cosmic significance, which it was a fascinating exercise to research and evaluate, was the Tunguska bolide impact of 1908. On the morning of June 30 an explosion occurred in a remote area of eastern Siberia. It was heard a thousand kilometres away, and pressure waves circled the planet twice before dissipating. Little was known about this event at the time, and before the Russians themselves were able to investigate it seriously, the Bolshevik Revolution prevented them sharing what they knew. The space race and the arms race created intense curiosity on the part of the Americans for any information about the explosion, and a small team of us at the Library of Congress did our best to document the effects and establish the cause. The first of these proved to be easier than the second. An area of one thousand square kilometres was totally incinerated, and trees were felled in a radial pattern by the blast up to fifty kilometres distant from ground zero. Many hundreds of square kilometres of coniferous forest burned fiercely for two days. A major reason for the

Americans' concern was that many features replicated those of a nuclear blast. After prolonged investigation, it was ascertained that Russian scientists had ascribed the explosion to a comet impact. For our part, lengthy discussions at the US Geological Survey library at Reston, Virginia led to a consensus that the event was the explosive vaporization of a stony meteorite just fifty metres in diameter at a height of eight kilometres above ground zero. Interestingly, after forty years this difference of opinion still remains.

A third topic that Congress asked us to report on in detail was the massive 1964 Alaska earthquake. At a magnitude of 8.3 on the Richter scale, it was comparable with the San Francisco quake of 1906. Only seven earthquakes of this magnitude or greater have occurred worldwide in the past thousand years. Although I have experienced several earthquakes, my reading of the scientific descriptions of the Prince William Sound event of 1964 made me glad that it was not one of them! I was asked to make some historic comparisons, and decided after some digging in the history areas of the Library that the worst earthquake in human history must have been one in 1201, caused by sudden tectonic movement on the Middle East section of the Great Rift. It devastated a strip from southern Egypt to northern Syria, causing an estimated 1,100,000 deaths.

The idea was mooted to use a series of colossal nuclear explosions to blow open the Bering Straits and change the hydrography, oceanography and glaciology of the Arctic Ocean. Before committing vast sums to such a scheme, DLC librarians were asked to evaluate the possible consequences, positive and negative. Personally I have rarely been in favour of giga-projects to transform the earth's environment, and I must confess that I was not overly enthusiastic about the Bering Straits scheme.

One job that I did enjoy was to evaluate the Ishuaq geochronology which identified the oldest rocks in the world in Greenland, carefully dated at 3,800 million years BP.[28] The geologists were from several nations, and their fieldwork had been published in some very obscure technical journals. So again, the Library of Congress was perhaps the only place in the world where this could have been done in the short time we had available.

This was certainly true of the largest of our research abstraction projects, an evaluation of the International Geophysical Year (1957–58). This was the largest integrated scientific project in history. Sixty-seven nations took part, and traditional enemies worked together in the interest of human knowledge and progress in a unique partnership. Perhaps more was learned about the cosmos, the planet and our physical environment in that one year than in all the previous history of mankind. In the years that followed IGY, data pouring into "DLC" from all over the world became a torrent that threatened to overwhelm the Library and its overworked staff. But, inspired by the challenge, we managed to cope. Sullivan has described IGY as *"a major turning point in history"*. Certainly it was an exciting time for a young scientist. All of us who were involved realized the significance of our work, and at the end of our evaluation project we could agree with Sullivan that *"science and scientists came out of the IGY as a potent influence in world affairs"*.[29] But much more emerged from the IGY than merely an enhanced prestige for scientists – and librarians. J. Tuzo Wilson, a distinguished Canadian geophysicist, was one of the masterminds of IGY. Looking back, as he wrote the definitive story of its enormous achievements, he made a confession which spoke for very many of us who shared his vision: *"if science has given unexpected power to man, it has to an even greater extent revealed the unimagined glory of God"*[30] That revelation has never left me and only grown deeper with the years.

Two very large projects in which I played a small part while at the Library of Congress were *The National Atlas of the United States of America,* and a report about ongoing climate change. My only comment on the *National Atlas* is to emphasize that the combined research that went into it would fill a small library. The final publication was a victim of drastic cost-cutting at Federal level, and, unfortunately, much of it was never published in any form.

In 1966 the global climatological community was sharply divided between coolers and warmers. The US Congress was anxious to know what the future held (for them, of course), but its members were sharply divided too. Were we moving rapidly towards a new ice age, or towards a scenario of rapid global warming? Computer technology was becoming available that helped us find an answer in the time frame that would satisfy a typical politician. Personally, I have always been a warmer, having lectured for years at my own University of the West Indies as a prophet of global warming, with publications to back it up. But in 1966 our report, assessing both possible trends but tentatively predicting warming, was quietly shelved by a Congress in denial at the prospect of a New Orleans type catastrophe.

My second period of service was as a Fulbright Research Fellow in the 1990s, nearly thirty years later. Once again the initiative came from the United States government. The focus this time was to quantify the destruction and deforestation of the tropical rainforests. There was unacceptably wide variation in the estimates, especially between the figures and rates supplied by the forestry departments of national governments and those obtained by various international and private agencies through remote sensing by satellite. To reconcile these sources was a daunting challenge. The Library of Congress was an ideal institution for this work. American embassies throughout the world sent national data, and the special section of the Library handling data from the various United Nations and other international agencies was kept quite astonishingly up to date.

A major problem was that the US government not unreasonably wanted verifiable satellite data to be accepted by national governments. Simply, this was impossible. Few governments want to be seen as permitting the reckless destruction of its rainforests and other valuable environmental resources. It was quite obvious that many forestry departments were conniving with illegal loggers and other destroyers. Some nations were (and still are) intent on selling off as quickly as possible their entire rainforest domains, ostensibly to alleviate rural poverty, but in reality to make a few wealthy individuals even wealthier. In 1993-94 I went around the world four times, visiting seventy countries. I learnt the art (and science) of negotiation the hard way. There was no hope of unanimity. Compromise became the buzz word. Eventually a massive collation emerged. As I was personally committed to "ground truth" (as far as it can be scientifically defined and described), not to fudged and imaginary statistics, the last stages of compiling my report for the Library were extremely challenging, to put it mildly. As the Americans would not accept the final draft, the report was eventually published in India.

27.14 Great Librarians

It is imperative that we also memorialize the three greatest librarians in the history of science.

Eratosthenes of Cyrene (276–195 BCE) was born at Shahhat in what is now Libya and is undoubtedly the most notable African-born intellectual in history. He was Director and chief librarian of the Alexandriana for forty-one years. He was first and foremost a geographer, in an age when geography was the most important and prestigious of all the sciences. Under the leadership of Eratosthenes, an oceanography department measured ocean tides, comparing the Indian and Atlantic Oceans. Geodesy was a well-established discipline, and a base line of latitude was established from Gibraltar to the Himalayas. This made possible the first accurate maps of the land masses of the planet. His calculations of the earth's size were not bettered until modern times. If Columbus had used Eratosthenes' globe, he may not have ventured on his transatlantic voyage, and how different the history of the Americas would have been!

Christian Jocher was librarian of the Universitätsbibliothek Leipzig from 1742 to 1758. I consider him to be the first "modern" librarian of science. He published *"the first alphabetical union catalogue"* and edited the first "modern" scientific encyclopaedia.[31] His work was crucial in establishing Germans in the forefront of world science right up to World War II, culminating in the great Leipzig professor Werner Heisenberg, and thus subsequently the leadership of America in the second half of the twentieth century.

Sir Hans Sloane (1660–1753) was the founder of the British Library. There are several personal reasons for my choice of Sloane. He was a careful scientist, and wrote up his discoveries meticulously, without rushing into publication. His *magnum opus* was *The Natural History of Jamaica,* published in 1725, described by Gardner as *"a marvellous work".*[32] His botanical field work was done in 1687–1688 when he was twenty-seven years old, in the course of which he discovered eight hundred species of plants new to science. It was eight years later when he published a taxonomic and descriptive catalogue in Latin. He was not only a naturalist, but a general scientist, interested in seismology after experiencing an earthquake in Jamaica, and also in anthropology and the social sciences.

Sir Hans, born in Ireland, married a native Jamaican widow, Elizabeth Rose, and enjoyed life along with his Jamaican stepchildren and grandchildren. In fact, he enjoyed life so much that, almost miraculously for the eighteenth century, he lived into his ninety-fourth year.[33] The fact is that Sloane was deeply interested in everything. He was physician in chief to the British Army, and did his job so well that he was promoted to Royal Physician to George II. He was a distinguished Fellow of the Royal Society, then its Secretary, a job he did so well that he became its President. Above all he was a bibliophile and almost certainly a speed reader, for, unlike many of his contemporaries, his books were for his use not for show or status. His private library was a well-organized and well-read collection of 30,000 books and 3560 manuscripts. The final reason for my choice of Sloane is that he decided to devote the entire collection to the service of science, and it formed the nucleus of one of the greatest libraries in the world. In 1759, six years after this grand old man's death, the great British Library opened its doors to the nation and the world.[34]

References

1. René Taton (ed.). Ancient and medieval science from prehistory to AD 1450,. London: Thames and Hudson, 1963.
2. Joseph Needham. *Science and Civilization in China.* 27 vols. Cambridge: University Press, 1954. There is a handy one-volume "distillation" by Robert Temple, with an introduction by Needham: China, land of discovery. Wellingborough: Patrick Stephens, 1986.
3. Temple, p.127.
4. Fu Tse Hung. *Golden Mirror of the Flowing Waters.* c.1400 CE, ch.92.
5. Needham, Vol. 1, p.132.
6. Shen Kua. *Dream pool essays.* 1086. Cited by Temple, pp. 168–169.
7. Temple, p.109, citing Needham.
8. It is said that this work eventually totalled fifty million characters.
9. John Henry Newman. *Macedonian and Roman schools.* London 1899, p. 94.
10. Ludwig Weniger. *Das alexandrinische Museum.* Berlin: Lüderitzische verlag, 1875, p.9.
11. Edward A. Parsons. *The Alexandrian Library: Glory of the Hellenic world.* London: Cleaver-Hume, 1952, p. 217.
12. Derek J. de Solla Price has described these instruments in various publications.
13. The "Second Temple" in Jerusalem had a huge hydraulic organ built in Alexandria. Jewish legend has it that at full power it could be heard all over the ancient city.
14. I Thessalonians 5:21.
15. The New Testament writers cite the Septuagint Greek version of the Hebrew Bible frequently. This version was made at the Alexandriana. On occasion the apostle Paul cites Greek writers.
16. This fascinating historical saga is recounted in L. Alan Eyre. "Isaac Edmestone Barnes in Kroonstad, Orange River Colony: the troubled life of a black Jamaican mining executive 1903 to 1909" in *Quarterly Bulletin of the National Library of South Africa,* 60(4), 2006, pp. 105–127. Dr. Isaac Barnes was an active member of the worldwide Christadelphian Brethren in Christ (see note 20). In 1889 he founded the congregation in Kingston, Jamaica. Besides his mining interests, Barnes' many publications ranged over philosophy, biblical exegesis, economics, and activism on behalf of the rights of the world's black people.
17. Known as the Grey Collection, donated by a former Governor of Cape Province.
18. Janos Bolyai was one of the discoverers of non-Euclidean geometry. His most important work was well known in German, but was not translated into English until more than thirty years after his death.
19. The Edict of Toleration 1557 and the Edict of Turda 1568.
20. Ferenc David was a leading figure in the Unitarius Egyhaz, in Transylvania, then an independent buffer state between the Turks and the Habsburg empire. Like David, many Szeklers were members of the Brethren in Christ, a Bible-oriented religious group with a rationalist, anti-trinitarian, mortalist and anabaptist theology, widely dispersed in Poland, the Ukraine, and elsewhere in Europe. See G. Huntston Williams. *The Radical Reformation.* Kirkville:

Sixteenth Century Journal Publications, 1992; L. Alan Eyre. *Brethren in Christ*. Adelaide: Christadelphian Scripture Study Service, 1982.

21. See Thomas Aquinas. Selected writings (trans. Robert P. Goodwin). Indianapolis: Bobbs-Merrill, 1965, p.7–28.

22. L. Alan Eyre. "A 1909 Cape Town publication and its author: a puzzling mystery solved" in *Quarterly Bulletin of the National Library of South Africa*, **59**(2), 2005, pp. 62–65.

23. There were also a very few Turkish and Japanese students registered at the university, but none of these are shown on the photographs.

24. James Bell Pettigrew. *Design in Nature*. 3 vols. London: Longmans, Green, 1908.

25. I consider the precipitous decline in the numbers of Lampyridae in Jamaica in my lifetime to be a tragedy.

26. Tony Rice. *Deep Ocean*. London: The Natural History Museum. 2000, p. 62.

27. The same route was used after Chernobyl in 1986. Much of this very informative but deeply disturbing material was put under wraps by "nuclear lobbies" in the USA and other western countries. However, it is not classified and can be found by persistent researchers.

28. Since the Greenland work was done, Samuel Browning believes that he has discovered an older rock, the Acasta gneiss, north of Yellowknife in Canada (3,900 million years BP). There seems to be some prestige factor involved, both nationally and personally, in identifying the world's oldest rock. See Tjeerd H. van Andel. *New Views on an Old Planet*. Cambridge: University Press, 1994, p. 257.

29. Walter Sullivan. *Assault on the Unknown: the International Geophysical Year*. London: Hodder and Stoughton, 1961, p. 415.

30. J. Tuzo Wilson. *IGY: the Year of the New Moons*. London: Michael Joseph, 1961, p. 27.

31. Universitäts Leipzig. *The University Library of Leipzig: the Profile of the Library*. Leipzig, 2003, p.2.

32. W. J. Gardner. *A History of Jamaica*. London: Frank Cass, 1971, p. 205.

33. George Metcalf. *Royal Government and Political Conflict in Jamaica 1729–1783*. London: Longmans, 1965, p. 82.

34. Originally and until fairly recently known as the Library of the British Museum.

28

Governance at Harvard University Library

Dudley Fishburn

28.1 Introduction

The library at Harvard University is an entirely private institution. With its collection of 15.5 million volumes housed in over 80 different sites it is, therefore, by far and away the largest non-governmental research concern in the world. Even in the public league it is among the big five: The Library of Congress, the British Library, the New York Public Library and the Bibliotheque Nationale de France. But size, though it pleases the macho heart, is not the most impressive thing about Harvard's library system. What matters is the use made of that size. This year there will be 5.3 million hits on the library's e-resources. In nine months alone 436,877 people clicked their way through the turnstiles at Widener Library, the open stack collection that lies at the heart of the system. And in the same period (July 2005 – March 2006) 794,000 items circulated from the overall library collection. These figures, showing a library besieged by users, are the most satisfying of the generally rather boastful statistics laid out in this opening paragraph. But just to conclude, here are some financial numbers: expenditure on library materials runs at about £14 million a year and the overall budget, almost all of it met from private funds, comes in at about £70 million a year ($135 million.)

How is all this governed? The explanation, particularly of one important part of it, The Visiting Committee, is the subject of this paper. The Visiting Committee is an animal that is quite foreign, indeed perhaps incomprehensible, perhaps abhorrent, to a non-American academic. It has no counterpart in universities outside the United States, though many other private university libraries – Yale, Princeton, Penn and more – have one in their governance structure.

28.2 The University Library Council

But first to the routine, understandable stuff of university governance. Each bit of the library system – the Medical School, the Business School, the Divinity School and so on – has its own budget, its own collection policy, its own staff and its own "Librarian". The largest of these libraries, by a long chalk, is that which sits within the Faculty of Arts and Sciences, the Harvard College Library. Take it for granted that each of these units has university administrators and budget-setters and Deans breathing down its neck. Each library will also have its committee of Faculty. And the whole system is pulled together by The University Library Council, 16 professional librarians. This group is chaired by the Director of the University Library. He has overarching responsibility for everything: in a British university like Cambridge the thought of such a figure would cause consternation. Interestingly, this top director is not a librarian at all. He has another full-time job as one of Harvard's most distinguished University professors, playing a major role in the Department of Government. For most of his library tenure, he has also taken a hugely popular undergraduate class twice a week on participation in American politics and has represented American political science on a national scale, as well as zipping off to lecture in Oxford or Paris. This structure is the standard or "plain vanilla" part of the libraries management. Too compressed a description to do it justice but, mutatis mutandi, familiar as a model.

28.3 The Visiting Committee

Now to the unfamiliar: that Visiting Committee. First amongst its attributes is its antiquity, because from its age comes much of its authority. (Within Harvard the committee is, in large part, what Walter Bagehot, the great 19th-century British constitutionalist and founder of *The Economist*, called the "dignified" part of the Constitution. So, age matters.) The Harvard library dates from the start of the university. Indeed it was the will of the Puritan preacher, John Harvard, a graduate of Emmanuel College, Cambridge, who died in Cambridge, Massachusetts in 1638 that kicked the whole thing off. He left his books – all 400 of them – to the college. (The college did not look after them very well: only one survives today.) The library, therefore, stood at the centre of the place's spirit and intellect from the start. By the first half of the 19th century, the Visiting Committee was in operation – and it has reported on a regular basis ever since.

In 1847 for example, the Committee came to call. The Harvard Librarian at the time, John Sibley, wrote in his diary: *"All the books are called in about three weeks before the visit."* That is, for the avoidance of doubt *all* the books in the university. *"The Librarian arranges them on the shelves in order. The Committee is divided into couples, one member holds the Catalogue, the other counts the books and examines. Generally there have been twelve persons or thereabout present. Last year each shelf was carefully examined. There is no compensation but the courtesy of a dinner is extended to the Committee."*

Though much has changed, more has stayed the same. Every year some 20 people descend on the Harvard Library. They have been appointed to that role by the University's senior governing body, the Board of Overseers, to whom they report and from whom they get their authority. (This being a private institution with its statutes unbroken since its founding, when the Overseers sit down as a body corporate, they are the university: they own it.) These 20 mostly serve nine-year terms. The Visiting Committee at the time of writing is as typical as at any other time. It consists of: four professional librarians (Reg Carr being one, others come from Princeton, Cornell, the Library of Congress), four bibliophiles or private collectors, a handful of successful entrepreneurs from Silicon Valley and from Wall Street, a number of philanthropists (that extraordinary American phenomena), and a few of the good and great: lawyers, Massachusetts bigwigs, people who have served in Washington, distinguished Harvard alumni, college presidents. And then scattered over this lot, as there should be on any good committee, are a number of people who seem to be there by serendipity: a Hollywood producer and the Chairman, myself, a non-academic Englishman (worse, a one-time Member of Parliament, worse still, a journalist) who knows not a thing about libraries and has not got a dollar to his name with which to be philanthropic.

Yet this motley crew annually inspects the library during a day and a half of meetings. We take evidence. We cross-question. We set the agenda, year by year. One year "What is a Science Library? Another "How good are our environmental controls?" All the professional Harvard librarians, the executives, put in an appearance, as requested. The university president will often stop by. There is a fair bit of "show and tell", a fair bit of "letting the hair down", things for the record, gossip not to be repeated. After any meeting the committee might choose to write a letter to the Overseers. One year in three it is required to write a 10–15 page report. In that year, the Overseers themselves, after reading the report, will call in – for an hour's grilling – the Chairman of the Committee and the Director of the Library. And there it rests. Or does it?

In our barren English academic world, where so much "governance" is reduced to the latest condescending circular from the Higher Education Funding Council, we may have forgotten how things work. So here is what actually happens. First, of course, the library staff prepares for the Visiting Committee many months in advance, indeed they are aware of its presence as individual members pass through Harvard, throughout the year.

As Chairman I say to the various library directors: "I hope this committee makes your hearts beat faster, partly out of love but partly out of fear". How could it not be like this when you are asking the Bodleian Librarian and a handful of your other professional peers into your parlour?

None of this needs to be said or written down to be effective. But imagine if Reg Carr were to request that a paragraph be included in the report drawing attention to the poor environmental conditions in the stacks of, say, the Fine Arts Library. That observation might end up in the university archive but on the way it would stop off on a great number of desks.

Then, of course, this random-seeming selection of people on the committee is not random at all. The Committee has not ever, not once, been used as a fund-raising group. To mention money-raising would be like the subject of a Bateman cartoon: The man who talked money at a Visiting Committee! Hair would stand on end, hackles would rise. This is not the forum for such things. This is something we English find hard to fathom. Why have all this paraphernalia of a Visiting Committee, if there is not a cheque for the university's coffers at the end of the day? Because if a committee member has created a Californian Hi-tech empire from scratch or has run an enormous fund on Wall Street, he or she is likely to have some good and vibrant ideas; and is likely to have a wide circle of equivalent friends. One day such a committee member may well want to support the university and its library – often in the most improbable, unlooked-for way. In my time as Chairman, perhaps some £10 million ($20m) has come this way. I would not know. This is not the business of the committee.

28.4 The Report

Then there is the report itself. Yes, it passes by the Overseers on the way to the archive. But it is also read by various Deans and administrators, by library staff, perhaps – who knows – by journalists. Remember this is a committee with no executive powers, no funds at its command. (HEFCE would merely pass by and sneer.) But in the 1997 report of the Visiting Committee these paragraphs appeared deep in the text:

"There are two blots on the library's landscape. Blot One: the physical condition of Widener library. Blot Two: the seeming insouciance of the University to do anything about it. Widener, the largest open-stack library in the world and perhaps the University's most famous landmark, was completed in 1915. It has no fire control system. (And the destruction by fire of a magnificent public library in Southern California this year was one more indication of how combustible libraries are and have been since the great library in Alexandria went up in flames in AD640.) Widener has no climate control system. Humidity soars up and down with the New England weather, drying the books out one moment, dampening them down the next. Here there is not the risk of rapid destruction by fire, but the certainty of a daily and unnecessary slow-burn of every book in the place. Widener has no surveillance system. The kind of closed-circuit camera that is put up in every grocery store to stop shop-lifting is not to be found anywhere in this great and valuable collection. Its electrical wiring and its plumbing are woefully out of date.

The Visiting Committee would not envy Harvard's President having to face a reporter from The New York Times the day after a major fire, flood or theft. How would he answer the following question? "Mr President, how is it that Harvard with a $8 billion endowment and a $2.1 billion fund drive could find the money to give its undergraduates a better restaurant but not to safeguard its most famous library?" An unfair question, of course. But not an easy one to answer. It is hard to imagine any other single thing that puts the University's reputation more at risk."

28.5 The Response

The result of this report by a non-executive, outside committee was electrifying. By 2005, after spending over £40 million ($80m), Widener, the world's largest open-stack library, had been refitted, rewired, equipped with air conditioning and renovated inch-by-inch – and all with private money.

28.6 Conclusion

So what does the Visiting Committee do? To paraphrase Gilbert and Sullivan "It does nothing in particular, and does it very well". It does not raise funds, though it has among its members some enormously generous Harvard benefactors. It does not second-guess the university's librarians, though there are on the committee some of the most distinguished professional librarians in the world. And though there are very considerable bibliophiles and collectors on the committee, it would be far too particular if any used that to pursue their own interests. Doing nothing in particular allows the Visiting Committee to do a great deal in general: to flit from the Business School to the Chinese library, from wrestling with conservation issues to investigating the university's digital programmes, from being an outside critic to being an inside friend. It is a model that has worked well for many of America's best universities since the 19th century; some of Britain's would be wise to adopt it in the 21st.

Higher Education Libraries and the Quality Agenda

John Horton

29.1 Introduction

As a linguist (though never, I trust, a pedant) I have never been impressed by the apparent force of the word "quality", or, more specifically, by its use or misuse in numerous contexts by those with a particular message to convey. It is essentially a neutral term, which has somehow come to acquire a positive connotation.

I have always been happy with Shakespeare's allusion to the unstrained nature of the quality of mercy; I can appreciate the irony of the exhortation to feel the width rather than the quality; and I can understand the industrial application of the concept of quality control. I have had more difficulty in appreciating the value of a product described as a quality item, or the subtleties of teen-talk in which first "ace" then "brill" then "quality" were seemingly and successively parroted to describe, for example, a good evening out on the town. The prefixing of epithets such as poor, low, good or high to the word quality does help to give a sense of direction, but the last of these has become so glib as to render the phrase virtually meaningless and, therefore, to provide the justification for the demanding of evidence.

This, in combination with the requirements of the new managerialism and public accountability, partly explains why higher education over the last fifteen years, has been subjected to, and to some degree profited from, an evidence-based process of inspection of its "quality".

However, it is only in recent years that there has emerged anything like a clear and generally accepted (on both "sides") definition of what this term means in the context of higher education. It is a characteristic which we have been successively required to assess, to audit, to assure, to enhance, and finally to embed.

The following text is intended not as a critical analysis of the process, but rather as a personal reflection by one who has fulfilled two roles during this period: the first, until recently, as an institutional auditor for the currently named

Quality Assurance Agency for Higher Education; the second as a University Librarian, amongst whose responsibilities the all-embracing "quality agenda" has been at the forefront.

29.2 Librarians and Quality Assurance

When I was first appointed as an auditor for the QAA nearly a decade ago, I was surprised to discover that I was the first librarian of any sort to be appointed to their panel, which at that time comprised well over a hundred auditors – indeed I remained in this splendid isolation for the next five years. Of course, the QAA, whilst striving to be representative, is not formally looking to appoint from every section of academic or related activity, and my appointment was not on the basis that I was a university librarian per se; nor, in fact, was my application submitted on that basis alone, but rather on the evidence that my post had given me wide experience of, or constant contact with, most other areas of university life and governances. In other words, I was not expected or asked to represent specifically the library / learning resources agenda when auditing, but to engage with the complete portfolio of institutional audit. I do remember some consternation at one audit: this particular university (as we all understandably do prior to audit) had done its homework on the details of the then three auditors who were to visit them and, having brought up my profile, assumed that this was an indication that it was the library which was going to be particularly examined.

However, it remains something of a surprise that a greater proportion of librarians are not appointed as auditors; or perhaps it is that they do not apply to be, and I do not mean this in a spirit of "if you can't beat them, join them". One learns as much from being an auditor as one gives to the process – indeed it is a privilege to be able to be afforded deep access to the workings of an institution other than one's own, particularly in what I believe remains essentially a process of peer review rather than of inquisition (though I did have concerns for the public relations of the QAA when after one audit a reply from the institution concerned specifically thanked the audit team for our unthreatening approach to the process). But at a time when so much more of the student experience depends upon their libraries, whether actual or virtual, as a result of developments and expectations in student-centred learning, evidence-based learning, project-oriented learning, etc., we are already noticing and can continue to expect a more thorough appraisal of our services; this would seem to be an argument for a larger representation of our understanding and expertise in the sphere of institutional audit and review.

29.3 Quality Audit

So what in general terms should we all expect from quality audit? There are now numerous, and helpful, codes of practice consultatively drawn up and published by the QAA. Do these indicate that the QAA itself, or more fairly as an agency of the funding councils and ultimately of the government, is seeking to make all universities the same, or at least to reflect a common structure and method of providing instruction and facilitating research? I believe not. We all know that that there is no such thing as a model university; similarly there is no such thing as a model library. Quite apart from "rankings", each university has its own more specific aims, and each library strives to reflect these in terms of its collections and services. Audit should, and generally does, judge us on those terms.

In more modern times there are clearly differing political views about what higher education is for. Personally, I am quite happy to live with Newman's idea of the university as containing some guiding principles – indeed, he even mentions skills as well as knowledge. It is to what that knowledge and those skills are applied that seems to be a basis of the modern arguments. In the new order the pressure is on to show how the universities apply their activities to the economic progress of the nation. This is fair enough – up to a point. But that is only one of the means to an end, and I apologize for drawing attention to the Charter of my own University which uniquely, and I am proud to say tenaciously, proclaims its object as the "advancement of learning and knowledge, and the application of knowledge to **human welfare**". That is its essence or "quality". Within that context the library becomes a central and indispensable resource upon which the lecturer draws to distil the learning to students, upon which the researcher relies as a platform from which to advance knowledge, and for which the librarian must take the professional responsibility in reflecting, proactively, the general and specific aims of the university.

That is the library's nature or quality in the neutral sense of the word. What quality has come to mean is that the library, as with the rest of the institution, has procedures in place to assure itself, and, more importantly its users, that it is fulfilling its role; by which I do not mean drawing up service-level agreements set at a low level in order to give it a fighting chance of doing what it says on the tin, but fully engaging with its users (stakeholders, if you must) in a genuine effort to provide them with what they require, whatever the level. As librarians we are all in the same business of ensuring that the University as a whole is successful and that the user experience is continually enhanced.

29.4 Audit Outcomes

The outcome of audit in its various forms when applied to libraries and related activity in higher education has over the years been largely positive. The cynic would allege that the reason for that is a comparatively lighter touch of audit when applied to support areas. There is some truth in this. It may owe something to the fact that as an academic support area the university library has a tradition and good record of looking after its users which is generally accepted. It may also reflect my earlier point concerning under-representation of librarians on audit and review panels, particularly when the library is audited as one part of a general process. However, the claim of a "lighter touch" cannot be justified when one considers the quantity, if not the quality, of audit or review.

During the time of subject review and offshoots such as "discipline audit trails", an individual academic department might feel that it could temporarily afford to "relax", in the knowledge that it would not be reviewed again for several years. The Library, on the other hand, having been part of a review for one subject, did not have to wait long before the next one covering a different subject (four or five such reviews in a single year was not an unusual load). If this were to have been a more research-oriented article I might have been tempted to assess the annual amount of library staff time devoted to preparation for audit and review, both locally and nationally, in the genuine hope that it can be shown to have been worth it. Given the number of agencies and other bodies engaged in audit and review (each, admittedly, with their own agenda and terms of reference: parts of HEFCE, QAA, OFSTED, professional bodies, even on occasion the Church of England) one could be forgiven for asking whether there is scope for greater co-ordination and sharing of outcomes in order to reduce the burden of evidential provision by the universities themselves.

29.5 Library Provision

This reminds me of a suggestion which I made some years ago to the then Chief Executive of the QAA: my point was that it might ease the burden on the library if it likewise were to have its own departmental review every few years covering all subjects, thus obviating the need for seemingly continual involvement on the occasion of each subject review. The idea of the totally separate review of the library was pronounced as an excellent idea – but unfortunately as an addition rather than as a replacement.

Although this problem has lightened a little for libraries in the context of the QAA, it remains regular in the context of accrediting bodies (both national and European) who, with justification and considerable acuity, are concerned with library provision (including financial resources) in relation to the quality of the programmes and of the graduates being produced for their particular professions. From AMBA and EQUIS in the business studies field, the Law Society, GSCC for social work, the NHS, through all the scientific and engineering professions, and beyond – all and more are regular monitors of library provision as an integral part of their accreditation – only in the humanities, it seems, are libraries relatively unaffected by accrediting bodies.

29.6 Quality Assurance and Enhancement of Library Services

So how do we attempt to assure and enhance the quality of our activities and services as librarians? Few of the following suggestions are particularly new, but are drawn from my experiences, as auditor and auditee, as having been shown to be aspects attracting particular attention. Taken together they help to demonstrate to the outside world a collective ethos, and a commitment to, including a sense of ownership of, the "quality agenda".

User surveys have their place, but there is the clouding factor of "questionnaire fatigue", when students are now presented with countless forms from other areas of the University. Low rates of response and the box-ticking structure often result in a dubious set of figures with a string of numbers after the decimal points (shades of Dewey), with little provision made for substantial comments in free text; but such surveys can be better received, and their results be more useful, when a library is asking for comments in relation to a new initiative, and particularly if the library is known for giving feedback from the feedback.

One of the most important series of documents in the audit process is the collection of minutes of each Departmental Staff / Student Liaison Committee. The relevant subject librarian should be a full member of every one of these, and should ensure that library and related matters are a standing item on the agenda, thus providing a meaningful conduit for student concerns as well as an opportunity for mutual reporting on new developments. An auditor will be looking for evidence that issues raised are dealt with, and appropriately recorded as resolved (or that feedback has been given as to difficulties in implementation). The Library's case to the University for more resources in relation to a particular concern is noticeably strengthened if it has arisen from a student-based committee, on the grounds that what starts off as an issue of resource will, if unheeded, become an issue of quality. In more general terms such membership furthers integration between the library and the academic department. In short, the library should be seen, and is likely to be audited as, not simply a place where information happens to be available if one asks for it, but as a natural extension of the teaching and research departments and their activities. Student representation on Library Advisory groupings is clearly useful, though this usually depends on the clout which such sub-committees have within the university decision-making structures. It is often useful for the student officer concerned with academic affairs to be informally invited to internal meetings of the library when support is needed to rectify or promote a particular concern or initiative.

The same applies to departmental academic committees, which are usually the starting point of proposals for new modules, courses and degree programmes. It is essential that the library is engaged at this early stage in order to advise on its ability to support these new developments. Subject librarians should also be full members of those university committees dealing with course approval and subsequently annual monitoring, as quite apart from matters of collection development, conventional or electronic, they may well be teaching and assessing subject-based information skills on such programmes, and, indeed, their teaching may be observed during an external review.

Of equal importance is the library's position in relation to collaborative provision, at home and abroad. In the overseas context in recent years there has been occasional adverse publicity relating to the quality of franchised provision which has prompted the auditing agencies, and other influential bodies such as the British Council, to sharpen their focus and attention. It is the expectation of audit that students at all levels on franchised courses and partner institutions, should experience a level of quality of provision as close as practicable to that experienced by students at the validating university itself. There is, therefore, a responsibility to ensure this, particularly in relation to new partnerships and programmes. A new site, at home or abroad, requires an impartial inspection on behalf of the host university for an assessment of its ability to deliver and support its programmes, and this includes library provision. It is clearly not going to impress an auditor to read a document or hear a comment indicating only that someone has "driven past" or "had a look in" the library, that it contains some relevant books and that some journals are probably available via internet access to the full-text holdings of the validating university – there will need to be a meaningful statement relating to plans for its development and a commitment to monitor its effectiveness. Once the programme is established, there will in the normal course of events be visits by academic co-ordinators from the home university. It will likewise bring credit to the home library if, for example, the subject librarian also makes a visit in order to bring local staff up to date with developments and provide any required training (partner institutions, particularly abroad, have even been known to offer the travel and subsistence costs for this!)

Related to this is the increasing attention of audit paid to the experience of distance learners. It is important for the library to have a documented policy on the services which it aims to provide to this category of student, and hard evidence as to how their needs have been identified and are being fulfilled. It is unlikely that the auditor will be able to question the distance learner directly – hence the need for sound and readily accessible documentation.

Similar attention is likely to be paid to the position of part-time learners. This category is likely to be more available personally to the auditors, who justifiably may ask to see a representative. Again, documentation relating to policy and monitoring evidence, against which the student view can be "tested", needs to be accessible and up to date. It also goes almost without saying that the library should be able to provide evidence of its proactive commitment to the particular needs of users with any form of disability.

The introduction of "top-up" fees is beginning to blur the students' perception of the distinction between "quality" and "value for money". This factor is acute in the case of overseas students from outside the EU, who, particularly if they are self-financed and paying the full market rate, may be entitled to feel that that the quality of their experience should be proportionately enhanced, or, more crudely, that they should be getting more for their money. Given that in certain cultures there is a demonstrable reluctance to complain in case it should jeopardize their academic progress, it should not be a surprise to institutions to whom this income is not just significant, but often a lifeline, if the quality of provision, standard or specialized, to overseas students, is a focus of audit, including their experience of the library, where statistically they can be shown to spend a large part of their time.

The recent initiative of the QAA in adding postgraduate research provision to its portfolio of quality assurance (albeit, for the moment, assessed through documentation rather than visitation) is a reminder to us, if any were needed, that our users are not a homogeneous group for whom one width or quality fits all.

29.7 Ongoing Issues

However, I am often asked as a QA auditor whether there is a particular issue which arises with students more persistently than any other. There is, and it is basic: there are never enough copies of recommended individual texts to go round. It is a question not of the range of the material but of its immediate availability – it is a classic case of a quantitative issue in terms of financial resources becoming a qualitative issue in terms of the student experience. It is one with which university libraries have been faced since the dawn of modularization, which brought with it a narrowing of the timescale of demand, often to a particular week, or even a particular day. An auditor will be aware of the resourcing issues, but will be looking to see whether the library is listening and what partial steps a library is taking to alleviate the problem. There are electronic part-solutions increasingly available, but these, too, come at an extra cost in terms of licensing, etc. An auditor or a subject reviewer, particularly from an accrediting body, may well ask for evidence of how an increased intake of students over a period in a particular subject has been reflected in the library allocation of resources to, and expenditure on, that subject.

29.8 Conclusions

To the potential readership of this volume it may appear somewhat impertinent to offer a word of general advice. But do beware the "hostage to fortune" argument. By which I mean: do not in your documentation be tempted to "hide" reference to an aspect where you think you may be vulnerable. Such documentation is supposed to reflect critical analysis rather than pure description, and self-assessment rather than self-congratulation. Auditors are fully, albeit sympathetically, trained to look for both the good and the not so good, and in my experience will give us as much credit to the institution or its library for having recognized a deficiency (particularly if accompanied by a strategy to deal with it) as they will for something which is working well and which can be characterized, reported and disseminated as good practice.

So, where do we go, or rather how are we to be led, from here? The essence of the latest round of quality audit is contained in the indispensable QAA Audit Handbook (1), and focuses on the institution's approach to "taking deliberate [presumably meaning conscious rather than slow] steps" to **enhance students' opportunities for learning,** and to **reflect** upon the effectiveness of this approach. This is yet another angle (not wholly original, but welcome).

If one is sometimes tempted to think in terms of a quality "industry" having developed over the last decade and a half, to wonder how on earth we managed to cope with delivering relevant and useful library services to our academic communities prior to that, and to question the benefits of the bureaucratization of common sense – well, temper that with the fact that audit has indeed provided the encouragement and stimulus to **reflect** upon what we do, to take advantage of externality on our sometimes narrowly internal view, and to remind us that our services and systems should be driven by the expressed needs of our users rather than by the expectation that those users will fit in with those services and systems which are convenient for us. What has informally motivated most of us as university librarians for years is now official – it's the student experience.

I do not think that the QAA, for example, would dissent from that. We are pushing in the same direction, and even if it droppeth not as the gentle rain from heaven, there is some mercy in quality, so let us at least for the moment leave it unstrained.

Reference

1.   QAA (2006) *Handbook for Institutional Audit: England and Northern Ireland.* Available online at http://www.qaa.ac.uk/.

Author Index

Baker, David 95
Barnard, John 327
Brindley, Lynne 65
Chen, Sherry 253
Coughlan, Jane 253
Deegan, Marilyn 219
Dilks, David 359
Earnshaw, Rae 241
Eyre, Alan 381
Field, Clive D. 303
Fishburn, Dudley 401
Follett, Sir Brian K. 55
Fox, Peter 75
Friend, Frederick 155
Frith, Gareth 273
Hall, John 345
Heaney, Mary 181
Horton, John 407
Iacono, Antonietta 273
Kroch, Carl A. 173
Law, Derek 107
Lossau, Norbert 11
Love, Steve 253
Macredie, Robert D. 253
Milne, Ronald 3
Ovenden, Richard 295
Pinfield, Stephen 119
Ratcliffe, Fred 137
Rusbridge, Chris 207
Simpson, Bill 85
Tanner, Simon 219
Thomas, Sarah E. 173
Tuck, John 163
Vince, John 241
Watson, Les 191
Wells, Mike 31
Wilson, Frankie 253